The Early History of Islam

With special reference to the Position of Ali, during the Life of The Holy Prophet Mohammed and after

In Two Volumes
(Bound in One)

by

Saiyid Safdar Hosein

An Impartial Review of the Early Islamic Period
Compiled from Authentic Sources

References profusely given and freely quoted in-extenso

Intended to Supply a Long Felt Need to educate the Moslen Youth in the elements of Islamic History and to arouse his interest for a deeper study of the subject

Low Price Publications

2012

First Published 1933
Reprinted in **LPP** 1995, 1998, 2006, 2012

ISBN 10: 81-7536-388-6
ISBN 13: 978-81-7536-388-5

Published by
Low Price Publications
A-6, Second Floor, Nimri Commercial Centre,
Ashok Vihar Phase-IV, Delhi 110052 (INDIA)
tel.: +91.11.27302453 fax.: +91.11.47061936
url: www.Lppindia.com e-mail: info@Lppindia.com

Printed at
Salasar Imaging Systems
Delhi

PRINTED IN INDIA

Vol. 1

Life of
The Holy Prophet
Mohammed

PREFACE.

My object in presenting this volume to the public is neither to make money nor to court fame. I am an obscure old man, who has finished with the world and its affairs, and is, in fact, past all ambition. My chief aim has been to put in a simple language and handy form the chief events in the life of the great Prophet of Islam.

It is intended primarily for the ordinary Moslem youth, who has neither the time nor the inclination to wade through a mass of standard works, which are mostly in Arabic and Persian; and whose information at present is derived from the few English books written by Europeans. These books have been written either by the Christian Missionaries, whose bias is obvious, or others who are far more dangerous, having subtler political motives. As an instance I may quote Sir William Muir, who has written volumes on the subject. He has exhibited a profoundly wilful ignorance by saying that Hazrat Ali had no important position in Islam as long as the Prophet lived.

The succession might be a controversial question, but all Moslems are unanimous in believing in the great services which Hazrat Ali rendered to the cause of Islam. Would it not savour of ingratitude if what he did was not acknowledged? Rather it would be incriminatory to ignore the meritorious services which he rendered often at the risk of his own life, which none other could hazard and without which Islam could not have been what it is today. Histories abound in unequivocal evidence to show beyond all posibility of doubt that Hazrat Ali was the unique hero of Islam, and was the favourite of the Prophet, who had made several attempts to define his position. I have endeavoured in this book to show the position of Hazrat Ali during the life time of the Prophet and after his death. For this purpose I had to give only brief accounts and merits of the eminent personages who were inaugurated as caliphs, one after the other, before Hazrat Ali succeeded.

I do not claim that this work is original. It is only a reproduction of the valuable information recorded by learned men in histories or collections of traditions on the subject, in different languages. My task in the writing of this volume has been that of a mere annalist. I have given bare facts and on most of the important subjects I have given quotations in the text or in foot-notes from the renowned European researchers such as Gibbon, Price, Muir, Irving, Ockley, Carlyle, Davenport and others in their own wording, for the satisfaction and interest of the reader. On account of diversity of sects in Islam with so many dissonant and clashing opinions, I have left it to the discretion of the reader to form his own opinion on the facts given.

من اُنچه شرط بلاغ است باتو میگویم   زهے مراد بفکرت اگرچه آمد خوش

The general indifference, nay apathy, of the average Moslem youth towards religious matters is patent to all, and if this little book succeeds in arousing the interest of even a few, I shall consider myself amply recompensed.

I should gratefully acknowledge the concise works of S. Zakir Hosain Ja'far of Delhi and K. B. Nawab Sheikh Ahmad Hosain, O. B. E., of Paryáwán, which furnished me with ready references quoted or copied in vernacular as foot-notes to the English text to satisfy the reader. I record my deep gratitude to Mr. Syed Kazim Raza, B. A., who gave me material literary help in my task, as also to Messrs. Haji Syed Jalaluddin Haider, M. A., Syed Abid Husain, B. A., L.L. B., and Syed Alay Ahmad, who very kindly undertook the trouble of going through the manuscript and giving me some useful suggestions in the arrangement of the book.

I may add a word on the system of transliteration which I have adopted in the rendering of the Arabic names in which several letters are uttered by non-Arabs with one and the same sound. To distinguish such letters I have used the following rendering with uniformity as far as possible:—

ث	is represented by		th
خ	"	"	kh
ذ	"	"	zh
ز	"	"	z
ض	"	"	dz
ظ	"	"	tz
ع	"	"	a comma as in apostrophe but not uniformly.
غ	"	"	gh
ق	"	"	q
ک	"	"	k

I have not, however, changed the spelling of the names or words naturalised in the English language, for instance :— Caliph for Khalifa ; Hegira for Hijra ; Mecca for Makka ; and so on.

LUCKNOW :
19th May 1933.

SAIYID SAFDAR HOSAIN.

CONTENTS.

CONTENTS of Vol. II.

CHAPTER XVIII—The Prophet's successors.

Abubekr, the First Caliph.

CHAPTER XIX—Omar, the second Caliph.

CHAPTER XX—OTHMAN, THE THIRD CALIPH.

CHAPTER XXI—ALI b. ABI TALIB.

CHAPTER I.

The Land of the Holy Prophet Mohammed's Birth.

Arabia, old and new.

Arabia, the birth-place of our Lord Mohammed, the Apostle of God, whose religion is professed by about $\frac{1}{5}$th of the world's population, is a peninsula in the west of Asia. It is bounded on the north by Asia Minor and Syria, on the east by the Euphrates and the Persian Gulf, on the south by the Arabian Sea, and on the west by the Red Sea. Formerly Arabia Proper was divided into three regions: (1) Arabia Felix or the fertile tract along the sea-coast and comprising the west and south-western coasts; (2) Arabia Petræa or the rocky tract which included the whole north-western portion; and (3) Arabia Deserta or the sandy desert consisting of the whole interior. It is now divided by modern geographers into seven provinces, *viz.*, (1) the Hejáz, (2) Yemen, (3) Hadzramawt, (4) Omán or the Kingdom of Muscat, (5) Central Arabia or the Kingdom of Nejd, (6) Iráq-i-Arab, *i.e.*, the region extending along the borders of Persia, (7) Bahrein or the provinces situated along the Persian Gulf.

The Holy Land.

The province of Hejáz is known as the Holy Land or the Land of Pilgrimage, deriving its importance from the holy places situated within it. Mecca, or Becca as named in the Qurán, the chief city of Hejáz, is the most ancient city, or admittedly one of the most ancient cities, of the world.

Mecca is celebrated for its sacred edifice the Ka'ba, which is a place of great concourse from as remote a period as that of Abrahám and his son Ismáel who built the Sanctuary.† Abrahám first called the people to visit the Holy House. Tradition represents Mecca as the centre of yearly pilgrimage from all Arabia and the surrounding countries from times immemorial, perhaps since the call from Abrahám.

The pilgrimage to the Ka'ba.

Ka'ba was thus the grand centre of religion, to visit which and to perform the rites connected there-with was at all times regarded as a sacred duty, as it still commands the reverence and devotion of the whole Moslem world. The Holy Qurán says: "Verily, the first house founded unto men (to worship in) was that which is in Becca, blessed, and a guidance to mankind. Therein are manifest signs, Abrahám's place (where he stood), and whosoever entereth therein, shall be safe; and from God is ordained a pilgrimage to the House, on those who have means to go thither." (*Sura III-90 & 91*). "And proclaim unto the people a solemn pilgrimage: let them come to thee on foot, and on every lean camel arriving from every distant route." (*Sura XXII-28.*)

The pilgrimage performed in Zhilhajja, the last month of the Mohammedan calendar, with an additional pilgrimage to Arafát (a small eminence of granite rocks in a valley within the mountainous tract, ten or 12 miles east of Mecca) was called Haj-al-Akbar or the Greater Pilgrimage and it is incumbent on every Moslem except for lawful excuse; while that performed at any season of the year without the pilgrimage to Arafát was called Omra or Haj-al-Asghar or the Lesser Pilgrimage. The Omra may be performed with merit at any season of the year but specially in Rajab, the seventh month of the Mohammedan year. The Haj must be performed in Zhilhajja.

Mecca owes its fame also to its being the birth-place of the holy Prophet Mohammed, as Medina, another principal

† According to Moslem writers it was first built on earth by Adam, exactly under the spot occupied by its perfect model in Heaven which was constructed two thousand years before the creation of the world.—*Zwemer's Arabia p. 35.*

town of the same province, has gained an importance next to Mecca for its being the place of residence of the Prophet and of his interment.

The sacred territory and the sacred months.

Mecca, together with the territory several miles around it, was held sacred on account of the Ka'ba. The sacred territory was called Harem. † Three consecutive months (the last two of one and the first of the following year) *viz.*, Zhilqa'da, Zhilhajja and Moharram ‡ and the seventh month *viz.* Rajab in each year, were regarded as sacred,—perhaps a system dating from the time of construction of the Edifice. "Verily, the number of months with God, is twelve, in the book of God, since the day He created the heavens and the earth; of these four are sacred..........." (*Sura IX-36.*) During these four months every sort of violence was forbidden, hostile activities and tribal feuds were suspended and universal amnesty prevailed throughout Arabia; and pilgrims from every quarter repaired to Mecca.

Subsequently a fair was established at Okátz in the suburbs of Mecca. All sorts of festivities were held there; poets recited their master-pieces, merchants had brisk business, and athletes exhibited their feats of prowess and strength. The people, who flocked to Mecca for pilgrimage, interested themselves in the great mart of Okátz, availing themselves of the privileges of the sacred months.

The people and their religion.

Modern Arabs are sprung from two stocks, *viz.*—(1) Qahtán or Joctan descendants of Noah, who are called Arab-al-Ariba, and (2) Adnán a descendant of Ismáel the son of Abrahám,

† The boundaries of this sacred territory are rather uncertain. Abdal Haq says that when, at the time of rebuilding of the Ka'ba, Abrahám (Khalil Allah) placed the Black Stone, its east, west, north and south sides became luminous, and wherever the light extended, became the boundaries of the sacred city! These limits are now marked by pillars of masonry, except on the Jiddah and Je'rána road, where there is some dispute as to the exact boundary. *Zwemer's Arabia p. 31.*

‡ According to Lane, the present luner months of the Mohammedan year were named by Keláb b. Morra, an ancestor of Mohammed, about two centuries before Islam.

who are called the Arab Mosta'riba. The latter settled round the Ka'ba, and Mohammed, the Holy Prophet, came of this stock.

The Arabs originally believed in one God, but at the time when our Lord Mohammed was born their religion had degenerated into Polytheism, Star-worship and Fetishism. They worshipped a number of godlings. Each sept or tribe had its own particular god. Idols were found in every house, and homage was paid to them in order to secure their pleasure and to avert their wrath. Above them all, however, they had a dim idea of a Supreme Being called Alláh. By Him they swore; and Covenants or Treaties were sealed in His name (Bismika Allahomma), because the lower gods belonged to one party only and not to the other, so they were not deemed suitable to be invoked in such cases; hence for these purposes the necessity for a universal God. Wellhausen says: "In worship Alláh had the last place, those gods being preferred who represented the interests of a particular circle and fulfilled the desires of their worshippers." They also worshipped angels, whom they called goddesses *i. e.*, the wives or daughters of God. They made their images and paid them divine homage. Al-Lát, a huge image of grey granite, the chief idol of the tribe of Thaqif at Táef and Al-Uzza, a block of granite some twenty feet long, were worshipped as the wives of the Supreme God. Hobal, a huge idol in the form of a man, brought from Syria and ostentatiously installed in a high place of honor, was worshipped in the Ka'ba, where numerous other idols and the images of Abrahám and Ismáel, each carrying in their hands divine arrows, were consecrated. Such was the state of religion of the Arabs before the Saviour Mohammed appeared amongst them to preach the doctrines of Monotheism, upright and sin-avoiding walk of life and the idea of responsibility for the Day of Judgment.

The Period of Ignorance.

The period of Polytheism, Tribal feuds, Infanticide etc., all of which obtained in the whole of Arabia before the advent of the great

Prophet Mohammed, was called by him the Period of Ignorance.

CHAPTER II.

The Prophet's Ancestors.

As, in connection with the advent of our Lord Mohammed, I have to deal particularly with the history of his forefathers—the Háshimites—it is desirable to describe here their origin and antecedents, as briefly as possible, in order to introduce them to the reader.

The Háshimites are known to be the true Ismáelites being descended from Kinána, who was 7th in lineal descent from Adnán, a descendant of Ismáel the son of the great prophet Abrahám. Kinána's great grandson Fihr was called Qoreish. The posterity of Qoreish (Fihr) formed scores of families or clans, all members of which were styled the Qoreishites or mere Qoreish. To facilitate distinction of one family or clan from the other, each clan is separately and more properly known by the name of its own distinguished head, though individually and collectively they are all Qoreish. Thus the descendants of Háshim (a Qoreishite of distinction) are called Bani Háshim; likewise the descendants of Omyya (Háshim's twin brother's son) are known as Bani Omyya. A genealogical table is given herewith to show clearly the particular clans of the Qoreish, who figure prominently in this history.

The ancestry of the Prophet.

Mohammed the great Prophet of Islam belonged to Bani Háshim, whose lineage is given below, connecting him directly with Adnán a descendant of Ismáel the *blessed* † son of Abrahám:—

MOHAMMED صلو ا علیه و آ له bin (son of) Abdalláh,

† *Vide Genesis XVII—18, 20* "And Abrahám said unto God, O that Ishmáel might live before thee! And God said, As for Ishàmel, I have heard thee. Behold, I have blessed him, and will make him fruitful, and will multiply him exceedingly: twelve princes shall he beget, and I will make him a great nation."

bin Abd-al-Mottalib, bin HASHIM, bin Abd-Manáf, bin Qosayy, bin Kelab, bin Morra, bin Ka'b, bin Loay, bin Ghálib, bin FIHR (QOREISH), bin Málik, bin Nadzr, bin Kinána, bin Kházima, bin Modrika, bin Ilyás, bin Modzar, bin Nazár, bin Ma'd, bin ADNAN, a descendant of Ismáel son of ABRAHAM.

Antecedents.

Qosayy, the grandfather of Háshim and the sixth in lineal descent from Fihr or Qoreish, was the Sheikh of Mecca and Chief of the surrounding territory. The five privileges of the custodian of Ka'ba were vested in Qosayy, *viz.* (1) the Hijába, *i.e.* the possession of the keys and the control of the Sanctuary; (2) the Siqáya and the Rifáda, *i.e.* the right of providing drink and food to the pilgrims; (3) the Qiyáda, *i.e.* the command of the troops in war; (4) the Liwá, *i.e.* the right of affixing the banner to the staff and of presenting it to the standard bearer; (5) the Dár-al-Nadwa, *i.e.* the presidency of the Council. His orders were paramount. Subsequently these offices were inherited by the grandsons of Qosayy, *viz.* Háshim (born about 442 A. D.), Al-Mottalib, Nawfal and Abd Shams.

† Háshim was alloted the right of providing drink and food to the pilgrims. He was rich and in a position to fulfil the trust with princely munificence, and to entertain the pilgrims royally. His princely hospitality surrounded him, in the eyes of all Arabia, with a peculiar halo of glory. His public-spirited charity during a famine, which lasted continually for three years in Mecca, still more increased his popularity. Háshim organised the mercantile expeditions of his people, so that every winter a caravan set out for Yemen and Abyssinia, while in summer a second visited Gháza, Angora and other Syrian marts.

Omyya's envy.

‡ The ever increasing fame and success of Háshim in all his undertakings provoked the envy of his twin brother Abd Shams and his

† Tabaqát Ibn Sa'd; Ibn Hishám.
‡ Tabaqát Ibn Sa'd.

son Omyyá. They were wealthy, no doubt, but instead of utilizing their wealth to useful purposes, they attempted to vie with their kinsman in munificence, and were at last treated with ridicule by the Qoreish, who watched their vain endeavours with contempt. Omyya was so much enraged at length, that he openly challenged Háshim to a trial of superiority. Háshim wished to avoid such a contest with one so much inferior to him both in years and dignity; but the Qoreish, who loved such exhibitions, would not let him stand aloof. He had therefore to consent, but with the stipulation that the vanquished party should give fifty black eyed camels and be for ten years an exile from Mecca. A Khozáite sooth-sayer was appointed as an umpire, who, having heard the pretensions of both, pronounced Háshim to be the victor. Háshim took the fifty camels, slaughtered them and fed all the people present. Omyya set out for Syria, and remained there in exile for ten years. This is the origin of that rivalry and feud between the Omyyad and the Háshimite factions which in after ages caused such a havoc amongst the Háshmites *viz.* the descendants of the Prophet in particular and their followers in general.

How Sheiba-al-Hamd was called Abd-al-Mottalib

At the time of Háshim's death (about 510 A. D.) his son was a mere child and away at Medina with his mother Selma bint Amr, a lady of distinction of the Banu Najjár clan of the Khazraj tribe. Háshim entrusted the offices held by him to his brother Al-Mottalib (the name should not be mistaken for Abd-al-Mottalib) with instructions to give the charge to the son. Al-Mottalib conducted the entertainment of the pilgrims in so splendid a style as to deserve the epithet Al-Faidz, 'the Munificent'. Meanwhile his little nephew Sheiba-al-Hamd (so called because his infantile head was covered with white hair) was growing up under the care of his widowed mother at Medina. Several years after his brother's death, Al-Mottalib brought him from Medina. The Meccans, seeing the beautiful lad with Al-Mottalib, presumed that he was a slave and told Al-Mottalib what a pretty bargain he had made. Al-Mottalib, however, informed them that the boy was his nephew Sheiba, the son of Háshim. They then minutely scrutinized his features and swore that he was the very likeness of Háshim. In this incident the name Abd-al-Mottalib (slave of Al-Mottalib) is said to have had its origin, and by this name the son of Háshim was hereafter called. †

Usurpation of Abd-al-Mottalib's rights.

Another instance of the ill feelings of the Omyyads (Bani Omyya) towards the Háshimites (Bani Háshim) may be found in the following incident :—

‡ Al-Mottalib transferred the offices to Abd-al-Mottalib in accordance with his father's will and continued to manage the affairs himself. But Al-Mottalib died soon after. The boy Abd-al-Mottalib had two other uncles—Abd Shams and Nawfal. The hostile disposition of the former was manifest, but unfortunately for the boy the latter also, being the confederate of Abd Shams, was not favourably disposed towards him. The four sons of Abd Manáf were divided into two parties, each of which was at variance with the other. Háshim and Al-Mottalib formed one party while Abd Shams and Nawfal formed the other. Nawfal, at the instigation of Abd Shams (father of Omyya) taking advantage of the boy's helplessness deprived him of his rights, usurping them himself; but he was compelled to recede on the interference of the boy's maternal relatives, to whom he had appealed to come to his aid from Medina.

Abd-al-Mottalib's vow. The well Zem Zem.

|| Thus installed in the office of entertaining the pilgrims, Abd-al-Mottalib discharged the functions for years. But he was destitute of power and influence; and, having but one son to assist him, he found it difficult to cope with the opposing faction of the Qoreish. He felt so deeply his

---

† Tabaqát Ibn Sa'd ; Ibn Hishám.

‡ Ibid.

|| Tabaqát Ibn Sa'd; Ibn Hishám; Rawdzat-al-Ahbáb.

weakness and inferiority in contending with the large and powerful families of his opponents as to vow that if Providence should ever grant him ten sons he would devote one of them to the Deity. His prayer was heard, and he began to have his sons one after the other. Meanwhile fortune smiled on him. He received in a vision the heavenly behest to dig for the well of Zem Zem, which for centuries had been choked up and even its site was not remembered. He made diligent search for the site of the well in the vicinity of the Ka'ba, and at length succeeded in discovering the masonry work. Aided by his son Hárith, the only grown up one, Abd-al-Mottalib, in spite of the opposition of the Qoreish, dug deeper and deeper till he came upon the two golden Ghezálls with the swords and suits of armour buried there by the Jorhomite king Amr b. Hárith, more than three centuries before. Thus was the well of Zem Zem discovered.

The plentiful flow of fresh water from the well was a great triumph to Abd-al-Mottalib. Hitherto, with considerable troubles, water was procured from the wells scattered all over Mecca and stored in cisterns near the Ka'ba for the pilgrims. Now all other wells were deserted and this alone resorted to, on account of its water being the best in taste and purity. The origin of Zem Zem is shrouded in mystery. Tradition says that its water first began to sprout from the ground underneath with the strokes of the heels of baby Ismáel, whom his father Abrahám had deserted along with his mother Hágar in this wilderness, while she ran hither and thither eagerly at the deceptive sights of the fleeting sand in search of water to slake her thirst. It was therefore held sacred and now it soon acquired additional sanctity ‡ sharing in the sacredness of the Ka'ba and its rites.

---

‡"Burkhardt ascertained that the level of Zem Zem continues the same even when there is the greatest drain on its waters, by comparing the length of the bucket-rope in the morning and again in the evening. The Turks regard this as a miracle, as it is used not only by the multitudes of pilgrims, but

Abd-al-Mottalib fulfilling his vow.

†Years rolled on and Abd-al-Mottalib found himself at last surrounded with the number of sons prayed for, the sight of whom daily reminded him of his vow, rashly taken at a time when he was alone and in trouble. He took his sons to the Ka'ba and a lot was cast for each of the sons to single out the one to be sacrificed. The fatal lot fell upon Abdalláh, who was the most beautiful and modest of the Arabian youth and the most beloved of Abd-al-Mottalib. It was very hard for Abd-al-Mottalib, but the vow must be kept. How else should it be fulfilled than by the sacrificial knife? His six daughters wept bitterly and clung around the father and persuaded him to cast lots between Abdalláh and ten camels, the current ransom for the blood of a man. If God accepted it, the boy was saved. The lot was cast, but only to the disappointment of the anxious family. It was repeated with an addition of ten camels, but the lot again fell upon the son. At

---

by every family in the city, for drinking and ablution, though held too sacred for culinary purposes. He learned from one, who had descended to repair the masonry, that the water was flowing at the bottom, and that the water is therefore supplied by a subterraneous rivulet. The water is heavy in its taste, and sometimes in its colour resembles milk, but it is perfectly sweet, and differs very much from that of the brackish wells dispersed over the town. When first drawn up, it is slightly tepid, resembling in this respect many other fountains in the Hejáz." *Travels p. 144 from Muir's Life of Mohammed.*

"Ali Bey says:—The well is about 7 feet 8 inches in diameter, and 56 feet deep to the surface of the water (which) is rather brackish and heavy, but very limpid. Notwithstanding the depth of the well, and the heat of the climate, it is hotter when first drawn up than the air....................................It is wholesome, neverthless, and so abundant that at the period of the pilgrimage, though there were thousands of pitchers-full drawn, its level was not sensibly diminished." *Muir Vol. ii p. 81.* "Sale, on the authority of Edrisi, states that the springs of Mecea are bitter and unfit to drink, except only the well Zem Zem." *Prel. Disc. p. 3 from Muir's Life of Mohammed.*

†Tabaqát Ibn Sa'd; Ibn Hishám.

each successive trial Abd-al-Mottalib added ten camels to the stake, but God appeared to refuse the offer of ransom and required the sacrifice of the man. At the tenth throw, however, with a ransom of hundred camels, the lot fell upon the camels. Abd-al-Mottalib had this lot cast thrice and each time it having fallen upon the camels, he was satisfied. He then joyfully slaughtered one hundred camels between Safá and Marwa and feasted the inhabitants of Mecca upon them. It was this Abdalláh who became the father of the Holy Prophet Mohammed. The sacrifice of the Prophet's father and his forefather Ismáel was held back but it was distined to be fulfilled with the greater sacrifice of his posterity at Karbala. فديناه بذبح عظيم "And We ransomed his son with a greater sacrifice." *Sura XXXVII—108.*

The fame and influence of Abd-al-Mottalib now began to be established; a large family of thirteen powerful sons added to his dignity; he became and continued to his death the virtual Chief of Mecca. The grand offices of the Siqáya and the Rifáda *i.e.* the exclusive privilege of supplying water and food to the pilgrims secured to the Háshimites a commanding and permanent influence under the able management of Háshim, of Al-Mottalib and now of Abd-al-Mottalib, who like his father Háshim was regarded as the Chief of the Sheikhs of Mecca.

Envy of the Omyyads.

†But the branch of Abd-Shams (the Omyyads), with their numerous and powerful connections, continued their manoeuvres against the Háshimites and eagerly endeavoured to raise the cry of heresy and impiety against them in order to disposess them of the guardianship of the Ka'ba. Following the example of his father, Harb son of Omyya attempted to dislodge him from his position by challenging Abd-al-Mottalib to prove his superiority to retain the office. But, to his great disappointment, the empire settled the contest in favour of Abd-al-Mottalib declaring him the

†Tabaqát Ibn Sa'd.

rightful possessor. Harb was deeply mortified and shunned the society of his opponent. This incident may be deemed to be a further cause for the burning hatred which smothered within the breasts of the Omyyads against the Háshimites, and later on, other occurrences of much more serious nature contributed to the mighty blaze, when the Omyyads found themselves strong enough to take revenge.

Harb, son of Omyya, was the head of the Omyyads at the time we speak of. He already held the office of chieftain in war, which contributed much to his splendour. Besides, he was a successful businessman and thus had both wealth and influence.

So long as Abd-al-Mottalib lived, he was regarded as

Changes. the virtual Chief of Mecca, but after his death there was no powerful head among the Háshimites to maintain the position. Hárith, the eldest son of Abd-al-Mottalib, was dead. Zobeir was the oldest and to him Abd-al-Mottalib had bequeathed his offices. Zobeir again left them to Abu-Tálib, but he was too poor to maintain the expensive position of furnishing the pilgrims with food and water. He waived his claim in favour of Abbás, who was older than Hamza and in fortune better than others. Abu Lahab, though the elder of the two, was not favourably disposed towards his brothers, being in closer association with the Omyyads and having married a daughter of Harb. But Abbás also proved unable to keep up the two offices. Rifáda passed into the hands of the rivals, while Abbás retained only Siqáya, involving the charge of the well Zem Zem, which was retained by him till the introduction of Islám, and then confirmed to his family by the Prophet. Thus the family of Háshim had fallen from its height, while their rivals, the Omyyads, with Harb son of Omyya as their head, had succeeded in gaining the long coveted ascendency. This state of things lasted till the conquest of Mecca by the Prophet over fifty years later.

——:o:——

CHAPTER III.

The birth of our Lord Mohammed and the first forty years of his life.

The great prophet of Islam, Mohammed (Peace on him and his Holy progeny), was born at Mecca, **Place and date.** in the year when Abraha b. al-Sabáh surnamed al-Ashram, the Abyssinian viceroy of Yemen, a Christian in faith, made the expedition against Mecca to destroy the Ka'ba. The year is known as Am-al-Fil after the name of the expedition, as the Arabs first saw the elephant on this occasion, and the invaders are mentioned in the Qurán as Asháb-al-Fil, who perished of Divine Wrath, vide *Sura CV*. in which a description of the event is given thus:—"Hast thou not seen how thy Lord dealt with the army of the elephant? Did He not cause their stratagem to go amiss? And He sent against them flocks of little birds, which cast down upon them small clay stones, and made them like unto the leaves of corn of which the cattle have eaten." Forty-five or fifty-five-days after the expedition, the Holy babe was born in the house known as She'b Abi Tálib on Friday at the dawn of morning.

The date of birth reckoned by the Shi'as as the most authentic, is the seventeenth of Rabi' I; while the Sunnis regard the twelfth of Rabi' I as the correct date. Both these sects are, however, divided among themselves about the exact date. According to the Christian era, Cassin de Perceval dates the birth at twentyninth of August 570 A.D.

I have given the paternal lineage of the Holy babe in the preceding chapter as well as in the Genealogical Table at the end of it. His mother Amena was the daughter of Wahab, a great grandson of Keláb of the same lineage as our Lord Mohammed.

Amena, the mother of Mohammed, never felt any heaviness on account of her pregnancy **Name.** and therefore she could not, for a considerable period, believe that she was pregnant, until she received the intelligence in a vision; and later on she dreamt of an angel directing her to name the babe 'Ahmad' or Mohammed when born. She was frightened at such dreams and to repel the effects thereof she was advised to wear some iron lockets, which she wore till delivery. The progenitor of Mohammed *i. e.* Ismáel was given his name in the like manner as also some other Prophets, *vide Genesis XVI-11*. "And the angel of the Lord said unto her, Behold, thou art with child, and shalt bear a son, and shalt call his name Ishmael; because the Lord hath heard thy affliction." Also see *Genesis XVII-19* "And God said (unto Abraham), Sárah thy wife shall bear thee a son indeed; and thou shalt call his name Isaac:" Also see *St. Matthew I-21*. "And she shall bring forth a son, and thou shalt call his name Jesus:"

As soon as he was born, a messenger was sent to Abd-al-Mottalib conveying the happy tidings of the blessed babe, which had brought with him a sudden light, † which illumined the whole place at the time. Abd-al- Mottalib hastened joyfully to the infant, took him in his arms to Ka'ba, offered thanks to God for the gift and named him Mohammed, which means in Arabic 'the praised'. This name was justified by the Prophet after his mission to mark him out as the promised ‡ Paraclete *vide New Testament,*

---

† W. Irving writes: "His mother suffered none of the pangs of travail. At the moment of his coming into the world a celestial light illumined the surrounding country, and the new born child, raising his eyes to heaven, exclaimed: "God is great! There is no god but God, and I am His Prophet."—*Life of Mohammed page 13.*

‡ "Other passages of Scripture understood by Moslems of their Prophet are:—

Deut. xxxiii-2,—where Sinai is said to mean Judaism, Seir (in Galilee) Christianity, and Párán (in Arabia) Islam.

Isia, xxi-6,—Where the 'rider on the ass' is Jesus, the 'rider on the camel' Mohammed.

Matt. xx: 1-16,—Where the *morning*, *noon*, and *even* are Judaism, Christianity and Islam.

John iv-21

John XIV-26, XVI-7. The seventh day after the glorious birth a feast, in celebration of the happy event, was given by Abd-al-Mottalib with great eclat.

Death of Abdallah.

† Mohammed's father Abdalláh, son of Abd-al-Mottalib, did not live to see the son's birth. Leaving his wife in pregnancy, Abdalláh had proceeded on mercantile business towards Syria. On his way back, he fell seriously ill and was left behind by the caravan at Medina with his father's maternal relations. On hearing of Abdallah's illness, Abd-al-Mottalib sent his son Hárith to fetch him to Mecca, but he was too late. Hárith returned to tell the sad news of his brother's death only to plunge the whole house into mourning. Abdalláh was but twenty-five years of age. His old father loved him fondly because of his being possessed of personal traits and accomplishments, which none of his brothers had. ‡To the young wife the news was a death blow. She could not survive him long. She was only very recently married to Abdalláh when he left her. The only consolation to her was the child. But the grief told upon her health to such an extent that the fountain of her breast dried up and she could not nurse the babe.

Nursing of Mohammed.

So he had to be entrusted first to Thowbiya, a maid servant of Abu Lahab, the babe's uncle, for a short period, and subsequently to Halima, a Bedouin woman, who took him under her care and brought him up amongst her own people, the noblest of the Bedouin races, the Banu Sa'd, who inhabited the hills south of Táef.

---

1 John iv-2, 3—Where Mohammed is said to be 'the spirit that is of God,' because he proclaimed that Jesus was a true man and not God." *Rodwell's Kor. p. 445.* Also *Habak, iii-3.*

† Tabaqát Ibn Sa'd.

‡ "So remarkable was Abdállah for personal beauty and those qualities which win the affections of women, that, if Moslem traditions are to be credited, on the night of his marriage with Amena, two hundred virgins of the tribe of Qoreish died of broken hearts." *W. Irving's Life of Mohammed p. 13.*

Bedouin women were accustomed to suckle the children of towns-folk for wages, and Halima was fortunate enough to get Mohammed in her charge inasmuch as she was comfortably prosperous, and—contrary to the habits of the bedouin tribes, who lived constantly at war with each other—quite peaceful at home so long as Mohammed lived with her. Halima kept Mohammed with her for about five years, and he was now grown up and did not need his foster mother's care. Halima reluctantly gave him back to his mother Amena.

Death of Amena.

† Soon after this, Amena proceeded to Medina (575 A.D.) to show her boy to the maternal relatives of his father, taking Mohammed with herself along with Omm Aiman, the slave girl of her late husband; or rather to console her heart, which yearned to have a look at the heap of earth beneath which her husband lay buried at Medina. During her short stay for about a month at Medina, Amena felt her heart failing and she hastened back, but she died at Abwá midway between Medina and Mecca and was buried there. Omm Aiman brought Mohammed back to Mecca, where the charge of the orphan was undertaken by his grandfather Abd-al-Mottalib, who had by this time reached the patriarchal age of four score. Mohammed was now in his sixth year and was treated by his grandfather with singular fondness. Omm Aiman was still his nurse.

Death of Abd-al-Mottalib.

‡ The guardianship of Abd-al-Mottalib lasted, however, only about two years, and he breathed his last (578 A. D.) leaving the orphan in his eighth year. Mohammed felt bitterly the loss and followed the bier weeping.

Abu Talib's guardianship.

‡‡ Abd-al-Mottalib on his death-bed embraced Mohammed for the last time and then entrusted him to the care of his son Abu Tálib, brother of Mohammed's father Abdalláh by the same

† Ibn Hishám; Ibn Sa'd; Rawdzat al Ahbáb.
‡ Tabari; Ibn Hishám; Ibn Sa'd.
‡‡ Tabari; Ibn Sa'd; Ibn Hishám.

mother, enjoining him to treat the orphan as tenderly as his own son. He said, "They must take care of that beautiful little boy: nothing in their kindred was more precious than he." Abu Tálib very affectionately promised to do this; and his subsequent behaviour showed how faithfully he kept his word. He liked the boy, loved him fondly, made him sleep by his own bed-side and took him wherever he went; and this continued until Mohammed was about twelve years of age.

[Abu Tálib's devotion to Mohammed in his youth, and his protection from the hostilities of the Qoreish against him will be seen later on. His wife Fátema bint Asad (the mother of Ali), also was no less zealous in her affections for Mohammed, whom she treated just as her own son.]

Mohammed's trip to Syria.

† Abu Tálib then undertook a journey on business to Syria (A. D. 582) and intended to leave Mohammed behind at Mecca, but the latter would not consent and clung to his uncle in a manner that deeply moved Abu Tálib, who could not see him crying, and took him to Syria. It is noteworthy that in this journey when the caravan halted at its last stage to Bostra, Abu Tálib happened to put up near a church of the Nestorian monks, one of whom, Boheira or Sergius by name, noticed that a piece of cloud was shadowing Mohammed. He came near him when he sat under a tree ‡ which bowed low as if to pay respects to Mohammed, thoroughly examined his features, happened to see the impression like a large mole of the size of a pigeon's egg between his shoulders (the seal or credential of his Divine Mission) and by some symptoms on his face was convinced that he was the person predicted in the Scriptures as the coming Prophet. After meditation and contemplation he advised Abu Tálib to protect the boy from dangers, which, he said, would be abundantly

† Ibn Hishám.

‡ Tirmizhi as quoted in Uswat-al-Rasul *Vol ii p. 167*.

awaiting him at the hands of his own people, whose deliverer he was destined to be.

Mohammed's bent of mind.

As Mohammed was born and brought up among the sacerdotal house-hold of the guardians of the Ka'ba sanctuary, and being gifted by nature with a thoughtful and meditative mind, the order and decorum of the house of Abu Tálib, the pious offerings and the devoutful prayers of his priestly self and relations, the rigid observance of sacred rites, and, above all, the sacred and awe-inspiring environments of the Sanctuary itself made a strong impression on the mind of Mohammed, tending him to devotion to the Omnipotent and Omnipresent Lord.

Sacrilegious war 585 A. D.

† When Mohammed was fourteen or fifteen years of age, a war, rather tribal feud, broke out between the Banu Kinána and the Banu Hawázin, in which Mohammed was perforce engaged to take part twice to help his uncle Zobeir. This war occurred within the sacred months and in the sacred territory and lasted with occasional engagements for a period of nine years. This was called Fijár or the 'Sacrilegious War'.

Hilf-al-Fudzul 595 A. D.

‡ As Mohammed was gifted by Nature with a sympathetic mind, his heart bled at the sight of frightful outrages, which he occasionally saw perpetrated heartlessly by his own countrymen on helpless victims. He earnestly wished and worked to improve, if possible, their morals, and to cultivate fear of God in them. Actuated by such feelings, he had, while but twenty years of age, wished to adopt some measures for the suppression of violence and injustice. It was at his instance, that Zobeir, the oldest of the surviving sons of Abd-al-Mottalib, formed a league to suggest to the principal Qoreish tribes the expediency of binding themselves by an oath to secure justice to the helpless. The Háshimites, the Banu Zohra and the Banu Tym took part in the League

† Abul Fida ; Tabari.
‡ Tabaqát Ibn Sa'd.

and swore that they would stand up as the champion of the injured, and would see that wrongs did not remain unpunished and that the claims of the oppressed were fully satisfied. The oath is known as Hilf-al-Fudzul. It proved useful both as a preventive against violence and as a means of enforcing restitution. In after days Mohammed used to say that he bore a happy remembrance of his having taken the initiative in the League of the Oath which was taken in the house of Abdalláh son of Jod'án to suppress violence and oppression.

Al-Ameen.

As Mohammed had acquired, under the guidance of his uncle Abu Tálib, a man of great mercantile abilities, fair knowledge and experience of mercantile transactions carried on by caravans, and was well spoken of by persons who happened to come in touch with him, some traders engaged him as their representative to conduct important business affairs in their behalf. Mohammed so successfully executed these trusts that people wondered at his intelligence and business capacity. They were perfectly satisfied with his honesty, and the whole of Mecca rang with praise for his being truthful, strong in moral character, honest in his dealings and reliable in every respect. The stainless character and the honorable bearing of the unobtrusive youth won the respect of his fellow citizens, and he received by common consent the title of Al-Ameen, *i. e.* the 'Trustworthy.'

Khadija 595 A. D.

† The fame of Mohammed's straight-forwardness and uprightness reached the ears of Khadija, a noble lady of Mecca who was a Qoreishite. Her father Khowailid was a son of Asad, who was a grandson of Qosayy. She was rich enough to carry on trade by caravans of her own, which were worked in charge of her slaves and servants. She needed an honest and intelligent man capable of undertaking the journeys on her behalf. She sent word to Mohammed through his friend Khazima b. Hakim, a relative of hers, offering him double the rate of the usual salary.

† Ibn Hishám; Tabari; Ibn Sa'd.

Mohammed, with the consent of Abu Tálib entered into her service, and, in charge of a trading caravan belonging to her, travelled to Bostra, on the road to Damascus. Meisara, a servant of Khadija, also accompanied him in charge of her property. In the course of his journey to Bostra, Mohammed was seen overshadowed by a cloud during the heat of the day, and Meisara, greatly wondering at the strange occurrence, related the fact to Khadija on his return. Reaching the destination, Mohammed, by judicious barter with the Syrian merchants, succeeded in doubling the usual profits on Khadija's goods.

There is a tradition which relates that, before disposing of the goods, there was a contention between Mohammed and the person who wished to take his wares. He desired Mohammed to swear by the two Meccan goddesses Lát and Uzza, but Mohammed bluntly refused to do so. This refusal is an incident which shows that he *never* believed in idols.

When Mohammed had disposed of the merchandise of his mistress, and, according to her command, purchased for her such things as she had directed, he returned to his native land in company with Meisara; and as they drew near Mecca, the grateful servant persuaded Mohammed to go ahead of the caravan from Marr-al-Tzohrán and be himself the bearer to his mistress of the glad tidings of the successful transactions. Khadija, surrounded by her maids, was sitting upon the upper story of her house, (which is still known and venerated as Mowlad-i-Fátema, or the birth-place of Fátema, a little to the north-east of Ka'ba), on the watch for the first glimpse of the caravan, when a camel was seen rapidly advancing, and as it approached, she perceived that Mohammed was the rider, with his brilliant face protected from the heat of the sun by a piece of cloud over him. She was struck with his beauty and all that she saw about him. He entered, recounted the prosperous issue of the business and enumerated the various goods, which agreeably to her taste, he had brought for her. She was highly pleased at the success. † Again she sent him in the same capacity towards Yemen, where also, by his tact and diligence, he attained a similar success to the great joy of Khadija.

Khadija proposes to Mohammed.

She was a lady distinguished by birth as well as by fortune. She had been already twice married and had borne several issues, but now she was a widow. Though she was forty, yet looked younger, and retained a fair and attractive countenance, and was possessed of good health. Many of the Qoreish nobles sought her in marriage, but she preferred to live in dignified and independent widowhood, and rejected all their offers. Mohammed was now in the bloom of his life, being in his twentyfifth year of age. He was endowed by nature with beauty and prepossessing appearance. Noble by birth he was noble in bearing and had elegent manners. Attracted by personal qualities and fascinated with the beauty and elegance of Mohammed, ‡ Khadija desired to marry him, and in order to sound his views, she deputed a maid servant of hers to approach him. "What is it O Mohammed," said this female, adroitly referring to the unusual circumstance of his being unmarried at so mature an age, "what is it which hindreth thee from marriage?" ' I have nothing," replied he, "in my hands wherewith I might marry." "But if that difficulty were removed, and thou wert invited to espouse a beautiful and wealthy lady of noble birth, who would place thee in a position of affluence, wouldst thou not desire to have her?" "And who," said Mohammed startled at the novel idea, "may that be"? "It is Khadija." "But how can I attain her"? " Let that be my care," returned the female. "I shall have no objection to such an union," answered Mohammed. The female departed and imparted the intelligence to Khadija, who lost no time in intimating to Abu Tálib, Mohammed's uncle and guardian, her desire of matrimonial alliance with Mohammed.

---

† Tabari; W. Irwing.

‡ Tabaqát Ibn Sa'd.

Mohammed marries Khadija.

† Abu Tálib, after consulting Mohammed, consented to the proposal, and the marriage took place (595 A. D.) with great eclat and feasts. Invitations were issued by Abu Tálib, and Khadija herself. ‡ Abu Tálib himself read the Sermon of the ceremony and paid down from his purse the dower of twelve and a half okks of gold equivalent to the price of twenty well bred young camels. This marriage proved very advantageous to Mohammed, for it raised him above the necessity of toiling for subsistence and gave him leisure to indulge in meditation to which he was originally inclined and which had been fostered in the course of his priestly uncle Abu Tálib's guardianship.

He lived in a most affectionate manner with his wife. She reciprocated the love gratefully, and her regard for him grew more and more as time passed on. The marriage was quite a happy one for the pair in every respect. She bore him her illustrious daughter Fátema, who was destined to be the fore-mother of the holy descendants of Mohammed. She bore him also two sons, *viz.* Qásim, after whose name Mohammed received his surname Abul Qásim, and Abdalláh. But both of them died in their infancy.

The birth of Ali.

It was perhaps on the occasion of the death of a babe that Abu Tálib's wife, Fátema bint Asad, who was pregnant, offered to make over to Mohammed her issue, whether male or female, in order to comfort him in his bereavement (as Fátema, his daughter was not yet born.) This offer proved to be the Decree of Providence later on. Fátema bint Asad felt how the babe, when still in the womb, compelled her to stand up in order to pay respect to Mohammed, whenever he happened to visit her; and never allowed to let her turn her face from Mohammed so long as he was there. Ordinarily it should have been

---

† Ibn Athir; Tabari.
‡ Zarqáni; Rawdzat al Ahbab.

the other way, because the aunt, being Mohammed's superior by relation, ranking almost as his mother, owed respect from him; but she knew not what power made her stand up at once before Mohammed, who was now about only thirty years of age.

This babe was none other than Ali, who was born within the holy precincts of the Ka'ba (600 A. D.), where none else was born, ever since its foundation thousands of years ago. He first opened his eyes on no other object but the face of Mohammed, when he took him caressingly in his arms. His first wash, after his birth, was performed by Mohammed with a prediction that this babe would give him his last wash. The prophecy was fulfilled on the death of Mohammed. The babe accepted no other food than the moisture of Mohammed's tongue, which he sucked for several days after his birth. Mohammed fondled him while an infant, in his lap; used to chew his food and feed Ali on it, made him often sleep by his side in the same bed and thus Ali enjoyed the warmth of Mohammed's body and inhaled the holy fragrance of his breath. When grown up, he shared the meals and was brought up under the personal care of Mohammed to share his high ethics and morals. Ali was ever ready to run the risk of his own life at times of danger for Mohammed and to him he was affectionately attached with unswerving faithfulness. The cousins were so fond of one another that they always lived together till death parted them.

Ali adopted by Mohammed. 605 A. D.

When Ali grew out of his infancy, Mohammed, to compensate his uncle, Abu Tálib, as much as possible, for the troubles he had undergone in taking care of him and giving him a genial training, took his cousin Ali, while he was only five years of age, under his own care to train him up to his own fashion and according to most of the assertions, adopted † him. As a severe

†Tabari ; Ibn Athir.

famine was afflicting the country at the time, Mohammed persuaded his uncle Abbás to relieve Abu Tálib of the cares of another of his sons. Thus Abbás took Ja'far.

Zaid b-Haritha.

At about the same period a boy named Zaid son of Háritha was presented to Mohammed, by his wife Khadija, as a slave. Originally he belonged to a respectable family of the tribe of a Khozáite branch called Kalb; but, being taken away in his childhood by a party of free-booters, was sold to Khadija. His father getting the clue came to Mecca, approached Mohammed and offered a considerable sum for his ransom, which was politely denied. ‡ Mohammed, who had already freed Zaid, allowed him the option of going home with his father; but Zaid did not like to lose the affectionate treatment experienced by him, and preferred to remain with Mohammed, who subsequently married him to Omm Aiman his old attendant girl. Osáma, the famous General, who was given command of the expedition against the Greeks by Mohammed just before his death, was the son of this Zaid, a fruit of this marriage. Zaid had fallen at Muta in command of a previous expedition against the same people.

Rebuilding of the Ka'ba. 605 A. D.

Mohammed was now about thirtyfive years of age, when a fortunate event increased his popularity amongst his tribesmen. The walls of the Ka'ba were low and in a dilapidated condition, being rendered insecure by a flood, which frequently committed similar ravages; as for instance in 1627 A. D. it damaged three sides of the sacred buildings. Owing to the absence of a roof, some thieves clambered over the walls and had stolen some of the precious relics, which were, however, recovered. It was therefore resolved that the walls should be raised to a greater height and covered over with a roof. In the meantime a Grecian ship was wrecked upon the shores of the Red Sea near Sho'aiba, the ancient harbour of

‡Sirat-al Halabiya; Tanqid-al-Kalám.

Mecca. Walid b. Moghira proceeded to the scene of the disaster, purchased the timber of the broken ship, and secured the services of her Captain, Báqum by name, who was a skilled architect, to assist in rebuilding the Ka'ba.

The numerous tribes of the Qoreish were divided into four bodies and to each was assigned the charge of one side. Thus one side was assigned to the Banu Abd Manáf including the descendants of Háshim, Abd Shams, Nawfal and Al-Mottalib and the Banu Zohra; a second to Banu Asad and Abd-al-Dár; a third tò Banu Makhzum and Banu Tym; and the fourth to Banu Sahm, Adi and Amr b. Loay. The old and dilapidated walls were demolished to the bed of green stones called the 'Foundation of Abraham' † and from thence the new walls were raised.

For the construction of the sacred enclosure, stones of grey-granite were hewn from the neighbouring hills and carried by the citizens upon their heads. Mòhammed, with the whole body of the Qoreish, assisted in the work. As customary, people loosened their undergarments and gathered them over their heads for protection against the weight and roughness of the stones. Mohammed, when reluctantly loosening his garment, happened to fall headlong on the ground and a voice from some invisible source was heard warning him not to expose his person. He at once got up and was never seen naked by any human being from his boyhood till his death.

---

† A tradition says that when a pickaxe struck the green stones of the foundation set close together like teeth, the whole of Mecca shook, as if by an earthquake. It is also stated that an inscription was discovered beneath one of the corner foundations, written in Syriac, which no one could decipher until a Jew made it out as follows:—"I am God, the Lord of Becca; I created it on the day on which I created the heavens and the earth, and formed the sun and the moon; and I have surrounded it with seven angels of the true faith; it shall not pass away until the two hills thereof pass away. Blessed be the inhabitants thereof in water and in milk." *Hishami.* Also there is a tradition that about forty years before the mission

Hajar-al-Aswad or the Black Stone.

† When the walls at the eastern corner rose to a sufficient height for fixing the Hajar-al-Aswad or the sacred Black Stone, there arose a dispute as to who should have the honor of placing the Black Stone in its new receptacle, each family of the Qoreish claiming the privilege. The contention grew so hot that bloodshed was imminent. For four or five days the construction was suspended. At last, Abu Omyya (a Banu Makhzum, brother of Walid the father of Khálid), the oldest citizen, suggested that any one who chances first to enter in the sacred enclosure by the gate of the Bani Sheiba (so called probably because it was built by Sheiba-al-Hamd, the original name of Abd-al-Mottalib) should be chosen to decide the difference, or himself to place the Stone. After a while, Lo! there appeared Mohammed, who happened to be absent on the occasion, and was the first man by the Gate within the enclosure. They exclaimed: "Here comes Al Ameen the arbitrator; we are content to abide by whatever he decides!" Calm and self-possessed, Mohammed received the commission and cheerfully availed himself of the chance, both of performing his own duty as a Divine Missionary (though this fact may not have been realized at the time); and of conciliating all the disputants of the four parties, by his expedient and judicious solution of the complicated problem, at one and the same time. He took off his mantle, spread it upon the ground and, placing the sacred stone on it, invited one chief from each of the four divisions to come forward to raise the four corners of the mantle high up to the wall. ‡ They complied, and Mohammed guided the Stone with his own hands to its proper place in the

---

of Mohammed, a stone was found in the Ka'ba inscribed with these words:—"He that soweth good, shall reap that which is to be envied; and he that soweth evil, shall reap remorse. Ye do evil, and (expect to) obtain good: Ah! that would be to gather grapes of thorns." *Muir's Life of Mohammed.*

† Ibn Hishám.

‡ Madárij-al-Nabowat; Rawdzatal-Ahbáb.

wall, at the south-east corner of the Edifice, five feet above the ground floor.

No doubt, youthful Mohammed's having been singled out to be the Judge among his own fellows for the decision of a sacred question, in spite of the aged and venerable chiefs, was apparently Providential, as he was the Chosen of God to be the prophet of His people. Though this fact appears to have passed unnoticed by them, yet this decision raised the character of Mohammed for his ready wit and prudent determination, and enhanced the esteem and respect in which he was held among his tribes-men.

"The Black Stone is undoubtedly the oldest treasure of Mecca. We have the Moslem tradition that it came down snow-white from heaven and was blackened by the touch of sin—according to one tradition, that of an impure woman, and according to another by the kisses of thousands of believers. It is probably an aerolite and owes its reputation to its fall from the sky." *Zwemer*. I will not endeavour to describe the Black Stone of the Ka'ba as an aerolite or an angel transformed into stone. Be it what it may; suffice it to say that it was held sacred by Abrahám and Ismáel, who are universally acknowledged as revered Prophets who fixed it there in the Ka'ba sanctuary, and it is held sacred ever since.

Mohammed's retirement for meditations.

The awe-inspiring environments of the Ka'ba and the sacred ceremonies performed by the people there had already made a deep impression upon the mind of Mohammed. But his later experience showed that all the various forms of worship were but a mockery or at least customary rites coming down from father to son. There was no sincerity in their worship. He felt deeply for their utter disregard and neglect of responsibilities to the Almighty Creator and the Day of Judgment. Traditions told him of the purer faith of their ancestor Abrahám, and he realized how that pure devotion was now corrupted and degenerated to gross idolatory and ferocious crimes prevailing in the country.

He longed for restoring the erring humanity to the right path, and to bring back the worship of the Almighty Lord as in the days of Abrahám.

In fact, he had all along been a thoughtful man and inclined to religious meditations. With a heavy heart, he now used to retire into solitude and silence, for prayers and meditations. Through the hours of loneliness in the desert, in the darkness of the night, and in the dazzling light of the day, his attention was ever rivetted to the natural evidences of the twinkling stars and bright constellation, the moon and the sun gliding silently along the deep blue sky; and all these pointed out to the existence of the All-managing Creator. They seemed to charge him with a special mission. Some low voice, which by the attentive listner is never passed unheard, would swell into grander and more imperious tones, when the tempest swept with its forked lightning and far rolling thunder along the vast solitude of the Meccan mountains.

Mohammed's favourite resort.

Mohammed's favourite resort was a cavern on Mount Hirá, overlooking the Ka'ba, at a distance of about three miles north of Mecca, where he frequently withdrew for prayers and meditations, where he lived much within himself reserved and meditative for considerable periods. In this cave often he passed whole nights, absorbed in profoundest thought, as if deep in communion with the All-pervading God of the Universe. During the month of Rajab and Ramadzán, he was wont to pass the whole month in this cave, amongst the dark and wild surroundings, resigning himself entirely to the will of the All-directing, All-powerful Judge of mankind. At length, he received visions in his dreams or heard voices from invisible source pointing to the traces of the object he sought for. Conceptions of the Most High dawned upon his mind as he cherished a deep and earnest faith in the Omnipotent and Omnipresent Lord, the only Being to be worshipped.

He was now regarded among the members of his family and relations, as well as in the circle of his friends and acquaintances as a very pious and saintly man. When he was in his thirty-eighth year, he began to be conscious of some light around him during the course of his devotional prayers.

CHAPTER IV.

The Mission and its first three years.

Be'that or the Mission.

In the fortieth year of his life, when Mohammed was passing, according to his wont, the month of Rajab in the solemn solitude of the cavern on Mount Hirá, praying, fasting, and meditating on Divine conception and human regeneration, it was in the deep silence and calm atmosphere of the 27th night of that month that all of a sudden he heard a voice calling him by name. He looked round but no one was to be seen. Again he heard the same voice and a flood of light broke in upon him with dazzling splendour. He composedly beheld a human form approaching. It was the angel Gabriel, who coming quite near Mohammed, held a silken scroll before him and asked him to read what was written thereon. Mohammed replied: "What should I read.?" Thereupon the angel pressed Mohammed hard to his own person so that he was bedewed with sweat. He felt his mind illumined with celestial light, and his eyes opened to the writing on the Scroll and he could recite اقرا باسم ربک الذی خلق ٥ "Read! in the name of thy Lord, who hath created"; خلق الانسان من علق ٥ "Created man from a clot of blood." اقرا و ربک الاکرم الذی علم بالقلم ٥ "Read! for thy Lord is the Most Generous, who hath taught the use of the pen"; علم الانسان مالم یعلم ٥ "Hath taught to man what he knew not." کلا ان الانسان لیطغي "Nay! Truly man walketh in delusion," ان راٰہ استغني "When he deems that he suffices for himself." ان الی ربک الرجعي

"Verily, unto the Lord they must all return." *Sura XCVI: 1-7*. When he finished the recitation, the heavenly messenger announced, "O Mohammed, Verily, thou art the Prophet of God! and I am His angel Gabriel."

This was the first revelation to Mohammed from Heaven, and the first descent of a passage of the Heavenly Book the Qurán. † The angel Gabriel was gone; the words which Gabriel required Mohammed to read remained graven on his heart.

Uncertain, whether all that had occurred in the night was a reality and that his heart-felt desire,—to restore the erring humanity to the right path and to bring back the true worship of the Almighty Lord as among the true followers of Abrahám,—was decreed, or whether it was all a mere delusion, he proceeded home, early in the following morning, very excited. On his way home he heard voices, 'Peace be unto thee, O Apostle of Alláh!' as if coming out of stones and trees, and the words of the Silken Scroll coming uppermost in his mind, he felt that he was ordained to promulgate Divine Unity. He reached his house, trembling as if frightened, and said to his wife Kdadija, "Hide me! Hide me.!" She promptly put on him some covering, and tenderly enquired of him the cause of this extraordinary behaviour. He recounted to her every thing that had happened.‡ Khadija comforted him. ¶"Joyful tidings dost thou bring!" exclaimed she, "By Him, in whose hand is the soul of Khadija, I will hence-

---

† The fellow citizens of Mohammed knew well that, duriug his forty years of life before the Revelations, he had never exercised himself in composing verses or orations, whereby he might have acquired such a command over language which in the Qurán is so manifest that none could compose a single line of equal merit and elegance in response to the well known challenge. Neither had Mohammed studied literature nor ever frequented the society of the learned men of the age. These facts conclusively prove that the Qurán is the Word of God taught to Mohammed (Peace on him and his holy progeny).

‡ Rawdzat al Ahbáb.

¶ W. Irving's *Life of Mohammed.*

forth regard thee as the prophet of our nation. Rejoice," added she, seeing him still cast down, "Alláh will not suffer thee to come to shame. Hast thou not been loving to thy kinsfolk, kind to thy neighbours, charitable to the poor, hospitable to the stranger, faithful to thy word, and ever a defender of the truth?"

Khadija had received the news with great joy, as she already believed in one God and denied Polytheism. She did already know that her old venerable cousin, Waraqa bin Nawfal, believed Mohammed to be a prophet. She hastened to inform him of the occurrence in detail. Having listened to her attentively, he exclaimed: "*Quddusun! Quddusun*! This was the *Namus-al-Akbar*, who came to Moses," and he readily believed in all that was communicated to him, expressing his view that it was the usual mode of revelation. He said, that as in former times God sent the angel Gabriel to make revelations to the great prophets, in the same manner Gabriel was now sent by God to Mohammed. †

Waraqa bin Nawfal knew the Hebrew language very well, and was well versed in the knowledge of the Jewish and Christian Scriptures. Having read in these sacred books the prophecies about the coming prophet, he found Mohammed's features tallying in all details with the prophecies; and he believed him to be the Promised Prophet. Whenever he happened to meet Mohammed, he kissed his brow in token of veneration. Waraqa professed Christianity, and his death took place soon after this event.

The date of the first Revelation according to several historians was the ‡27th of Rajab (610 A. D.) it being Monday on that date. According to others it was 17th, 18th or 19th of Ramadzán or the 12th of Rabi' I. There is no difference as to the day.

Mohammed's mission is generally considered to begin

---

† Tabari, Ibn Jarir.

‡ (Shi'a) Hayát-al-Qulub; (Sunni) Mawáhib-al-Ladunniya and Muntaqi.

with this date, which marks the commencement of an era known as the year of Be'that (Mission). Henceforward, after an interval of some time from the first Revelation, a succession of revelations followed throughout his life.

Revelations. The revelations were received in several ways: sometimes like impressions made by Divine agency on the mind of the Prophet while sleeping; sometimes Gabriel appeared in human form to communicate the Revelation, and sometimes in his real angelic appearance, being invisible to other eyes than those of the Prophet; sometimes the Prophet was overpowered with a condition of brain and nerves, and was senseless to all outward appearances with a pallor on his face, which reflected an intense anxiety of mind. This mode was much painful, as on the coldest day his forehead was bedewed with sweat in such moments. The times or periods of Revelation also varied. He had the revelation even while on horseback or on the back of his mule or camel.

The first † Believers. It has been already mentioned how Khadija believed in her husband's Apostolic Mission when she learned from him the details soon after the occurrence. She followed him the same day in his prayers. His cousin Ali, aged about ten years, followed him next as readily as Khadija. Then Zaid bin Háritha, the freed slave, who also lived under the same roof with Mohammed, embraced his faith.

"Indeed Ibn Abbás, and Anás, and Zaid bin Arqam, and Salmán-al-Fársi, and others have said that he (Ali) was the first who embraced Islam, and some say that there is a *consensus* for this." *Major Jarret's trans. of Suyuti's His. of Cal. p. 171.*

* The illustrious Ali was thus the first who readily embraced his faith and believed in Mohammed's being the Apostle of God.

---

† Isti'áb; Tafrih-al-Azhkiya; Bahjat-al-Mahâfel; Ibn Hishám; Tabari; Rawdzat-al-Ahbáb; Abul Fida; Ibn Athir.

* قال ابن حجر العسقلانی فی الاصابه علی ابن ابیطالب ا لقرشی الهاشمی ابوالحسن اول الناس اِسلا ما فی قول الکثیر من اهل ا لعلم ولد

* Mohammed used to say that the three men *viz.*, Ezakiel, Habib Najjár and Ali, who came forward first to bear testimony to the faith of their prophets, Moses, Jesus, and himself respectively were noted as † Siddiq. Ali repudiated the claim of any other to this epithet. ‡

قبل البعثة بعشر سنين على الصحيح فربي فی حجر النبي صلي الله عليه و آله و سلم و لم يفارقه —

ترجمه — ابن حجر عسقلاني كتاب الاصابه مين لكهتے هين كه كثير اهل علم كے قول كے مطابق ابوالحسن علي بن ابيطالب اسلام لانيوالون مين اول شخص هين — اونكی ولادت بعثت نبوي سے دس سال پهلے هوئي — اُنهون نے رسول مقبول هي كے آغوش مين پرورش پائي اور كبهي آنحضرت سے جدا نهين هوے — (تاريخ احمدي صفحه ١۴) —

* في الدر المنثور للسيوطي وفتح القدير للشوكاني - اخرج ابن ابي حاتم عن ابن عباس في قوله تعالے - والسابقون السابقون قال يوشع بن نون سبق الي موسي و مومن آل يس سبق الي عيسي و علي بن ابيطالب سبق الي رسول الله صلعم — و اخرج ابن مردويه عن ابن عباس في قوله والسابقون السابقون قال نزلت في حزقيل مومن آل فرعون و حبيب النجار الذي ذكر في يس و علي بن ابيطالب و كل رجل منهم سابق اُمته وعلي افضلهم سبقا — و اخرج البخاري في تاريخه عن ابن عباس قال قال رسول الله صلي الله عليه و سلم الصديقون ثلاثه حزقيل مومن آل فرعون و حبيب النجار صاحب آل يس و علي بن ابيطالب —

ترجمه — تفسير در منثور سيوطی و فتح القدير شوكاني مين هے كه ابن ابي حاتم نے والسابقون السابقون (س ١٠-٥٦) كي تفسير مين عبدالله ابن عباس سے روايت كی هے كه سابق الاسلام تين بزرگ هين (١) يوشع بن نون جنهون نے حضرت موسي كي رسالت پر ايمان لانے مين سبقت كي (٢) مومن آل يس جنهون نے حضرت عيسي كی رسالت پر ايمان لانے مين سبقت كي - (٣) علي بن ابيطالب جنهون نے همارے رسول مقبول كي رسالت پر ايمان لانے مين سبقت كي — اور ابن مردويه نے آيه مذكور كي تفسير

---

† Ahmad Hanbal in his Manáqib; Nasái in his Khasáes; Hákim in his Mustudrak; Qotaiba in his Ma'árif.

‡ Ibn Athir.

It is noteworthy that Mohammed presented himself as a prophet, first only to the inmates of his own house, to those who were most familiar with his infirmities—if any—as a man; and it is all the more creditable as being a proof of the purity of his character in domestic life; otherwise they would have been the last to believe in his assertions.

Conversion of Abubekr.

Later on, Abubekr b. Abu Qoháfa, a friend of the Prophet, was easily persuaded to become his disciple, at the age of thirty-eight years. The story connected with his conversion to Islam runs thus: || While on a trip to Yemen, Abubekr met an old and learned sage of the Azd tribe, who predicted to him that a prophet was to appear in the near future at Mecca, with a young man and another of advanced age to help him. When Abubekr came back to Mecca, he paid a visit to his friend Mohammed, who invited him to his religion, Islam, declaring himself the Prophet.

مین ابن عباس سے روایت کی ھے کہ یہہ آیت حزقیل مومن آل فرعون اور حبیب النجار مومن آل یس اور علی بن ابیطالب کی شان مین نازل ھوئی ھے اور انھین سے ھر ایک اپنی امت کا سابق الایمان ھے اور علی اُن سب مین بحیثیت سبقت ایمانیہ افضل ھین - اور بخاری نے اپنی تاریخ مین ابن عباس سے جناب رسول مقبول کا یہہ ارشاد روایت کیا ھے کہ صدیق تین بزرگ ھین (۱) حزقیل مومن آل فرعون (۲) حبیب النجار مومن آل یس (۳) علی بن ابیطالب — (تاریخ احمدی ص ۱۶)-

فی فتح البیان للصدیق حسن خان والدر المنثور للسیوطی عن ابن ابی لیلی سباق الامم ثلاثہ لم یکفروا باللہ طرفۃ العین علی بن ابیطالب و ھوافضلھم و مومن آل فرعون و صاحب یس و ھم الصدیقون

ترجمہ — تفسیر فتح البیان صدیق حسن خان فیز تفسیر در منثور سیوطی میں بتفاوت الفاظ ابن ابی لیلی سے مروی ھے کہ تین شخص ایسے ھیں جنھون نے بقدر طرفۃالعین بھی خدا کے ساتھہ کفر کا ارتکاب نہیں کیا - ایک تو علی بن ابیطالب جو اُن سب میں افضل ھیں دوسرے مومن آل فرعون تیسرے صاحب یس اور یہی لوگ صدیق ھیں — (تارخ احمدی ص ۱۷)

|| Sirat-al-Halabiya; Osad-al-Ghába; Tárikh-al- Khamis, etc.

Abubekr asked him for some proof, and the Prophet at once related to him the prediction of the sage of Yemen, though he himself was not a witness to the incident, being all along at Mecca during the absence of Abubekr. Abubekr then accepted Islam and became a follower of Mohammed.

"Ibn Asákir on a reliable ascription from Mohammed bin Sa'd bin Abi Waqqás records that he said to his father Sa'd: Was Abubekr As-Siddiq the first of you in embracing the faith? He said: No, for there were more than five in the faith before him, but he was the best of us in Islam." (*Major Jarret's trans. of Suyuti's History of Cal. p. 33*).

* Ibn Khathir says, "It is clear that Mohammed's family believed before every other—his wife Khadija, his freed man Zaid, and the wife of Zaid, Omm Aiman, and Ali and Waraqa". (*Major Jarret's trans. of Suyuti's His.*)

"Ibn Abi Sheiba and Ibn Asákir record on the authority of Sálim bin Abi Ja'd that he said: I asked Mohammed bin Hanifa: Was Abubekr the first of the people to adopt Islam? He replied: No. I said: For what reason then is he exalted and preferred, so that no one speaks of any but Abubekr? He replied: Because he was the most excellent of them in Islam from the time he embraced the faith until he attained to his God." (*Major Jarret's trans. of Suyuti's His. of Cal. p. 33*).

† Ibn Abd-al-Bar, a scholar of the Maliki School of Thought, has recorded on the authority of Mohammed b. Ka'b Qartzi that he was asked to state whether Ali was the first man who embraced Islam or Abubekr. He replied that Ali was certainly the first; and he added that some eminent Companions of the Prophet *viz.*, Salmán Fársi, Abu Zharr, Miqdád, Khabáb, Jábir, Abu Sa'id Khudri, and Zaid b. Arqam have also testified that Ali was surely the foremost of the men to embrace Islam; and they exalt him and give him preference over all the rest of the Moslems.

† Isti'áb.

It is an admitted fact that Ali in his childhood came into the guardianship of Mohammed, who, as a parent, brought him up under his personal care after his own heart in moral, social and religious matters. He lived under the same roof, slept on the same bed with Mohammed and shared his meals. Thus, from his early childhood, Ali followed Mohammed in his faith as well as in every other respect; and continued to follow him after Mohammed announced himself a prophet. Ali, therefore, cannot be said to be a convert, because conversion implies a change in religion, while in Ali there had been no change whatever. These appear to be the circumstances under which Ali claimed to have joined Mohammed in prayers seven years before any other did join. Consequently no one but Ali can claim to be the First Moslem.

It is contended by some that by raising this controversy, though vain, an attempt is made to create in masses a doubt, which is aimed to diminish the esteem to which Ali is entitled as being the first Moslem.

Ja'far joining the Faith.

Sometime after the incidents related above, Abu Tálib happened to see his son Ali and his nephew Mohammed performing their prayers together, in a secluded place. Ali stood on the right side of Mohammed. He watched in silence their novel method of Service—bending on their knees, then standing erect, then prostrating themselves till their forehead touched the ground. Witnessing their absorption and humility in Divine presence, he was so impressed with their devotional worship that he † bade Ja'far, another of his sons, who accompanied him, to join Mohammed on his left. When they finished their prayers, Ali, by way of an explanation, said to his father, "I believe in the Unity of Alláh and that my cousin Mohammed is His prophet, whom I follow." "Follow him, my son!" replied Abu Tálib, "he will lead thee to the right path and will not call thee to aught save what is good."

† Ibn Athir; Tabari; Sirat al Halabiya.

Abu Tálib—as the guardian—carefully watched the behaviour of Mohammed subsequent to the prediction of the Nestorian monk, and finding him superior in virtues to the average youth, nay! rather finding him that he was regarded as a saintly man, and knowing that he was now already the acknowledged spiritual guide of some people, no doubt, believed Mohammed to be the Messenger of God; and therefore he voluntarily gave his consent to his sons Ja'far and Ali to follow Mohammed.

CHAPTER V.

Public Preachings, and Persecutions by the Qoreish.

Mohammed proclaiming himself a prophet.

* In the fourth year of his Mission, the prophet Mohammed was commanded by Alláh to give a warning to his near relations: "Warn thy relatives of nearer kin," *Sura XXVI-213*; so he invited them all to an entertainment, with a view to carrying out the Commandment. A banquet, consisting of a large cup full of milk with bread made of one Sá' (about $3\frac{1}{2}$ seers) of wheat flour and meat, was arranged by Ali, according to the instructions given him by the Prophet. Forty of his relations,

* قال ابوالفدا فی تاریخه کانت دعوة رسول الله صلعم الی الاسلام سراً ثلاث سنین ثم بعدها امر الله رسوله باظهار الدعوة

ترجمه — علامه ابوالفدا اپنی تاریخ میں لکھتے هیں که تین برس تک آنحضرت نے مخفي طور پر دعوت اسلام فرمائي - اسکے بعد پروردگار عالم نے آپکو باعلان دعوت اسلام کا حکم دیا — (تاریخ احمدي ص ۱۷)

فی معالم التنزیل للبغوي و لباب التاویل للخازن البغدادي و دلائل النبوة للبیهقی و جمع الجوامع للسیوطی و کنزالعمال لعلی المتقی و تاریخ الملوک والرسل للحافظ ابن جریر والکامل لابن الاثیر الجزري و الکتاب المختصر فی اخبار البشر لابی الفدا و فی الکتب الاخر من التفاسیر والاحادیث والسیر عن علي بن ابیطالب قال لما نزلت هذه الایة علی رسول الله صلعم وانذر عشیرتک الاقربین دعانی رسول الله - فقال یا علی

Banu Abd-al-Mottalib, attended. The Prophet's uncles, Abu Tálib, Abbás, Hamza and Abu Lahab, were present among them. Mohammed kept this seemingly frugal repast before them and tasted himself from it, beginning with the name of Alláh, the Compassionate, the Merciful بسم الله الرحمن الرحيم . They all followed and ate to their fill, but to their surprise nothing was finished; everything appeared still as it was when served. Abu Lahab got up exclaiming that Mohammed had enchanted them all, and the party broke up. Mohammed could not say a word and they were all gone; but he soon invited them again to a like entertainment, and this time he addressed them thus:

ان الله امرنی ان انذر عشیرتی الاقربین فضقت بذلک ذرعا و عرفت انی متی
اناديهم بهذا الامر اري منهم ما اكره فصمت عليها حتي جاءني جبريل فقال
لي يا محمد الاتفعل ماتومر يعذبك ربك فاصنع لنا صاعا من طعام واجعل
عليه رجل شاة واملاء لنا عساس لبن ثم اجتمع لی بنی عبدالمطلب حتي
ابلغهم ما امرت به ففعلت ما امرنی به ثم دعوتهم له وهم يومئذ
اربعون رجلاً يزيدون رجلاً او ينقصونه فيهم اعمامه ابوطالب و حمزة و
العباس (رض) و ابولهب فلما اجتمعوا اليه دعانی بالطعام الذی صنعته
فجئت به فلما وضعته تناول رسول الله صلعم جذبة من اللحم فشقها
باسنانه ثم القاها فی نواحی الصحفته ثم قال خذوا باسم الله فاكل القوم حتی
مالهم بشئی حاجته و ايم الله ان كان الرجل الواحد منهم لياكل مثل ماقدمت
لجميعهم ثم قال اسق القهم فجئتهم بذلک العس فشربوا حتی رووا جميعاً
و ايم الله ان كان الرجل الواحد منهم يشرب مثله فلما اراد رسول الله ان
يكلمهم بدره ابولهب فقال سحركم صاحبكم فتفرق القوم و لم يكلمهم
رسول الله فقال الغد يا علی ان هذا الرجل قد سبقنی الی ما سمعت
من القول فتفرق القوم قبل ان اكلمهم فعدلنا من الطعام مثل ما صنعت ثم
اجمعهم ففعلت ثم جمعتهم فدعانی بالطعام فقربته ففعل كما فعل بالامس
فاكلو او شربوا ثم تكلم رسول الله فقال يا بنی عبدالطلب انی قد جئتكم
بخير الدنيا والاخرة و قد امرنی الله تعالے ان ادعوكم اليه فايكم يوازرنی
علی امري هذا و يكون اخی و وصيي و خليفتی فيكم فاحجم القوم عنها
جميعاً فقلت و انا احدثهم سناً يا نبی الله انا وزيرک عليه قال فاخذ
برقبتی فقال ان هذا اخيی و وصيی و خليفتی فيكم فاسمعو اله واطيعوا

"O Sons of Abd-al-Mottalib! I know no man in all Arabia who brought for his kindred a more excellent thing than that which I have brought for you. It will serve you in this life and in the life to come. Will you believe me, I ask, if I tell you that an enemy of yours is to fall upon you by day or by night?" They all replied with one voice that they believed him to be a truthful man. Thereupon he said, "then know you all that Alláh has sent me to guide man to the right path, and has commanded me to call first my near relations, to invite them to His holy will and to warn them against His wrath. You have seen the miraculous feast you are entertained with, persist not in your infidelity. O sons of Abd-al-Mottalib! Alláh has never sent a Messenger but that he appointed one, his brother, heir and successor to him from amongst his own relations. Who therefore will henceforth be assisting me in my noble work, and become my brother, my heir and my successor? He will be to me just as Aaron was to Moses."

فقام القوم یضحکون و یقولون لابی طالب قد امرک ان تسمع لعلي و تطیع—

ترجمہ—تفسیر معالم التنزیل بغوي و تفسیر خازن بغدادي و دلائل النبوۃ بیہقی و جمع الجوامع سیوطی و کنزالعمال علاؤالدین علی متقی و تاریخ الرسل و الملوک ابن جریر طبري و تاریخ کامل ابن آثیرجزري و تاریخ ابوالفدا نیز دیگر کتب تفسیریہ و حدیثیہ و تاریخیہ مین حضرت علی علیہ السلام سے مروي و منقول ھے کہ جب آیہ وانذر عشیرتک الاقربین نازل ھوا تو جناب رسالتمآب نے مجھے بلاکر ارشاد کیا کہ اے علی پروردگار عالم نے حکم دیا ھے کہ اپنے قرابتدارون کو (اوسکے عذاب سے) دراؤں لیکن قوم کی حالت دیکھکر اور یہہ سمجھہ کر کہ جب مین اونکو حکم خدا پہونچانے کے لئے بلاونگا تو اون سے اطوار نا ملایم دیکھون گا میري ھمت پست اور طاقت ضعیف ھوگئی اور مینے سکوت اختیار کیا حتي کہ جبریل امین نے (مکرر) نازل ھوکر مجھے آگاہ کیا کہ اے محمد اگر تم حکم الہی کے پہونچانے مین تامل کروگے تو یہہ امر موجب عتاب ربانی کا ھوگا—بس اے علی اب تم ایک صاع طعام اور ایک

Mohammed proclaiming Ali his successor.

Mohammed, who had delivered the speech with full religious fervour, was disappointed to find the whole assembly silent, some wondering, others smiling with incredulity and derision.

No one was forthcoming to accept him as spiritual guide. Mohammed seemed to feel for them. At this juncture Ali, the favourite cousin of the Prophet, stepped forward, but Mohammed bade him wait till one of his elders come forward. The Prophet vainly tried thrice. At last, Ali, disliking the ridiculing attitude which the assembly were now adopting, impatiently came forward for the third time and enthusiastically declared that he

---

ران بکري کی اور ایک بڑا پیالہ دودہ کا تیار اور مہیا کرکے بنی عبدالمطلب کو میرے پاس جمع کرو تاکہ مین اونکو حکم الٰہی پہونچادون- چنانچہ مین نے حکم نبوي کے موافق عمل کیا اور بنی عبدالمطلب جو ایک کم یا ایک اوپر چالیس مرد تھے جمع ہوے- جنمین آنحضرت کے چچا ابو طالب حمزۂ عباس اور ابولہب بہی تھے- حسب ایماے رسول مقبول کہانا حاضر کیا گیا تو آنحضرت نے ایک تکڑا گوشت کا اوٹہا لیا اور اوسے اپنے دانتون سے پارہ پارہ کرکے اطراف ظرف مین ڈالدیا اور فرمایا بسم اللہ کہاتے جاؤ چنانچہ سب لوگوں نے سیر ہوکر کہایا باوجودیکہ بخدا وہ کہانا اور دودہ اتنا ہی تہا کہ فقط ایک شخص کے کہانے اور پینے کو کفایت کرتا- اس کے بعد آنحضرت نے اونسے کلام کرنا چاہا تو ابو لہب نے مبادرت کرکے کہا کہ تمہارے صاحب (آنحضرت) نے تمپر سحر کیا ھے — یہہ سنتے ھی تمام قوم متفرق ہوگئی اور آنحضرت کو اونسے کلام کرنیکي نوبت نہ آئي- دوسرے دن جناب رسول خدا نے فرمایا کہ اے علی روز گذشتہ کیطرح مکرر سامان دعوت مہیا کرو اور بنی عبدالمطلب کو بلاؤ- چنانچہ مینے حکم نبوي کے موافق پہر انتظام کرکے سبکو جمع کیا اور جب وہ خورد و نوش سے فارغ ہوے تو آنحضرت نے اونسے یہہ تقریر کی کہ اے بني عبدالمطلب مین تمہارے پاس دنیا اور آخرت کي نیکي لایاہون اور اللہ تعالے نے مجہے اس بات پر مامور کیا ھے کہ تمہین اوسکي طرف بلاؤن پس تم مین ایسا کون شخص ھے جو اس امر مین میري وزارت کرے اور

10 B. H.

not only did believe in Mohammed to be the Apostle of God, but that he offered himself, body and soul, to the good pleasure of the Prophet. †"O Prophet!" said he, "I am the man; whosoever rises against thee, I will dash out his teeth, tear out his eyes, break his legs, rip up his belly. O Prophet, I shall assist thee, and I will be thy vizir over them." ‡Thereupon Mohammed, throwing his arms round the generous youth and pressing him to his bosom exclaimed: "*Behold my brother, my vicegerent and my successor* (*or Caliph*). *Let all listen to his words and obey him.*" Hearing this, the whole assembly, with loud contemptuous laughter, ironically exhorted Abu Tálib to bow down before his son Ali, and yield him obedience. Thus dispersed Mohammed's guests with hatred in their minds and derision on their faces.

Thomas Carlyle in his 'Heroes and Hero-worship' says: "The assembly broke up in laughter. Nevertheless it proved not a laughable thing; it was a very serious thing. As for this young Ali, one can not but like him.

میرا بهائي اور وصي اور خليفه هو آنحضرت کو کسي نے جواب نه دیا مگر میںنے باوجود سب سے کمسن هونیکے عرض کیا که یا نبي الله اس کام کیلئے میں حضور کي وزارت کو حاضر هون یهه سنکر جناب رسالت مآب صلعم نے میري گردنپر دست شفقت رکهکر فرمایا که (اے قوم) دیکهو تم لوکونمیں یهه علي میرا بهائي میرا وصي اور میرا خلیفه هے تم سب اسکا حکم سنو اور اطاعت کرو- یهه سنتےهی لوگ قهقهه لگاکر اوٹهه کهڑے هوے اور ابوطالب سے کهنے لگے که لو تمهیں حکم دیا گیا هے که اپنے فرزند (علي) کي فرمانبرداري و اطاعت کرو—(تاریخ احمدي ص ۱۷ و ۱۸)

نیز ملاحظه هو

تفسر لباب التاویل جلد ۳ صفحه ۳۷۱ - حبیب السیر جلد ۱ جزو ۳ صفحه ۱۶ - تفسیر ثعلبي - گبن جلد ۳ صفحه ۴۹۹ - اوکلے ص ۱۵ کارلائل ص ۷۸ - ایرونگ ص ۳۷ - گلمن ص ۸۳ ڈیون پورٹ ص ۵—

---

† Gibbon by W. Smith, p. 458.

‡ Tabari; Ibn Athir; Abul Fida.

A noble minded creature, as he shows himself now and always afterwards; full of affection, of fiery daring. Something chivalrous in him; brave as a lion, yet with a grace, a truth and affection worthy of Christian Knighthood."

Mohammed's preaching in public.

Mohammed was not at all discouraged by the scornful treatment meted to him by his own near relatives. He now began to preach in public at Mecca. With his naturally noble mien, pleasant address and cheerful manners, he always succeeded in gathering around him a large number of listeners. But so long as he preached the doctrines of Islam, *viz.* the acknowledging of only one true God, the All-powerful, All-knowing Judge of mankind, Resignation to His will, Devotion to His worship requiring a life of prayer and alms-giving, honesty and uprightness in manners, the gatherings listened to him with patience and attention. But the denial of Polytheism and idolatrous worship was ultimately unavoidable in his speeches; and no sooner did they find him talk lightly about their gods and their ungodly worship, than they began to jeer at him. They turned to insult him, but he patiently continued his preachings, which, in spite of all opposition, did not prove altogether fruitless.

Indirect assault on Mohammed.

The Prophet was gaining ground, though at a very slow pace. Some people including one of the prominent Omyyads, Othmán son of Affán, embraced his faith. The Qoreish, especially the Omyyads, who bore old enmity to the Háshimites, grew alarmed. But they could not dare do Mohammed serious harm on account of Abu Tálib's protection of him. Serious harm to him would necessarily have involved them in a family feud, which was not to be lightly risked. So they formed a plan of indirect but efficacious campaign affecting Mohammed in his domestic life. Abu Lahab—the only Háshimite opponent of Mohammed and an intimate friend of the Omyyads, having married a sister of Abu Sofyán the head of the Omyyads—†with the connivance of his wife compelled his two sons Otba and Oteiba to divorce their wives, Omm Kulthum and Roqyya respectively, who were the daughters of Khadija by her first husband and Mohammed's step daughters. These had been married to Otba and Oteiba long before Mohammed's claim as a prophet. Mohammed must have felt this domestic trouble keenly. But soon after Roqyya was married to Othmán b. Affán and later on, after the death of Roqyya, Omm Kulthum, the other girl, was also married to Othmán.

Persecutions.

Regardless of domestic affairs, the Prophet kept on his preachings with as much fervour as ever. The Qoreish now violently acted against him and began strenuously to oppose the teachings and innovations of Mohammed. They insulted him in public, threw dust and dirt at him and over him while in prayers, made loud cries, hooted or sang wild songs to drown his voice while he was preaching; but to their great discomfiture they could not prevent him. ‡Failing in their attempts to silence Mohammed by words, threats, insults and assaults, they tried to pacify him by tempting offers of wealth, power and position or marriage with most beautiful woman; but he rejected these overtures all scornfully.

Violence against the followers of Mohammed.

¶ Now, finding all their efforts of no avail, they began to use violence against his followers and to treat them with contempt. Such of the followers, who did not hold an independent position or had no member of the family to come forward and support them, were the chief victims; and the brunt of their wrath fell upon them. They were seized and imprisoned. Some were encased in coats of mail and were made to lie down upon the arid sand or rocks under the heat of the tropical noon-day sun. The torture thus

† Zakir Hosain's His. of Islam, vol. II p. 47.

‡ Rawdzat-al-Ahbáb; Ibn Hishám.

¶ Ibn Hishám; Ibn Athir; Madárej al Nabowat.

inflicted by the heated metal with the scorching sun above and the burning sand below can be better imagined than described. The converted bondsmen and the bondswomen of the Qoreish found no mercy at the hands of their masters, who brutally tortured and beat them. For instance: (1) Omar b. Al-Khattáb used to beat his slave-girl, a convert Lobina by name, to such an extent that he himself got tired of it. (2) Bilál, a convert, who was a bondsman of Omyya b. Khalf, was cruelly tortured, exposed in the glare of the midday sun upon the scorching gravel of the Meccan valley. When the torment was enhanced by intolerable thirst, the wretched sufferer was required to acknowledge the idols of Mecca; still Bilál never recanted, but, in the depth of his anguish, he cried 'Ahad! Ahad!' One, One, the only God! Mohammed (Peace on him and his holy progeny), having come to know all about him, was so much moved to pity that he managed to relieve him of the painful tortures by purchasing him. (3) Yáser and his wife Somyya, both resolutely refusing to recant, were tortured to death by the Qoreish. † Somyya was tied between two camels and was cruelly pierced with a lance. These were the first Moslem victims of the Qoreish animosity. Their son, Ammár, when tortured and forced to recant, fearing to share the fate met with by his parents before his own eyes and wishing to escape so cruel a death, obeyed the dictates of his persecutors, ‡ though his heart agreed not with his tongue. The Prophet, on being told that Ammár had denied the Faith, said that it was impossible, for Ammár was full of faith from the crown of his head to the soles of his feet, faith being intermixed with his very blood and flesh. When Ammár appeared weeping and crying before him, the Prophet recited: "Whosoever denieth God, after he hath believed, ***except him who is forced against his will and whose heart remaineth steadfast in the Faith***, and whosoever shall voluntarily profess infidelity, on those shall be Wrath

† Al Beidzáwi.

‡ Ibid. and Zamakhshari.

from God, and they shall suffer great torment." *Sura XVI-108.* He wiped off the tears from Ammár's face and consoled him saying: "Thou art not guilty if they forced thee."

Emigration to Abyssinia. 615 A. D.

In the circumstances, it was no more possible for the followers of Mohammed to live in peace any longer in Mecca; nor was it safe for himself to conduct his preachings at a place where the listeners might be exposed to assaults. The Prophet therefore advised his followers, who had no protection in Mecca, to seek refuge and shelter elsewhere. Abyssinia was the place proposed for this purpose, and unanimously agreed upon. Accordingly, in the fifth year of Be'that (Mission) in the month of Rajab, (about 615 A. D.) a party of eleven men and four women, including Othmán and his wife Roqyya made their escape to Abyssinia. They were received with marked kindness by Najáshi (Negus), the Christian king of Etheopia, who himself after some time embraced Islam and became a follower of Mohammed.

†Encouraged by this kind reception of the refugees at Abyssinia, the Prophet permitted others of his followers to migrate thereto for their safety. Consequently thirtythree men and eighteen women left Mecca individually or in small groups and fled to Abyssinia. Ja'far b. Abu Tálib with fifty others followed them. Thus one hundred and sixteen refugees reached Abyssinia in safety.

Qoreish deputation to Abyssinia.

‡The Qoreish found themselves baffled by the Moslem converts escaping to Abyssinia, and sent an embassy headed by Amr bin As and Abdalláh bin Omyya with costly presents to the king of Etheopia. Amr and Abdalláh in the presence of the king first prostrated themselves to pay him their profound respects, then opened their mission by exhibiting their rich presents, and explained that some of their tribes-men, having

† Tabari; Tárikh-al-Khamis; Rawdzat al-Ahbáb.
‡ Ibn Athir.

adopted a new faith which taught them to think lightly of Jesus and his mother Mary, had forsaken their ancestral true religion and escaped to his country. They requested the king, in the name of the Qoreish nobles of Mecca, that the fugitives might be delivered up to them. The king was a just man. He sent for the Moslems to hear from them the defence against the heresy of which they were accused. They came in a body headed by Ja'far, the brother of Ali and a son of Abu Tálib, a cousin of Mohammed the Prophet. None of the Moslems prostrated himself before the king, but saluted him in their usual manner, 'Peace be with thee'. The king was not offended at this, rather admiring their manners, explained to them the charges brought against them by their own country-men. †Ja'far, who was a man of noble mien, pre-possessing countenance and persuasive eloqnence, stood forth and expounded the doctrines of Islam with zeal and enthusiasm. The king, who was a Nestorian Christian, as already observed, found the doctrines similar to those of his own religion and opposed to the polytheism of the Qoreish. He wished Ja'far to recite some passage from the Revelations to the Prophet. Ja'far recited passages from Sura XIX, which touched the heart of the king so much so that he could not help shedding tears. He was pleased to hear Ja'far explaining his arguments; and, instead of delivering up the Moslems to the members of the Embassy, received them into his favour over and above the protection they already enjoyed. He dismissed the Embassy from his court returning the presents they had brought.

The Prophet at Dar-al-Arqam.

After the exile of as many as one hundred and sixteen members of the small party of the Prophet's adherents, his position in Mecca became much weakened. The Qoreish, on the other hand, feeling keenly the unexpected and disgraceful repulse of their envoys at the Abyssinian court,

† Tabari; Ibn Hishám.

bent on avenging themselves upon Mohammed, by persisting in their attempts to oppose his preachings more vigorously than before. He, therefore, in the sixth year of Be'that (Mission) sought shelter in the house of one of his converts named Arqam near the sanctuary of Ka'ba, where he could conduct his prayers and teachings peacefully.

† One day, while the Prophet was sitting outside the house, Abu Jahl, the head of the great and wealthy family of Banu Makhzum, happened to pass by and used abusive language to him. He felt it very sorely, but did not utter a single word of remonstrance. A slave girl of Abdalláh b. Jod'án, who lived nearby, however, was much affected by this uncalled for insult from Abu Jahl; and a short while after, she narrated the incident to Hamza—an uncle of the Prophet—who was passing by her house on his way home from a sporting excursion. Hamza, who was a man famous among the Arabs for his great valour and chivalry, felt deeply the outrageous treatment Mohammed had received from Abu Jahl. He proceeded straight to the house of Abu Jahl and, remonstrating with him, hit him with his bow, striking a blow on his head. His adherents stood up to avenge Abu Jahl, but he stopped them and told Hamza, in order to reconcile him, that he had abused Mohammed only because he vilified their gods. Hamza, thereupon, boldly declared that he himself despised the stony gods, and challenged Abu Jahl to do against him what he could; and in order to proclaim himself publicly Mohammed's champion, Hamza read aloud the Kalima, 'There is no god but one true God and Mohammed is His prophet,' and announced himself a Moslem. Thenceforward he proved to be a staunch Moslem till his last moments.

This was a very fortunate event for Mohammed and the Moslems, particularly at this juncture when matters were assuming so gloomy an aspect for this little company, to get, as a helping hand from Heaven, such a notable adherent to their cause.

† Tabari; Ibn Hishám; Tárikh al Khamis.

Omar's errand to kill Mohammed. 6th year of Mission.

† Having been subjected to humiliation at the hands of Hamza, Abu Jahl now resolved to do away for good with the ever-spreading contagion of Mohammed's innovations, and set a reward of one hundred camels or one thousand ounces of gold in cash for Mohammed's head. Omar b. Al-Khattáb, who was as deadly hostile to Mohammed as Abu Jahl, his maternal uncle, undertook to win the prize for this deed of blood. He was at this time thirty three years of age. He took his sword and set off towards the house of Arqam. On his way Omar met Sa'd b. Abi Waqqás to whom he told his errand not knowing that he was a follower of Mohammed. Sa'd first warned him against the risk he was running then advised him to look first after his own sister and her husband, who, he said, were already the followers of Mohammed. Omar, realising the advisability of the warning, turned to his sister's house and happened to overhear the teachings of a Chapter (*Sura XX*) from the Qurán tutored by one Khabbáb to his pupils Amena, the sister of Omar, and Sa'id b. Zaid her husband. Omar abruptly entering the house and proceeding direct to Sa'id engaged in wrestling with him, and throwing him down on his back sat on his breast to kill him, when his wife interceded. She was slapped to bleed, but she in a fit of anger cried, "O son of Khattáb! Do what thou soughtest to do, for verily I have changed my faith," and professed that both of them—*i.e.*, she herself and her husband—were no doubt Moslems.

Omar's conversion. 6th year of Mission.

‡ Omar, feeling ashamed of himself to have driven her to such effrontery, stood aside and asked her to recite what she was learning. She recited the verses with a solemnity that affected the very core of his heart. The passage which she recited was the first fourteen

---

† Ibn Hishám; Tárikh al Khamis.

‡ Tarikh al Khamis; Ibn Hishám.

verses of Sura Ta Ha which begins thus:

In the name of God, the Compassionate, the Merciful.
Ta. Ha. Not to sadden thee have We sent down this Qurán to thee,
But as a warning for him who feareth;
A missive (from) Him who hath made the earth and the lofty heavens,
The All-merciful who is enthroned on high!
To Him belongeth whatsoever is in the heavens and whatsoever is in the earth, and whatsoever is between them both, and whatsoever is beneath the humid soil!
And thou needest not raise thy voice (in prayer); He verily knoweth the secret (of thy heart), Yea that which is most hidden!
God! There is no God but Him! Most excellent His titles!
Hath now the history of Moses reached thee?
When he saw a fire, and said to his family, "Tarry ye (here), verily I perceive a fire:
Haply I may bring you a brand from it, or by the fire find guidance."
And when he came to it, he was called to, "O Moses!
Verily, I am thy Lord: therefore pull off thy shoes. Lo, thou art in the holy valley Towa;
And I have chosen thee; hearken then to what shall be revealed.
Verily, I am God: there is no God but Me: therefore worship Me, and offer up thy prayer to none but Me.

Omar was quite amazed at the excellence of the language which had a supernatural effect, which he could not resist himself. At last he asked both of them to take him to Mohammed. Khabbáb, who had hid himself in the house when he had seen Omar approaching, now came forth. They took him to the house of Arqam, where he met Hamza at the door. He was conducted to the presence of the Prophet. Omar was so much overawed that he shuddered before the Prophet, who caught him by his hand and said: "Wilt thou not cease O Omar! until God sendeth upon thee calamity and chastisement such as He sent upon Walid b. Moghira"; and invited him to Islam which he accepted reciting the Kalima: "There is no god but one God, and Mohammed is the Apostle of God." The conversion of Omar took place only three days after Hamza had proclaimed himself a Moslem.

Qoreish deputations to Abu Talib. 7th year of Mission.

†After the conversion of Hamza and Omar, the Prophet ventured twice to offer his prayers, along with some of his followers, publicly in the Ka'ba; and the necessity for conducting the religious gatherings privately, especially in the house of Arqam disappeared. He again appeared in public to preach, and Islam was making a steady progress among the various Arab tribes. This enraged the Qoreish more than ever. Now they changed their tactics and thought it advisable to approach Abu Tálib, the Prophet's uncle and protector and the head of his family. They warmly solicited him to impose silence on Mohammed or to withdraw his protection from him. Abu Tálib pacified them somehow, but did not, however, make any mention of this to Mohammed, who continued to carry on his work in his usual manner.

The Qoreish watched for some time, but at length when they saw no change in the attitude of Mohammed, they lost all patience. They went in a body again to Abu Tálib, and adopting a threatening tone demanded of him to make his nephew desist from attacks on their gods, or to let Mohammed alone. Abu Tálib thereupon sent for his nephew and mentioned to him all that the Qoreish charged him with. He suggested that he might make his conduct less offensive to the Qoreish in order to avoid a family feud. Mohammed then strongly put forward his

†Abul Fida; Habib-al-Siyar; Asni-al-Matálib.

convictions, and said flatly that he would not leave the Commandments of God unobeyed, and that he was bound to carry them out till his last moments. "Though they should array the sun against me on my right hand and the moon on my left," said he, "to draw me back from my undertaking, yet would I not do so until God shall carry it to a successful issue, or I give up my life for it." (Abul Fida). Mohammed thought that his uncle, for fear of family feud, wanted to withdraw his protection, so he said to him that he depended solely on the protection and help from God, the Almighty, even if his uncle was unwilling to continue his guardianship.

† So saying, Mohammed turned to go away with a heavy heart, but Abu Tálib called him back and without any further argument promised him to stand by him against all his enemies and to defend him against all assaults till his death. Abu Tálib himself believed in his nephew's convictions, and he accordingly made the Meccans understand that his nephew was really a messenger from God; and therefore they should take him as their spiritual leader and guide.

With this cold answer from Abu Tálib, the Meccans were utterly at a loss to understand what to do now against Mohammed and his followers. "Abu Sofyán, the head of the Omyyads, seized the opportunity to throw discredit, not merely upon Mohammed or such of his kindred as had embraced his faith, but upon the whole line of Háshim, which, though dissenting from his doctrines, had, through mere clannish feelings, protected him. It is evident the hostility of Abu-Sofyán arose, not merely from personal hatred or religious scruples, but from family feud. He was ambitious of transferring to his own line the honors of the city so long engrossed by the Háshimites." *W. Irving's Life of Mohammed p. 56*. So far as can be gathered from the available information, it was at this time that the opposition against the Prophet's propagation of his Faith reached its highest pitch.

---

† Abul Fida ; Habibal Siyar ; Asnial Matalib.

The Interdict and Ban.

Urged by Abu Sofyán, the heads of the different families decided to form a league to break off all connection with Mohammed, his followers and the Háshimites, as they would not consent to separate themselves from Mohammed. † They entered into a solemn compact not to have any sort of intercourse with them—neither to sell to nor to buy anything from, nor to contract matrimonial alliance with them. In the seventh year of Be'that about 616 A.D. the Covenant was written, signed and sealed, and to give it an air of solemnity it was safely kept in the Ka'ba.

‡ Abu Tálib now took Mohammed to his quarters known as She'b Abi Tálib; and the Háshimites, submitting to the Interdict for the sake of Mohammed, also withdrew to the same quarters. Only one of their number, Abu Lahab, separated himself from them and made common cause with the Meccans.

Now the ostracised Háshimites were entirely alienated from the rest of their townfellows; they were the ex-communicated people, doomed to suffer all the privations. The fortress, She'b Abi Tálib, was also beleaguered occasionallay by the Qoreish, to enforce the Ban in all its rigour, and to prevent the possibility of supplies. They found themselves sometimes reduced to starvation for want of supplies, which they could only purchase at exhorbitant prices from foreign traders during the days of Truce *viz*. in the months of Rajab and Zhilhajja of each year.

They were constantly watched by the Qoreish, and dared not walk out. Abu Tálib feared even night attacks and was on his guard for the safety of Mohammed, and often changed his bed-room as a precaution against sudden violence. This state of affairs lasted for about three years, beginning with the close of the seventh year of Be'that and ending in the tenth year, when Mohammed had entered into his fiftieth year of age.

---

† Tabari; Ibn Hishám.

‡ Ibid.

It should be mentioned here that the Prophet, during these years did not neglect his Mission. He set himself to improve the minds of his relations by preaching Monotheism in order to effect their submission to his Faith; and, whenever he happened to go out during the Truce days, he would mingle among the pilgrims, deliver his sermons, propound his doctrines and proclaim his revelations on suitable occasions.

Some of the most noted Miracles. 9th year of Mission.

"In this way," says W. Irving in his book 'Life of Mohammed' on pages 57-60, "he made many converts, who, on their return to their several homes, carried with them the seeds of the new faith to distant regions. Among these converts were occasionally the princes or heads of tribes, whose example had an influence on their adherents. Arabian legends give a pompous account of the conversion of one of these princes which, as it was attended by some of the most noted miracles recorded of Mohammed, may not be unworthy of an abbreviated insertion."

"The prince in question was Habib Ibn Málik, surnamed the Wise, on account of his vast knowledge and erudition; for he is represented as deeply versed in magic and the sciences, and acquainted with all religions, to their very foundations, having read all that had been written concerning them, and also acquired practical information, for he had belonged to them all by turns, having been Jew, Christian, and one of the Magi. It is true he had had more than usual time for his studies and experience, having, according to Arabian legend, attained to the age of 140 years. He now came to Mecca at the head of a powerful host of twenty thousand men, bringing with him a youthful daughter, Satiha, for whom he was putting up prayers at the Ka'ba, she having been struck dumb and deaf, and blind, and deprived of the use of her limbs."

"Abu Sofyán and Abu Jahl, according to the legend, thought the presence of this very powerful, very idolatrous, and very wise old prince, at the head of so formidable a host, a favourable opportunity to effect the ruin of Mohammed. They accordingly informed Habib the Wise of the heresies of the pretended prophet; and prevailed upon the venerable prince to summon him into his presence, at his encampment in the Valley of Flints, there to defend his doctrines; in the hope that his obstinacy in error would draw upon him banishment or death."

"The legend gives a magnificent account of the issuing forth of the idolatrous Qoreishites, in proud array, on horseback and on foot, led by Abu Sofyán and Abu Jahl, to attend the grand inquisition in the Valley of Flints; and of the Oriental state in which they were received by Habib the Wise, seated under a tent of crimson, on a throne of ebony, inlaid with ivory and sandal-wood, and covered with plates of gold."

"Mohammed was in the dwelling of Khadija when he received a summons to this formidable tribunal. Khadija was loud in her expressions of alarm; and her daughters hung about his neck, weeping and lamenting, for they thought him going to certain death; but he gently rebuked their fears, and bade them trust in Alláh."

"Unlike the ostentatious state of his enemies, Abu Sofyán and Abu Jahl, he approached the scene of trial in simple guise, clad in a white garment, with a black turban, and a mantle which had belonged to his grandfather Abd-al-Mottalib and was made of the stuff of Aden. His hair floated below his shoulders, the mysterious light of prophecy beamed from his countenance, and though he had not anointed his beard, nor used any perfumes, excepting a little musk and camphor for the hair of his upper lip, yet wherever he passed, a bland odour diffused itself around, being the fragrant emanations from his person."

" A silent awe, continues the legend, fell upon the vast assemblage as the Prophet approached. Not a murmur, not a whisper was to be heard. The very brute animals were charmed to silence; and the neighing of the steed, the bellowing of the camel, and the braying of the ass, were mute."

"The venerable Habib received him graciously; his first qnestion was to the point. "They tell thou dost pretend to be a prophet sent from God. Is it so?"

"Even so," replied Mohammed. "Alláh has sent me to proclaim the veritable faith."

"Good," rejoined the wary sage, "but every prophet has given proof of his Mission by signs and miracles. Noah had his rainbow; Solomon his mysterious ring; Abraham the fire of the furnace, which became cool at his command; Isaac the ram, which was sacrificed in his stead; Moses his wonder-working rod; and Jesus brought the dead to life, and appeased tempests with a word. If, then, thou art really a prophet, give us a miracle in proof."

"The adherents of Mohammed trembled for him when they heard this request, and Abu Jahl clapped his hands and extolled the sagacity of Habib the Wise. But the Prophet rebuked him with scorn. "Peace! dog of thy race!" exclaimed he; "disgrace of thy kindred and of thy tribe." He then calmly proceeded to execute the wishes of Habib."

"The first miracle demanded of Mohammed was to reveal what Habib had within his tent, and why he had brought it to Mecca."

"Upon this, says the legend, Mohammed bent toward the earth and traced figures upon the sand. Then raising his head, he replied, "Oh Habib! thou hast brought hither thy daughter, Satiha, deaf and dumb, and lame and blind, in the hope of obtaining relief of Heaven. Go to thy tent; speak to her, and hear her reply, and know that God is All Powerful."

"The aged prince hastened to his tent. His daughter met him with light step and extended arms, perfect in all her faculties, her eyes beaming with joy, her face clothed with smiles, and more beauteous than the moon in an unclouded night." *W. Irving.* (Peace on Mohammed and his holy descendants)

The second miracle demanded by Habib was that the Prophet should cover the noontide heaven with supernatural darkness and cause the moon to appear upon the top of the Ka'ba. The Prophet prayed. Instantly complete darkness covered the day-light and the glorious orb of the moon shone above the Sanctuary. The Prophet made a sign with his finger and the orb was divided into two halves so that Mount Abu Qobeis stood between them. After a while he again made a sign and the two halves were re-united. † Some deep fissures still exist in the moon as if to indicate the rejoining.

The miracle of Sundering the the Moon. 9th year of Mission.

The prince and four hundred and seventy of his adherents as well as some Meccans, being thoroughly convinced, embraced the faith of the Prophet. Abu Jahl and Abu Sofyán exclaimed that it was all an enchantment of Mohammed; they were too hardened in unbelief. The incidents related above are said to have occurred about five ‡ years before Hegirat.

---

† In connection with this miracle of the sundered moon by the Prophet, it may be mentioned here that indirect evidence of its having actually happened is available from no less an author than the celebrated astronomer Sir J. F. Herschel, who thus writes in his Outlines of Astronomy (Fourth Edition 1851), on page 247, in a footnote, when discoursing about the moon: "There is an optical illusion of a very strange and unaccountable nature which has often been remarked in occultations. The star appears to advance actually upon and within the edge of the disc (of the moon) before it disappears, and that sometimes to a considerable depth. I have never myself witnessed this singular effect, but it rests on most unequivocal testimony. I have called it an optical illusion; but it is barely possible that a star may shine on such occasions through *deep fissures* in the substance of the moon." Deep fissures in the moon! Does not this expression clearly indicate a rejoining of the moon after it was sundered into two? and when the two pieces reunited, they did not reunite perfectly but left deep fissures.

‡ Mawáhib Ladunnyia.

Miraculous removal of the ban. 619 A. D.

At the close of the third year of Interdict, in the tenth year of Be'that (Mission) Mohammed told his uncle, Abu Tálib, that Alláh had shown His disapproval of the convention against him, and had sent worms to eat out every word of the Document placed in the Ka'ba, excepting His own name written thereon. Abu Tálib, believing his nephew as the receiver of Revelations from heavens, unhesitatingly went to the Qoreish and told them what Mohammed had spoken; and added that if what he was telling them was found true on examination of the Covenant, they would be bound to withdraw from their compact and lay aside their enmity towards Mohammed and his followers; and if proved false, he, on his part, would be bound to deliver up Mohammed to them. Mot'im b. Adi, Zam'a b. Aswad, Abul Bakhtari and some others of the Qoreish neighbours, who felt deeply for the bitter lamentations of the half-starved children of the ostracised Háshimites and sympathized with them in their sufferings, accompanied Abu Tálib to see that his just demand should not be refused by the Qoreish. To these proposals of Abu Tálib, however, they all agreed most willingly, and at once went to inspect the Document. But to their great astonishment they found it worm-eaten; only the name of Alláh was still there and no more. Abu Tálib was overjoyed at this miracle worked by supernatural agency in favour of the Prophet Mohammed, while the Qoreish looked confused and bewildered. They said that it was an enchantment of Mohammed, but, at the persistence of Abu Tálib and his party, they, after all, declared the Document null and void. The ban being removed, all the Háshimites took to their houses, and Mohammed (Peace on him and his holy progeny) was once more free.

CHAPTER VI.

The four years before the Hegirat.

Return of Emigrants from Abyssinia.

When the Qoreish interdict was removed and the Háshimites were free to have intercourse with the citizens of Mecca, the news reached Abyssinia that Mohammed the Prophet was on peace with the Meccans. As the emigrants at Abyssinia longed to see their home again, this news was welcome to them. Consequently twenty-nine emigrants including Othmán and his wife Roqyya, who were most anxious to come back, returned from exile, in the tenth year of Be'that to Mecca, only to find matters still the same as at the time when they had made their escape. They, however, seeking protection of some reliable Meccans lived in Mecca until the Prophet directed them to migrate to Medina.

Other emigrants returned from Abyssinia in the fifth year of the Prophet's hegirat to Medina, with the exception of Ja'far b. Abu Tálib and about twenty others of his party, who came back last of all in the seventh year after Hegirat when the Prophet was engaged in war with the Jews of Khaibar.

Death of Abu Talib.

In the fiftieth year of his life and the tenth of Be'that, some months after the withdrawl of the Interdict, the Prophet lost his affectionate uncle Abu Tálib, who died at the patriarchal age of 87 years—an uncle who had nurtured him in his childhood, trained him in his youth, settled him in a comfortable family life when he was grown up, and steadfastly protected and defended him from the hosts of his enemies. Mohammed keenly felt this loss.

Abu Tálib's attitude towards his nephew Mohammed, narrated in the foregoing pages, as well as some of his preserved verses prove, says Abul Fida, that he believed and acknowledged Mohammed as the true Apostle of God and his religion as the best of all the religions of the

4 B. H.

Universe. No doubt, Abu Tálib died actually in the Faith with the Kalima on his lips. The following verses which, amongst many others, are ascribed to him clearly prove his belief in Mohammed:

و لقد علمت بان دين محمد   من خير اديان البرية دينا

I believe that Mohammed's Faith is the best of all the religions of the Universe.

الم تعلموا انا وجدنا محمداً   نبياً كموسى خط في اول الكتب

Don't you see that we have found Mohammed a prophet like Moses; he is already predicted in previous Scriptures.

وابيض يستسقى الغمام بوجهه   ثمال اليتامى عصمة للارامل

His is the illumined face which is the medium for the rains; he is spring for the orphan and a protector for the widow.

[NOTE.—Once during his childhood on the occasion of a scarcity of rains Abu Tálib took Mohammed to the Ka'ba and standing with his back touching the wall of the sanctuary lifted up Mohammed in his lap and sought him to be a medium in his prayers to the Almighty for the rains. Mohammed joined him in his prayers with his face upturned. The prayers were not finished when the clouds began to appear and the rain fell in torren This incident is alluded to in the above verse.]

فمن مثله في الناس اي مومل   اذا قاسه الحكام عند التفاضل

People who tried his virtuous worth, could find none him amongst mankind.

حليم رشيد عاقل غير طايش   يوالي الها ليس عنه بغافل

Meek, virtuous, wise and prudent; He whom he loves is not indifferent to him.

وشق له من اسمه ليجله   فذو العرش محمود و هذا محمد

To exalt him He derived his name from His own; the One on High is called Mahmud while He named him Mohammed.

The Year of Mourning. 10th year of Mission.

He had to suffer yet another and still more serious a loss only three days after the death of Abu Tálib. His loving wife Khadija breathed her last, leaving her only daughter Fátema. Her loss left Mohammed inconsolable as he was fondly attached to her. "Mohammed wept bitterly at her tomb, and clothed himself in mourning for her and for Abu Tálib, so that this year was called the Year of Mourning." *W. Irving.* She was the powerful supporter of her husband's cause and was his benefactress. She was the first and foremost to accept the truth of his Divine Mission, and believed in him as the Apostle of God. Mohammed treated her with considerable respect, which was reciprocated by her grateful regard and esteem for him; and thus they enjoyed the twenty-five years of their happy married life. He retained the memory of her goodness and of her unwavering faith to his death; and reckoned her as one of the four holy women perfect in faith with whom God has deigned to bless this earth, *viz.* Asia, the wife of Pharaoh, Mary, the mother of Jesus, Khadija the wife of Mohammed, and Fátema his daughter, the wife of Ali.

The Prophet at Taef.

† After the death of both of his best supporters, the Qoreish became more mischievous and troublesome than ever before. The Prophet began to feel his position untenable in Mecca, and determined to seek refuge elsewhere. He, therefore, set out with Zaid, his freedman, to Táef, which was one of the strongholds of idolatry about seventy miles east of Mecca, where the stony image of Al-Lát covered with gems and jewels was believed to be inspired with life and was worshipped. He preached his doctrines there for a week or so. The votaries of the idol which Mohammed denounced were greatly irritated and they had him driven out of the town bruised and bleeding, being pursued and hailed with stones until he found shelter in a vineyard belonging to some noble Meccan. In the deepest despondency at this cold and brutal behaviour of the inhabitants of Táef, he took back the road to Mecca.

---

† Tabaqát Ibn Sa'd.

Genii embracing Islam.

On his way home he halted one night in a grove at Nakhla, where after his usual prayers he was reciting the verses of the Qurán, when a party of seven or nine genii happened to pass en route to Yemen. They seemed affected by the melodious tone and the excellence of the language of the recitation, and appearing before the Prophet accepted his doctrines; and on reaching their destination propagated them amongst their kins-folk, who all embraced Islam:

"And when We turned aside unto thee a party of the genii, listening to the Qurán; and when they were present at it, they said (to one another), Hark! and when it was ended, they turned back unto their people preaching."

"They said, O our people, verily we have heard a Book (read unto us) sent down after Moses, confirming what was (delivered) before it, directing unto the truth and the straight path."

"O our people! respond to the crier of God and put faith in Him; He will forgive you your sins, and will deliver you from a painful torment."

"And whosoever respondeth not to the crier of God, shall by no means frustrate (God's vengeance) on earth; neither is there for him a protector beside Him. These (will be) in plain error." *Sura XLVI: 28-31.*

The Prophet again at Mecca. 10th year of Mission.

At the dawn Mohammed again started towards Mecca, and reaching Mount Hirá he stopped there and sent Zaid to negotiate with some of the friendly citizens for protection, as he could not venture to enter the town where he knew full well that his return would be unwelcome to others and unsafe to himself. Zaid, after prolonged negotiations, was, however, successful to secure the help of Mot'im b. Adi, one of those who had sided with Abu Tálib in obtaining removal of the Ban against the Háshimites. He came to Mohammed, offered him security and took him to his own house in Mecca.

Now the Prophet could appear in public only during the period of Truce, *i.e.* the months of Rajab and Zhilhajja, and preached the doctrines of his Faith to the pilgrims as well as to the Meccans. Abu Lahab and Abu Jahl, the inveterate enemies of Mohammed and his Faith followed him about and contradicted him. They posted the Qoreish on pilgrim routes to warn them against Mohammed whom they represented as a dangerous magician.

Ayesha's betrothal.
11th year of Mission.

Since the death of Khadija, to whom Mohammed was fondly attached, he looked cheerless and sorrowful. Abubekr, who watched for an opportunity to cement his friendship, would not lose this singular chance of providing consolation for him. He, therefore, made an offer of his daughter Ayesha to him. Though she was a girl of only about seven years of age, but the customs of the country recognized such an alliance. † At his persuasive earnest solicitations Mohammed consented, but he contented at the time with only the betrothal; the consummation of the contract took place at Medina after the Hegirat. This was an act of Abubekr's characteristic foresight. With the example of Abubekr before him, Omar was also desirous of having a like influence in the harem of the Prophet, and later, somehow, he had his daughter Hafsa given the Prophet to wife, the mention of which will come in its proper place.

Men of Medina embracing Islam.
620 A. D.

‡ In the eleventh year of his Mission, whilst the Prophet was preaching at Aqaba, a place between Mina and Arafát, six Khazrajites of Yathrib, who happened to come to Mecca on pilgrimage, listened to him attentively. Hearing patiently the fundamental principles of Mohammed's Faith and his own sentiments, they were struck by the truth of his words and they embraced Islam. On their return to Yathrib (Medina) they diffused the Doctrines of

† Spirit of Islam.

‡ Ibn Hishám; Tabari.

2 B. H.

Islam among their people and told of their conversion to the faith of Mohammed, with high praises for his truth, saintly character, brotherly love, inoffensive behaviour and attractive personality.

First-Pledge of Aqaba. 621 A. D.

† Next year, the twelfth of Be'that, seven persons, drawn by curiosity at the reports given by the six converts, came to Mecca from Yathrib, along with the five of those who last year had embraced Islam. They paid visits to the Prophet at the same Aqaba and were highly pleased at his teachings. They embraced his Faith and gave him their pledge to acknowledge no god but the one Omnipotent and Omnipresent Lord, the Alláh, and to obey the God's Messenger in his commands to the rigid observance of prayers and to live sin-avoiding life *i. e.* not to commit adultery, nor fornication, nor infanticide, nor stealing and to abstain from calumny and slander. This homage is known in the history as the first Pledge of Aqaba. All the twelve men pledging themselves to the Prophet in faith and firm adherence to him returned as propagandists of Islam to their home Yathrib (or Medina) about 250 miles north of Mecca. Two of the Prophet's disciples *viz.* Mos'ab b. Omeir, a grandson of Háshim and Abdalláh b. Omm Maktum, were sent along with them to teach the Qurán and the fundamental doctrines of Islam. These propagandists were required to inform the Prophet of their success in their efforts at the same place in the following pilgrimage season.

The Me'raj. 621 A. D.

In Mecca on the 27th of Rajab in the twelfth year of his Mission, while Mohammed finished his night prayers in the house of his cousin Omm Háni, the daughter of Abu Tálib, and when the rest of the inmates were asleep, the angel Gabriel appeared to him and took him to the Ka'ba, made him ride on a beautifully shaped, human-faced, white-winged horse called Boráq, and guided him towards Jerusalem, where

† Ibn Hishám; Ibn Athir; Abul Fida.

they descended at the temple. After presiding over an assembly of bygone prophets in prayers, Mohammed again rode on and was carried to the heavens, where he was shown the beauties of Paradise and the horrors of Hell. *Among the Celestial Lights, where he received from God new Precepts and Commands and order for five daily prayers for his people, he saw his own name together with that of Ali inscribed in the Kalima: "There is no god but one God and Mohammed is His prophet with Ali as his Right-hand."

---

* فی الشفاء للقاضی عیاض و لا خلاف بین المسلمین في صحته الاسراء بهٖ صلعم اذ هو نص القران و فیه عن ابی الحمراء قال قال رسول الله صلعم اسری بی الی السماء اذا علی العرش مکتوب لا اله الاالله محمد رسول الله ایدته بعلی —

ترجمه—شفاے قاضی عیاض مین هے که اهل اسلام مین معراج نبوی کی صحت کے متعلق اختلاف نهین هے - کیونکه اسکا ثبوت نص قران سے هے نیز کتاب مذکور مین ابوالحمرا سے مروي هے که جناب رسول کریم نے فرمایا-که جب میئنے (شب معراج مین) آسمانون کی سیر کی تو عرش پر لکها هوا دیکها —

لا اله الا الله محمد رسول الله ایدته بعلی -

فی الدرالمنثور للسیوطی اخرج ابن عدي و ابن عساکر عن انس (رض) قال قال رسول الله صلعم لما عرج بي رایت علی ساق العرش مکتوبا لا اله الا الله محمد رسول الله ایدته بعلی —

ترجمه—تفسیر در منثور سیوطی مین بروایت ابن عدی و ابن عساکر انس بن مالک سے جناب رسالت ماب کا یهه ارشاد منقول هے که جب مجهکو معراج هوئی تو میئنے ساق عرش پر لکها هوا دیکها - لا اله الا الله محمد رسول الله ایدته بعلی (یعنے سواے الله کے کوئی معبود نهین هے محمد اوسکا رسول هے اور الله تعالے نے اپنے رسول کی نصرت علی سے فرمائی)— (تاریخ احمدی ص ۲۴)

2 B. H.

Having seen what was shown to him of the heavens, the Prophet was carried back to his residence, to find that his absence involved no more time than a moment. This night of journey of the Prophet is known as the Lailat-al-Me'ráj, and there is a mention of it in the Qurán.

> "Pure (of all defects) is He who carried His servant by night, from the sacred mosque (of Mecca) to the farther temple (of Jerusalem), the circuit of which We have blessed, that We might show him some of Our signs; Verily, He is the Hearer, the Beholder."
> *Sura XVII-I.*

No Moslem must have any doubts as to its truth. There is still a foot print of the Prophet, on the stone of a rock at Jerusalem, from over which he mounted the Boráq to proceed on his journey to the Heavens. A mosque built by Caliph Omar to preserve the memory of the print on the stone, still stands at the place.

*But there are, however, some notable names of persons, who did not believe in the Prophet's bodily ascent to the Heavens, their idea being of a spiritual journey in which they believed his spirit was shown the things above. Such an idea was held by Ayesha Siddiqa, daughter of Abubekr Siddiq, a wife of the Prophet, as well as by Mo'áwiya, the famous son of Abu Sofyán.

---

* قال ابوالفدا فی تاریخه و قد اختلف اهل العلم فیه هل کان بجسده ام کان رویاء صادقة والذی علیه الجمهور انه کان بجسده و ذهب اخرون الی انه کان رویاء صادقة و عن عایشه (رض) انها کانت تقول ما فقد جسد رسول الله و لکن الله اسری بروحه ونقلوا عن معاویة ایضاً انه کان یقول ان الاسرا کان رویای صادقه—

ترجمه—مورخ ابوالفدا لکهتا هے که اهل علم کا اس باب مین اختلاف هے که معراج جسم کے ساتھ هوئی یابطور سچے خواب کے تهی - جمهور کی راے تو یهي هے که معراج جسمانی هوئی مگر بعض لوگ اسطرت بهی گئے هین که معراج محض سچا خواب تها - چنانچه حضرت عایشه سے مروي هے که جناب رسالت ماب کو معراج جسدي نهین هوی - بلکه

It will not be out of place to note here that, at the period when Me'ráj took place, Ayesha was a child of about seven years, living with her parents and relations and not with the Prophet, to whom she was delivered up at Medina, as his wife, about two years later. Ayesha's father, Abubekr, however, believed in the bodily ascent and some say that the title of Siddiq, or the Truthful, was given to him specially for corroborating the story of ascent.

"Mos'ab b. Zobeir and others say that the people, concurred in naming him As-Siddiq (witness to the truth), because he hastened to testify to the Apostle of God......" *Major Jarrett's trans. of Suyuti's His. Cal. p. 25.*

Mo'áwiya was not born at the time when Me'ráj took place. He was born a year later (the year that the Prophet sought refuge in the Cave) of his heathen parents, who were deadly hostile to the Prophet at the time. He became a convert to Islam some ten years later.

الله تعالے نے آنحضرت کی روح کو شب معراج مین سیر کرایا-اور معاویہ سے بہي ایسا هی منقول ھے کہ معراج سچے خواب کے طور پر هوئي—

اخرج ابن اسحق و ابن جریر عن عایشة انها قالت ما فقد جسد رسول الله و لکن الله اسري بروحه—(تاریخ احمدي ص ۲۳)

ترجمه—ابن اسحق اور ابن جریر نے حضرت عایشه سے روایت کیا ھے کہ شب معراج مین رسول الله کا جسد اقدس بدستور اپنی جگه پر رها اور الله تعالے نے آپکی روح کو آسمانون کي سیر کرائي—

قال ملا علی القاری في الشرح الفقه الاکبر و خبر المعراج ای بجسد المصطفی صلعم یقظه الي السماء ثم الی ماشاء الله تعالے فی المقامات العلی حق ای حدیثه ثابت بطریق متعدده فمن رده اي ذلک الخبر و لم یومن بمقتضی ذلک الاثر فهو ضال مبتدع—

ترجمه—ملا علي قاري شرح فقه اکبر مین لکهتے هین کہ واقعه معراج جسدي یعنے رسول مقبول کا بحالت بیداري سماوات اور مقامات عالیه کی سیر فرمانا حق ھے اور اسکی حدیث طریق متعدده سے ثابت ھے پس جو شخص کہ معرآج جسماني کي تردید کرے اور اوسکی صحت پر ایمان نه لاے وه گمراه اور بدعتی ھے—(تاریخ احمدي ص۲۴)

2 B. H.

† In the foot-note below, an abbreviated selection from

---

† In the mid-watches of the night, Mohammed was roused by a voice crying, "Awake, thou sleeper!" The angel Gabriel stood before him. He brought Mohammed a white steed of wonderful form and qualities, unlike any animal he had ever seen; and, in truth, it differs from any animal ever before described. It had a human face, but the cheeks of a horse: its eyes were as jacinths, and radiant as stars. It had eagle's wings, all glittering with rays of light; and its whole form was resplendent with gems and precious stones. From its dazzlig splendour and incredible velocity it was called Boráq, or Lightning.

The animal approached and submitted to be mounted; then rising with Mohammed on its back, it soared aloft far above the mountains of Mecea. As they passed like lightning between heaven and earth, Gabriel cried aloud, "Stop, oh Mohammed! descend to the earth, and make the prayer with two inflections of the body." They alighted on the earth, and having made the prayer—"Oh friend and well beloved of my soul!" said Mohammed, "why didst thou require me to pray in this place?" "Because it is Mount Sinai, on which God communed with Moses."

Resuming their aerial course, they arrived at the gate of the holy temple at Jerusalem, where, alighting from Al-Boráq, Mohammed fastened it to the rings where the prophets before him had fastened it. Then entering the temple, he found there Abraham, and Moses, and Isa (Jesus), and many more of the prophets. After he had prayed in company with them for a time, a ladder of light was let down from heaven, until the lower end rested on the Shakra, or foundation-stone of the sacred house, being the stone of Jacob. Aided by the angel Gabriel, Mohammed ascended this ladder with the rapidity of lightning.

Being arrived at the first heaven, Gabriel knocked at the gate. Who is there? was demanded from within. Gabriel. Who is with thee? Mohammed. Has he received his mission? He has. Then he is welcome! And the gate was opened. As Mohammed entered, an ancient man approached him, and Gabriel said, "Here is thy father Adam, pay him reverence." Mohammed did so, and Adam embraced him, calling him the greatest among his children and the first among the prophets. In this heaven were innumerable animals of all kinds, which Gabriel said were angels, who, under these forms, interceded with Allah for the various races of animals upon earth. Among these was a cock of dazzling whiteness, and of such marvellous height, that his crest touched

the detailed account of this nocturnal journey of the Pro-

---

the second heaven, though five hundred years' journey above the first. This wonderful bird saluted the ear of Alláh each morning with his melodious chant. All creatures on earth, save man, are awakened by his voice, and all the fowls of his kind chant hallelujahs in emulation of his note. [A similar bird is mentioned, says Dr. Prideaux, in the tract of Bava Bartha of the Babylonish Talmud, wherein we have a story of such a prodigious bird, called Zig, which, standing with his feet on the earth, reacheth up to the heavens with his head, and with the spreading of his wings darkeneth the whole orb of the sun, and causeth a total eclipse thereof. This bird the Chaldee paraphrast on the Psalms says is a cock, and that he crows before the Lord; and the Chaldee paraphrast on Job tells us of his crowing every morning before the Lord, and that God giveth him wisdom for that purpose.]

They now ascended to the second heaven. Gabriel, as before, knocked at the gate; the same questions and replies were exchanged; the door opened, and they entered. Here they found Noah, who, embracing Mohammed, hailed him as the greatest among the prophets.

Arrived at the third heaven, they entered with the same ceremonies. Here was seated an angel of immeasurable height, whose eyes were seventy thousand days' journey apart. He had at his command a hundred thousand battalions of armed men. Before him was spread a vast book, in which he was continually writing and blotting out. "This, oh Mohammed," said Gabriel, "is Azrael, the angel of death, who is in the confidence of Alláh. In the book before him he is continually writing the names of those who have lived their allotted time, and who, therefore, instantly die."

They now mounted to the fourth heaven. Among the angels who inhabited it was one five hundred days' journey in height. His countenance was troubled, and rivers of tears ran from his eyes. "This," said Gabriel, "is the angel of tears, appointed to weep over the sins of the children of men, and to predict the evils which await them."

Reaching the fifth heaven, Mohammed was received by Aaron with embraces and congratulations. The avenging angel dwells in this heaven, and presides over the element of fire. Of all the angels seen by Mohammed, he was the most hideous and terrific. His visage seemed of copper, and was covered with wens and warts. His eyes flashed lightning, and he grasped a flaming lance.

phet, written by *W. Irving* in his '*Life of Mohammed*' chiefly

---

He sat on a throne surrounded by flames, and before him was a heap of red-hot chains. Were he to alight upon earth in his true form, the mountains would be consumed, the seas dried up, and all the inhabitants would die with terror. To him, and the angels his ministers, is intrusted the execution of divine vengeance on infidels and sinners.

Leaving this awful abode, they mounted to the sixth heaven. Here was a great angel, composed half of snow and half of fire; yet the snow melted not, nor was the fire extinguished. Around him a choir of lesser angels continually exclaimed, "Oh Alláh! who hast united snow and fire, unite all thy faithful servants in obedience to thy law." "This," said Gabriel, "is the guardian angel of heaven and earth." Here was the prophet Musa (Moses), who, however, instead of welcoming Mohammed with joy, as the other prophets had done, shed tears at sight of him. "Wherefore dost thou weep"? inquired Mohammed. "Because I behold a successor, who is destined to conduct more of his nation into paradise than ever I could of the backsliding children of Israel."

Mounting hence to the seventh heaven, Mohammed was received by the patriarch Abraham. This blissful abode is formed of divine light, and of such transcendent glory that the tongue of man cannot describe it. One of its celestial inhabitants will suffice to give an idea of the rest. He surpassed the whole earth in magnitude, and had seventy thousand heads; each head seventy thousand mouths; each mouth seventy thousand tongues; each tongue spoke seventy thousand different languages, and all these were incessantly employed in chanting the praises of the Most High.

While contemplating this wonderful being, Mohammed was suddenly transported aloft to the lotus-tree, called Sedrat, which flourishes on the right hand of the invisible throne of Alláh. The branches of this tree extend wider than the distance between the sun and the earth. Angels more numerous than the sands of the sea-shore, or of the beds of all the streams and rivers, rejoice beneath its shade. The leaves resemble the ears of an elephant; thousands of immortal birds sport among its branches, repeating the sublime verses of the Qurán. Its fruits are milder than milk and sweeter than honey. If all the creatures of God were assembled, one of these fruits would be sufficient for their sustenance. Each seed incloses a houri, or celestial virgin, provided for the felicity of true believers.

Mohammed and his celestial guide now proceeded to Al Mamour, or the House of Adoration; formed of red jacinths or rubies, and surrounded by innumerable lamps, perpetually burning. As Mohammed entered the portal, three vases were offered him, one containing wine, another milk, and the third honey. He took and drank of the vase containing milk. "Well hast thou done; auspicious is thy choice," exclaimed Gabriel. "Hadst thou drunk of the wine, thy people had all gone astray." The sacred house resembles in form the Ka'ba at Mecca, and is perpendicularly above it in the seventh heaven. It is visited every day by seventy thousand angles of the highest order. They were at this very time making their holy circuit, and Mohammed, joining with them, walked round it seven times.

Gabriel could go no further. Mohammed now traversed, quicker than thought, an immense space, passing through two regions of dazzling light, and one of profound darkness. Emerging from this utter gloom, he was filled with awe and terror at finding himself in the presence of Alláh, and but two bow-shots from His throne. A feeling of ecstatic bliss followed while a sweetness and fragrance prevailed around, which none can understand but one who has been in the Divine presence.

Mohammed now received, from the Deity himself, many of the doctrines contained in the Qurán; and five prayers were (finally) prescribed as the daily duty of all true believers.

By the ladder of light he descended to the temple of Jerusalem, where he found Boráq fastened as he had left it, and mounting, was borne back in an instant to the place whence he had first been taken.

This account of the nocturnal journey is chiefly according to the words of the historians Abulfida, Al Bokhári, and Abu Horeira, and is given more at large in the *Life of Mohammed* by Gagnier. The journey itself has given rise to endless commentaries and disputes among the doctors. Some affirm that it was no more than a dream or vision of the night; and support their assertion by a tradition derived from Ayesha, a wife of Mohammed, who declared that, on the night in question, his body remained perfectly still, and it was only in spirit that he made his nocturnal journey. In giving this tradition, however, they did not consider that, at the time the journey was said to have taken place, Ayesha was still a child, and, though espoused, had not become the wife of Mohammed.

Horeira is given here for the interest of the reader.

The soil of Yathrib proved very fertile for Islam.

Propagation of Islam in Medina. 621 A. D.

Mos'ab b. Omeir, soon after his arrival at Yathrib (Medina), began to preach in public the new religion of Mohammed; and with the assistance and example of the twelve propagandists, had a great success. The men who were

---

Others insist that he made the celestial journey bodily. According to Ahmad bin Joseph, the nocturnal visit to the temple (Jerusalem) was testified by the patriarch of Jerusalem himself. "At the time," says he, "that Mohammed sent an envoy to the emperor Heraclius, at Constantinople, inviting him to embrace Islamism, the patriarch was in the presence of the emperor. The envoy having related the nocturnal journey of the prophet, the patriarch was seized with astonishment, and informed the emperor of a circumstance coinciding with the narrative of the envoy. 'It is my custom,' said he, 'never to retire to rest at night until I have fastened every door of the temple. On the night here mentioned, I closed them according to my custom, but there was one which it was impossible to move. Upon this I sent for the carpenters, who, having inspected the door, declared that the lintel over the portal and the edifice itself had settled to such a degree, that it was out of their power to close the door. I was obliged, therefore, to leave it open. Early in the morning, at the break of day, I repaired thither, and behold, the stone placed at the corner of the temple was perforated, and there were vestiges of the place where Al Boráq had been fastened. Then said I, to those present, this portal would not have remained fixed unless some prophet had been here to pray.' "

Traditions go on to say that when Mohammed narrated his nocturnal journey to a large assembly in Mecca, many marvelled yet believed, some were perplexed with doubt, but the Qoreishites laughed it to scorn. "Thou sayest that thou hast been to the temple of Jerusalem," said Abu Jahl "prove the truth of thy words, by giving a description of it." For a moment Mohammed was embarrassed by the demand for he had visited the temple in the night, when its form was not discernible; suddenly, however, the angel Gabriel stood by his side, and placed before his eyes an exact type of the sacred edifice, so that he was enabled instantly to answer the most minute questions.

already expecting the Promised One of the Scriptures, when they heard of Mohammed and his doctrines identified him with the expected prophet, and many of them soon embraced Islam. Oseid bin Hodzeir, a nobleman of the town, and Sa'd bin Mo'ázh the prince of the Aws tribe were the first important converts and their example was followed by the whole of their big families known as the Bani Abd-al-Ashhal. Similarly Abu Qais and most of his adherents were the later converts.

Second Pledge of Aqaba. 622 A. D.

Next year, the thirteenth of Be'that, in the month of Zhilhajja—the festal celebration days of Mecca—seventy-three men and two women, from among the converts of the Aws and Khazraj tribes of Yathrib, accompanied Mos'ab b. Omeir to Mecca, with a Jewish caravan of 300 or 500 pilgrims, headed by their chief Ibn Obay. Immediately on their arrival at Mecca they approached the Prophet, paid him profound reverence and desired him to accompany them to Yathrib. The invitation was opportune—a Godsend—as the Qoreish, failing in all their attempts to thwart the progress of Mohammed's religion and realising their failures to check the influence he and his followers were gaining everywhere, had begun to contemplate open violence to the Prophet and even his murder. It was, therefore, unsafe for Mohammed to stay much longer at Mecca.

To consider over the proposal of the converts of Yathrib, their next visit was fixed to take place at the Aqaba on the third night *i. e.* the one after the day of Sacrifice. While proceeding to keep the appointment Mohammed took with him his uncle Al-Abbás, who was now the head of the family and formally Mohammed's protector. He silently watched the proceedings of the conference. The Yathribites solemnly affirmed to defend the Prophet from his enemies and to guard him against all perils. They desired the Prophet to give them his word that if he was claimed back by men of his native town he would not abandon his new allies. The Prophet promised and asked them to consider himself thence-forward wholly as one of themselves as bound by the ties of interest, honor and blood. Then they asked what would be their reward if they were killed in his service and cause. To this query his reply was that Paradise would be the reward to all those who might be killed in defending the Prophet in the cause of Islam. All the people were highly pleased with the frank answers of the Prophet and they reiterated the oath of allegiance and fidelity, placing one by one their hands in the hands of the Prophet. This is known in the history as the Second Pledge of Aqaba. Realising the earnestness of the Yathribites and their devotional adherence to Mohammed, Abbás solemnly transferred his nephew from under his protection to that of theirs in Yathrib. The pact having been unanimously confirmed, the Prophet's hegirat or emigration to Yathrib (Medina) was definitely settled.

† Notwithstanding the secrecy with which the negotiations at the Aqaba were carried on in the dead of night, some Qoreish spy, just after the proceedings were over, shouted out that he would denounce them. 'Fear him not, he is the foe of God,' said the Prophet and the assembly broke up. Next morning, while on their home-ward journey with the returning caravan, the Yathribites were pursued by the Meccans, but the pursuit was fruitless. The Meccans, however, had got wind of the affairs transacted at the Aqaba, and they were alarmed at the idea that Mohammed was securing friends beyond their reach.

Establishment of brotherhood. 622 A. D.

* Now the Prophet, collected his Meccan adherents and established brotherhood between each two of his followers. Thus Abubekr and Omar were enjoined brothers; Hamza and Zaid b. Háritha; Othmán and Abd-al-Rahmán;

* قال العلامة القسطلاني في ارشاد الساري لشرح صحيح البخاري اخي رسول الله صلعم بين ابو بكر و عمر (رض) و بين حمزة و زيد بن

† Ibn Hishám; Ibn Khaldun.

Zobeir and Ibn Mas'ud; Obeida b. Hárith and Bilál; Talha and Sa'id b. Zaid; Mos'ab b. Omeir and Sa'd b. Abi Waqqás; Abu Obeida and Sálim etc., etc., were made brothers to one another. † *His own brotherhood the Prophet bestowed upon Ali.*

CHAPTER VII.

Qoreish designs to murder Mohammed, and his escape to Medina.

Commencement of Emigration to Medina. 622 A. D.

The Qoreish now renewed their persecutions with greater determination and with redoubled ferocity, more especially towards the adherents of Mohammed. Their chief object was to prevent their country-men from migrating to Medina. But their violence served only to precipitate matters. The Prophet, who had already made provision for the safety of his followers,

حارثة (رض) و بين عثمان و عبدالرحمن بن عوف (رض) و بين الزبير و ابن مسعود (رض) و بين مصعب بن عمير و سعد بن ابی وقاص (رض) و بين عبيدة بن حارث و بلال (رض) و بين ابي عبيدة و سالم مولي ابی حذيفة (رض) و بين سعيد بن زيد و طلحه بن عبيد الله (رض) و بين علی و نفسه صعلم—

ترجمه—علامه قسطلاني كتاب ارشاد الساري شرح صحيح بخاري مين لكهتے هين كه جناب رسالت ماب نے دو دو مهاجرين مين رشتهٔ برادرانه قائم كيا - چنانچه حضرت ابو بكر اور حضرت عمر كو باهم بهائی قرار ديا - اور حضرت حمزه و زيد بن حارثه كو - اور عثمان و عبدالرحمن بن عوف كو- اور زبير بن العوام و ابن مسعود كو- اور عبيده بن الحارث و بلال كو - اور مصعب بن عمير و سعد بن ابي وقاص كو - اور ابو عبيده و سالم مولی ابی حذيفه كو - اور سعيد بن زيد و طلحه بن عبيد الله كو باهم بهائي قرار ديا -اور اپنے اخوت كا شرف آنحضرت نے علی بن ابيطالب كو عطا فرمايا — (تاريخ احمدي ص ٢٥)

† Tárikh al Khamis; Habib al Siyar.

as well as for himself, with the men of Yathrib by their solemn pledge at Aqaba, and had enjoined brotherhood between each two of his adherents for the furtherance of sympathy between them, now gave them permission to repair to Yathrib for their safety.

No sooner had they received permission to migrate than some of the followers of Mohammed took their departure to Yathrib. Thus, in the spring of the thirteenth year of his Be'that, began the Hegirat or Exodus to Yathrib (Medina). The Meccan converts who migrated to Medina were called Mohájirs; while the men of Medina who undertook to defend the Prophet from his enemies were called Ansárs or the Auxiliaries. Subsequently all Medina converts were distinguished by the surname Ansárs. The emigration went on quietly and unostentatiously; within two months about one hundred and fifty Meccan Moslems succeeded in reaching Yathrib. At last Omar's departure publicly, together with twenty other converts of his party, alarmed the Qoreish.

The Prophet remained in Mecca waiting for God's command *re* his hegirat. Ali, his favourite brother, and Abubekr were alone left behind in Mecca to keep him company.

Conspiracy to murder Mohammed. 622 A. D.

† Meanwhile the Qoreish, beholding with alarm the exodus of the followers of the Prophet and dreading the consequences of the new alliance of Mohammed and his followers with the people of Yathrib, formed a strong conspiracy to prevent his escape to Yathrib, under any circumstances. They kept close watch over the movements of the Prophet and took measures to secure his person in order to put him to death. They held a council to discuss how they should do away with Mohammed. One opined that he should be imprisoned in a cell having but a little hole, through which he should be given scanty food till he died. Another suggested that he should be

† Tabari; Ibn Hishám; Tárikh-al-Khamis; Rawdzat al Ahbáb.

banished. These proposals were rejected by others lest he should possibly find means of release and help to avenge. At length they decided to force into the Prophet's dwelling the same night, and appointed one man from each of their separate families to join in the murderous attack upon Mohammed in order to baffle the Háshimites to avenge themselves upon any particular member or family, as it would be obviously impossible for them to incur the risk of entering into feud with all the families.

This secret conspiracy was hardly at work, when the angel Gabriel appeared to the Prophet, informed him of the scheme against him, and communicated to him the permission of Alláh to his hegirat or exile from Mecca to Yathrib that very night. It is mentioned in the Qurán thus:

> "And when the Infidels plotted against thee, that they might detain thee (as prisoner) or put thee to death, or turn thee out; and they plotted (against thee) but God laid a plot (against them); and God is the best layer of plots. (*i. e.* God's watchfulness outwits the wicked in frustrating their designs against the virtuous)." *Sura VIII—30.*

Escape of the Prophet.

* By the time the murderers began to assemble before the dwelling of the Prophet, he apprised his favourite cousin, Ali, of the impending danger, and of his intention to leave the house at once for good. He directed Ali to lie down on the bed in his place and cover himself with his (the Prophet's) well known green mantle. Unhesi-

* قال ابن الاثير في الكامل فلما كان العتمة اجتمعوا على بابه يرصدونه متي ينام فيثبون عليه فلما رأهم رسول الله صلم قال لعلي بن ابيطالب نم علي فراشي واتشح ببردي الاخضر فنم فيه فانه لا يخلص اليک شي تكرهه و امره ان يودي ما عنده من و ديعة و امانة وغير ذلک و خرج رسول الله صلعم فاخذ حفنة من تراب فجعله علي روسهم و هو يتلو هذه الايات يس والقران الحكيم الي قوله فهم لا يبصرون ثم انصرف فلم يروه —

tatingly † Ali carried out the instruction and Mohammed, repeating the first eight verses of Sura Ya Seen of the Holy Book, sallied forth unobserved by the assailants as if they were stricken with blindness.

> "And We have set a barrier before them, and a barrier behind them; and We have covered them with darkness; wherefore they shall not see." *Sura XXXVI–8.*

* When all the assassins had been assembled, "they (in the words of W. Irving) paused at the door and looking through a crevice, beheld, as they thought, Mohammed wrapped in his green mantle, and lying asleep on

---

ترجمہ—ابن اثیر جزري تاریخ کامل مین لکھتے هین که جب رات کي تاریکي هوئي تو کفار قریش اس اراده سے در دولت نبوي پر مجتمع هوے که پیغمبر صاحب اپنے بستر پر لیٹتین تو وه حمله کرین – رسول الله نے اونکا مجمع دیکھکر علي بن ابیطالب سے کہا که تم میرے سبز چادر اوڑه کر میرے بستر پر سو رهو اور اطمینان رکھو که تمکوکوي گزند نه پهونچیگا – نیز حضرت علی کو حکم دیا که جسکی جو امانت اور ودیعت هے اوسکو ادا کردینا—اس کے بعد آنحضرت گھر سے باهر نکلے اور آپنے سوره یس کي ابتدائي آیتین فهم لا یبصرون تک پڑه کر ایک مٹھی خاک کفار کے سرون کي جانب پھینکدي اور راه مدینه اختیار کي کفار قریش مین سے کسی نے بھی آپکو نه دیکھا (تاریخ احمدي ص ۲۷)—

* في الدرالمنثور لسیوطي اخرج الحاکم و صحیحه عن ابن عباس (رض) قال شري علی (رض) نفسه و لبس ثوب النبي صلعم ثم نام مکانه وکان المشرکون یحسبون انه رسول الله صلعم و کانت قریش تریدان تقتل النبي صلعم —

ترجمه—تفسیر در منثور سیوطی مین بروایت حاکم بسند صحیح ابن عباس سے مروي هے که علي بن ابیطالب نے اپني جان کو رسول الله پر فدا کیا اور رسول مقبول کي چادر اوڑه کر اونکی جگه سورهے مشرکین قریش سمجھتے تھے که آنحضرت سو رهے هین اور اس اراده مین تھے که (نعوذ بالله) آنحضرت کو قتل کرین — (تاریخ احمدی ص ۲۷) —

† Tabari ; Tárikh-al-Khamis; Ibn Hishám; Ma'álim-al-Tanzil; Rawdzat-al-Ahbáb.

his coach. They waited for a while consulting whether to fall on him while sleeping or wait until he should go forth. At length they burst open the door and rushed towards the coach. The sleeper started up, but instead of Mohammed, Ali son of Abu Tálib stood before them. Amazed and confounded they demanded, "Where is Mohammed!?" "I know not," replied Ali sternly, and walked forth, nor did any one venture to molest him."

John Davenport describes the incident in the following words: "After surrounding the house, the assassins then forcibly entered it, but finding instead of their purposed victim, the youthful Ali, calmly and resignedly awaiting the death intended for his Chief, so much devotedness excited the pity even of those men of blood, and Ali was left unharmed."

Ali's devotion.

*Ali's devotion to the Prophet without fear to run therefrom the risk of his own life was much appreciated †by the All-knowing Judge of man, the merciful God, who sent down the angels Gabriel and Michael to guard him from the murderous mob; and informed the Prophet on his way to Medina of His ‡approval of Ali's resignation to His will, with the words

* في اسد الغابه لابن الاثير الجزري و احياء العلوم للغزالي و تاريخ الخميس للديار بكري بات علي كرم الله وجهه علي فراش رسول الله صلعم فاوحى الله تعالي الى جبريل و ميكائيل عليهم السلام اني اخيت بينكما و جعلت عمر احد كما اطول من عمر الاخر فايكما يوثر صاحبه بالحيوة فاختار كلا هما الحيوة واحباها و اوحي الله عزوجل اليهما افلا كنتما مثل على بن ابيطالب اخيت بينه و بين نبي محمد فبات على فراشه يفديه بنفسه و يوثر بالحيوة اهبطا الي الارض فاحفظاه من عدوه فكان جبريل عند راسه و

† Tafsir Kabir Fakhruddin Rázi.

‡ Ibn Athir; Ghizáli's *Ahya-al-Uloom*; Tarikh-al-Khamis etc.

contained in *Verse 203 of Sura II of the Quran.*

"And of men there is one who selleth his soul for the sake of seeking the pleasure of God; and God is gracious unto his servants."

میکائیل عند رجلیه و جبرئل (علیہ السلام) یقول بخ بخ من مثلک یا بن ابی طالب و اللہ تعالی یباهی بک الملایکته فانزل اللہ تعالی علی رسوله و هو متوجهه الی المدینة في شان علی :

و من النلس من یشري نفسه ابتغاء مرضات اللہ واللہ روف بالعباد —

ترجمه — اسدالغابه ابن اثیر جزري اور احیاء العلوم غزالي اور تاریخ الخمیس مین هے که جب حضرت علي بستر نبوي پر سوئے تو خدانے جبرئیل و میکائیل کیجانب وحی فرمائي که مینے تم دونون مین رشتۂ برادرانه قائم کیا اور تم مین سے هر ایک کي عمر به نسبت دوسرے کے طویل کي - پس تم دونون مین کون ایسا هے جو اپنے ساتھي پر اپني جان نثار کرے — یهه خطاب الهي سنکر جبرئیل و میکائیل نے اپني اپني زندگاني کو عزیز سمجھا اور ایثار بالحیوة کو گوارہ نه کیا — پروردگار عالم نے پھر اونکي جانب وحي فرمائي که کیا تم دونون علي بن ابیطالب کی طرح نهین هوسکتے - دیکھو مینے محمد و علی مین مواخات قائم کی اور علی اسوقت بستر نبی پر اس غرض سے لیتا هے که ایثار بالحیوة کرکے اپنی جان کو اپنے بھائي پر فدا کرے - اب تم دونون زمین پر جاؤ اور شر اعدا سے علی کي حفاظت کرو- پس بحکم الهی دونون ملک مقرب نے نازل هوکر بستر علی کے بالین و پائین قرار لیا اور جبرئیل علیه السلام فرماتے تھے که مرحبا مرحبا کون هے مثل تیرے اے ابوطالب کے بیتے جسکے ساتھه اللہ تعالے ملائکه پر مباهات فرماتاهے — چنانچه حق سبحانهٔ تعالے نے اپنے رسول مقبول پر جبکه وہ مدینے جارهے تھے علی کي شان مین یهه آیت نازل فرمائي —

و من الناس من یشری نفسه ابتغاء مرضات اللہ و اللہ روف بالعباد -

(یعنے لوگون مین سے ایک ایسا بھی هے جو خدا کي رضا جوي کے لئے اپنی جان تک فروخت کر دیتا هے اور خدا اپنے بندون پر بڑا شفقت فرمانیوالا هے — (تاریخ احمدي ص ۲۰)

The cave on Mount Thowr.

Leaving the house the Prophet met Abubekr, whom he required to accompany him, and both of them proceeded in the dead of night, as quickly as they could, towards the south, a direction opposite to Medina towards which Mohammed thought the Meccans would naturally suppose him to have gone. Speeding about an hour and a half, they approached a rocky summit of Mount Thowr, by a rugged and difficult path. There they found a low cavern with an opening hardly sufficient to admit them singly. † Abubekr crept into it first, cleansed it sweeping all round, then the Prophet entered and took shelter into it along with Abubekr. During the night, the spider worked a thick web over the opening of the cave, a bushy plant grew up near it and a pigeon laid eggs forming its nest thereat, so that the cave to all appearances looked deserted for long.

The Qoreish, exasperated at the sudden and successful escape of their intended victim, set a reward of hundred camels for Mohammed's capture, alive or dead. ‡ Scouts were set on to search out the fugitive in every direction, and they explored every haunt in the neighbourhood, some miles round the city. They arrived near the cave wherein the Prophet was hidden. Abubekr became uneasy and fearful of the imminent danger of being discovered. He began to whine and said trembling to the Prophet, "What if our pursuers should find us out? We are but two." "Don't be afraid," replied he, "Alláh is with us." Approaching the cave, the Providential spider's web and the pigeon's nest with eggs convinced the Qoreish scouts that the place was solitary for a long time. They turned back without looking into it.

The Prophet's Hegirat. 622 A. D.

Mohammed passed three days with his calm unwavering trust in God in this cave upon the barren rock of the wild tract together with Abubekr naturally in suspense. At the close of the third day when the heat of the pursuit

† Rawdzat-al-Ahbáb; Madárij-al-Nabowat; Habib-al-Siyar.
‡ Ditto; Tárikh-al-Khamis; Sirat Mohammediya.

had subsided and the busy curiosity of the first agitation relaxed, †† Ali provided them with camels in charge of a guide to lead them to Medina by an unfrequented route. By the evening of Monday, the 5th of Rabi I or 21st of June 622 A. D. they were well started on their journey.

On the second day of their journey, when they were thinking themselves beyond the probability of being pursued, ‡ they beheld in the distance behind them the fast approaching form of a man—Soráqa b. Málik—who, tempted by the reward set upon the head of the Prophet, had not yet given up the search. At the sight, Abubekr again began to tremble for fear of being captured, and cried out, "We are lost." Mohammed comforted him again saying, "Don't be afraid, Alláh is with us." So saying, the Prophet prayed to God for protection; and Lo! as the pursuer advanced, his charger reared and sank motionless on the ground and the rider was helpless. Bewildered and astounded, Soráqa was convinced of heavenly interference, and entreated the forgiveness of the Prophet, promising not to betray him. The Prophet prayed for him and his charger got up, and he rode back to Mecca. Mohammed was again free to pursue his course along the sea coast.

A Miracle. † Before this encounter with his pursuer, the Prophet had reposed for a while at Qadid in a tent belonging to a noble lady, Omm Ma'bad, of that place. When he got up to resume his journey, he performed ablutions preparatory to his after-noon prayers, throwing water over a plant close by the tent. The plant was found the next day to have grown up to a tree laden with fruits and with leaves bigger than ever it had. The people, who tasted its fruits, found them to be very delicious and having a pleasant flavour. The tree was henceforth considered as blessed, and the sick got cured

†† Tabari; Sirat Mohammediya.

‡ Abul Fida; Ibn Athir; Ibn Khaldun; Tárikh-al-Khamis etc.

† Zamakhshari in *Rabi'al Abrar*; Tárikh-al-Khamis.

with its fruits and leaves. It soon acquired a wide fame. People from distant places thronged around it. Some ten years afterwards it shed its fruits all of a sudden. The incident coincided with the day of the Prophet's death. About thirty years later, on the day of Ali's assassination, fruits of the tree again fell down all at once, and it never produced any fruit again. The people, however, contented themselves with its leaves for getting cure of their diseases. At last, on the day of the murder of Hosain, the grandson of the Prophet, at Karbalá, a red fluid was found flowing profusely from its trunk and the tree dried up.

CHAPTER VIII.

The Prophet's arrival and settlement in Medina.

Arrival at Qoba. 622 A. D.

† Mohammed reached Qobá, a suburb of Medina, about two miles from the city, situated in a fertile valley and famous for its orchards and fruit gardens, on Monday, the 12th of Rabi' I, at the end of the thirteenth year of his Be'that (Mission) at the close of fiftythird year of his age. His camel sat down on its own accord at a place called Al Taqwa, where the Prophet got down and put up in the house of Kulthum b. Hadam or Sa'd b. Khathima. Abubekr proceeded on to Medina and put up in the house of Khabib b. Osáf or Zaid b. Khárja at Sonh, another suburb of Medina. For four days the Prophet halted at Qobá to take rest after the anxieties and the fatigue of the long journey of more than 250 miles.

Boreida b. Al Hasib.

‡ Here at Qobá arrived Boreida b. Al Hasib from Mecca with his seventy followers in pursuit of Mohammed. But appearing before him, all of them embraced Islam. The Prophet

† Ibn Hishám; Tabari; Ibn Khaldun; Táríkh al Khamis.
‡ W. Irving.

1 A. H.

was delighted at this first sign of his success on setting foot in the suburbs of Medina.

Salman Farsi.

† Next came Salmán, a venerable old man, a Persian merchant by origin and a Christian by faith, but now a bondman of a Jew of Medina. He was anxiously expecting the Prophet promised in the Scriptures, and on appearing before Mohammed identified him as the Promised Prophet, and unhesitatingly accepted his Faith.

Victualling in the cave.

The Prophet's brother and vicegerent Ali, who was left behind by him to restore the properties placed in trust with him, to their owners, ‡ managed to supply food to the refugee and his companion in the cave, as naturally none other could be confided with the secret of the hiding place, as it involved the precious life of Mohammed. There is also another version of the story. Some maintain that a particular lady used to provide food to the refugees in the cave. But it does not appeal to common sense that a female (a girl of 13 or 14 years, probably unmarried), could possibly have dared traverse the wild tract, with a double journey, alone and unprotected, during nights, to carry the food under the very nose of the Qoreish scouts, specially in the circumstances attendant upon the situation of the cave, which was admittedly at a distance of one and a half hour's journey of a hurrying man, and located on the sum-

---

† "He (Salmán, the Persian) was of a good family of Ispáhan, and, in his younger years, left the religion of his country to embrace Christianity; and travelling into Syria, was advised by a certain monk of Amoria to go into Arabia, where a prophet was expected to arise about that time, who should establish the religion of Abrahám; and whom he should know, among other things, by the *Seal of Prophecy* between his shoulders. Salmán performed the journey, and meeting with Mohammed at Qobá, where he rested in his flight to Medina, soon found him to be the person he sought, and professed Islam." Sale from Ex. Ibn Isháq *vide Gagnier*.

‡ Tabari ; Sirat Mohammediya ; Hayát al Qulub.

mit of a Mount which could be reached only through the wilderness and by the zigzag paths. Ali was the only suitable man (aged about 23 years), the confidante of the Prophet, to have undertaken the task, ‡ as also to have provided the fugitive and his companion with transport and a reliable guide for their escape to Medina.

Ali at Qoba.

* Having satisfactorily accomplished the responsibilities entrusted to him, and having arranged for the safe departure of the Prophet's family members to Medina, Ali hastened forward on foot to Medina travelling only in the night and hiding himself in the day lest he should fall into the hands of the Qoreish, who had severely || maltreated him on the disappearance of the Prophet. He reached Qobá three days after the arrival of the Prophet there, with his feet sorely lacerated and † bleeding. The Prophet, overjoyed to see him, received him with open arms, and finding him tired and exhausted, shed tears manifesting his affection for him; and subsequently applied the moisture of his mouth to the wounds of Ali's feet with his own hand and prayed for him. This produced instantaneous relief.

---

* قال ابن الاثير الجزري فی اسد الغابه و خرج علي في طلب رسول الله صلعم بعد ما اخرج اليه اهله يمشي الليل و يمكن النهار حتي قدم المدينة فلما بلغ النبي صلعم قدومه قال ادعوالي عليا قيل يا رسول الله لا يقدران يمشي فاتاه النبی صلعم فلما راه عتنقه و بكی رحمته لما يقدسيه من الورم و كانتا تقطران دما فتفل النبی صلعم فی يديه و مسح بهما رجليه و دعاله بالعافيه فلم يشتكهما حتی استشهد رضی الله عنه

ترجمه—اسد الغابه ابن اثير جزري مين هے كه حضرت علي (بعد اداے امانات) جناب رسالت ماب كے اهل و عيال كو بجانب مدينه روانه كركے خود بهي آنحضرت كي حضوري حاصل كرنيكے لئے (تنها اور پياده) مكه سے مدينه كو روانه هوے—رات بهر چلتے تهے اور دن كو قيام كرتے تهے يهانتك كه بعد طی منازل مدينه پهونچنے كی اطلاع هوئی تو فرمايا

‡ Tafsir Durr Manthur Suyuti vol ii.
|| Spirit of Islam.
† Ibn Khaldun; Habib al Siyar.

1 A. H.

"When the Prophet fled to Medina, he commanded him (Ali) to remain behind at Mecca for somedays, in order to discharge for him certain trusts and charges and bequests which were incumbent on the Prophet, and then join him with his family, and he did so and was present with the Apostle of God at Bedr and Ohod and all the expeditions except Tabuk, for verily the Prophet had *appointed him his vicegerent at Medina.*" (*Major Jarret's trans. of Suyuti's His: Cal. p. 171.*)

Foundation of a Mosque at Qaba

* The converts at Qobá desired the Prophet to lay the foundation stone of a mosque for them. He asked his Companions to ride on his camel and to make a round. Abubekr and Omar, who were among the Companions—visitors from Medina—mounted by turn on the back of the camel, but it did not move. Then the Prophet asked Ali, his vicegerent to make the attempt. As soon as Ali set his foot in the stirrup, the camel stood up and the Prophet directed Ali to let it go by itself without guiding it. Ali let the rein and the camel went round a small piece of ground and coming back to its starting point knelt down. The Prophet marked the site and fixing the position of the Qibla laid the foundation stone for the mosque to be built there. There is a mention of this mosque in the Qurán vide Sura IX-109 last portion.

که علي کو میرے پاس لاؤ-لوگون نے عرض کیا که یا رسول الله اب اونمین چلنے کي قدرت نہین هے - یهه سنکر رسول مقبول خود حضرت علی کے پاس تشریف لاے اور بغلگیر هوکر فرط محبت سے رونے لگے کیونکه اونکو اس سفر مین ایسي تکلیف هوئي تهي که دونون پاون سوج گئے تهے اور اونسے خون ٹپکتا تها— آنحضرت نے اپنا لعاب دهن حضرت علي کے پیرونمین اپنے دست مبارک سے لگایا اور اونکی صحت و عافیت کیلئے دعا کی چنانچه پهر وه وقت شهادت تک کبهي ان شکایتونمین مبتلا نهین هوے—(تاریخ احمدي ص ۳۰)

---

* شیخ عبدالحق محدث دهلوي در جذب القلوب آورده که بروایتے اهل قبا از آنحضرت صلعم التماس نمودند که مسجدے براے ایشان بنا

†The news of the arrival of the Prophet soon spread far and wide, and the proselytes in Medina having ascertained the day of his solemn entry into their city and impelled by the sense of duty in paying profound reverence to him, hastened to accord a befitting welcome to the Prophet. On the 16th of Rabi' I, the Prophet left Qobá a little before noon. Boreida b. Al Hasib with his seventy neophytes formed a procession ahead, carrying as Standard his lance with a piece from his turban fastened to its upper end.

It being Friday, the Prophet halted at Ránawná, a place midway between Qobá and Medina and performed his Friday prayers, followed by a Sermon to the Moslems, who were present on the occasion. ‡ This Friday Service and the Sermons were the first, to be observed always thereafter ; and Friday is commemorated as a holiday ever since. Most of the Medinian converts and almost all the Meccan Moslems, who had migrated to Medina, had come to this place to receive the Prophet and had joined him in the Service.

The Prophet's entry into Medina.
622 A. D.

When the Prophet, after the Service, was proceeding to Medina, the whole spectacle with its ceremonious solemnity looked really grand, like a triumphal procession headed by a monarch, increasing in its majestic

فرماید - اشارت به صحابهٔ کرام کرد و فرمود یکے از شما براین ناقهٔ من سوار
شود و بگرداند - ابو بکر صدیق برخواست و برپشت ناقه نشست - ناقه
بر نخاست بعد ازوے عمر فاروق سوار شد نیز بر نخاست - بعد ازان
علی مرتضے برخاست - همین که پاے در رکاب آورده ناقه برجست - فرمود
زمام اورها کن که وے مامور است هرجا که گردد - آخر هم بر مدار سیر
ناقهٔ مسجد قبا بنا فرمود و با هل قبا امر کرد تا سنگها جمع کردند -
پس بغزه که در دست داشت خطے براے تعین قبله بر کشید و سنگے بدست
مبارک برگرفت و بر موضع بنا نهاد - (تاریخ احمدی ص ۳۰)

† Rawdzat al Ahbáb ; Tárikh al Khamis.

‡ Tabari ; Rawdzat al Ahbáb.

grandeur as it approached the city, where thousands of spectators had assembled to have a look at the great prophet of Islam. This was no other than Mohammed (on him and his holy descendants be the eternal peace), who had been banished into exile from his own dear home by his own people, under the most serious persecutions, with a price upon his head, escaping death only about a fortnight ago. But the extreme persecutions, instead of obstructing the natural course of things, generally precipitate them. It is true especially in religious propaganda. Such had been the case with Mohammed, who now entered Medina as a †Spritual Monarch swaying the hearts of the people, Moslems and non-Moslems alike. History of the World records no greater example of the triumph of truth.

Medina, prior to the settlement of the Prophet there, was called Yathrib; after his settlement it was known as 'The city of the Prophet,' or Medinat al Nabi. Now it is generally named 'Medina Monawira,' the illuminated, as a luminous haze hanging over the town meets the eye of the devout Moslem pilgrim on his approach to the city.

Each tribe, which he passed through, desired the honor of his presence and requested him to take up his abode with them. The homeless, refusing all these offers, said that the camel, which he rode on, was inspired and would take him to the proper quarter. The camel proceeded on to the eastern quarter and knelt down in the open courtyard of the Banu Najjár, near the house of Khálid b. Zaid known in the history as Abu Ayyub Ansári, the then head of the Banu Najjar family—the family to which Mohammed's grand father Abd-al-Mottalib's mother Selma belonged. He was delighted to be the fortunate one to have the honor of the Prophet's presence; and Mohammed

†"God came from Teman, and the Holy One from Mount Paran-Selah. His Glory covered the heavens, and the earth was full of his praise." Habakkuk III—3.

Note: The hills surrounding Mecca are called Fárán Mountains.

took up his temporary residence in his house for about seven months, until a mosque, with proper quarters for himself, was built in the court-yard where the camel had stopped.

The Prophet's Mosque.

† The court-yard, with some palm trees growing over it, was the property of two orphans, Sohal and Sohail, who desired to make a present of it to the Prophet, when they learned that he wished a mosque to be built over the spot. But the Prophet would not accept the offer and paid them ten mithqáls in gold, the price settled for the plot. After the purchase the ground was cleared of the trees, and a mosque, fifty-four yards in width and sixty yards in length was built over it with clay bricks and mud, and roofed with palm-wood rafters, covered with palm branches and leaves and clay. It was not sufficiently solid to keep out rain. The trunks of palm tree were used as pillars to support the roof. The construction work of the mosque was distributed among the converts—the Mohájirs and the Ansárs—the Prophet too had his share of the work. But he himself was seldom allowed to work, as Ammár Yásir, an early convert and a faithful Companion of the Prophet, used to accomplish the Prophet's share of work in addition to his own. ‡ Ammár was the first and foremost to begin the foundation of the mosque.

A Prophecy.

¶ It was on this occasion that the Prophet, while affectionately putting off the dust fallen over Ammár's body, prophesied that that Companion was destined to fall under the sword of rebels, which actually happened some thirty-eight years later.

Close to one side of the mosque, apartments were constructed for the Prophet and his family; and on the other side rooms were provided for the poor adherents who had no house of their own. They numbered about

---

† Rawdzat-al-Ahbáb; Tárikh-al-Khamis.
‡ Ibn Hishám.
¶ Tirmizhi; Muslim; Bokhári.

seventy at the time and later on their number reached approximately to four hundred. These rooms of the adherents were termed 'Suffa.'

Though the mosque was very simple in structure, made of rough and rude material, yet it is the most glorious in the annals of Islam, as having been the first mosque built by the Prophet himself and his revered Companions; where he and his Companions spent the greater part of their time in devotional worship of the Supreme Lord; where the Prophet performed Friday service and delivered sermons to a large congregation every week; where thousands of people received and accepted the doctrines of Islam, and, giving up their old established idolatrous practices, fervently embraced the faith professed by the Prophet; where the holy Prophet lived all his life after his Hegirat from Mecca and where still he lies buried.

When the mosque and residential houses were complete, the Prophet shifted from his temporary residence at the house of Abu Ayyub Ansári to his permanent residence, together with his family members, who had already arrived there. At this time he had only one wife, Sawda. His betrothed wife Ayesha was still with her father Abubekr living in Sonh, but later on, after the consummation of her nuptials at the age of nine years, some eight or nine months after the Prophet's arrival in Medina, she was unostentatiously brought over to one of the quarters close to the mosque.

Closing of the doors opening into the Prophet's Mosque.

Later on, some Companions of the Prophet also built their houses close to the Mosque with doors opening into the courtyard. Sometime afterwards, * one day while they were leisurely sitting in the Mosque, a voice was heard: "Ye people! Close

* محدث دهلوي در جذب القلوب ذكر كرده اورده اند كه اصحاب همه در مسجد نشسته بودند ناگاه منادي ندا در داد ايها الناس سدوا

your doors opening into the Mosque." The people were struck with wonder to hear the voice, but they sat dumb without stirring to carry out the Command, till they heard again the injunction to close the doors on pain of Divine Wrath. Terrified at this warning, they all approached the Prophet, who was in his apartment. Ali also came out of his apartment which was separated from the Prophet's rooms by a partition wall since the date of Fátema's marriage with him. He stood by the Prophet when he ordered that all the doors opening into the Mosque, excepting that of Ali and his own, should be closed. The people began to murmur. The Prophet was angry at their attitude and addressed them thus:—"Verily, God ordered His apostle Moses to build a holy Mosque, and he allowed Moses, Aaron and the two sons of Aaron *viz.* Shabbar and Shabbir to live therein. I was likewise ordered to construct a holy mosque wherein myself and my brother Ali and his two sons, Hasan and

---

ابوابکم انتبا هے در مردم پیدا آمد لیکن هیچکس بر نه ایستاد- بار دیگر ندا آمد—ایها الناس سدوا ابوابکم قبل ان ینزل العذاب — مردم همه بر آمدند و بملازمت آنحضرت مبادرت کردند- علی مرتضي نیز آمد و بر سر انحضرت ایستاد- فرمود تو چه استادهٔ برو و بخانه خود بنشین و در خانهٔ خود را بحال خود بگذارد و درمیان مردم ازین معنی گفتگوے افتاد و دریغے در دلها راه یافت آنحضرت در غضب شد و به منبر رفت و حمد و ثنائے مولا گفت و گفت حق سبحانه و تعالي وحی فرستاد بر موسي علیه السلام که مسجد بناکن موصوف بهٔ صفت طهارت و ساکن نشود در وے جز تو و هارون و پسران هارون شبر و شبیر همچنین وحی کرد بر من که مسجدے سازم طاهر که ساکن نشود در وے جز من و علی و پسران او حسن و حسین پس بمدینه آمدم و مسجدے گرفتم و مرا در آمدن و گرفتن مسجد اصلا اختیارے نه بود- من نمیکنم مگر انچه بکنانند و نمی دانم مگر انچه بدانانند- پس والله من درها را نه بسته ام ونه کشاده ام و علي را من نه آورده ام اورا خدا آورد من چه کنم (تاریخ احمدی ص ۳۲)

Hosain are allowed to live. *Verily, I do only what I am ordered to do. I never undertake to act on my own wish. Certainly I have not ordered of my own accord to close your doors or to let Ali's door open. It is God who granted Ali an abode in the Holy Mosque." Consequently, the Companions, whose houses skirted the quadrangle of the Mosque, closed their doors.

"It is recorded on the authority of Sa'd, that the Apostle of God said to Ali : It is not lawful for any to be in the Mosque while under the obligation of performing a thorough ablution (*i. e.* غسل جنابت) except for me and for thee." *Major Jarret's trans. of Suyuti's His. p. 175.*

"Omar b. Al-Khattáb said: Verily, Ali hath been endowed with three qualities, of which had I but one, it would be more precious to me than were I given high bred camels. It was asked of him what they were; he replied: His marriage with Fátema, the daughter of the Prophet; his remaining in the Mosque while that is permitted to him which is not lawful for me; and his carrying the Standard on the day of Khaibar." *Major Jarret's trans. of Suyuti's His. p. 175.*

---

* اخرج النساي فی الخصایص عن زید بن ارقم قال کان لنفر من اصحاب رسول الله صلعم ابواب شارعة فی المسجد فقال رسول الله صلعم سدوا ابواب الاباب علی فتکلم بذلک الناس فقام رسول الله صلعم فحمد الله واثني علیه ثم قال اما بعد فانی امرت بسد هذه الابواب غیر باب علي و قال فیه قائلکم والله ما سدوته و لا فتحته و لکني امرت فاتبعته —

ترجمه — نسائی نے خصایص میں زید بن ارقم سے روایت کي هے که بعض اصحاب رسول کے دروازے مسجد نبوی کی جانب تهے رسول مقبول نے علی بن ابیطالب کے سوا اور سب اصحاب کو حکم دیا که اپنے اپنے دروازون کو بند کردین - اسپر اصحاب نے کچه کلام کیا تو آنحضرت نے کهڑے هوکر بعد حمد و ثنائے الهی فرمایا که مینے حکم ایزدي کے مطابق تم لوگون کے دروازے بند کرائے اور علی کا دروازه کهلا رکها تمنے اس باب مین (فضول) چون و چرا کي مینے نه کوئی دروازه بند کیا نه کهولا بلکه خدانے جو حکم دیا اوسکی تعمیل کی — (تاریخ احمدی ص ۳۱)

Authority of Mohammed.

In Medina the Aws and the Khazraj were the predominant Arab tribes, which formed the bulk of the population of the city. They originally belonged to Banu Qaila Arabs of Yemen, who, some centuries before Mohammed, had immigrated to Yathrib, now called Medina, and had driven away the Jews, who partly remained scattered among the Arabs under their protection, and partly in independent communities, such as the Bani Qainoqá, the Bani Nadzir and the Bani Qoraitza; but the majority of the Jews had gone out and settled in other places, such as Wádi-al-Qora, Khaibar, Fadak, Taima etc.

The Banu Qaila Arabs were divided into two branches, the Aws and the Khazraj, who were bitterly on enmical terms with one another. Shortly before the arrival of Mohammed, the battle of Bo'áth, during the seventh year of the Prophet's Mission, between the two sections had shattered the power of the Khazraj, who were now contemplating to make Ibn Obay king of Medina in order to be guided by him in consolidating their strength, as they were still more numerous than the other party. At this juncture, the appearance of the Prophet and the conversion of the majority of the Aws clan turned the tide in favour of the Prophet and he was at the right moment to settle the feuds and restore order. Hitherto the Arabs used to lay all complicated cases of their disputes for decision before their Káhins or Priests. Now they brought such cases to Mohammed as their religious leader. Mohammed had an acute and piercing wit and was a man of excellent judgment, naturally endowed with sound understanding. He heard their arguments and was helped by Providence to solve their riddles. His judgments were always acceptable to the contesting parties. His judicious reasonings and equitable decisions still more raised his position in the eyes of the people and strengthened their belief in his holiness as a Messenger of God. He successfully reconciled the Aws and the Khazraj tribes, and restored peace and order among them. He was therefore the restorer of Law and Justice where there had been nothing but violence and hatred before. He had come to be the veritable Hákim-be-amr-Alláh over them, and his authority was acknowledged by all the inhabitants of Medina.

Brotherhood between the Mohajirs and Ansars.

*The Prophet here inculcated the fundamental principle that brotherhood depended not on blood but on faith; and the relationship of Moslems with non-Moslems was entirely disowned. The rights of family inheritence, within Islam, were expressly valid and sacred. These mandates resulted in a considerable extension of the Moslem community. He established brotherhood individually between the Mohájirs of Mecca and the Ansárs of Medina; for instance, between Abubekr Mohájir and Khárja b. Zaid Ansár; between Omar b. Al-Khattáb

---

* فی الاستیعاب لابن عبدالبر اخی رسول الله صلعم (بمکته) بین المهاجرین ثم اخی (ثانیا بالمدینة) بین المهاجرین والانصار و قال فی کل واحدة منهما لعلی انت اخي في الدنیا والاخرة و اخی بینه و بین نفسه

ترجمه— استیعاب عبدالبر مین هے که (جسطرح) رسول مقبول نے (بمقام مکه) مهاجرین مین مواخات فرمائي تهی (اوسیطرح مدینه مین بهی) بین المهاجرین والانصار رشته اخوت قایم فرمایا اور دونون موقعون پر آنحضرت نے اپنا بهائي علی بن ابیطالب کو قرار دیکر ارشاد کیا که تم میرے بهای هو دنیا مین بهي اور آخرت مین بهي — (تاریخ احمدي ص ٣٣) —

قال ابوالفدا و اخي رسول الله (بالمدینة) فاتخذ علی بن ابیطالب اخا وصار ابوبکر و خارجه بن زیدا لانصاری اخوین و عبیدة بن ا لجراح وسعد بن معاذ الانصاري اخوین و عمر بن الخطاب و عتبان بن ا لمالک الانصاري اخوین و عبدا لرحمن بن عوف و سعد بن الربیع الانصاري اخوین و عثمان بن عفان و اوس بن ثابت الانصاري اخوین و طلحه بن عبیدا لله و کعب بن مالک الانصاري اخوین و سعید بن زید وابي بن کعب الانصاري اخوین —

Mohájir and Otbán b. Málik Ansár; between Othmán b. Affán Mohájir and Aws b. Thábit Ansár. †*His own brotherhood the Prophet bestowed upon Ali,* his cousin, as previously he had done in Mecca, declaring according to Suyuti, "*Thou art my brother in this world and in the next.*"

The Moslems were sympathetic and considerate to each other after the brotherhood was enjoined. They were so zealous in their faith that they disregarded every thing that before Islam, or outside of it, was looked upon as holy. In fine, they were animated with a strange spirit of firmness to their adherence to the Prophet and of cohesiveness to hold together. Gibbon gives the account in the following words: "To eradicate the seeds of jealousy, Mohammed judiciously coupled his principal followers with the rights and obligations of brethren; and when Ali found himself without a peer, the Prophet

---

ترجمہ—ابوالفدا نے لکھا ھے کہ آنحضرت نے مابین مہاجرین وانصار دو دو آدمیونمین رشتہ برادرانہ قائم کیا چنانچہ حضرت علي کو اپنا بھائي ھونیکا شرف عطا فرمایا اور حضرت ابوبکر وخارجہ بن زید انصاري کو باھم بھائي قرار دیا اور اسیطرح ابوعبیدہ بن الجراح وسعد بن معاذ انصاري کو اور عمر بن الخطاب و عتبان بن مالک انصاری کو اور عبدالرحمن بن عوف وسعد بن ربیع انصاري کو اور عثمان بن عفان و اوس بن ثابت انصاري کو اور طلحہ بن عبید الله و کعب بن مالک انصاري کو اور سعید بن زید وابي بن کعب انصاري کو آپسمین بھاي بھاي قرار دیا۔ (تاریخ احمدي ص ۳۳) —

في كتاب خلاصته الوفا باخبار دار المصطفے السمهودي اخي رسول الله صلى الله عليه وسلم بين اصحابه من المهاجرين والانصار فقال تاخوا في الله اخوين اخوين ثم اخذ بيد علی بن ابيطالب فقال هذا اخی —

ترجمہ—علامہ سمهودي کی کتاب خلاصته الوفا مین ھے کہ جناب رسالت ماب نے مہاجرین و انصار مین رشتہ برادرانہ قایم کیا اور ارشاد کیا کہ دو دو آدمي آپسمین دینی بھائي بنجاؤ پھر آنحضرت نے علی بن ابیطالب کا ھاتھہ پکڑ کر فرمایا کہ یہہ میرا بھاي ھے (تاریخ احمدي ص ۳۳) —

†Ibn Hishám; Nasái; Ahmad Hanbal; Hákim.

tenderly declared that *he would be the companion and brother of the noble youth.* The expedient was crowned with success; the holy fraternity was respected in peace and war, and the two parties vied with each other in a generous emulation of courage and fidelity." *W. Smith's* p. 460. The ordinance of brotherhood is given thus in the Qurán.

> "Verily, those who believe and have emigrated and have tried with their substance and their souls for the cause of God, and those who have given them shelter and been helpful, shall be near of kin (heirs) the one to the other." *Sura VIII—73.*

In obedience to this ordinance, every two persons, between whom brotherhood was established, enjoyed the rights of inheritance—the one to the other—till the revelation after the battle of Bedr of the following verse—

> "The Prophet is nearer of kin to the Faithful, than they are to their own souls; and his wives are their mothers; but those who are related by blood are nearer of kin (heir), the one to the other, according to the Book of God, than other believers and the refugees." *Sura XXXIII—6.* †

The Hypocrites.

Notwithstanding all this, feelings of antipathy were also traceable among a considerable number of the community. Ibn Obay—Abdalláh b. Obay Salol—a powerful and rich man, who exercised great influence over the Khazraj tribe, was envious of Mohammed, who had intervened at the time when Ibn Obay was dreaming of being made king of Medina. He and the men of his party treated the Prophet to all outward appearances with utmost respect, but in their inmost hearts they were unfavourably disposed. They could not, however, take open action against the Prophet for want of decided opinion and sufficient strength. These men were called 'Monáfiqien' or the Hypocrites.

† The heirship ordinance as in the former verse was repealed by the latter, but Ali being related to the Prophet by blood his right of heirship to the Prophet remained intact.

† During the second year of Hegirat, a call to prayers, as tutored to the Prophet by the angel Gabriel, was introduced; and Bilál, the negro, was appointed to call the Moslems to each of the daily prayers with his sweet melodious grand voice.

Call to Prayers.

At first no particular place or quarter of the world was observed by the Moslems to turn their faces to, when they prayed. At Medina the Prophet directed them to turn towards Jerusalem, which was observed as their Qibla till the middle of the month of Sha'bán in the 2nd year of his Hegirat. ‡ At about this time, while engaged in performing his noonday *i.e.* Tzohr prayers, he was commanded by Alláh to direct his followers to turn their faces towards the Ka'ba in Mecca. Since then Ka'ba is strictly observed as Qibla towards which the Moslems turn themselves for prayers and for prostrating themselves till their forehead touches the ground in token of their humility and submission to the All-powerful Lord, the Creator of all beings.

Ka'ba as Qibla.

> "We have seen thee turning thy face towards Heaven; but We shall assuredly have thee turn to a Qibla which thou shalt like. So turn thy face towards the sacred Mosque (of Mecca), and where-ever ye be, turn your faces in that direction; and verily, those who are given the Book do of certainty know that it is the truth from their Lord, and God is not regardless of what they do." "Even though thou shouldest bring every sign to those who have been given the Scriptures, yet they will not follow thy Qibla,—and thou shalt not follow their Qibla—nor will one of them follow the Qibla of the other. And surely, if thou follow their wishes, after the knowledge of what hath come to thee, verily, then wilt thou become of the unrighteous." *Sura II—139 & 140.*

---

† Ibn Hajar; Zárqáni.
‡ Ibn Hishám; Tabari; Ibn Sa'd; Zarqáni.

2 A. H.

Fasts of Ramadzan

The compulsory observance of the fasts in the month of Ramadzán was also ordained at about the same time. *See verses 179-181 of Sura II of the Quran.*

The first year and a half of Hegirat to Medina was spent by the Prophet in settlement, in restoring peace and order among the citizens, in establishing Law and Justice and in consolidating his strength; over and above his religious functions and the regulating of the observance by the Moslems of prayers, fasts and alms, and their devotion to the worship of the Supreme Lord, which was the chief aim of his life.

Marriage of Fatema.

† The betrothal of Fátema, the only daughter of the Prophet, with his cousin and faithful disciple, Ali, took place in the month of Ramadzán 2 A. H., but the nuptial ceremonies were performed two months later in Zhilhajja. This alliance—as revealed to the Prophet—was ‡ ordained by God, who, he said to Fátema, had informed him of His choice from the noblest on the earth of two blessed men, one being her father (himself) and the other her husband (Ali); and that He had decreed his (the Prophet's) lineal descendants to spring forth from the couple (Ali and Fátema) and not direct from himself.*

---

† Rawdzat-al-Ahbáb; Tárikh-al-Khamis.

‡ Tabari; Tibráni; Ahmad b. Hanbal; Ibn Asákir etc.

* اخرج الطبرانی فی معجمه الکبیر عن ابن مسعود قال قال رسول الله صلعم ان الله امرنی ان ازوج فاطمه من علی و عن جابر قال قال رسول الله صلعم جعل ذریته کل نبی فی صلبه و جعل ذریتي فی صلب علي بن ابیطالب

ترجمه طبراني نے معجم کبیر مین عبد الله بن مسعود سے جناب رسول خدا کي یهه حدیث شریف روایت کي هے که حق تعالے نے مجهے حکمدیا که فاطمه کا نکاح علی سے کرون - نیز جابر سے آنحضرت کا یهه قول مبارک روایت کیا هے که هرنبي کی ذریت اُسکے صلب مین قرار دیگئي اور میری ذریت علی بن ابیطالب کے صلب مین ودیعت کیگئي (تاریخ احمدي ص ۳٦)

The wedding ceremonies of the only daughter of Mohammed well demonstrate the ideal simplicity with which they were conducted. The wedding feast was of dates and olives; the nuptial coach was a sheep-skin; the ornaments, the general outfit and the articles of necessity for the bride consisted of only a pair of silver armlets, two shirts, one head tire, one leather pillow containing palm leaves, one grinding mill, one drinking cup, two large jars and one pitcher. This was all, concordant with the circumstances of the Prophet Mohammed and his son-in-law Ali, who had to sell his coat of mail to raise the dowry required of him.

The true grandeur of the marriage lay not in the ostentations, but in the blessings of Heaven for which the marriage is the most memorable in the annals of Islam. The couple—tied in matrimonial alliance by God—were destined to be the parents of an illustrious progeny termed the sons of the Prophet, who are distinguished from the rest of the Moslem world as Imáms or the Commanders of the Faithful, and the rightful successors of the Apostle of God. They are universally acknowledged by Moslems as the fountain head of piety and wisdom. Hasan and

---

فی الریاض المستطابه لیحیی العامري اختصه (رسول الله صلعم) بتزویج سیده نساء العالمین و اخبر ان ذلک یوحی من الله تعالے وان الله جعل ذریته نبیه في صلبه—

ترجمه— ریاض مستطابه مین ھے که جناب رسالت ماب نے سیده نساء العالمین کي تزویج حضرت علی کے ساتھه مخصوص فرماکر خبردي که یهه تزویج حسب حکم ایزدي ھے اور پرور دگار عالم نے اپنے نبي کی ذریت کو علی بن ابیطالب کے صلب مین ودیعت فرمایا- (تاریخ احمدي ص ۳۶)

در مدارج النبوة آمده که از وقایع سنه ثانیه نکاح فاطمه زهرا و علي مرتضي است رضی الله عنهما و روایت میکند انس رض که بودم من نزد رسولخدا صلی الله علیه و سلم پس در گرفت آن حضرت را حالتے که در میگرفت او را نزد وحی و ربوده شد از خود پستر کشاده شد آن حالت بحال خود آمد و فرمود یا انس آمد مرا جبریل علیه السلام از نزد پروردگار

Hosain, the sons of the couple, played in the lap of the Prophet, who showed them proudly from his pulpit and called them the Chiefs of the Youths of Paradise. The parents themselves were as exalted as their children. The Prophet used to say, "I am the city of knowledge and Ali is its gate." Ali, the gallant hero as he proved himself on all occasions of undaunted valour, had won for himself the title of 'Lion of God' from the Prophet. Fátema, who possessed the love and confidence of the Prophet, was ranked as one of the four noble ladies 'Perfect in Faith' with whom God had deigned to bless this earth, *viz* † Asia, the wife of Pharaoh; Mary, the mother of Jesus; Khadija, the wife of Mohammed; and Fátema, the wife of Ali.

عرش و گفت بدرستے خدایتعالے امر میکند ترا که تزویج کنی فاطمه را
با علی ـــ و در بعض رویت آمده که آمد رسولخدا صلی الله علیهٔ و سلم
روز نکاح فاطمه وعلي بعد از عشا بسوئے خانهٔ ایشان پس بر داشت ظرفے
از اب و انداخت آب دهن مبارک خودرا و خواند معوذتین را و دعا کرد و
امر کرد علی را که بیاشامد آن آب را و وضو کند بعد ازان امر کرد
فاطمه را که بیاشامد آن آب را و وضو کند ازان پستر کفت خداوندا
این هر دو ذات از من اند و من از ایشانم خداوندا چنانکه دور کردي
از من پلیدي را و پاک ساختی مرا پاک گردان این هر دو را و بیرن آر
از ایشان ذریت بسیار پاک و از حضرت فاطمه این هم ارشاد کرد که
برگزید خدایتعالے از زمین دو مرد را یکے ازان پدر تست و دیگرے زوج تو
(تاریخ احمدي ص ۳۷)

† Asia, the daughter of Mozáhem. The commentators relate, that because she believed in Moses, her husband cruelly tortured her, fastening her hands and feet to four stakes, and laying a large mill-stone on her breast, her face, at the same time, being exposed to the scorching beams of the sun: these pains, however, were alleviated by the angels shading her with their wings and the view of the mansion prepared for her in paradise, which was exposed to her on her pronouncing the prayer in the text: at length God received her soul; or, as some say, she was taken up alive into paradise, where she eats and drinks. *Sale from Jalal-uddin-al-Zamakhshari.*

CHAPTER IX.

Jehad. Battle of Bedr and other important events ending with the second year of Hegirat.

Anxieties of Mohammed.

After his Hegirat to Medina, the Prophet saw that the Qoreish of Mecca had sent out parties of scouts with temptations of a handsome reward to secure his person dead or alive, and one of them—a party of seventy men—reached Medina in pursuit as already observed. † He knew that the Qoreish were in secret communication with Abdalláh b. Obay, the hypocrite, instigating him to rise in revolt against him, to turn him out of Medina; and that they used threats to fall upon Medina in case he failed to meet their wishes. He was not therefore unmindful of their persistence in persecutions and of the enmity they bore towards him. He had received intelligence too that the Qoreish were busily forming alliance with the Bedouines inhabiting on their way to Medina; he was aware that they had already shown their colors by venturing recently to advance so far as to the pasture grounds of Medina under the leadership of Kurdz b. Jábir Fihri and carrying away the camels and cattle, and setting the neighbouring grounds to fire.

He, naturally, must have feared lest they should venture to surprise him at Medina, which was situated on their much frequented route to and from Syria, where they took their merchandise in caravans of considerable force. Even the fact that some Jews and Arabs, who did not like his growing authority in Medina, had migrated to Mecca and joined the Qoreish, accentuated the apprehended danger of being taken unawares.

"In the state of nature," says Gibbon, "every man has a right to defend, by force of arms, his person and his possessions, to repel or even to prevent, the violence of his

† Sunan Abu Dáud Báb-al-Tafsír.

enemies and to extend the hostilities to a reasonable measure of satisfaction and retaliation." In the case of the Prophet, it was not to defend himself alone. He had to protect his fellow citizens, who had suffered such great troubles and lost so much for the faith. It was to defend his Medinian followers, who, in giving him hospitality, laid themselves open to the attacks of the enemies. It was to guard their common faith to escape being annihilated; to save his religion from being choked; and last of all, to save himself from being treated in the same manner as his illustrious predecessor, Jesus Christ. To accomplish this aim, he keenly felt the necessity of having recourse to the most effective measures—the sword—† similar to the other prophets before him. But he could not take up arms in the absence of permission from the Supreme Authority, on which all his activities were based.

---

† See Book of the Old Testament: 'Numbers,' Chapter 31.

1 And the Lord spake unto Moses, saying,

2 Avenge the children of Israel of the Midianites: afterward shalt thou be gathered unto thy people.

3 And Moses spake unto the people, saying, Arm some of yourselves unto the war, and let them go against the Midianites, and avenge the Lord of Midian.

4 Of every tribe a thousand, throughout all the tribes of Israel, shall ye send to the war.

5 So there were delivered out of the thousands of Israel, a thousand of *every* tribe, twelve thousand armed for war.

6 And Moses sent them to the war, a thousand of *every* tribe, them and Phinehas the son of Eleazar the priest, to the war, with the holy instruments, and the trumpets to blow in his hand.

7 And they warred against the Midianites, as the Lord commanded Moses; and they slew all the males.

8 And they slew the king of Midian, beside the rest of them that were slain; namely, Evi, and Rekem, and Zur, and Hur, and Reba, five kings of Midian; Balaam also the son of Beor they slew with the sword.

9 And the children of Israel took all the women of Midian captives, and their little ones, and took the spoil of all their cattle, and all their flocks and all their goods.

More than a year and a half passed off at Medina in intense anxiety. At last came the permission, as appears from the following passage, amongst others, in the Qurán:

Permission to take up arms.

"Permission to fight is given to those who are fought against, because they have been wronged; and, verily, God has the power to help them. Who have been turned out of their homes without other reason than that they say God is their Lord." ***Sura XXII: 40, 41; and Sura II: 186, 187, 212 and 213.***

"Nothing appears more natural," says a learned lecturer, "if God in His mercy meant to humanize the barbarous inhabitants of Arabia, and raise them from the abyss of immorality and superstition into which they had sunk down, than that His choice should fall upon a man full of determination and of unswerving fidelity to the task

---

10 And they burnt all their cities wherein they dwelt, and all their goodly castles, with fire.

11 And they took all the spoil, and all the prey, both of men and of beasts.

12 And they brought the captives, and the prey and the spoil, unto Moses, and Eleazar the priest, and unto the congregation of the children of Israel, unto the camp at the plains of Moab, which are by the Jordan near Jericho.

13 And Moses and Eleazar the priest, and all the princes of the congregation, went forth to meet them without the camp.

14 And Moses was wroth with the officers of the host, with the captains over thousands, and captains over hundreds, which came from the battle.

15 And Moses said unto them, Have ye saved all the women alive?

16 Behold, these caused the children of Israel, through the counsel of Balaam, to commit trespass against the Lord in the matter of Beor, and there was a plague among the congregation of the Lord.

17 Now therefore kill every male among the little ones, and kill every woman that hath known man by lying with him.

See also Book of the New Testament. The Gospel according to 'St. Matthew,' Chap. 10. 34 Think not that I am come to send peace on earth: I came not to send peace, but a sword.

with which he was entrusted, a man endowed with a genius equal to every change of circumstances, capable of enduring hardship and of serving others without regard for his own interests, and ready to resist the oppressor even physically, if necessary, on behalf of his people." The holy Prophet Mohammed never used his sword but for defence. Professor J. W. Arnold, a Christian by faith, has most ably proved that Islam was propagated without the sword.

The Nakhla.

Having been permitted to take up arms againat his enemies, the Prophet arranged small parties from among his faithful adherents, and sent them as scouts to observe the activities of the Meccans and specially of the caravans issuing from or coming back to Mecca. Though the Prophet strictly enjoined each party to avoid unnecessary violence, yet it was highly improbable that no party should have an encounter with the Qoreish.

† A small group of eight or twelve men was sent to Nakhla, a place between Mecca and Táef, with instructions to get information about the caravans passing that side. The men had an encounter with four Meccans carrying raisins from Táef to Mecca. One of the Meccans—a nobleman of distinction named Amr b. Abdalláh—was slain in the fight and one escaped; two were taken prisoners to the Prophet. The day of the encounter was mistaken by the party as the last day of Jamádi II, but the Meccans alleged that it was the first day of the holy month of Rajab in which every sort of aggression was forbidden. The action was thus taken as an encroachment on the sanctity of the holy month.

The Prophet was angry with Abdallah b. Johash, the head of the party, for having disregarded the sacred privilege, and compensated the murder. In the meantime, the Prophet had a Revelation which purported to justify the action in the face of the banishment of the Faithful

† Tabari; Ibn Athír; Habíb-al-Siyar; Ibn Khaldun.

from the sacred edifice, the Ka'ba, which was brought about by the wickedness of the Meccans. Subsequently one of the two prisoners, who were still detained, embraced Islam and remained at Medina, while the other was released on payment of the ransom money.

The Battle of Bedr. 2 A. H.

In spite of the compensation paid for the murder of one Meccan at Nakhla, the Qoreish were furious and contemplated dire revenge. They pretended to be irritated still more by a rumour, which was totally unfounded, that the caravan returning from Syria, richly laden with precious goods, would be way-laid by Mohammed's followers, in retaliation of the loss of their property on account of their exile from Mecca; so they began to mobilize. The Prophet, on the other hand, received information of the activities of the Meccans. He did not think it advisable to wait in Medina for an attack by the enemy; because he did not like the idea of a new-comer, as he really was, to cause trouble to the inhabitants, who would inevitably have to suffer the hardships of a siege or war in such a case. Moreover, he presumed that the sympathizers with the Meccans were more numerous than his own adherents in Medina—a fact which, if correct, would prove dangerous to his cause. He had received information too that Abu Sofyán, the bitterst of his enemies, was on his way back to Mecca, with his thirty mounted guard escorting a caravan from Syria; and that he would have to pass by the route near Medina. Consequently the Prophet resolved to meet the enemy out of Medina, and he set out with three hundred and thirteen of his adherents, consisting of eighty-two Mohájirs and two hundred and thirty-one Ansárs, the auxiliaries of Medina (61 from the Aws and 170 from the Khazraj tribes.)

This small force was marshalled out of Medina with the youthful Ali holding the † Banner of the Prophet. In

† Tabari; Kámil, Ibn Athír; Ahmad Hanbal; Durr Manthur, etc.

the whole army only two men appeared on horse-back, the rest mounted seventy camels by turn on the journey. Othmán b. Affán could not join the army, his wife Roqyya being seriously ill.

When the army reached the fertile vale of Bedr, a favourite watering place and camping ground on the caravan route, three stations northward from Medina, the Prophet ordered halt, taking up a suitable position near a stream of fresh water, to await the arrival of the enemy *viz.* the Qoreish army from Mecca or Abu Sofyán from Syria. Here he was informed, by his scouts, of the caravan that was approaching on one side, and of the huge Qoreish army that was advancing on the other.

Considering thoughtfully to meet one or the other, the Prophet had a consultation ‡ with his chief Companions, who appeared reluctant to face the large force of the enemy, more than thrice their number, and insisted obstinately on pursuing the Caravan. But their courage was revived and stimulated by the hopeful words of the Prophet to receive Divine help in the contest. He decisively preferred the execution of Duties involved on him by God's command for Jehád on a larger number of Meccan infidels than confronting Abu Sofyán and his small horde of followers.

---

‡ In answer to the question of the Prophet as to what was to be done in the circumstances, Abubekr said: 'The Prophet knoweth better—I have received intelligence that the Qoreish are fast approaching. They are only two stages from us.' Omar added: 'O Prophet! The prestige of the Qoreish is involved in the affair, they have never bent their haughty necks to servitude and, since they had become infidels they never turned believers. They are sure to set themselves stubbornly against you. You should therefore have adequate equipment to meet them.' At these expressions the Prophet appeared exceedingly angry. Miqdád b. Amru, then, addressed the Prophet thus: 'We should not tell the same as the children of Israel did tell to Moses, *i.e.*, 'Go thou and thy Lord to fight, for we will sit here quietly,' but, by God who sent thee to guide us, we should tell: 'Go thou and thy Lord to fight and we shall fight thy foe on thy

Sura VIII :—

5 As thy Lord brought thee forth from thy
house with truth, and, verily, a party of the
believers were averse (to thy directions);
6 They disputed with thee concerning the truth,
after it was made plain, as if they were
driven to death and looked (it with their
eyes).
7 And when God promised you one of the two
parties, that it should be yours, and ye
desired that the (one) which had no arms
should be (delivered) unto you; but God
desired to prove the truth in His words,
and to cut off the uttermost part of the
unbelievers;
8 That He might prove the truth and disprove
falsehood, although the wicked were averse
(thereto).
9 When ye asked help from your Lord, and He
answered you: Verily, I will assist you with
a thousand Angels following one another.

It was prudent for the Prophet to have chosen this course of action, as Abu Sofyán was clever enough to get

---

right and on thy left, and on thy front and in thy rear, till the Lord makes thee victorious.' Hearing this speech of Miqdád, the Prophet smiled and bestowed his blessings upon him; and again turned to consult with them, now applying himself chiefly to the Ansárs, who formed the major portion of his force, and who, he apprehended, might think themselves not pledged at Aqaba to assist him against any other than such as should attack him in Medina. But Sa'd b. Mo'ázh stood up in behalf of the Ansárs, told him that they had received him as the Apostle of God and have sworn him fealty and obedience, consequently they were all to a man ready to follow him, wherever he pleased, though it were into the sea. Upon this the Prophet made known to all his men his resolve to face the Meccan forces, assuring them of victory. 'The multitude shall surely be routed, and (they) shall turn (their) back. *Sur. LIV-45.*' Tabari; Sirat Mohammedia; Tafsir Durr-e-Manthur.

scent of the impending danger beforehand. He kept himself well informed of Mohammed's movements, and had summoned speedy help from Mecca. Leaving, however, the usual route, he guided his caravan through a less frequented sea-coast pathway and passed safely off the danger.

The Meccans, who were already mobilizing, as observed, receiving Abu Sofyán's message, hastened to his relief with eight hundred and fifty foot and one hundred horse in command of Abu Jahl. Though Abu Sofyán informed them of his safe passage by a circuitous route west of Bedr, and advised them to return home, yet Abu Jahl and his army, intent upon avenging the Nakhla murder, continued their march till they reached Bedr and faced the hostile gathering.

Next day, Friday, the seventeenth of Ramadzán 2 A. H. or 13 of January 624 A. D., they moved slowly over the ground, which the rain in the last night had made heavy with mud and difficult to pass over. The same cause had rendered the sand hills in front of the Moslems lighter and more firm to walk upon. The Meccan army laboured under another disadvantage in having the rising sun before them, while the Moslem army faced toward the west. The main body, however, of the Qoreish army, blowing their trumpets, approached the opponents and both the forces were in battle arrayed. † The Prophet seated himself under a canopy, thatched with palm branches, which was erected and closely guarded by Sa'd b. Mo'ázh. Abubekr did not join the ranks of the combatants but seated himself by the Prophet. Three Qoreish warriors, Otba the father-in-law of Abu Sofyán, Walid, his son, and Sheiba, the brother of Otba, advancing in front, challenged the bravest of the Moslems to single combat. They were all men of high rank and position among their tribe. Three Ansars of Medina stepped forward in response to the challenge; but they refused to accept them as their equals, and called the Meccan rene-

† Zakir Hosain's *Tarikh-al-Islam.*

gades (as they called them) to come forward if they dared. Upon this Ali and Obeida, cousins of the Prophet, and Hamza his uncle responded to the challenge, and the fight began. After a fierce and prolonged contest, Ali and Hamza succeeded in overpowering their antagonists, Walid and Sheiba respectively, whom they slew. They then went to the aid of Obeida, who was severely wounded and nearly overcome by Otba. They slew Otba and took away Obeida, who died of his wounds four days after. Now the battle was raging furiously and the Qoreish were pushing on, the Moslems being pressed hard.

The Prophet, who was eyeing the field anxiously, prayed to God for succour; and, coming out of the thatched canopy, cast a handful of gravel into the air towards the enemy saying: "Confusion seize their faces;" and called out to his men, "Courage my children, ! Close your ranks, discharge your arrows and the day is yours." Both the armies heard his thundering voice. † They fancied that they beheld angelic warriors. The line of the Qoreish wavered and a number of their bravest and noblest fell; they took to flight ignominiously, and in their haste to escape they threw away their armour and abandoned their transport animals with all their camp and equipage.

‡ Seventy of the bravest Qoriesh were slain, and fortyfive taken prisoners. Their commander, Abu Jahl—the Pharaoh of his people—had fallen in the battle and his head was taken to the Prophet. His original name was Amr alias Abul Hakam *i. e.* 'Father of Wisdom,' son of Hishám; it was changed by the Moslems in contempt to 'Abu Jahl' *i. e.* 'Father of Folly,' and by this name he was ever known afterwards. On the Moslem side fourteen men—six Mohájirs and eight Ansárs—were killed. [In *Sura VIII* : *9—13* of the Qurán there is a mention of the Divine Succour accorded to the Prophet in this battle.]

† Abul Fida.
‡ Rawdzat-al-Ahbáb.

The day was now closing, so the Moslems cast the enemy's dead into a deep pit called

Qalib well at Bedr.

Qalib. The Prophet looked on as the bodies were brought up and cast in. Abubekr stood by, and examining their faces called aloud their names. "Otba! Sheiba! Walid! Omyya! Abu Jahl! etc." exclaimed the Prophet, as one by one the corpses were cast into the deep and dark pit, † "Alas! Have you now found true what your lords promised you? What my Lord promised me, that, verily, have I found to be true. Woe unto ye! Ye rejected me, your Prophet! Ye cast me forth and others gave me refuge; ye fought against me and others came to my help!" ‡ "O Prophet!" said Omar, who was also standing by, "Dost thou speak unto the dead?" "Yea, verily," replied the Prophet, "for they realize what I spake unto them, better than thee."

Though it was the first engagement of the youthful Ali, he showed excellent results so that he was praised by all.

Ali's prowess.

He killed no less than sixteen—though some historians give him credit for thirty-six ¶—of the bravest and the most prominent of the Qoreish army.

While returning to Medina, at Safrá, a station between Bedr and Medina, the Prophet had two of the most obnoxious prisoners, Oqba b. Abi Mo'eit and Al Nadzr b. Al Hárith beheaded.

The Prisoners of Bedr.

The rest of the prisoners were taken to Medina, where they were released on payment of the ransom money. Among the captives were * Abbás, an uncle of the Prophet, Nawfal b. Hárith, and Aqil b. Abu

---

† Ibn Hishám.

‡ Madárij-al-Nabowat; Rawdzat-al-Ahbáb quoted by Zakir Husain in his *History of Islam*.

¶ Habib-al-Siyar; Matálib-al-Saul; Kifáyat-al-Tálib.

* Ali b. Abi Tálib, the nephew of Abbás, bitterly reproached his uncle with stinging words, upon which Abbás retorted: "You rip up our ill actions, but give no credit of our good deeds; we free the captives, we adorn the Ka'ba, we regularly visit the Holy

Tálib, the cousins of the Prophet, and Abul As, the husband of Zainab a daughter of Khadija. Abbás was a man of tall stature and stout built. He was captured by Abul Yasar, a man comparatively thin and lean and of short stature. When asked how such a man could overpower him, Abbás said that his captor looked to him a giant at the time.

> "Already ye have had a wonder in the two armies, which fought, one for God's true path and the other infidels; they saw (the faithful) twice their like in (their) eyesight; for God strengthens with His help whom He pleaseth. Surely herein is an example unto those who have sight." *Sura III-11.*

Abbás was asked to pay the ransom money for himself and for his nephews *viz.* Nawfal and Aqil. He replied that if he paid up the demand he would be reduced to beg alms of the Qoreish as long as he lived. But to his great astonishment, the Prophet revealed to him the secret of the gold, which he had confided to his wife at midnight at the time of his departure with the Meccan army, and then recited *Verse 71 of Sura VIII of the Quran*: "O Prophet! Say unto the captives, who are in your hands: If God knows of any good in your hearts, He will give you better than what hath been taken from you; and He will pardon you; for God is Forgiving and Merciful." † Now Abbás, confirmed in his belief that Mohammed was the true Apostle of God, declared that none could know of the transaction except God, and readily embraced Islam along with his nephews. Some years later, when Abbás found himself possessed of large fortunes he

---

Edifice and we entertain the pilgrims with providing drink to them." This occasioned the revelation of the following passage: "Do ye reckon the giving of drink to the pilgrims and the visiting of the sacred Mosque like him who believeth in God and the Last Day and fighteth for the way of the Lord; they are not equal in the estimation of God: God guides not the wrong doers." *Sura IX-19. Al Beidzawi.*

† Habib-al-Siyar.

reflected on this recitation of the Prophet and admitted that the prophecy was fulfilled.

To effect the release of Abul As, his wife Zainab sent some of her ornaments including a necklace given her in dowry by her mother Khadija. The Prophet identified the necklace, and sadly remembering Khadija, handed it back to Abul As to be given back to Zainab, and released him on condition to send Zainab to him. Zaid b. Háritha accompanied Abul As on his return to Mecca and brought Zainab to Medina. She did not go back to her husband till he embraced Islam, sometime before the conquest of Mecca, when he was again brought before the Prophet as a captive.

Distrbution of war booty.

At this same place (Safrá) the booty, which consisted of weapons and camels taken in the battle, was distributed in equal shares to each of his followers by the Prophet, and he reached back in Medina after fifteen or nineteen days' absence. In the meantime, Roqyya, the wife of Othmán, had died, on account of whose illness Othmán could not join the battle.

War Sequels.

The battle of Bedr is the most important in the history of Islam, and therefore the most famous among the Moslems. This victroy opened to the Prophet the gates of progress in spreading his Faith, as most of the bitterest and influential opponents of his religion had fallen in this war. This first victory of the Prophet helped immensely to strengthen his position. In Medina, the hypocrites and the non-Moslems, who were not favourably disposed toward him, were greatly discouraged to contemplate any overt action against the Prophet. Meccan veterans, who so long hatefully scorned Mohammed and his followers, were quite humiliated by the defeat inflicted on them by a comparatively unexperienced and numerically smaller force than theirs.

The defeat of the Qoreish at Bedr was actually a death below to Abu Lahab—the only Háshimite, who was a bitter opponent of the Prophet—and he died of grief at the loss of his friends and relations in the persons of Walid, Sheiba and Otba, after a short illness of a week.

Sawiq or Meal War.

† The next man, who felt the defeat very seriously, was Abu Sofyán. His heart burnt with rage, for the man whom he scorned and detested had inflicted such a severe blow. He swore he would neither anoint himself nor go near his wife till he was avenged upon Mohammed, though later he realized that he was rash in his oath of abstinence. To keep his vow, however, he set out towards Medina in Zhilhajja 2 A. H. with two hundred horse. Reaching within three miles of Medina to its north east at Oreidz, he fell in with one Ansár and his servant whom he killed, set fire to some huts and cut down some palm trees. The Prophet receiving information of it went out against them, but they fled in haste throwing away their sacks of meal to accelerate their flight. These sacks were picked up by the Moslems, and from this circumstance this was called the Meal-war. Thus Abu Sofyán fulfilled his vow, but he meditated another expedition on a larger scale.

CHAPTER X.

The Jews of Medina. The battle of Ohod, and other important events ending with the third year of Hegirat.

The Jews.

The Jews in Medina, living in independent communities or scattered under the protection of the Arabs, were powerful. They were industrious people and conducted trade, by virtue of which they had acquired wealth. Though they formed only a small part of the population yet they exercised great influence over the Arabs. Only a few of them, including one of their monks 'Abdalláh b. Salám, had embraced

† Ibn Hishám.

Islam. The majority did not believe in Mohammed, the prophet promised in their Scriptures, because they always expected the Promised One to come from the Israélites, and who, they thought, would rise from Syria, like other previous prophets with Hebrew as his language.

Marking their arrogant attitude and wishing to conciliate them, Mohammed issued a Firmán proclaiming his protection to the Jews, and granting them rights to be included in the nationality with the Moslems, and allowing them freedom in the exercise of their religious rites. The Jews gladly accepted the privileges offered in the Firmán and entered into a treaty with the Prophet to keep peace. For some time they appeared to be content, but soon with the growth of the Prophet's power they became jealous of him, and attempted to discredit him before his followers. Disputes arose between them and the Moslems, resulting in mutual dislike and hatred. The Jews treated the Moslems and even the Prophet himself with sneer, whenever they could do so.

The Banu Qainoqa' Jews 2 A. H.

About a month after the Prophet's return from Bedr, a dispute broke out between the Moslems and the Banu Qainoqá' Jews, who lived in a strongly built suburb of Medina. They had indecently assaulted a Moslem girl and one man on each side of the disputants was killed in the affray which ensued. The Prophet summoned them to his presence, but the Jews behaved contemptuously and haughtily, disregarding the Treaty which they had entered into. The Prophet was thus compelled to take serious steps against the revolting tribe. He laid siege to their dwellings and after about a fortnight they had to surrender. Being guilty of treasonable behaviour against the newly established authority, acknowledged by the bulk of the people, they deserved exemplary punishment, but with the arbitration of Abdalláh b. Obay they were turned to exile towards Syria.

Other Jewish tribes, who lived in Medina, began to be restive. † Ka'b b. Ashraf, a most inveterate enemy of the Prophet and his religion, a wealthy and influential poet and leader of the Nadzirite tribe went to Mecca and intrigued with the Qoreish against the Prophet; and by circulating elegies, lamenting the hard fate of the Meccans, who had fallen in Bedr, and reflecting very severely on the Prophet, stirred ill feelings towards him. Coming back to Medina, he boldly recited epigrams against the Prophet and his followers and addressed amatory sonnets to their women in public. The undeserving sarcasms stinged the Moslems, who at length lost all patience and assassinated him. (14th Safar, 3 A. H.)

The fate of Ka'b b. Ashraf

In such unpleasant circumstances, there was lef tno room for the Prophet to doubt that the Treaty was null and void, owing to the abuse of the privileges of the Firmán by the Jews. Consequently they were outlawed, with the result that tribe after tribe left Medina to seek refuge with outlying Jewish habitations. The more powerful and wealthy Jews, however, did not leave Medina, resolving to defy the Prophet's authority.

The Jews outlawed.

Hinda, the wife of Abu Sofyán, cried night and day for vengeance on Ali and Hamza, at whose hands her father Otba, her uncle Sheiba and her brother Walid had fallen in the battle of Bedr. Abu Sofyán contemplated revenge and began to persuade his people to devote to the preparation of war the whole of their profit of the year; and communicated with coast tribes to co-operate with him, as his allies, in the campaign against Mohammed.

The Meccans' preliminary arrangements for Ohod campaign.

‡ The Meccans, to provide funds for the next great action against the Prophet as well as to make up their

† Tárikh-al-Khamis; Ibn Hishám.

‡ Tárikh-al-Khamis.

pecuniary losses at Bedr, were busily carrying on their trade. Instead of the now unsafe usual caravan route, they explored a new road to Syria through the desert and along the Euphrates. But they could not escape the notice of the vigilant Moslems, who at last over-took them at Qaráda on the outskirts of Nejd, some eight stages from Medina, under the leadership of Zaid b. Háritha in the month of Jamádi II, 3 A. H. The Caravan escort took to flight and Zaid had a rich booty to take to Medina.

The Ohod campaign. 3 A. H.

Abu Sofyán, irritated by the sense of private and public loss of wealth, now hurried his preparations for the campaign against Mohammed. His allies of the coast tribes together with Banu Kinána and Banu Tiháma having assembled, his whole army was three thousand strong, seven hundred of whom were armed with coats of mail and two hundred were mounted on horse back, besides one thousand camels that attended the march. He had been joined at this time by an influential man from Medina with a considerable number of followers. Thus Abu Sofyán set out for Medina at the head of this strong force, the right wing of which was commanded by Khálid b. Walid and the left by Ikrima b. Abu Jahl. His wife, the revengeful Hinda, with fifteen matrons of Mecca, brought up the rear, incessantly all of them sounding their timbrels to animate the troops and to magnify the greatness of Hobal, the most popular deity of Ka'ba. On their way to Medina, when the army reached Abwá, Hinda wanted to dig out of grave the remains of Amena, the Prophet's mother, who lay buried their for over fifty years; but with some difficulty she was kept from this wickedness. The army, at last reached its destination unchecked, and encamped at Zhul Holeifa, a village about five miles North-East of Medina, in the green corn fields by Mount Ohod, on Wednesday the 4th of Shawwál 3 A.H.

The Prophet's march.

† The Prophet was at Qobá when he received information of the Qoreish expedition from his uncle Abbás, who lived at Mecca. He hurried back to Medina and consulted his adherents as to whether he should wait the enemy's attack on the town and defend himself within the city, or meet the enemy out of the town. His own inclination was to the former proposal and many of his adherents held the same opinion; but the majority of his adherents urged him on to meet the enemy out of the town, and the resolution was adopted; though when the Prophet was ready to march out, they changed their mind and spoke to the Prophet, but he marched out with about one thousand men, headed by Ali as the Standard bearer, ‡ to meet the enemy. Abdalláh b. Obay Salol, at the head of some Khazrajites and some of his Jew allies numbering in all about three hundred men, had joined the Prophet's force. But the Prophet refused to receive help from the Jews unless they embraced Islam. Thus Abdalláh with his 300 followers turned back; and the Prophet, with his seven hundred men reaching Mount Ohod, secured a position on the declivity of the hill, placing the Qoreish between his army and Medina, so that Mount Ohod stood on the back of his army facing Medina. The Prophet posted fifty of his archers to guard the narrow defile of the mountain in the rear of his left flank and ordered the bowmen to quit their post on no account unless summoned by him.

The Battle of Ohod. 3 A. H.

|| The Prophet reached Ohod in the morning of Saturday, the 7th of Shawwál, 3 A. H. (January or February 625 A. D.) and found the Meccan forces face to face, ready to advance for the battle. The Qoreish advanced in the form of a crescent and the right wing of

† Rawdzat-al-Ahbáb.
‡ Habib-al-Siyar.
|| Ibn Athir; Ibn Hishám; Tabari.

3 A. H.

their cavalry was led by Khálid b. Walid, a notorious warrior. Abu Amir, a Meccan champion, stepping forward with his fifty archers, showered the arrows first towards the Moslems, who returned the shot as thickly and promptly. Thus the fight began. The Meccan archers turned back and their standard bearer, Talha b. Abi Talha, coming forth, challenged the Moslems. Ali stepped forward and struck off one of his legs. He fell down and another champion hoisted the standard. He was killed by Hamza. A third now took the Flag and he was slain by Ali. Thus nine or ten standard bearers fell one after the other only by Ali's sword ‡. It is a noteworthy incident that Talha the first standard bearer of the Meccans lost one of his legs by a stroke of Ali's sword, fell down and his lower garment being loosened he became naked. Ali, instead of finishing him, turned his face from him and hit him no more. The Prophet marked the event and exclaimed, "Alláh o Akbar" Great is the Lord, and when asked Ali why he had spared the man, he said the man was nude and entreated him for the sake of Allah to spare his life. Ali and Hamza, the champions of Bedr, unsparingly dealing out death, worked a havoc among the enemy. Hamza, however, while duelling with Sabá b. Abd-al-Uzza a Meccan champion, was treacherously speared from behind by Wahshi, an Etheopian slave, who lurked behind a rock with that intent, having been promised by Hinda, the wife of Abu Sofyán, his freedom, if he could revenge the death of her father or brother slain by Ali and Hamza in the battle of Bedr. Now Ali, taking Abu Dajána, Mos'ab b. Omeir and Sahel b. Honeif, Mohammedan champions with him, charged the enemy. The weight of the charge broke the centre of the enemy, the whole host wavered and Ali with his Moslem champions, gained the enemy's camp. They made the Meccan army turn and fly, leaving their camp to the Moslems, who at once proceeded to appropriate it.

‡ Tabari; Ibn Athir.

† But their eagerness for spoil turned the tide of victory, which was already gained by Ali and his Moslem champions. The archers posted at the defile deserted their picket to join in the plunder, leaving the subaltern, Abdalláh b. Jobeir, in spite of his protests, with only about ten men. Khálid, the Meccan commander of the cavalry, who behind the defile was waiting a suitable chance to effect his charge, succeeded in dexterously emerging through and cutting down the small guard of the ten men, and charged furiously the rear of the Moslems. Mos'ab b. Omeir, a champion of Mohammed, who bore a great resemblance to him, fell dead. Ibn Soráqa proclaimed aloud that Mohammed was slain. The flying Meccans turned back. Their banner, which was lying low on the ground, was picked up by a Meccan matron named Omrá bint Alqamá and then lifted high up by a slave named Sowáb and the idolators clustered round it. * Most of the Moslems including the Prophet's chief Companions Abubekr, Omar, Othmán and Abu Obeida took to flight. ‡

---

* فی المستدرک للحاکم و قرة العینین لشاه ولی الله الدهلوي عن عایشة قالت قال ابو بکر الصدیق لما جال الناس عن رسول الله صلعم یوم احد کنت اول من فاء الیه فبصرت به من بعد فاذا انا برجل اعتنقنی من خلفی یرید رسول الله صلعم فاذا هو ابو عبیدة بن الجراح—

ترجمه —مستدرک حاکم اور قرة العینین شاه ولي الله صاحب دهلوي مین حضرت عایشه سے مروي هے که فرمایا حضرت ابو بکر نے - جب بروز جنگ احد لوگ رسول مقبول کو چهوڑ کر متفرق هو گئے تو اونمین سے اولاً مین رسول خدا کي خدمت مین واپس آیا اور میري نگاه دور سے آنحضرت پر پڑي-پهر ایک شخص نے پیچهے سے آکر مجهے دبایا جو پیغمبر صاحب کے حضور مین حاضر هونا چاهتا تها-مینے مڑ کر دیکها تو وه ابو عبیده بن الجراح تها—(تاریخ احمدي ص ۴۲)

† Ibn Athir; Tárikh-al-Khamis.

‡ Tabari; Tárikh-al-Khamis; Tafsir Kabir; Minháj-al-Nabowat.

This sudden change of fortune checked the Moslems, who found themselves surrounded by the Meccans. It was all confusion so that it was not easy to distinguish the friend from the foe. Discipline could not be restored.

* Some were saying that Mohammed would not have been killed † had he been a true Prophet; ‡ others were talking of seeking pardon of Abu Sofyán and taking refuge

---

فی الدر المنثور للسیوطی والتفسیر الکبیرلابن جریر قال عمر رضي الله عنه لما کان یوم احد هزمناهم ففررت حتی صعدت الجبل فلقد رأیتني انزو کانني اروی —

ترجمه — تفسیر در منثور سیوطی و تفسیر ابن جریر مین مروي هے که حضرت عمر نے فرمایا که جب جنگ احد مین کافرون نے مسلمانونکو شکست دي تو مین بهاگ کر پهاڑ پر چڑه گیا اور اوسوقت میری حالت یهه تهی که پهاڑی بکري کیطرح کودتا پهرتا تها —

في التفسیر الکبیر للفخر رازي و من المنهزمین عمر رضي الله عنه الا انه لم یکن فی اوایل المنهزمین و لم یبعد بل ثبت علي الجبل ومنهم ایضاً عثمان رضی الله عنه انهزم مع رجلین یقال لهما سعد و عقبه انهزموا بعیدا ثم رجعوا بعد ثلاثه ایام —

ترجمه — تفسیر کبیر مین فخر رازی فرماتےهین که گریز کرنے والون مین حضرت عمر بهي تهے مگر وه ابتدا مین نهین بهاگے اور دور نهین گئے بلکه بهاگ کر پهاڑ پر رکے رهے نیز گریز کرنیوالونمین عثمان بهی تهے جو سعد (ابن ابی وقاص) اور عقبه کے ساتهه دور تک بهاگ گئے اور تین دن کے بعد واپس تشریف لاے — (تاریخ احمدي ص ۴۲)

* طبري جلد ۳ ص ۱۹ و ۲۰ و تاریخ الخمیس جلد ۱ ص ۴۸۸ و ۴۸۹ نیز تاریخ کامل مین هے که جب انحضرت صلعم کے قتل هونیکي خبر مشهور هوئی تو بعض مسلمانون نے کها کاش همارا کوئی قاصد عبدالله بن ابي کے پاس جاتا که همین ابو سفیان سے پناه دلوا دیتا اور بعض هاتهه پر هاتهه رکهکر هو بیٹهے اور بعض منافقون نے کها که اگر محمد نبی هوتا

† Tabari; Ibn Hishám.

‡ Tárikh-al-Khamis.

with him. (*Sur. III–138* refers to these people thus: "And Mohammed is no more than an Apostle; already there have passed before him Apostles: what then! if he dies or is killed, will ye turn back on your heels? But he who turneth back on his heels will not harm God at all; surely God will reward the grateful." *Sur. III–142* refers to them thus: "O ye who believe, if ye follow those who disbelieve, they will turn ye back upon your heels, and ye shall be turned back losers.")

† Some of the Prophet's adherents, however, resolved not to survive him and they fought and perished in the struggle. Anas b. Nadzar, uncle to Anas b. Málik, having seen Omar b. Khattáb and Talha b. Obeidalláh sitting leisurely along with some others, asked them what they were doing. They said they had nothing to do since Mohammed was slain. Hearing these words Anas addressed them aloud thus: "My friends! Though Mohammed be slain, certainly Mohammed's Lord liveth and dieth not: therefore value not your lives since the prophet is dead, but fight for the cause for which he fought; then he cried out, O God! I am excused before Thee, and acquitted in Thy sight of what they say; and drawing his sword fought valiantly till he was killed." *Sale p. 52, from Al-Beidzawi.* The Angel Gabriel appeared to the Prophet

---

تو قتل نه هوتا پهر چلو اپنے بهائیونکی طرف اور پهر جاؤ اپنے پهلے دین پر
انس بن مالک کے چچا انس بن نضر ایک مقام سے گذرے که وهان عمر
بن خطاب اور طلحه بن عبید الله بعض دیگر مهاجرین و انصار کیساتهه
هاتهه پر هاتهه رکهے بیتهے تهے - پس کها که تم لوگ کیون بغلونمین هاتهه
دے بیتهے هو - بولے کیا کرین رسول الله تو شهید هوگئے - کها پهر تم جی کر
کیا کرو گے انکے بعد اوتهو جسطرح وه دین کی حمایت مین شهید هوئے
هین تم بهی مرجاؤ - اگر محمد مارے گئے تو محمد کا خدا تو زنده هے وه
تو نهین مرتا پهر کها بار الها جو کچه یهه مسلمان و منافق کهتے هین
انکی نسبت مین تجهسے عذر کرتا اور برأت ڈهونڈهتا هون یهه

† Tabari-vol-iii; Ibn Athir; Tárikh-al.Khamis.

3 A. H.

with the verse which meant to inform him that among his followers there were persons who looked only after this life and also those who took care for the next life. (Sur-iii-146 "Of you were those who chose this present world and of you were those who adopted the world to come hereafter.")

Ali praised by Angels.

* Ali, who was still defending bravely, ran to the Prophet who was all alone, and stood by his side. † The Prophet queried him why he did not fly away with others, to which he replied that he belonged to him and had no business with the others and that he being a

---

کہکر دشمن پر حملہ کیا یہانتک کہ شہید ہوگئے - بروایت ابن ہشام انکے ستر زخم لگے تھے اکہترویں زخم مین شہید ہوے - خمیس مین ۸۰ سے اوپر تلوار نیزہ اور تیر کے زخم لکھے ہین —

قال ابن الاثیر الجزري في الکامل و انتهت الهزیمة بجماعته من المسلمین فیهم عثمان بن عفان وغیره الي الاعوص فاقاموا به ثلاثا ثم اتوا النبي صلعم فقال لهم حین راهم لقد ذهبتم فیها عریضه —

ترجمه — ابن اثیر جزري نے تاریخ کامل مین ذکر کیا ہے کہ ہزیمت یافتہ اور مفرور مسلمانون نے جنمین حضرت عثمان بہی تھے موضع اعوص پہونچکر دم لیا اور وہانسے تین دن کے بعد رسول مقبول کی خدمت مین واپس آے جنکو دیکھتے ہی آنحضرت نے فرمایا کہ تم لوگون نے بہاگنے مین خوب لمبي تانی (تاریخ احمدي ص ۱۴۳)

---

* شیخ عبدالحق محدث دهلوی در مدارج النبوت نقل فرموده که در روز اُحد از گروه مخالف چنان پیکار شدید واقع شد که مسلمانان رو به هزیمت آوردند و حضرت رسول صلعم را تنها گذاشتند حضرت در غضب آمد و عرق از پیشانی همایونش متقاطر گشت دران حالت نظر کرد علی بن ابیطالب را که بر پهلوے مبارکش ایستاده است فرمود که تو چرا به برادران خود ملحق نه گشتی یعنے فرار نه کردی علی گفت —

لا کفر بعد الایمان ان لی بک اسوة

† Tabari; Ibn Athir; Madárij-al-Nabowat, Habib-al-Siyar; Rawdzat-al-Ahbáb.

Believer would not like to turn a Disbeliever or an infidel. Presently, one after another, two parties of the Qoreish bent to attack the Prophet. He asked Ali to defend him, and the gallant hero repulsed them with such intrepidity that he was praised ‡ by Angels, whose voice was heard saying: "*Zhulfiqar is the only effective sword and Ali the unique champion.*"

Ali helped by Gabriel.

† Ali received sixteen wounds, four of which were so serious that he was falling down from his horse, but on each of these occasions a beautiful youth took hold of him, lifted him up to his saddle and soothed him with these encouraging words: "Go on fighting, O hero! God and His prophet appreciate thy services." This was none other than Gabriel the Evangel, who praised Ali to the Prophet for his enthusiasm and ardent devotion to him at the time

---

یعنے آیا کافر شوم بعد از ایمان به تحقیق که مرا به تو اقتدا ست بایاران مغرور چه سروکار باشد -درین اثنا جمعے از کفار متوجه آنحضرت صلعم شدند آنحضرت فرمود اے علی مرا ازین جمع نگاه دار و حق خدمت بجا آر که وقت نصرت است پس علی متوجه آن قوم شد و چنان قلع و قمع نمود که جمعےکثیر به دوزخ رفتند و باقي ماندگان متفرق گشتند- میگویند که دران روز شانزده زخمها بر تن مبارک جناب امیر رسیدند از آنجمله چهار زخم بسیار کاري بردند که بوقت رسیدن هر زخم جناب امیر از فرش زین به زمین آمدند و هر چهار بار جبرئیل علیه السلام وے را برداشت و سوار میکرد ومیگفت که اے علي جنگ‌کن‌که خدا و رسولخدا از تو خوشنود هستند و چون این حال جانفشانی علي مرتضي جبرئیل امین بحضور ختم المرسلین رسانید آنحضرت فرمود که علی چرا جانفشانی نه نماید که وے از من است و من از وے جبرئیل گفت و من از شما و علی هر دو هستم و منقول است که در همین جنگ رضوان به منقبت علي مرتضي میخواند که

لا سیف الا ذوالفقار و لا فتی الا علی الکرار

---

‡ Habib-al-Siyar ; Rawdzat-al-Ahbáb.
† Madárij-al-Nabowat; Ma'árij-al-Nabowat.

3 A. H.

when all others had deserted him. The Prophet told Gabriel: "No wonder! Ali comes of me and I myself come of him." *i. e.* both of us are part and parcel of one and the same Celestial Light; upon which Gabriel added that he also comes of both of them, *i. e.* he also was created from the same Light as Mohammed and Ali.

The Prophet wounded.

In the melee above refered to, Obba b. Khalf, a Meccan champion, rushed towards the Prophet aiming at him with his spear; but he was himself killed with his own spear, which the Prophet snatched out of his hands and dealt him a blow, striking him dead. Another tradition ‡ says that he had received a wound from the Prophet's own hand but died of the same wound on his return to Mecca. Soon after this, the Prophet was wounded by a stone from a sling aimed at him by Otba* brother of Sa'd b. Abi Waqqás, which struck the Prophet on the mouth, cutting his lips and shattering two of his front teeth. †† He was wounded on the face also by an arrow, the iron head of which could not be extracted by himself, and he lay bleeding for some time on the ground. † Blessed the timely aid and friendly hand of Ali, who, repulsing the enemy, came back and finding the Prophet in this condition conveyed him to a place of safety, ex-

---

* قال ابن الوردی فقتل من المسلمین سبعون و من المشرکین ثمان و عشرون و اصابت حجارة المشرکین رسول الله صلعم حتي وقع و اصیبت و شبح و جهه و کلمت شفته والذی اصابه عتبه بن ابی وقاص اخو سعد

ترجمه— ابن‌الوردي اپني‌تاریخ مین لکهتےهین که جنگ اُحد مین ستر اهلِ اسلام اور اٹهائیس مشرک قتل هوے اور عتبه بن ابي وقاص برادر سعد بن ابی وقاص نے پیغمبر صاحب کو ایسا پتهر مارا که اُنحضرت کا چهره مبارک زخمی هوگیا اور هونٹه پهٹ گئے، — (تاریخ احمدي ص ۱۴۳)

‡ Al Bedzáwi.

†† Ibn Athir; Tárik-al-Khamis.

† Tárikh Islam by Zakir Hosain (*Vol. ii. page 100.*)

tracted the arrow-head, staunched his blood and tended him, aided by his wife Fátema, the daughter of the Prophet. No doubt, Ali proved himself now, as before and as hereafter, the defender or Right-hand of the Prophet on all occasions of danger, in confirmity with God's Decree which the Prophet had seen inscribed on Heavens in the night of his Me'ráj. (*Vide page 66*) The reader may also bring to his memory Ali's running the risk of his own life in defending the Prophet, on the occasion of his escape from Mecca, by laying himself upon the couch in place of the Prophet, covering himself with the Prophet's well known green mantle, and thus keeping the Meccans for some hours to neglect the search in pursuit of the Prophet, who succeeded during the interval to hide himself in a cave on Mt. Thowr. (*Vide page 80.*)

The end of the battle.

The Moslems, finding out that the Prophet was only wounded and not killed, began to rally round him. The Meccans, having no courage to route them, contented themselves with the honour of snatching back the victory from Mohammed; and left the field after mangling and mutilating the dead bodies of the Moslems. Halting at Rowhá, 8 miles homeward from Ohod, Abu Sofyán felt uneasy for the utter fruitlessness of his campaign and began to meditate a raid upon Medina. The Prophet, on the other hand, suspecting some treachery at the enemy's hasty retreat, resolved on immediate action and therefore pursued them as far as Hamra-al-Asad, the next morning, where he was informed that the Meccans receiving intelligence of his advance had already taken their road home.

The Meccans lost twenty eight men in the battle; of these, twelve had fallen under the sword of Ali. Seventy martyrs fell from among the Moslems. The bravest of the Moslems, who fell dead in the battle, were Hamza b. Abd-al-Mottalib, Mos'ab b. Omeir, Sa'd b. Al-Rabi', Ammára b. Ziyád and Hantzala a son of Abu Amir, the Meccan champion, who was the first to come forward from the ranks of the Meccans with fifty archers to charge the

Moslems. Among the slain, the body of the Prophet's uncle Hamza b. Abd-al-Mottalib was found mutilated. The fiend Hinda, wife of Abu Sofyán, had his liver taken out, sucked it and quenched her thirst for the vengeance of her father who was killed by Hamza in Bedr. The Prophet collected all the dead bodies of the Moslems and buried them, offering prayers for each. He observed that the martyrs were his Companions, for whose perfection in faith he would bear witness on the Day of Judgment. * Abubekr, hearing this, asked if he was not his Companion, and the Prophet replying in the affirmative said: "But I can't see what you will innovate after me."

---

* اخرج مالک فی الموطاعن ابي النضر مولی عمر بن عبید الله انه بلغه ان رسول الله صلعم قال لشهداء احد هولاء اشهد علیهم فقال ابوبکر الصدیق یا رسول الله السنا باخوانهم اسلمنا کما اسلموا وجاهدنا کما جاهدوا فقال رسول الله بلی و لکن لا ادري ما تحدثون بعدي—

ترجمه—موطاے مالک میں ابو نضر سے مروي هے که جناب رسالت ماب نے شهداے اُحد کے حق مین فرمایا که یهه وه لوگ هین جنکے کمال ایمان کی مین گواهی دونگا - حضرت ابو بکر نے کها که آیا رسول الله کیا هم اونکے بهائی یعنے مثل اونکے نهین هین جسطرح وه اسلام لاے هم بهی اسلام لاے جسطرح اُنهون نے جهاد کیا همنے بهی جهاد کیا آنحضرت نے فرمایا که هان مگر میں نهیں جانتا که تم میرے بعد کیا احداث کروگے—(تاریخ احمدي ص ۴۵)

محدث دهلوي در جذب القلوب فرموده که در خبر است که آنحضرت بر مصعب بن عمیر که از شهداے احد است بایستاد و این آیت خواند من المومنین رجال صدقوا ما عاهدوا الله علیه (الایته) و فرمود اللهم ان عبدک ونبیک یشهد ان هولاء شهداء و فرمود که بیائید بر شهداے احد وسلام کنید بر ایشان تا آسمان برپاست هر که بایشان سلام کند رد سلام وے بروے بکنند - بعد ازان جاے دیگر بر سر شهداے دیگر بایستاد و فرمود اینها اصحاب من اند که روز قیامت بر ایشان گواهی دهم - ابو بکر صدیق گفت یا رسول الله ما نه اصحاب تو ایم فرمود بلے شما اصحاب من اید و لیکن ندانم که شما بعد از من چه کنید—

Wailings for the dead.

* Finishing his engagements at Ohod in five or six days, the Prophet came back to Medina where he heard the wails of the women of Banu Abd-al-Ashhal for their dead; and he expressed his regret that Hamza had none to wail for him. Sa'd b. Mo'ázh felt this, went at once to his women folk and brought them to the Prophet's house to mourn the death of Hamza by weeping and crying, and the Prophet blessed them for this. † The example was followed by all the women of the Ansárs at Medina.

Canal over the graves at Ohod.

** During the reign of Mo'áwiyá, a canal was planned passing through the grave yard in the Ohod valley. The Governor wrote to Mo'áwiya that unless the graves of the martyrs are levelled to the ground the canal cannot pass

---

* اخرج ابن سعد فی الطبقات سمع رسول اللہ صلعم البکاء فی بنی عبدالاشهل علی قتلاهم فقال رسول اللہ صلعم لاکن حمزة لابواکي لہ فسمع ذلک سعد بن معاذ فرجع الی نساء بني عبد الاشهل فساقهن آلی باب رسول اللہ صلعم فبکین علي حمزة فسمع ذلک رسول اللہ صلعم فدعا لهن وردهن فلم تبک امراة من الانصار بعد ذالک علی میت الا بدأت بالبکاء علی حمزة ثم بکت علی میتها —

ترجمہ—ابن سعد نے طبقات مین ذکر کیا ھے کہ جب رسول اللہ نے مدینہ پہونچکر زنان بنی عبدالاشہل کا رونا سنا جوکہ اپنے مقتولین کو رو رهی تهین تو فرمایا کہ افسوس حمزہ کا کوئي رونیوالا نہیں ھے یہہ سنکر سعد بن معاذ صحابی زنان بني عبدالاشهل کے پاس گئے اور اونکو در دولت نبوی پر لاے چنانچہ اُنهون نے وهان آکر حضرت حمزہ پر نوحہ و بکا کیا جسے سنکر پیغمبر صاحب نے اُن عورتونکے لئے دعاے خیر مانگي اور اونکو اُنکے گهرون کیجانب واپس فرمایا—پس بعد ازان انصار کی عورتون مین سے کوئی ایسي نہ تهی جو بغیر حضرت حمزہ پر نوحہ کئے هوے اپني میت کیلئے روتی —

** اخرج ابن سعد في الطبقات عن جابر بن عبدالله قال لما اراد معاویة ان یجري عینہ التی باحد کتبوا الیہ انا لا تستطیع ان تجریها

† Tabari; Ibn Athir; Rawdzat-al-Ahbáb.

through that tract. Consequently a Proclamation was issued and the corpses of the martyrs were dug out for removal to other place. † Despite a lapse of more than two score and five of years they were found fresh and unaffected, and when taken out they looked as if they were fast asleep. Hamza's corpse was bleeding in the foot, which was struck accidentally in the digging.

Omm Kulthum

Roqyyá, the wife of Othmán b. Affán having died in Ramadzán, 2 A. H., the Prophet gave Omm Kulthum in marriage to Othmán in Rabi' I, 3 A. H. She lived with her husband for about six years and died in 9 A. H. leaving no issue. As a matter of fact both the girls were the Prophet's step daughters but they were by courtesy called his daughters. Othmán was called by the people Zhulnurain *i. e.* a possessor of two lights.

Hafsa.

‡ In the month of Sha'bán the Prophet married Hafsá the widow of Jaish b. Hozháfa Sahmi, who had died at Medina some time after the battle of Bedr. She was a daughter of Omar b. Al-Khattáb, who first offered the girl to Abubekr

---

الا على قبور الشهداء قال فكتبولى نبشوهم قال فرأيتهم يحملون على اعناق الرجال كانهم قوم ينام و اصابت المسحاة طرت رجل حمزة بن عبدالمطلب فانبعثت دماء —

ترجمه— ابن سعد نے طبقات میں جابر بن عبدالله سے روایت کیا هے که جب معاویه نے اپنے زمانه حکومت مین بمقام احد نهر جاري کرنیکا اراده کیا تو عامل نے لکھا که نهر کا نکالنا غیر ممکن هے جبتک که شهداے احد کے قبور پر سے نه نکالی جاے - اسکے جواب مین معاویه نے لکھا که قبرون کو کھود ڈالو— اس حکم سے یهه حالت دیکھی گئي که لوگ مردونکو قبرون سے نکالکر اپنے کندھون پر لادے لئے جاتے تھے اور وه مردے ایسے معلوم هوتے تھے که گویا سورهے هین پس اس اثناء مین جبکه قبرین کھودي جارهي تھین ایک کدال حضرت حمزه کے پاے مبارک مین لگی جس سے خون تازه جاري هوا—

† Tárikh-al-Khamis; Minháj-al-Nabowat; Madárij-al-Nabowat.
‡ Tárikh-al-Khamis.

and then to Othmán but the offer was rejected by both. Omar mentioned this to the Prophet, as a complaint, who, in order to oblige him, accepted her as his wife. * She was, however, divorced by the Prophet on account of her temper later on; but on the entreaties of her father the Prophet took her in his harem. She died in Sha'bán 45 A. H., at the age of 60 years.

Hasan son of Ali born.

In the middle of the month of Ramadzán, 3 A. H., a son was born to Ali by his wife, Fátema, the favourite daughter of the Prophet. The babe was named Hasan. His next brother when born next year was named Hosain; † both these names were adopted after the Divine Will. These names were never before borne by any one else.

CHAPTER XI.

The Jews again. The Entrenchment Defence, and other important events during the fourth and the fifth years of Hegirat.

The Jews, as already observed, grew more and more jealous of the ever increasing strength and power of the Prophet. The more distinguished and wealthy Jewish tribe of the Banu Nadzir, who lived in Medina, defying the authority of the Prophet, contemplated his ruin by any means, foul or fair. Their leader, Ka'b b. Ashraf, had intrigued with the Meccans, as already observed. The Meccan invasion of Ohod took place after he was assassinated, thus the Banu Nadzir were kept from openly joining the invasion. Had he been alive, they would have certainly revolted against Mohammed or joined the Qoreish in

* اخرج احمد في المسند عن عاصم بن عمران رسولله صلعم طلق حفصة بنت عمر بن الخطاب ثم ارتجعها —

ترجمه — مسند احمد بن حنبل میں عاصم بن عمر بن الخطاب سے مروي هے که پیغمبر صاحب نے حفصه سے نکاح کرنیکے بعد اونکو طلاق دیدیا تها مگر پهر رجوع فرمایا —(نیز ملاحه هو اسدالغابه جلد ٥)

† Tarikh-al-Khamis; Suyuti.

their expedition. Though the invasion was successful to some extent as a campaign, yet in no way did it affect the power of the Prophet, whose authority remained intact as before.

Expulsion of Banu Nadzir Jews.

† The Nadzirite Jews, who lived some three miles from Medina, planned a scheme to murder the Prophet treacherously in a friendly invitation. They invited him to dinner and arranged his seat in a court-yard just below a sloping roof to facilitate the rolling of a mill-stone over him in order to kill him. The Prophet, when seated at the place along with some of his Companions, became somehow acquainted with the treacherous design, and suddenly leaving the place took his way home, alone and unperceived, as he saw that the Jews did not mean any harm to his Companions. His Companions, after a while, discovering the cause of his sudden disappearance, grew alarmed and followed his example.

The Prophet resolved to turn them out of Medina, and ordered their departure within ten days on pain of death. They paid no heed to the order and resolved to resist. They were besieged within their walls, and after fifteen days they had to surrender and were expelled in the summer of 4 A. H. or 625. A. D. (*Sura LIX-2 and 3.*) They were allowed to take with them their moveables except arms. Most of them proceeded to Khaibar, where they had landed property; and some marched to Syria. Their immoveable property was confiscated. Buildings were distributed among the Mohájirs, who still possessed no house in Medina since their migration. Some Ansárs, who had nothing of their own, were also provided with the dwellings.

Death of Ali's mother. 4 A. H.

The mother of Ali, Fátema bint Asad, who had affectionately nurtured Mohammed since the death of Abd-al-Mottalib died this year. The Prophet had her covered with his own shirt, after her wash preparatory to her burial.

† Ibn Athir.

He took part in the digging of her grave, and when it was ready, he first himself lay down in the vault and prayed for her. When he was asked the reason for this unusual attention and favour to the deceased, the Prophet said that she was unto him a mother.

Hosain son of Ali born.

On the 3rd of Sha'bán, 4 A. H. a second son was born to Ali by Fátema, the Prophet's daughter. He was named Hosain. He was born after only six months' pregnancy. It is said that no child, given birth to after so short a pregnancy, ever lived long, except the Prophet Yahya bin Zakarya and Hosain b. Ali. Gabriel appeared to the Prophet when he was kissing the babe on his throat. The angel congratulated the Prophet but could not help weeping at the sight. † The Prophet asked him the reason and the angel predicted the massacre of Hosain after the death of the Prophet and of his parents. He was given a handful of clay from the earth where the massacre was to take place. * On receiving the intelligence he felt sad, wept and cursed the Banu Omyya. The clay was

---

* علامه صديق حسنخان در حجج الكرامه فرموده كه خبر شهادت حسين عليه السلام پيش ازان به چند سال آنحضرت صلعم داده بود و بر بني اُميه و قاتلان وے نفرين و لعنت كرده-(تاريخ احمدي ص ۴۹)

اخرج ابو نعيم عن ام سلمه قالت كان الحسين والحسن يلعبان في بيتي فنزل جبريل فقال يامحمد ان امتك تقتل ابنك هذا من بعدك و اومي الي الحسين و اتاه بتربته فشمها ثم قال ريح كرب وبلاء و قال يا ام سلمه اذا تحولت هذه التربته دماً فاعلمي ان ابنى قد قتل فجعلتها في قارورة —

ترجمه—ابو نعيم نے ام سلمه سے روايت كی هے كه حسن اور حسين ميرے گهر مين كهيل رهے تهے ناگهان حضرت جبريل نے نازل هوكر رسول الله كي خدمت مين عرض كيا كه آپكي امت آپكے فرزند حسين كو آپكے بعد قتل كريگی پهر تهوڑي مٹي آنحضرتكو دي جسے سونگهكر آپنے فرمايا كه اس سے كرب اور بلا كي بو آتی هے اور ارشاد كيا كه اے ام سلمه

† Rawdzat-al-Ahbáb; Baghwi in his Mo'jam.

preserved in a bottle by Omm Selma, wife of the Prophet, who told her to preserve it so long as it did not turn blood red, which was the symbol of Hosain's death.

The Meccan Invasion. 5. A. H.

The Jews were not idle after being expelled, as related above. They formed a coalition with the other tribes who were banished from time to time; and they left no stone unturned to annihilate their common enemy the Prophet. They stirred up the Jews of Khaibar to join them against him. They sent deputations to the Bedouin tribes and to the Qoreish in Mecca. They succeeded in concluding a treaty with the Meccans, binding them conjointly to oppose Mohammed to the last. They also succeeded in bringing about an alliance with the great Bedouin tribes of Ghatafán, Solaim, Bani Qais and Bani Asad to suppress Islam. It was contemplated to attack Medina in a body to destroy the Prophet and his religion at its very source.

The Meccans, four thousands strong, including three hundred horse and fifteen hundred camels, were joined by six thousand of the allies from the Jews and the Bedouin tribes; and the three armies set out, ten thousand strong, under the command of Abu Sofyán in the month of Shawwál, 5 A. H. (Feby. 627 A.D.)

The Entrenchment Defence.

† The Prophet received intelligence of the invasion before the approach of the enemy, but barely in time to prepare for their reception. He resolved this time to defend himself at Medina, so he began preparations for a siege. The stone houses of the town were built so close to one another as to make a high and continuous strong wall for a long distance, excepting the North-west corner, where a wide open space could afford the enemy an easy ingress. At this place, with the happy suggestion of Salmán Fársi,

---

جب یهه مٹی خون هوجاے تو سمجهنا که میرا بیٹا حسین شهید هوا —
ام سلمه نے اُس مٹی کو شیشه مین رکه لیا —(تاریخ احمدي ص ۱۴۸)

† Tabari ; Ibn Athir ; Rawdzat-al-Ahbáb.

who was familiar with the mode of defending cities in other countries, a trench, fifteen feet in width and fifteen feet in depth, was dug. The work was portioned out amongst the Moslems, the Prophet himself sharing it by carrying the excavated earth. In six days the trench was finished, deep and wide throughout almost the whole length of the defence. The houses outside the town were evacuated, and the women and children were accommodated for safety on the tops of the double storied houses within the Entrenchment. These arrangements were hardly completed when the approach of the enemy was reported. The Moslem army was immediately marshalled and entrenched behind the ditch; and the Prophet encamped in the centre of the entrenchment in a tent of red leather on a space appearing like a crescent. The camp had the rising ground of Sila' on its rear and the trench in front.

The enemy on beholding the trench was struck dumb with astonishment. This mode of defence was not known to the Arabs, and they were at a loss to understand how to overcome the difficulty; they therefore laid siege. Unable to come to close quarters for some time, they directed their attacks perseveringly with the discharge of archery. Meanwhile, Abu Sofyán attempted to instigate the Jewish tribe of Qoraitza to break their pact of allegiance to Mohammed.

The Qoraitza Jews breaking their pact of neutrality.

The Nadzirite Hoyay b. Akhtab, the most zealous promoter of opposition against Mohammed, was sent to negotiate with Ka'b b. Asad, the prince of the Qoraitza Jews, and he succeeded in winning him over to the side of Abu Sofyán disregarding the pact of neutrality with the Prophet. It was agreed that the Qoraitza would assist the Qoreish after ten days' preparation, and would attack the rear of the Moslem army from the north-western quarter of the town, which lay on the south-east side of their fortress and was easily accessible to them.

Rumours of this reached the Prophet, who deputed two chief men of the Aws and the Khazraj, Sa'd b. Moázh and Sa'd b. Obáda respectivey, to ascertain the truth. They proceeded to the Jews and, after making searching enquiries, came back and reported to the Prophet that the temper of the Jews was even worse than feared. This news alarmed him. The apprehensions having been confirmed, it was necessary to guard against surprise or treachery. North-western quarter of the town, which lay on the side of the Jewish stronghold, was the least capable of defence. To protect the families of his followers throughout the city, the Prophet could do nothing but to detach a considerable number of men from his force of three thousand, which was barely adequate for the long line of entrenchment. To meet this emergency, he had to detach two parties, one of three hundred men under Zaid bin Háritha, his freed man, and another of two hundred men under a chief of Medina, to patrol the streets and lanes of the town night and day.

Hardships of the siege.

Thus the number of the force at the Defence was reduced to 2,500 men against the 10,000 of the enemy. The prolongation of the siege was still more troublesome to the Moslems, as the already inadequate number of men guarding the outposts of the Entrenchment line got no relief, though they were wearied with keeping vigilant watch unceasingly day and night. Besides hunger on account of having fallen short of provisions, they had to suffer badly from the heat of the sunny days and the chill of the cold nights in the open air.

The Enemy clearing the ditch.

More than a fortnight had thus elapsed, when at length a select party of the besiegers' horsemen found out the narrowest and weakly guarded part of the Ditch. Amr b. Abd Wudd, Nawfal b. Abdalláh and Dzarár b. Al-Khattáb led by Ikrima b. Abu Jahl, putting spurs to their steeds, succeeded in leaping over the Trench and galloped vauntingly in front of their enemy. Amr, reining forward towards the Moslems, challenged them to single combat. Abu Sofyán with Khálid b. Walid waited on the other side of the Trench to witness the issue of the fight.

Ali wins the day.

† The Moslems at the sight of Amr were awe-struck and motionless. None of them ventured to come forward as his antagonist, as he was famous for his prowess and was reckoned among the Arabs as one equal to one thousand antagonists. The Prophet asked his prominent Companions to step forward. None but Ali stood up, but the Prophet bade him wait. Again Amr roared for his opponent and again Ali was forthcoming, but the Prophet stopped him. At his third call, he tauntingly asked the Moslems whether none of them wished to enter Paradise as a martyr. Still no one was found to respond to the challenge except Ali, who impatiently stepped forward. Now the Prophet permitted him, * and putting his own turban upon Ali's head, his own coat of mail over Ali's body, armed him with his own sword the Zhulfiqár and sent him to his adversary. "It is a struggle between Faith and Infidelity; the embodiment of the former bounds to crush the entirety of the latter," ‡ exclaimed the Prophet (برز الایمان کله الی الشرک کله) while Ali, the illustrious hero of Islam was proceeding onward to Amr b. Abd Wudd, the famous giant of the

* في سيرة النبوية فاذن له رسول الله صلعم و اعطاه سيفه ذوالفقار و البسه درعة الحديد و عممه بعمامة و قال اللهم أعنه عليه اللهم هذا اخی و ابن عمی فلا تذرنی فردا و انت خير الوارثين —

ترجمه سيرة النبويه مين هے كه جب رسول مقبول نے حضرت علي كو جنگ كي اجازت دي تو اپني تلوار يعني ذوالفقار اونكو عطا كي اپنی زره اُنكو پهنای اور اپنا عمامة اُنكے سر پر بانده كر دعا كي كه خداوندا عمرو كے مقابله مين علی كی مدد كر خداوندا يهه ميرا بهائی اور ابن عم هے پس تو مجهكو اكيلا نه كر اور تو بهترين وارث هے - نيز دوسري

† Rawdzat-al-Ahbáb; Tárikh-al-Khamis; Rawdzat-al-Safá; Habib-al-Siyar.

‡ Sirat-al-Mohammediya; Hayát-al-Haiwán.

Infidels. Then lifting up his hands he prayed: "O God! Obeida my cousin was taken away from me in the battle of Bedr; Hamza my uncle in Ohod. Be merciful not to leave me alone and undefended. Spare Ali to defend me. Thou art the best of Defenders."

†When the two (Amr and Ali) stood face to face Amr said to Ali: "Nephew, (as he was a friend of Abu Tálib, the father of Ali) By God, I do not like to put thee to death." Ali replied: "But by God, I am here to kill thee". Amr, enraged at this reply, immediately alighted and having hamstrung his horse, in token of his resolve to conquer or to die, advanced towards Ali. They immediately engaged, and, in turning about to flank each other, raised such a dust that they could not be distinguished, only the strokes of their swords were heard. At last the voice of Ali, sounding Alláh-o-Akbar 'Great is the Lord, was heard, which was a signal of his victory. When the dust was subsided, Ali was seen with his knee upon the breast of his adversary severing his head. The Divine Decree لا اله الا الله محمد رسول الله ايدته بعلى which the Prophet saw inscribed in letters of Celestial Light on Heavens in the night of Me'ráj was found by him on every such occasion fulfilled.

‡ Beholding the fate of their renowned champion, his comrades in the enterprise rushed back to escape, spurred their horses and all gained the opposite side of the Ditch except Nawfal, whose horse failed in the leap and got a fall in the ditch. Being overwhelmed with a shower of stones by the Moslems, he cried out "I had rather die by the sword than thus." Hearing this appeal Ali leaped into the ditch and dispatched him.

روایت مین هے که آنحضرت نے اپنے عمامه کو آسمان کي جانب بلند کرکے مناجات کی که پروردگار میرے تونے عبیده کو مجهه سے بدر کے دن اور حمزه کو بروز احد لے لیا اور اب یهه میرا بهائی علی هے پس خداوندا مجهے تنها نه چهوڑ اور تو بهترین وارث هے —

† Ibn Athir; Abul Fida.

‡ Rawdzat-al-Ahbáb; Izálatal Khifa; Tárikh-al-Khamis.

Contrary to the custom, Ali did not strip Amr of his armour or clothes. ‡ When Amr's sister came to the corpse, she was struck with admiration at the noble behaviour of her slain brother's adversary; and finding out who he was, she felt proud of her brother having met his fate at the hands of the person who was known as the Unique Champion of spotless character. She expressed herself thus:

The sister of Amr b. Abd Wudd.

لو كان قاتل عمرو غير قاتله   لكنت ابكى عليه آخر الابد
لكن قاتله من لا يعاب به   من كان يدعى قديها بيضةالبلد

(Had his conqueror been other than the one who killed him, I would have wept over Amr for all my life. But (I feel proud that) his antagonist was the unique spotless champion.)

† The ever-victorious Ali, the 'Lion of God,' was thus signalized in this Defence, as on previous occasions in the battles of Bedr and Ohod. * The Prophet declared that Ali's deeds of valour in the struggle on the 'Day of the Ditch' were much more in worth than the devotional worships performed till the end of this world by all his followers.

Ali's valour praised by the Prophet.

---

* در مدارج النبوة (نيز در روضة الاحباب) آمده كه در غزوه خندق از علي مرتضي مبارزها و مقاتلها واقع شد كه از حد قياس و عقل بيرون چنانكه در اخبار واقع شده است كه فرمود سيدا لمرسلين لمبارزة على بن ابي طالب يوم الخندق افضل من اعمال امتي الى يوم القيامة و آن حضرت صلعم دعاها كرد در حق علي مرتضي و شمشير خود را كه ذوالفقار نام داشت بوے عطا نمود—

ایک روایت مین بجاے اعمالِ امتي کے من عبادة الثقلين (جن و انس كي عبادت سے) واقع هوا هے اور بعض روايت مين بجاے لمبارزة على کے بضربته علي وارد هوا هے—

‡ Tárikh-al-Khamis.

† Madárijal Nabowat; Hákim in his Mustadrak; Firdows-al-Akhbár; Rawdzat-al-Ahbáb.

The enemy's last attempt.

Nothing further was attempted by the enemy that day; but great preparations were made during the night, Khâlid with a strong party of horse vainly attempting at night to clear the Ditch. Next morning the Moslems found the whole force of the enemy marshalled against them along the line of entrenchment. They sought to gain the Moslem side of the Trench, but were repelled at every point. The Trench fully served its purpose; it could not be crossed, and during the whole operations only five Moslems were lost. The enemy, notwithstanding their large numbers, were paralysed by the vigilance of the Moslem outposts. They pretended to regard the Trench as an unworthy subterfuge, being a foreign artifice with which no Arab was acquainted.

Infidelity of ths Qoraitza Jews.

Meanwhile, Abu Sofyán demanded of the Qoraitza Jews the fulfilment of their engagement to join in a general attack on the following day; but the Jews doubted the Qoreish and their allies and feared, if the struggle proved a failure, the besiegers might conveniently withdraw and leave them to their fate. They accordingly demanded hostages in security against such an event, and pleaded their Sabbath as a pretext for fighting the following day. This attitude aroused, in turn, the suspicions of the Qoreish that the Jews, for making their peace with Mohammed, were demanding hostages of them for the purpose of handing them over to Mohammed. Abu Sofyán and his confederate Chiefs were greatly disheartened. Their hope was so long centered on the Qoraitza Jews falling upon the city in the rear of the Prophet; it was now changed into the fear of hostilities from the treacherous Qoraitza themselves.

Troubles in the enemy's camp.

Dispirited at the loss of their bravest General, Amr b. Abd Wudd, and wearied, as they were, after the two vigorous but unsuccessful attempts, the Qoreish and their allies had no courage to attempt another general assault. Discord was also rife amongst them. The Bedouines had no forage for their camels and horses, which were dying daily in considerable numbers. Provisions were running short. Above all, the weather was intolerably troublesome to them. Night set in upon them cold and tempestuous. A storm of wind and rain blew dust in their faces, overturned their tents, extinguished their fires, overthrew their cooking vessels, and put their horses astray. They exclaimed that it was all through the witchcraft and enchantment of Mohammed, who will be shortly seen falling upon them with his whole force, and they were greatly struck with terror.

* The Prophet was in earnest prayer for the last three days appealing to the help of the Almighty in such words: "O Lord! Revealer of the sacred Book, who art swift in taking account: turn the confederate host! Turn them to flight O Lord, and make them quake!" † The fourth night, when he finished his prayers, he asked Abubekr if he would go to the enemy's camp to spy out their activities. He replied: "I ask pardon of God and

---

* تفسیر درالمنثور جلد ٥ ص ١٧٥ مین هے — ابراهیم تیمی راوی هے که اُسکے باپ نے حضرت حذیفه سے کہا که اگر هم رسول الله کیخدمتمین پہونچتے تو حضرت کی خدمت کرتے - حذیفه نے کہا شب جنگ خندق هم رسول الله کے ساتهه تھے حضرت نماز پڑه رهے تھے اور یهه ایسی سرد رات تهی که اس سے قبل یا بعد کبهی ایسی سرد رات همنے نهین دیکھی — حضرت هملوگونکیطرف ملطفت هوے اور فرمایا هے کوئی مرد جو اس قوم کیطرف جاے اور خبر لاے خدا اُسکو همارے ساتهه قیامت مین جگه دیگا - حضرت کے اس کلام پر کوئي نه اُتها پهر حضرت نے اس کلام کا اعاده کیا کسینے جواب نه دیا آپنے فرمایا اے ابو بکر — ابو بکر نے کہا استغفر الله و رسوله - حضرت نے فرمایا اگر چاهو تو جاو - پهر فرمایا اے عمر - وه بهی استغفرالله کهکر ره گئے تب آپ نے فرمایا اے حذیفه تو همنے کہا لبیک اور حاضر هوے حالانکه سردی کی شدت سے کانپ رهے تهے - حضرت نے اپنے

† Tafsir Durr Manthur ; Sirat Mohammediya ; Sirat-Al-Halabia Tárikh Al Khamis ; Rawdzat al Ahbáb.

58

5 A. H.

His prophet." He promised Paradise to the person who might venture out for the purpose, and addressed Omar, who also replied in the like manner. The third person called was Hozhaifa, who readily responded to the call and proceeded to the Camp of the enemy in the darkness of the night, where he saw the devastations wrought by the tempest, and found Abu Sofyán in a gloomy mood. He came back to his Camp, and reported in detail to the Prophet what he had seen of the enemy. He was delighted to find his appeal to God being answered. " O true believers ! remember the favour of God towards you, when hosts (of infidels) came upon you and we sent against them a wind, and hosts (of Angles) which ye saw not, and God beheld what ye did." (*Sura xxxiii–9.*)

دست مبارک سے ہمارے سر اور چہرہ پر مسح کیا اور فرمایا جاکر اس
قوم کی خبر لا اور کوئی نئی بات نکرنا جبتک ہمارے پاس نہ پھر آو -
پھر آنپے دعادی کہ خدایا اسکی حفاظت کر آگے سے اور پیچھے سے اور دائن
اور بائین فوق اور تحت سے جبتک یہہ پھر آے - حذیفہ کہتے ہین ہم
جب اُدھر روانہ ہوے تو ایسی گرمی معلوم ہوتی تھی کہ گویا حمام مین
جا رہے ہیں- وہان جاکر کیا دیکھتے ہین کہ خدا نے اُنپر ایسی ہوا کو
مسلط کیا ہے کہ خیمہ کی طنابین ٹوٹ گئین جانور اُنکے بھاگ گئے برتن اُنکے
اُلٹے پڑے ہین کوئی چیز اُنکے پاس نہین ہے سب کو ہوا نے تباہ کردیا ہے
ابو سفیان کو دیکھا کہ آگ سلگاے ہوے تاپ رہاہے - ہمنے چاہا کہ ایک
تیرسے قصہ طے کردین مگر حضرت کا کلام یاد آیا جس سے تیر کو ہمنے پھر ترکش
مین رکھہ لیا - ایک شخص نے اُن کفار مین سے کہا کہین کوی جاسوس
نہ ہو تو ہر شخص نے اپنے اپنے ساتھی کا ہاتھہ پکڑ لیا ہمنے بھی اپنے پاس
والے آدمی کا ہاتھہ پکڑا اور پوچھا کون ہے تو اسنے کہا سبحان اللہ کیا
نہین پہچانتا کہ ہم فلان شخص ہین- وہ قبیلہ ہوازن سے تھا - بعد اسکے
ہم وہاں سے واپس آے اور رسول اللہ سے سارا قصہ بیان کیا حضرت اسقدر
ہنسے کہ اُس اندھیری رات مین آپکے دندان مبارک چمکنے لگے - حضرت نے
ہمکو اپنے قدم مبارک کے پاس سلایا اور اپنی رداے مبارک ہمپر ڈالی ہم
مارے سردی کے قدم مبارک سے اپنا شکم اور سینہ ملارہے تھے صبحکو خدا نے
اُس لشکر کو ہزیمت دی - (تاریخ اسلام جلد ۲ ص ۱۰۹ ایس ذاکر حسین)

Siege raised by the enemy.

Either discomforted with the severity of the weather or struck with terror at this manifestation of Heavenly Wrath, Abu Sofyán precipitately decided to raise the siege and to march back at once. Summoning the ally Chiefs, he made known to them his resolve. Issuing orders to break up the camp and immediately mounting his camel, he hastily took his way to Mecca followed by his armies; Khálid, with two hundred horse, guarded the rear against pursuit. The Ghatafáns and the Bedouin allies retired to their deserts; not a single soul was to be seen at the field in the morning.

It was with great joy that in the morning the Moslems discovered the sudden disappearance of the enemy and found themselves unexpectedly relieved. They broke up their Camp, in which they had been suffering the hardships of the siege for the last twenty four days in the month of Shawwál-Zhilqa'da, 5 A.H. (or February-March 627 A. D.), and as soon as they received permission from the Prophet to leave the ground beside the hill of Sila' they dispersed with the greatest alacrity to their homes.

Bani Qoraitza Jews. 5 A. H.

† Soon after his return from the Entrenchment, while laying aside his armour, the Prophet was washing his hands and face in the house of his beloved daughter Fátema, whom he used to visit before proceeding to his own quarter on return from an expedition or excursion, the Angel Gabriel brought him a Command to proceed immediately against the Qoraitza Jews. The Prophet instantly sent Ali with his Standard, and himself with his army followed him, and laid siege to the fortress of the Jews, who had not calculated the chance of a siege and soon began to feel its hardships. They sought to capitulate. But their recent treacherous conduct was not forgotten. It had caused the greatest anxiety to the Moslems till only the previous day. Had they fallen upon the rear of the Moslem lines, in fulfilment of their pact with the Qoreish,

† Abul Fida; Habib-al-Siyar; Tabari.

5 A. H.

they would have brought about the utter ruin of the Moslems. Nobody, placed in a position as the Prophet was during the days of Entrenchment, could have forgiven their treachery as already observed. Now it was their turn to suffer the consequences. The Prophet refused them any consideration. Still, when they begged that Abu Lobába of the Aws tribe, with whom they claimed their ancient friendship, might be allowed to visit and counsel them, the Prophet willingly gave his assent. Abu Lobába went and counselled, not with his tongue but symbolically with his hands drawing across his throat, † meaning that they were doomed so they must act desparately.

But their guilty conscience would not let their spirits rise. At last, after twenty five days they offered to surrender, if Sa'd b. Mo'ázh the chief of their allies —the Bani Aws—might be appointed to decide their fate. To this the Prophet agreed. They came out as prisoners, and Sa'd was summoned for the decision. Sa'd was severely wounded at the Trench and was under treatment. When he appeared on a mule, weak and jaded, supported by his friends with his portly and commanding figure, he was thronged round by the men of his tribe, who urged him to deal leniently with the prisoners, reminding him of their friedship and of the services rendered by them from time to time as in the battles of Bo'áth. When he approached, the Prophet commanded him to pronounce his judgment on the Bani Qoraitza. Sa'd turned to his people, who were still urging him for mercy upon the Jews, and said to them if they would bind themselves solemnly to accept whatsoever he should decide. After a general murmur of assent, Sa'd decreed that the male captives should be put to sword, women and

† Having thus betrayed the Prophet, Abu Lobaba felt conscious of his crime and coming back he proceeded direct to the Prophet's mosque in Medina, where he tied himself to a pillar, repentantly weeping and crying. He remained in this condition seven days without diet till he was forgiven.

children be sold as slaves and their goods be confiscated and divided among the besiegers. This sentence was accordingly put into execution.

The Nadzirite chief, Hoyay b. Akhtab, the culprit who had instigated the Qoraitza to break the pact of neutrality with the Prophet and had brought upon them this calamity, was among the slain, along with Ka'b b. Asad the chief of the Qoraitza.

Zainab bint Johash.

Zainab, a girl of extraordinary beauty, was the daughter of Omima bint Abd-al-Mottalib, the grandfather of the Prophet. She was thus a cousin to Mohammed, who brought her up in her girlhood, under his personal supervision. When she grew up to womanhood, the Prophet proposed her marriage with Zaid, his emancipated slave, who was looked upon with paternal affections by him. She resented this marriage at first, but was subsequently persuaded to the union. She was, however, never happy and treated her husband with contempt. Every day there were quarrels and Zaid complained against her to the Prophet expressing his desire to divorce her. The Prophet dissuaded him from this. At length, when Zaid could no longer bear the unceasing brunts of his wife, he divorced her in 5 A. H. Thinking himself to be the cause of his cousin's unhappiness resulting from the union against her will, the Prophet was uneasy, and recompensed by marrying her himself.

It may be explained here that a slave was always looked upon with contempt by his master and the general public, and was never given a status of equality with them even after emancipation, what to say of inter-marriage. The Prophet, by giving Zaid his own cousin in marriage, had set an example for the people not to treat a slave as one degraded or inferior to themselves. Besides this, there were many debasing customs prevalent in Arabia before the advent of the Prophet. For instance, the eldest son inherited his father's widows. Likewise the adopted son inherited all the properties and titles of his adopting father, who had no issue of his own, depriving all other rightful heirs from inheritance. The people on the whole were deeply sunk in cruelty and vice. Female infanticide was no crime among them. To condemn and abolish such vices and immoralities, as well as to remove the spiritual torpor, the Prophet was born in Arabia. He was now commanded by the Supreme Lord in a revelation ("And when Zaid had settled the necessary matter (divorce) concerning her, we married her to thee, that there might not be a hinderance to the Faithful concerning the wives of their adopted sons, when they have decided the necessary matter concerning them. And the cammand of God is to be performed." *Sura XXXIII - 37.*) to marry Zainab, on purpose to set an example to the Moslems, who might not forthwith treat an adopted son as a real one. The Prophet consequently married Zainab bint Johash after the lapse of the requisite term of her separation from Zaid.

CHAPTER XII.

The Hodaibiya treaty and other important events in the sixth year of Hegirat.

Bani Mostaleq Jews.

The Jews of the Bani Mostaleq tribe of a neighbouring province meditated a raid on Medina. The Prophet, having received intelligence of their activities, sent Boreida b. Al Hasib to ascertain the truth. Boreida on his return confirmed the news. The Prephet therefore marched against them on the 2nd of Sha'bán, 6 A. H. with Ali as his Standard bearer. A battle was fought in which ten Jews were killed along with their leader Hárith b. Abi Dzarár. The Jews, after the fall of their leader, took to flight, and the Moslems returned victorious with two hundred captives, one thousand camels and five hundred sheep. Jowairiya, the daughter of the Jewish

Chief was among the captives. † Her father Hárith had entreated the Prophet not to treat her as a slave. She embraced Islam and was married to the Prophet to maintain her dignity and queenly position among her kindred tribesfolk, who were all released in commemoration of the marriage.

Hypocrisy of Abdallah b. Obay. 6 A. H.

During the return journey, a servant of Omar, fighting with one of the Ansárs, occasioned a quarrel between the Ansárs and the Mohájirs. Abdalláh b. Obay Salol, the Hypocrite, siding with the Ansárs, taunted the Mohájirs as people that would, with their growing power, encroach upon the Ansárs if they did not take necessary measures to check their aggressions. His words were reported to the Prophet, and Omar suggested to send some one to strike off the head of Abdalláh. ‡ The Prophet rejected the suggestion saying: "People will say that Mohammed puts to death at his pleasure those who are with him." Soon after, the son of Abdalláh, a staunch follower of the Prophet, hearing all about this, came to the Prophet and told him that if he had any thoughts of condemning his father to death, he would be the first man to obey his order. The Apostle of God bade the young man not to think badly of his father and be kind to him.

Ayesha accused of wantonness.

‖ Another noteworthy incident which occurred in the same journey is the accusation laid on Ayesha, wife of the Prophet, who accompanied him in this expedition. According to the narrative given by Sale in his Notes on *Sura XXIV* it runs as follows:

"Mohammad having undertaken an expedition against the tribe of Mostaleq, in the 6th year of the Hegira took his wife Ayesha with him, to accompany him. In their return, when they were not far from Medina, the army removing by night, Ayesha, on the road, alighted from her camel

† Ibn Sa'd; Ibn Hajar; Ibn Monda.
‡ Sahih Bokhári. ‖ Tabari; Ibn Athir.

and stepped aside on a private occasion; but, on her return, perceiving she had dropped her necklace which was of onyxes of Tzafár, she went back to look for it; and in the meantime her attendants, taking it for granted that she was got into her pavilion, set it again on the camel, and led it away. When she came back to the road, and saw her camel was gone, she sat down there, expecting that when she was missed, some would be sent back to fetch her; and in a little time she fell asleep. Early in the morning, Safwán b. Mo'attal, who had stayed behind to rest himself, coming by, and perceiving some body asleep, went to see who it was, and knew her to be Ayesha; upon which he waked her, by twice pronouncing with a low voice these words: 'We are God's, and unto Him must we return.' Then Ayesha immediately covered herself with her veil; and Safwán set her on his own camel and led her after the army, which they overtook by noon, as they were resting."

"This accident had like to have ruined Ayesha, whose reputation was publicly called in question, as if she had been guilty of adultery with Safwán."

The Prophet was exceedingly chagrined and his mind was not at ease. W. Irving writes: "This account given by Ayesha, and attested by Safwán b. Mo'attal, was satisfactory to her parents and particular friends; but was scoffed at by Abdalláh and his adherents, the hypocrites.† Two parties thus arose on the subject and great strife ensued. As to Ayesha, she shut herself up within her dwelling, refusing all food and weeping day and night in the bitterness of her soul. Mohammed was sorely troubled in mind, and asked counsel of Ali in his perplexity. The latter made light of the affair, observing that his misfortune was the frequent lot of man. The Prophet

† Mosattah, the son of a maternal cousin of Abubekr, Zaid b. Rifá'a, Hamna bint Johash and Abdalláh b. Obay accused Ayesha with wantonness and Hassán, the poet, recited epigrams against her. Abdalláh b. Obay was the first, who raised the scandal and inflamed it to the utmost out of his hatred to Mohammed.

was but little consoled by this suggestion. He remained separated from Ayesha for a month; but his heart yearned toward her; not merely on account of her beauty, but because he loved her society. In a paroxysm of grief, he fell into one of those trances which unbelievers have attributed to epilepsy; in the course of which he received a seasonable revelation, which will be found in a Chapter of the Qurán. It was to this effect:— (*Sur. XXIV:11*) They who accuse a reputable female of adultery, and produce not four witnesses of the fact, shall be scourged with four score stripes, and their testimony rejected. As to those who have made the charge against Ayesha, have they produced four witnesses thereof. If they have not, they are liars in the sight of God. Let them receive therefore the punishment of their crime. The innocence of the beautiful Ayesha being thus miraculously made manifest, the Prophet took her to his bosom with augmented affection. Nor was he slow in dealing the prescribed castigation. It is true, Abdalláh son of Obay was too powerful a personage, to be subjected to the scourge, but it fell the heavier on the shoulders of his fellow calumniators. The poet Hassán was cured for sometime of his propensity to make satirical verses, nor could Hamna, though a. female and of great personal charms, escape the infliction of stripes, for Mohammed observed that such beauty should have been accompanied by a gentler nature. ***The revelation at once convinced the pious Ali of the purity of Ayesha, but she never forgot nor forgave that he had doubted; and the hatred thus implanted in her bosom was manifested to his great detriment in many of the most important concerns of his after life.''***

The Prophet's pilgrimage to Mecca.

† In the sixth year of Hegira, the Prophet had a dream that with his followers he made circuits round the Ka'ba, and performed all the ceremonies of the pilgrimage. Next morning he communicated the dream to his followers,

† Ibn Athir; Izálat-al-Khifa; Madárijal Nabowat; Habibal Siyar; Rawdzat-al-Ahbáb.

who were very glad to have the tidings, as they already longed to revisit their native town and home, which they were forced to leave six years back. It was the first day of the month of Zhilqa'da, in which war was unlawful throughout Arabia, much more within the sacred territory of Mecca; consequently Omra, or the Lesser Pilgrimage might be undertaken during this month without any risk of hostilities from the Qoreish or Meccans. Hasty preparations for pilgrimage were made, as the Prophet gave it out that he intended nothing but to make the pilgrimage. Early in the month, arrangements for the journey being completed, the Prophet led about fourteen hundred of his followers to Zhul Holeifa on the road to Mecca. They had taken seventy camels for the sacrifice. They carried no arms but sheathed sword of a traveller. Only one of his wives, Omm Selma, accompanied the Prophet in this pilgrimage.

Hostility of the Meccans.

The intelligence of the Prophet's march soon reached Mecca. Notwithstanding the unwarlike and peaceful attitude of the pilgrims, and the absence of arms with them, the Qoreish suspected treachery, and being alarmed, they got together a considerable force; and taking up arms, encamped about six miles out of Mecca, occupying a position on the Medina road. To check the advance of the Prophet, a body of 200 cavalry under Khālid b. Walid and Ikrima b. Abu Jahl pushed forward. The Prophet continued his march till a spy informed him of the movements of the Meccans, and shortly after, the Meccan cavalry itself was in sight.

The Prophet's halt at Hodaibiya.

Further advance being now impossible, as the Prophet did not come to give them battle, he turned towards the right. Reaching Al Hodaibiya, on the verge of the sacred territory surrounding Mecca, his camel Al Qaswa stopped there of its own accord and knelt down as if refusing to step farther. The people said she was wearied but the Prophet took it for a Divine omen that he should not proceed farther. He therefore encamped at Al Hodaibiya. There was no water available at the place, though there were some wells, but they were choked up with sand. The Prophet taking an arrow from his quiver, had it planted in one of the wells and the water immediately bubbled up to the great relief of the whole camp. Here the Qoreish sent three messengers—one after the other—to the Prophet to enquire of his intention in coming thither. Orwa, a chief from Táef, one of the three messengers, said to the Prophet that the Meccans were desperate and that they had resolved to perish rather than allow him to enter. He went on saying that the Meccans would not suffer the rabble accompanying him to approach the city, and swore that he was seeing him, as it were, deserted by them all as soon as the Meccans fell upon them. At this Abubekr started up and warmly resented the imputation. The Prophet, however, answered each of the messengers that it was purely out of a devout wish for visiting the holy Sanctuary and performing the sacred rites connected therewith that he had undertaken the pilgrimage. The messengers even saw the row of sacrificial camels with marks upon their necks of having been long tied up for this pious object. They expressed their conviction in the sincerity of Mohammad's peaceful intentions; but the Qoreish, they said, were firm and would not listen to them.

Negotiations with the Meccans.

The Prophet also sent one of his own men (Kharrash b. Omyya on his own camel named † Tha'lab) to give the Qoreish an assurance that he had come with no hostile design, but they treated him roughly, maimed the camel on which he rode and even threatened his life. He would have been killed had not the Ahabish interposed and helped him to escape. ‡ Upon this the Prophet desired Omar to go upon the same errand, but he excused himself saying that he was not on good terms with the Qoreish and named Othmán as a suitable envoy. Othmán was at last

† Uswat-al-Rasul Vol. III p. 10.

‡ Ibn Athir; Rawdzat-al-Ahbáb; Habib-al-Siyar; Ibn Hishám.

sent and he delivered the message to the Qoreish that the Prophet had come to pay a visit to the holy house and that after slaying the sacrificial camels the Prophet together with his followers would go back. But the Qoreish replied that they had sworn not to allow Mohammed to enter the city that year and that if he (Othmán) wished to visit the Ka'ba he might do so. Othmán declined the offer saying that he could not do so without the Apostle of God first performing the rites at the Sanctuary; and returned to the Camp. Meanwhile, considerable delay having occurred in his return, it was rumoured in the Moslem camp that he had been murdered by the Qoreish. The Prophet was much afflicted at this news.

Pledge under the tree.

‡The necessity of giving battle to the enemy being thus imminent, he summoned all the pilgrims around him, and taking his stand under a tree, took oath from each, of unflinching adherence to him—never|| to flee and fighting to the end. This pledge is called 'the Pledge under the Tree' (as referred to in *Sura XLVIII-18*: "Now God was well pleased with the Believers when they did swear fealty to thee under the tree; and He knew what was in their hearts; and He sent down Sakinah on them and rewarded them with a speedy victory'), and is memorable in the history of Islam, illustrating the devotion and loyalty shown by the followers of the Prophet, who boasted of their religious fervour and thought themselves deserving of salvation, *though the more reasonable among them were sensible of the malicious prosecutions practised by the followers of the Prophet later after the

---

* اخرج البخاري في صحيحه عن العلاء بن المسيب عن ابيه قال لقيت البراء بن عازب رضي الله عنهما فقلت طوبى لک صحبت النبی صلعم و بايعته تحت الشجرة فقل يا ابن اخی انک لا تدری ما احدثنا بعده—

ترجمہ—صحیح بخاري مين علاء بن مسیب سے مروي هے که مين نے براء بن عازب سے ملاقات کی اور اُن سے کها که خوشا حال تمهارا که تمنے

‡ Abul Fida; Habib-al-Siyar; Ibn Jarir.
|| Tabari; Ibn Athir; Ibn Hishám.

'Pledge under the Tree' and after the Prophet's death. The men who were not present on the occasion regretted having missed the chance. Soon, after the ceremony of the Pledge was over, Othmán's reappearance relieved the whole Camp from all suspense and anxiety.

Peace negotiations concluded at Hodaibiya.

A party of eighty Meccans was found, later on, beating up the Moslem Camp, seeking to cut off any stray followers. All the men were surrounded, taken prisoners and brought before the Prophet, who very wisely treated them generously and released them. The Qoreish appreciating the generosity and having learnt the purport of the Pledge, fearing a battle, sent Sohail b. Amr and some other representatives to conclude a treaty of peace with Mohammed. After a long discussion the terms of peace were settled and the Prophet required Ali, his vicegerent, to write down the Treaty at his dictation, which was begun thus: *'In the name of God, the most Gracious and Merciful,' Sohail objected to this and said that it

---

رسول مقبول کي صحبت اور بیعت تحت شجره کا شرف حاصل کیا هے یهه سنکر براء نے کہا که لیکن اے بهتیجے تم نهین جانتے که هم لوگون نے آنحضرت کے بعد کیا احداث کیا — (تاریخ احمدي ص ۵۴)

---

* فی الکامل لابن اثیر الجزری فدعا رسول الله صلی الله علیه و سلم علی بن ابیطالب فقال اکتب — بسم الله الرحمن الرحیم — فقال سهیل لانعرف هذا و لکن اکتب باسمک اللهم فکتبها ثم قال اکتب هذا ما صالح علیه محمد رسول الله سهیل بن عمرو فقال سهیل لونعلم انک رسول الله لم نقاتلک و لکن اکتب اسمک و اسم ابیک فقال لعلی امح رسول الله فقال لا امحوابدا فاخذه رسول الله صلعم فکتب موضع رسول الله محمد بن عبد الله و قال لعلي لتبلین بمثلها —

ترجمه — تاریخ کامل مین هے که جب رسول مقبول نے سهیل کي درخواست صلح منظور کرلی تو حضرت علی کو بلاکر ارشاد کیا که لکهو- بسم الله الرحمن الرحیم - سهیل بولا که هم یهه نهین جانتے - لکهو بسمک اللهم - چنانچه یهی لکها گیا - پهر جناب رسالتمآب نے حضرت علی سے

should begin as the Meccans used to do, thus: "In Thy name, O God!" The Prophet yielded and asked Ali to write "Bismeka Alláhomma." Next he dictated to write: "This is the Treaty made between Mohammed the Apostle of God, and Sohail son of Amr." Sohail again raised an objection and said that had the Meccans acknowledged him as Apostle of God they would not have taken up arms against him.† Instead of 'the Apostle of God,' Sohail asked the Prophet to have his father's name written. The Prophet again yielded but Ali had already written the words 'Mohammed the Apostle of God' The Prophet ‡bade Ali to erase the words under objection, but, as Ali hesitated, the Prophet himself taking the writing materials obliterated the words and had the words 'son of Abdalláh' substituted in place of 'the Apcstle of God.' He *prophesied ¶ at the same time, addressing Ali, that he should similarly have to yield on a similar occasion in

کہا کہ لکھو یہہ وہ صلحنامہ ہے جسکی بنا پر محمد رسول اللہ نے سہیل بن عمرو سے مصالحت کی۔ سہیل نے کہا کہ اگر ہم تمکو رسول اللہ جانتے تو قتال پر کیون آمادہ ہوتے لہذا بجاے رسول اللہ کے اپنا اور اپنے والد کا نام لکھو۔ پیغمبر صاحب نے حضرت علي سے فرمایا کہ اچھا رسول اللہ کے لفظ کو نکالڈالو۔ انہون نے کہا کہ میري مجال نہین جو لفظ رسول اللہ کو محو کرسکون۔ یہہ سنکر آنحضرت نے کاغذ لے لیا اور لفظ رسول اللہ کی جگہ محمد بن عبداللہ لکھہ کر حضرت علی سے فرمایا کہ اے علی تمکو بھي ایک وقت ایسا ھي معاملہ پیش آئیگا (تارخ احمدي ص ٥٤)

* صاحب معارج النبوة آوردہ کہ آنحضرت فرمود کہ اے علي ترا ھم در وقتے این چنین معاملہ پیش خواھد آمد —

فی الخمیس قال و اقبل یوجهه علی علی فقال یا علی سیکون لک یوم مثل هذه الواقعة —

ترجمہ — تاریخ الخمیس مین ھے کہ جناب رسول مقبول نے حضرت علي کیجانب نظر فرماکر ارشاد کیا کہ اے علی تمکو بھي اس قسم کا واقعہ روبکار ھونیوالا ھے (تاریخ احمدی ص ٥٥)

† Abul Fida.

‡ Habib-al-Siyar; Tazkirat-al-Kirám.

¶ Rawdzat-al-Ahbáb; Habib-al-Siyar; Ibn Athir.

his own time. This prophecy was fulfilled when a treaty was concluded between Ali and Mo'áwyia over thirty years later.

Peace terms of the Hodaibiya Treaty.

‡ The following terms were put down in the treaty. There shall be no aggression on the part of any of the two parties for the next ten years, neither shall attack the other or their allies. Whosoever wishes to join Mohammed and enter into a league with him shall have the liberty to do so; and likewise whosoever wishes to join the Qoreish and enter into a treaty with them shall be at liberty to do so. If any one goes over to Mohammed and is claimed back by his guardian he shall be sent back to his guardian; but if any one from the followers of Mohammed returns to the Qoreish, he shall not be sent back. Mohammed and his followers shall go back this year without entering the holy precincts. Next year Mohammed and his followers may visit Mecca for three days, when the Qoreish shall retire therefrom. But they may not enter it with any arms, save those of a traveller *viz.* each man with a sheathed sword.

Some Companions' doubts in belief.

|| Some of the eminent followers of the Prophet expected, as the result of his dream, nothing short of a complete victory over the Meccans. But now, finding that the Meccans were prevailing upon the Prophet, who was suing for permission and they were not allowing him to enter the holy precincts, they were disgusted to be disappointed after a great deal of fatigue and botheration. * Omar b. Khattáb expressed himself plainly that he had never before suspected so strongly the truth of Mohammed's

---

* فى تاريخ الخميس للديار بكري والدر المنثور للسيوطى روي عن عمر انة قال والله ماشككت منذ اسلمت الا يوميئذ فاتيت النبى فقلت الست نبي الله حقا قال بلي قلت السنا على الحق و عدونا علي الباطل قال بلي قلت اليس قتلانا فى الجنة و قتلاهم في النار قال بلى قلت فلم نعطى الدنية فى ديننا قال انى رسول الله و لست اعصيه و هوناصري—

‡ Ibn Athir; Tazkirat-al-Kirám.

|| Abul Fida; Ibn Athir; Rawdzat-al-Ahbáb.

6 A. H.

being the Apostle of God; and he even ventured to address † him thus: "Art thou not a true Apostle of God?" The Prophet replied, "I am, no doubt." Omar asked, "Are we not in the right and our adversaries in the wrong?" The Prophet said, "Of course we are in the right and our adversaries in the wrong." Omar concluded, "Why should we then put a blot upon our Faith and bear

---

تاریخ الخمیس اور تفسیر در منثور سیوطي مین هے که حضرت عمر نے فرمایا که بخدا مین جب سے اسلام لایا آجکے سوا مجھے کبھي شک نهین هوا چنانچه مینے پیغمبر صاحب کے پاس جاکر کھا که کیا آپ نبی برحق نهین هین ؟ آنحضرت نے فرمایا که بیشک هون — مینے کھا که کیا هم حق پر اور همارے مخالف باطل پر نهین هین ؟ اور کیا همارے مقتول جنتي اور اُنکے مقتول دوزخی نهین هین ؟ آنحضرت نے فرمایا که هم ضرور حق پر هین اور همارے دشمن باطل پر اور همارے مقتول جنتی هین اور انکے مقتول جهنمی — مینے کھا که پھر دین مین نقص وخست چه معنی دارد (یعنے آپ کیون صلح کرتے هین) آنحضرت نے فرمایا که مین الله کا رسول هون اُسکي نافرماني نهین کرتا اور وه میرا معین و مددگار هے — (تاریخ احمدي ص ٥٦) —

فی روایة البخاري قال عمر بن الخطاب فاتیت النبي صلعم فقلت الست نبی الله حقا قال بلی قلت السنا علی الحق و عدونا علی الباطل قال بلي قلت فلم نعطی الدنیة فی دیننا اذا قال انی رسول الله و لست اعصیه و هو ناصري —

ترجمه — صحیح بخاري کي حدیث مین هے که حضرت عمر نے فرمایا که بروز صلح حدیبیه مین نے پیغمبر صاحب سے کھا که کیا آپ نبي بر حق نهین هیں؟ آنحضرت نے فرمایا که بیشک هون — مین نے کھا کیا هم حق پر ارر همارے دشمن باطل پر نهیں هیں — آنحضرت نے فرمایا که بیشک هم حق پر اور همارے مخالف باطل پر هین؟ مین نے کھا پھر کیون اسوقت هم دین مین نقص اور خست گوارہ کرین — آنحضرت نے فرمایا که سنو مین خدا کا رسول هون اُسکے حکم کے خلاف کچھه نهین کرتا اور وه میرا مددگار هے —

† Sahih Bokhári; Ibn Hishám.

the brunt of humiliation?" The Prophet answered, "I am but a messenger of God and can do nothing against His will; He will help me." Omar however, was not satisfied with the Prophet's answers, as he again held similar indignant conversation with Abubekr:—"What! Is not Mohammed the Prophet of God? Are we not Moslems? Are they not Infidels? Why then is our Divine religion to be thus lowered? (*Hishami p. 325.*) Had these terms been fixed by any other than by Mohammed himself,—even by a Commander of my own appointment, I would have scorned to listen to them." *K. Wackidi p. 120. From Muir Vol. IV p. 38.*

While the Treaty was being drawn up, Abu Jondal, son of Sohail, who was a Mohammedan convert and was confined by his father at Mecca, got loose and came to the Mohammedan camp. He was discovered and was reclaimed by his father Sohail in virtue of the terms of the Treaty. The Prophet ordered his return to his guardian. Abu Jondal began to cry. The Prophet exhorted the young man to keep patience, promising him that God would soon give him liberty and prosperity, as to all

---

في عمدة القاري لشرح صحيح البخاري للعيني قال عمر رضي الله عنه لقد دخلني امر عظيم و راجعت النبي صلعم مراجعته ماراجعته مثلها قط—

كتاب عمدة القاري شرح صحيح بخاري مين علامه عيني لكهتے هين كه حضرت عمر نے فرمايا كه بروز صلح حديبيه ميرے دلمين خطره عظيم گذرا اور مينے پيغمبر صاحب كے ساتهه ايسي مراجعت كى كه پهلے كبهي نه كي تهي—(تاريخ احمدي ص ٥٦)

شيخ عبدالحق محدث دهلوي درمدارج النبوة آورده كه عمر بن الخطاب گفت كه در آمد در آنروز در دل من امر عظيم و مراجعت كردم با حضرت صلعم كه هرگز مثل آن نه كرده بودم و رفتم به نزد رسول و گفتم كه آيا تو پيغمبر برحق نيستى- فرمود بلى هستم گفتم نه ما بر حقيم و مخالفان ما بر باطل گفت بلي پس گفتم چرا ما اين مذلت و حقارت كشيم وباين طور صلح كرده باز گرديم -آنحضرت صلعم فرمود اے پسر خطاب بدرستيكه

under the same circumstances. * But Omar leapt over to him, comforted him with such ideas as these: "The blood of these infidels is no better than the blood of dogs," *Muir Vol. IV p. 42*; and induced him to kill his father, to set the whole peace transactions at naught. Abu Jondal did not consent to this proposal. The treaty was completed, the text having been written by Ali. It was witnessed by the most prominent Companions of the Prophet, notwithstanding the fact that they regarded the peace as a most dishonorable and humiliating one. A copy of the Treaty was given to Sohail, who then took his departure along with his comrades. The original document was kept by the Prophet.

† Having made the Treaty, the Prophet desired to perform such ceremonies of the pilgrimage as the nature of the circumstances permitted. He gave order to his Companions to slay their sacrificial camels and to shave their heads, but he was grieved to see that nobody paid heed to his command. He felt this disobedience so much that he made a mention of it to his wife Omm Selma, who accompanied him in this pilgrimage. But when he slew his

---

من فرستادہ خدایم و بے فرمان وے نمیکنم و وے ناصر و معین من است
و مرا ضائع نخواهد کذاشت—(تاریخ احمدي ص ۵۵'
بروایت روضتہ الاحباب حضرت عمر نے فرمایا۔

ما شککت فی نبوۃ محمد کشکي یم الحدیبیہ۔

یعنے جیسا شک مجھکو آنحضرت کي نبوت مین صلح حدیبیہ کے دن
هوا اتنا شک مجھے کبھی پہلے نہین هوا تہا۔(تاریخ اسلام جلد ۲ ص ۱۱۷)

---

* در روضتہ الاحباب آمدہ کہ پس عمر بن خطاب رضی اللہ عنہ
از جاے خویش بر جست و با ابوجندل میرفت و میگفت صبرکن (الي ان قال)
و اورا بہ سبیل تعریض و کنایت تحریص میکرد بر آنکہ پدر را بکشد و
و آن صلح درهم نوردد (الي ان قال) لکن وے بکشتن پدر بخیلي نمود۔
(تاریخ احمدي ص ۵۷)—

† Tabari; Ibn Athir; Rawdzat-al-Ahbab.

own camels and shaved his own head first, all his Companions gradually followed his example. Having thus completed the rites of pilgrimage, the Prophet, after a stay of twenty days at Hodaibiya, began his march homeward together with all his followers. On his way home, at the close of his first stage of march, the Prophet had the revelation of *Sura. XLVIII,* which begins with the words "Verily we have given unto thee a manifest victory," and on the very back of the camel he read it aloud. Some of his Companions wondered and asked if this was the victory, and the Prophet said that without any doubt it was a glorious victory. ‡ Omar and others reminded the Prophet of his promise to enter Mecca unmolested and unopposed, to which he replied that God had promised that indeed; continuing he said: But when did He promise that it should be in that very year?

Effects of the treaty of Hodaibiya.

Subsequent events did, however, evidently prove that the peace at Hodaibiya was the Prophet's glorious victory over the Meccans: By virtue of the Treaty every individual, each family, clan or tribe was at liberty to side with the Prophet, to profess his creed, to influence others to acknowledge him as his spiritual leader, to offer prayers in accordance with his teachings without any risk of persecution from the unbelievers, who were now powerless to ill treat them or to put a ban on them. Every Moslem was now at liberty to have free intercourse with non-Moslems. Thus mutual friendly relations having been re-established, peace and tranquility was restored by virtue of the Treaty.

صفحه ۱۵۷ کا بقایا مضمون :—

فی سیرة ابن هشام قال فکان عمر یقول مازلت اتصدق و اصوم و اصلي من الذي صنعت یومئذ مخافة کلامی الذي تکلمت به —

ترجمه—سیرة ابن هشام مین هے که حضرت عمر کها کرتے تهے که جو فعل مجهه سے بروز حدیبیه سرزد هوا اوسکے خوفسے مین همیشه صدقے دیتا رها اور صوم و صلوة ادا کرتا رها (تاریخ احمدي ص ۵٦)

‡ Habib-al-Siyar; Tazhkirat-al-Kirám,

In a considerably short time the whole of Hejáz was sounding with the praise of the Prophet who was helping them out of the oblivion of heathenism to the blissful light of Monotheism. Islam was now making steady progress throughout the land. There was no man of sense and judgement amongst the idolators, who did not entertain a deep consideration to the dictates of the Prophet. Immediately after the Treaty, the Bani Khozá'a, who for a long time were inclined to the new Faith, entered openly into an alliance with the Prophet. This was the first practical result of the Treaty. In short, within two years after the Treaty, the Divine Mission of Mohammed proved much more successful than it had hitherto been during the nineteen years of his apostolic career. This was all the glorious result of the Peace, which was considered dishonorable, humiliating and lowering the standard of the Divine religion—the same Treaty, which, in spite of his chief Companions' remonstrances, the Prophet unhesitatingly concluded with the Meccans.

بلغ العلى بكماله صلوا عليه و آله

Obviously it was the result of the same Treaty that two years later he was followed by ten thousand men in the Conquest of Mecca, while on the present occasion he could have brought with him not more than about only one and a half thousand followers. A great victory it was indeed, surpassing all others in its far-reaching effects. Without fighting and bloodshed, it made the infidels yield and recognize the once abused, persecuted and banished Mohammed as an independent Power, with whom they concluded a Treaty, giving him the right of occupying the following year, their city for three days undisturbed.

CHAPTER XIII.

Embassies to Foreign Countries; the Khaibar campaign; Omratal Qadza and other important events ending with the seventh year of Hegira.

Foreign Countries invited to Islam.
7. A. H.

With the Treaty at Hodaibiya, the Prophet got rid of the troubles from the Meccans; he was now able to direct his attention to a more wide-spread propaganda of his religion, the chief object of his Divine Mission. He, therefore, determined to invite the surrounding States and Empires to the Divine Faith by sending embassies with despatches from him. As the despatches, unless attested by a Seal, were not recognized by foreign courts, the Prophet, at the close of the sixth year of Hegira, had a ring made of silver with the words "Mohammed the Apostle of God," engraved thereon. Letters were written and sealed, and in the beginning of the seventh year, in the month of Moharram, six embassies were simultaneously despatched: to Najáshi, the king of Etheopia; to Yamáma; to Chosroes, the monarch of Persia; to Cæsar, the Roman Emperor; to Syria, and to Egypt. The messengers, selected to convey the despatches, could speak the language of the country to which they were deputed.

Amr b. Omyya was sent to Abyssinia with two despatches—one purporting to invite the king of Etheopia to the Divine religion; and in the second despatch the Prophet desired that the emigrants, remaining still in Abyssina, might now be sent back to Medina, adding a singular request that the King would betroth to the Prophet Omm Habiba, the widow of Obeidalláh, who had migrated there and subsequently died. The King received the embassy with utmost hospitality and replied to the first despatch in terms of humble acquiescence, giving assurance of his having already embraced Islam, and expressing his regret not to be able to attend in person to

7 A. H

receive the blessings of the Prophet. In compliance with the other despatch, the King performed the betrothal ceremony of Omm Habiba as desired, and provided two ships for the return of the emigrants headed by Ja'far, who reached Medina during the Autumn of 7 A. H. in the month of Jamádi I or August 628 A. D.

Salit b. Amr was sent to Yamáma with a despatch to Hauzha, the Christian Chief of the Bani Hanifa. He received the embassy with cordiality and praised the Prophet;but at last dismissed the messenger with a reply that he was ready to follow the Prophet, if he only made him a partner of his privileges, because, he added, he already enjoyed reverence as lord and orator of his people, being an eloquent poet of his tribe.

Abdallàh b. Hozháfa took the despatch to Persia. When it was delivered to Chosroes, the King, and its contents read over to him, he tore it into pieces. The messenger returned and reported to the Prophet. He prayed, "Likewise, O God ! Rend Thou his Kingdom from him." It happened, a few years later, that the Persian dominions were torn entirely to pieces. Chosroes sent orders to his governor of Yemen to restore the Prophet to his right mind, or to send him in chains to the Royal Court. Bázhán, the Persian governor of Yemen, thereupon sent a courteous despatch to the Prophet, who, on receipt of the despatch, smiled and invited the ambassador to Islam, telling him that Chosroes was no more alive, that only last night he had been stabbed by his son, the heir-apparant. The Prophet bade the ambassador go back to tell the tale to his master and to ask him to tender his submission to the Apostle of God. The ambassador went back and reported this to Bázhán, who in the meantime had received despatches from the new Emperor. Either convinced by the prophecy or actuated by motives of self interest, he signified his adhesion to the Prophet and embraced Islam, denouncing the authority of the Persian Emperor.

Dehya Kalbi, who was sent to Emperor Heraclius, the Christian monarch of the Roman empire, was received by the Emperor with respect. The Emperor appeared inclined to the new Faith; but after ascertaining the views of his courtiers, who were indifferent to it, he dismissed the ambassador with some valuable presents for the Prophet.

Shujá' b. Wahab was sent to Syria with a letter inviting Hárith VII, Prince of the Bani Ghassán, to Islam. He was very angry on reading the contents of the letter, which he forwarded to Emperor Heraclius, asking his permission to send an expedition to chastise its author. The messenger was detained. On receipt of a reply from the emperor, who did not approve of the suggestion, Hárith dismissed the messenger with some presents. The Prophet, on being informed of the attitude of Hárith, said that his kingdom had gone from him, and a short time after it was known that Hárith was dead.

† Hátib b. Abi Balta'a was the ambassador to Alexandria, the seat of the government of Egypt. Maqawqas, the Roman viceroy, received the embassy with profound respect, read the letter and wrote in answer promising to give consideration to it. He wrote that he knew that a Prophet was yet to arise, but he expected his appearance from Syria. To give substantial proof of his respectful feelings, he dismissed the messenger with several presents for the Prophet; among which were two young and beautiful Coptic (the race to which Maqawqas himself belonged) sister girls. One of them was named Mary, who had the honor of being married to the Prophet; the other named Sirin was given to Hassán the peot; a white mule, which was a rarity in Arabia, was also among the presents. The mule was named Duldul. It was used by the Prophet and after his death by his grandson Hosain.

---

† Tárikh-al-Khamis; Habib-al-Siyar; Tabari.

Since after his immigration to Medina, the Jews, as already observed, were jealous of the evergrowing power and authority of the Prophet and were constantly giving him trouble; most of them were consequently expelled. A party of the Banu Nadzir Jews, having been expelled from Medina, had settled among their brethren at Khaibar, about 96 Arabian miles or 8 stages north-east of Medina. They formed an alliance with several powerful Bedouin tribes and instigated them as well as the Qoreish of Mecca against the Prophet and unsuccessfully besieged Medina at the close of the year before last.

Causes of the Khaibar campaign.

After their retreat, their chief, Abul Haqiq, who had taken a prominent part in the siege of Medina, along with Hoyay b. Akhtab, incited the Bani Fezára and other Bedouin tribes to raid the property of the peaceful citizens of Medina. In Rabi' I, of the sixth year of Hegira, Oyaina, the Chief of the Bani Fezára, had fallen upon the milch camels of the Prophet and taken off the whole herd, killing the keeper and carrying away his wife as a prisoner. In Rabi' II, of the same year, the Banu Ghatafán likewise, were gathering for the purpose of carrying away from the pasture grounds the camels belonging to Medina. Mohammed b. Maslama was deputed with ten men to check their attempts. All his men were slain and he himself was so severely wounded that he was left for dead and subsequently escaped. About Ramadzán, 6 A. H. Abul Haqiq reached the end of his life His successor Osair b. Zárim, together with the Bani Ghatafán, the Bedouin allies of the Jews of Khaibar, was reported in Shawwál, 6 A. H. to be designing fresh movements against the Prophet and his followers.

Expedition against the Jews of Khaibar.

By virtue of the Hodaibiya treaty the Meccans, who were the most formidable enemies of the Prophet and the most powerful allies of the Jews, were cut off from assisting the Jews in their hostilities against the Prophet. Providence had thus furnished the Apostle of the Lord with an opportune chance to put to an end the troubles from the Jews of Khaibar. In Moharram 7 A. H. he, therefore, undertook an expedition against them with 1600 strong. Reaching Sahbá, he found several ways in different directions. Engaging, however, a guide, the army proceeded on to Khaibar, marching in the night and halting during the day. On their way they met a man, who was suspected and who afterwards confessed to be a spy. On promise to spare his life, he stated that the Jews had already received tidings of the Prophet's intention to avenge the wrongs done to his men and that they had sought succour from their Bedouin allies, of whom Oyaina had already arrived with his force, and the Banu Ghatafán were expected shortly. When the Prophet reached Raji', a place between Khaibar and the habitations of the Bani Ghatafán, he ordered halt. The Bani Ghatafán, who were by this time ready to go out to assist their allies at Khaibar, finding their own home in danger, held back (*Tabari*). Leaving a contingent at Raji', the Prophet moved forward and surprised the Jews of Khaibar at their doors early one morning with fourteen hundred of his followers, including about two hundred mounted soldiers. The Jews, issuing forth in the morning from their houses, were struck with dismay on finding themselves confronted all of a sudden with so large a force.

Sorties of the Jews.

The valley of Khaibar was studded with fortresses strongly situated on rocky hillocks, which numbered about ten, and some of them such a Al-Qamus, Al-Qatieba, Al-Watih and Solálim were deemed impregnable. Outside help was now impossible. The Jews, counting upon their numbers—far greater than that of the comparatively small horde of the enemy—upon their valour as well as upon their strongholds, resolved to resist. But, when besieged in any of their citadels, they could not resist longer and eventually evacuated it after one or two sorties. Thus all the inferior fortresses, with which the Moslems had begun their attacks, fell one after the other into their hands.

7 A. H.

At last the Jews rallied round their Chief, the king of their nation, named Kinána, son of Al Rabi' and grandson of Abul Haqiq. He lived in a strongly fortified citadel of Khaibar named Al-Qamus, having high and frowning walls, built on a steep rock which was deemed impregnable and was well defended by outworks and well guarded by brave soldiers, as it contained his treasures. As soon as the Prophet happened to cast a glance at the fortification, he first of all offered prayers to the All-powerful Lord, supplicating successful delivery of the citadel into the hands of the Moslems; and as long as he remained encamped before it, he used to offer prayers daily over a great stony rock named Mansela, and made daily seven circuits round it. A mosque was in after times erected at the spot in memory of the Prophet's worshipping place, and it became an object of veneration to the pious Moslems.

Khaibar citadel

The siege of Al-Qamus was the most trying task for the Moslems, who had never before forced their way into such a stronghold. It lasted for some time and tried the skill and patience of the Moslems, who had fallen short of provisions, and the country all around was laid waste by the Jews during the period—about a month—when they were engaged in storming the minor fortresses. The Jews had destroyed even their date palms round their citadel to starve the enemy; and, having resolved to fight desperately, they had posted themselves in front of the citadel. The besiegers attempted to force their approach, but every attack was repulsed. *The Prophet, who was during these days suffering badly with headache, handed over his Standard to Abubekr b. Abu Qoháfa directing him to lead the assault, but he was vigorously repulsed by the Jews and forced to retreat. Next the Prophet sent his

The siege of the citadel

* في تاريخ ابي الفدا خرج رسول الله صلعم فى منتصف المحرم منها الي خيبر (الى ان قال) و ربما كانت تاخذه صلعم الشقيقة فلما نزل خيبر اخذته فاخذ ابو بكر الصديق الراية فقاتل قتالا شديدا ثم رجع

men headed by Omar b. Al-Khattáb carrying his standard, but the result was no better than a forced † retreat. The soldiers, coming back to the Prophet, charged ¶their leader, Omar, with want of courage, while Omar blamed them of their cowardice. The Prophet, having thus been disappointed by the failure of his most prominent Companions, exclaimed: "‡Tomorrow I shall hand over my Flag to one who loves God and His prophet, and who is the beloved of the Lord and His prophet, a fearful constant charger who never turns his back upon a foe; at his hands the Lord will give victory." Every one of the Prophet's chief Companions was anxious to be signalized on the morrow as the

---

فاخذها عمر بن الخطاب فقاتل فتالا اشد من الاول ثم رجع فاخبر ذلک رسول الله صلی الله علیه و سلم فقال اما والله لاعطین الرایة غداً رجلاً یحب الله و رسوله و یحبه الله و رسوله کرار غیر فرار یاخذها عنوة فتطاول المهاجرون والانصار الیها فجاء علی و هو رمد قد عصب عینیه فقال له صلعم لدن مني فدني منه فتفل فی عینیه فزال وجعها ثم اعطاه الرایة—

ترجمه—علامه ابوالفدا اپنی تاریخ مین لکھتے هین که پیغمبر صاحب وسط محرم مین غزوه خیبر کیلئے نکلے تھے اور آنحضرت کو کبھی کبھی درد شقیقه عارض هوجاتا تھا - اتفاقاً جسروز خیبر پهونچے اوسروز بھی شکایت مذکوره لاحق هوگئي پس حضرت ابو بکر نے علم لیکر شدید مقاتله کیا لیکن بے نیل مرام واپس آے پھر حضرت عمر علم لیکر گئے اور پهلے سے زیاده جدال و قتال کے بعد لوٹ آئے - جب پیغمبر صاحب کو ان حالات کی اطلاع هوئي تو آنحضرت نے فرمایا که بخدا مین کل ایسے شخص کو علم دونگا جو خدا و رسول کو دوست رکھتا هے اور خدا و رسول اوسکو دوست رکھتے هین وه پے در پے حملے کرنیوالا هے بھاگنے والا نهین هے اور وه ثابت قدمي کیساتھه فتح کریگا—

---

† Tabari; Sirat Mohammediya; Rawdzat-al-Ahbáb; Tárikh-al-Khamis.

¶ Tabari; Sirat Mohammediya.

‡ Wáqidi; Bokhári; Muslim; Ahmad b. Hanbal, Nasái, Tirmizhi; Tabari; Ibn Athir; Suyuti etc.

7 A. H.

'beloved of God and His prophet.' They passed the night in great anxiety as to which one was to prove the blessed being. No one thought of Ali, the cousin and the vicegerent of the Prophet, the hero of all previous wars, because he was badly suffering with sore eyes and could not see anything. Some † traditions say that he was absent from the Camp on this occasion, being at the time in Medina. The Prophet, however, saying Nád-i-Ali called Ali, who appeared on the scene with his eyes badly sore. The longed for morning dawned with the twinkling stars round the Prophet, each gleaming to be particularly taken notice of. Sa'd b. Abi Waqqás, to invite attention specially towards him, threw himself over the ground, pretending to have fallen and then got up. But the Prophet appeared not to take notice of any particular individual. When he broke up silence and asked for Ali, all of them with one voice answered that he was badly suffering with the sore eyes, and that he was utterly unable to look around. The Prophet commanded them to bring him. Selma b. Ako'

یہ سنکر مہاجرین و انصار حصول رایت کے متمني ہوے اتنے مین حضرت علی آے جنکي آنکھین آشوب کي ہوئي تہین - پیغمبر صاحب نے اونکو اپنے پاس بلایا اور آب دہن مبارک اونکي آنکھو نمین لگایا جسکے لگاتے ہي درد چشم زائل ہوگیا اور آنحضرت نے اونکو علم عطا فرمایا —

اخرج النسای في الخصائص عن ابي بريدة قال حاصرنا خيبر فاخذ الراية ابو بكر و لم يفتح له فاخذه من الغد عمر فانصرف و لم يفتح له و اصاب الناس شدة و جهد فقال رسول الله صلعم اني دافع لوائی غداً الى رجل يحب الله و رسوله و يحبه الله و رسوله لا يرجع حتى يفتح له و بتناطيبة انفسنا ان الفتح غدا فلما اصبح رسول الله صلى الله عليه وسلم صلي الغداة ثم جاء قائما و دعا باللواء فهامنا انسان له منزلة عند رسول الله صلى الله عليه و سلم الا وهو يرجو ان يكون صاحب اللواء فدعا علي بن ابيطالب رضي الله عنه و هو رمد فتفل و مسح فی عینیه فدفع اليه اللواء —

ترجمہ — کتاب الخصائص مین ابو بریدہ سے روایت ہے کہ جب ہم لوگون نے قلعہ خیبر کا محاصرہ کیا تو حضرت ابوبکر علم لیکر گئے مگر

†Ṭabari; Madárijal-Nabowat; Tárikh-al-Khamis; Rawdzat-al Ahbáb.

fetched him hand in hand. The Prophet, ‡ taking Ali's head into his lap, applied the saliva of his mouth to his eyes. Instantaneously his eyes got so clear as if he had never suffered from the disease. It is said that throughout his life he never had the trouble again after this event.

Ali specially deputed to conquer.

The Prophet ¶ confided his sacred Banner into the hands of Ali, armed him with his sword the Zhulfiqar, and thus designated him the man whom God and His prophet loved. He directed Ali to lead the assualt and to fight till the Jews acknowledged submission. Ali, clad in a scarlet vest over which was buckled a cuirass of steel, issued forth with his followers and scrambling up the great stony rock in front of the fortress planted the †Standard over its top, resolved never to recede until the citadel was taken.

بغیر فتح کے واپس آے - پھر دوسرے دن حضرت عمر علم لیکر گئے وہ بھی بے نیل مرام لوٹ آے اور مسلمانون کو شدید محنت و تکلیف اُٹھانی پڑی پس پیغمبر صاحب نے فرمایا کہ کل مین ایسے شخص کو علم دونگا جو خدا اور اُسکے رسول کو دوست رکھتا ھے اور خدا و رسول اُوسکو دوست رکھتے ھین وہ بغیر فتح کئے واپس نہ آئگا - یہہ سنکر ھملوگون نے اس خوشی مین رات بسر کی کہ کل روز فتح ھے - جب صبح ھوئی تو رسول مقبول بعد فراغ نماز تشریف لاکر کھڑے ھوے اور علم کو منگایا اوسوقت ھر صحابی مقرب اسی فکر و تمنا مین تھا کہ علم اوسیکو ملے - اتنے مین پیغمبر صاحب نے علی کو بلایا اونکو آشوب چشم کی شکایت لاحق تھی آنحضرت نے آب دھن مبارک ھاتھہ مین لیکر اونکی آنکھونپر پھیرا اور اونھي کو علم عطا فرمایا (تاریخ احمدي ص ٥٨)

فی سیرۃ ابن ھشام قال رسول اللہ صلعم لاعطین الرایۃ غداً رجلاً یحب اللہ و رسولہ یفتح اللہ علی یدیہ لیس بفرار فدعا رسول اللہ صلعم علیا و ھو رمد فتفل فی عینیہ ثم قال خذ ھذہ الرایۃ فامض بھا حتی یفتح اللہ علیک —

‡ Ibn Hishám; Tabari; Nasái; Abul Fida etc.

¶ Ibn Hishám; Tabari etc.

† Ibn Hishám; Tabari; Rawdzat-al-Safá; Tárikh-al-Khamis.

The Jews sallied forth to drive down the assailants. *A Jewish monk asked Ali his name, which he gave out as Ali b. Abi Tálib or Haidar.‡ The Monk, hearing the name, omened his men that the assailant would not withdraw without gaining the ground. However, Harith, a Jewish champion, who had vigorously repulsed the previous attacks, stepped forward and slew several of his Moslem antagonists. Perceiving this, Ali himself advanced and, in hand to hand fight with him, slew him and came back to his lines. The brother of Hárith was a man of gigantic

---

ترجمہ—سیرۃ ابن ہشام مین ہے کہ جناب رسالتمآب نے فرمایا کہ کل مین ایسے شخص کو علم عطا کرونگا جو خدا اور اُسکے رسول کو دوست رکھتا ہے اور جسکے ہاتھون پر خدا نے فتح مقرر کی ہے اور وہ بھاگنے والا نہین ہے چنانچہ دوسرے دن پیغمبر صاحب نے حضرت علی کو طلب فرمایا اونکی آنکھین آشوب کی ہوی تھین - رسول مقبول نے آب دہن مبارک اونکی آنکھون مین لگاکر فرمایا کہ اس رایت کو لیکر جاو اور جنگ کرو تا اینکہ خدا تم کو فتح دے—(تاریخ احمدی ص ٥٩)

* درمدارج النبوۃ است کہ پس علی علم بر گرفتہ روان شدو بہ پاے حصار قموص آمد و علم را بر تودہ از سنگریزہ کہ دران جا بود بزد - یکے از احبار یہود کہ بلاے حصار بود پرسید کہ اے صاحب علم تو کیستی - گفت منم علی بن ابیطالب پس ان یہودي باقوم خویش گفت سوگند بہ توریت کہ شما مغلوب شدید این مرد فتح ناکردہ بر نہ خواہد گشت-ظاہرا آن راہب صفات علي و شجاعت وے را میدانست کہ در توریت وصف اورا خواندہ بود-

پس اول کسیکہ از حصار بیرون آمد حارث یہودي بود برادرمرحب کہ سنان نیزہ وے سہ من بود آمد و بہ جنگ پیوست و چند نفر را از اہل اسلام شہید ساخت-پس علي مرتضی بر سر اوراند و بیک ضرب وے را بہ دوزخ فرستاد-مرحب چون بر قتل برادر واقف شد باجماعہ از شجعان خیبر اسلحہ پوشیدہ در صدد انتقام بیرون آمد-گویند کہ وے درمیان خیبریان مبارزے بود بغایت دلاور بلند بالا و تناور و در شجاعت و مبارزت از میان ابطال این اہل بطلان ہمتانہ داشت و آنروز

‡ Zákir Hosain's Tárikh Islam Vol. II p. 122; Ibn Hishám.

stature and huge form. He was unequalled in valour among the Jews. To revenge the death of his brother, he came out, covered from his neck to the waist with a double coat of mail, having on his head a helm of proof with a double turban wound round it, and set with a stone in the middle for protection from the stroke of a scymitar. He had a huge sword girt on both his sides and brandished a big spear with triple-forked sharp pointed heads. Stepping forward from the Jewish lines, he challenged his adversaries to single combat. "I am Marhab," he cried, "as all Khaibar knoweth, a warrior bristling with arms in a furiously raging war." None among the Moslems could dare come forward to confront him. †Ali himself advanced from the Moslem line in response to his vainglorious challenge saying, انا الذی سمتنی امی حیدره + ضرغام آجام ولیث قسوره "I am he whom his mother named Haidara, a lion of the wilderness; I weigh my foes in a gigantic balance (*i.e.* I make short work of my enemies)." Ali's words were not meaningless. Ali knew, through inspiration, that Marhab had lately dreamt of a rugged lion tearing him to pieces; so he reminded Marhab of the dream in order to overawe him. The words had their effect; as when the two combatants accosted each other, Ali measured him with the eye and found him wavering. As they closed, Marhab made a thrust at Ali with his three-pronged lance, which Ali dexterously warded off, and before he could recover.

دو زره پوشیده بود و دو شمشیر حمائل کرده و دو عمامه بر سر بسته و خودے بر بالاے این نهاده و رجز گویان در معرکۂ جنگ در آمد و هیچ‌کس را از اهل اسلام طاقت نه شد که باوے معارضه نماید و درمیدان قتال در آید - پس علی مرتضی رضوان الله علیه نیز رجزے خواند و مقابل وے شد- مرحب پیشدستی نموده خواست که تیغے بر سر علی زند پس امیر کبیر سبقت جسته ذوالفقار بر سر آن ملعون غدار فرود آورده چنانکه از سر و خود و دستارش گذشته تا بحلق و بروایتے تا به رانهاے وے و بروایتے تا به قابوس زین او رسید و دو نیم ساخت -پس اهل

† Tárikh al-Khamis; Sirat Mohammediya.

himself, Ali dealt him a blow with his irresistible scymitar, the Zhulfiqár, which divided his buckler, passed through his doubled turban, through the helm of proof and skull; cleaving his head went down to his chest or down to his saddle, as some ¶ traditions say, severing him in twain. He fell lifeless to the ground and the winner announced his victory by his usual shout "Allah-o-Akbar," *i.e.*, Great is the All powerful Lord. And every one knew that Ali was victorious.

Ali's superhuman feats of Prowess.

The Moslems now rushed forward in a body and there was a melee. Seven of the Jews' most distinguished warriors *viz.* Marhab, Antar, Rabi', Dzajij, Dáud, Morra and Yásir, having fallen by Ali's sword the Jews retreated into the citadel with the Moslems hotly in pursuit. In the heat of the battle a Jew dealt a blow on Ali's arm severing his shield, which fell to the ground and another Jew ran away with it. † Ali being enraged, performed superhuman feats of prowess; he jumped over a trench, approached the iron gate of the fortress, wrenched a gate off its hinges and used it as a buckler through the remainder of the battle.

اسلام با حضرت امیر در میدان آمده دست به قتل جهودان دراز کردند و حضرت امیر هفت کس از رؤساے شجعان یهود را به قتل آورد و باقي ایشان هزیمت نموده روے به قلعه آوردند- وے رضی الله عنه در عقب ایشان میرفت؛ در این حالت یکے از مخالفان ضربے بردست مبارک وے زد چنانچه سپر از دست بر زمین افتاد- یهودي دیگر سپر را بزده رو بگریز نهاد- حضرت امیر در غضب آمد و یک حالتے از عالم قدرت ربانی بقوت روحانی وارد شد که از خندق جستے نموده بر دروازه حصار افتاد و یک در آهنی حصار را بر کند و سپر خود ساخت و به جنگ پیوست—

¶ Madárij-al-Nabowat etc.

† Ibn Hishám; Ibn Athir; Abul Fida; Tárikh-al-Khamis; Rawdzat-al-Ahbab.

*Abu Ráfe', one of those who stormed the fort with Ali, testifies that, after the war, he examined the gate and tried with seven other persons to turn it over but the attempt failed. The citadel was captured and the victory was decisive. The Jews lost ninety three men, while on the Moslem side only nineteen were killed throughout the campaign.

Ali's services appreciated.

† After capturing the citadel when Ali came back victorious to his Camp, the Prophet, seeing him coming, came out of his tent with open arms to receive him. Warmly embracing Ali, the Prophet kissed his brow and declared that his services to the Divine Cause were appreciated by the Almighty Judge as well as by himself His prophet.

---

* في سيرة ابن هشام و تاريخ الكامل و تاريخ ابى الفدا عن ابى رافع قال خرجنا مع علي بن ابيطالب رضى الله تعالي عنه حين بعثه رسول الله صلعم برايته فلما دنا من الحصن خرج اليه اهله فقاتلهم فضربه رجل من يهود فطرح ترسه من يده فتناول على عليه السلام بابا كان عند الحصن فترس به عن نفسه فلم يزل فى يده و هو يقاتل حتى فتح الله عليه ثم القاه من يده حين فرغ فلقد رايتنى فى نفر سبعة معي انا ثامنهم نجهد على ان نقلب ذلك الباب فما نقلبه —

ترجمه — سيرة ابن هشام اور تاريخ كامل ابن اثير اور تاريخ ابوالفدا مين ابو رافع سے مروي هے كه جب پيغمبر صاحب نے حضرت علی كو علم ديكر خيبريون سے جنگ كے لئے بهيجا تو هم بهى اونكي معيت مين تهے پس جسوقت حضرت علی قتال كرتے هوے قريب قلعه پهونچے ايک يهودي نے حضرت علی كے دست مبارک پر ايسي ضرب لگائی كه ڈهال هاتهه سے گر گئي - آپنے فوراً ايک دروازه باب خيبر كا كهينچ ليا اور اوسكو بجاے سپر هاتهه مين ليكر قتال كرنے لگے حتي كه خدا نے آپكو فتح نمايان عطا فرمائی - پهر جنگ سے فارغ هونيكے بعد آپنے اوس دروازه قلعه كو هاتهه سے پهينكديا اور وه اسقدر بهاري تها كه هم آتهه آدمی ملكر اوسكو كسيطرح ادهر سے اودهر پلٹ نه سكے - (تاريخ احمدي صفحه ٦١)

† Madárijal Nabowat; Rawdzat-al-Ahbáb; Rawdzat-al-Safá; Ma'árij-al-Nabowat; Habib-al-Siyar.

7 A. H

Ali shed tears of joy at the intelligence. *The Apostle revived their* (his followers, who had unsuccessfully retreated in previous attempts) *faith by the example of Ali, on whom he bestowed the surname of the Lion of God.*" Gibbon, D. & F. of Roman Empire Vol. V. p. 365.

Surrender of the Jews.

‡ After the defeat, the fortress surrendered on condition that the inhabitants were free to leave the country, giving up their whole property to the conqueror, taking each one camel load of food stuffs with him. Concealment of the valuables was to be deemed an infraction of the conditions, and the violator was liable to capital punishment. People preferring to live in the country might occupy and reside in the houses possessed by them, and might cultivate the land in their occupancy, but no immoveable property was to be owned by them, they being treated as tenants bound to cede half of their products to the conqueror, who may put them to exile at his will and pleasure.

Kinana.

Kinána, the Chief of the Jews, was suspected of having concealed his treasure, which, in spite of a careful search, could not be discovered. He was, at last, asked what had become of the vessels of gold, which he used to lend to the people of Mecca. He protested that all his wealth had been expended in the subsistence of his army. He was then told that his life would be at stake if anything was discovered. He agreed to this. Subsequently one of his traitorous friends revealed the place where a great amount of Kinána's wealth was deposited. When it was discovered, Kinána was †delivered up to the vengeance of a Moslem named Mohammed b. Maslama whose brother Mahmud b. Maslama, he had curshed to death by hurling ove r him a mill stone. The Moslem struck off his head with one stroke of his scymitar.

Safiya.

Kinánas' wife Safiya, the daughter of the Nadzirite chief Hoyay b. Akhtab, embraced Islam and was married to the Prophet. She most readily and cheerfully enjoyed her new position,

‡ Abul Fida. † Tabari.

which she expected, as a matter of fact, since she had dreamt of the moon falling form the heavens into her lap, and on relating the dream to her husband, Kinána had upbraided her violently with coveting the embrace of the Prophet of Hejáz. She bore the mark of a bruise upon her eyelid caused by Kinána's striking her when she had narrated the dream to him.

Attempt at poisoning the Prophet.

While the Prophet was at Khaibar, an attempt at his life was made by a Jewess, who dressed a lamb, poisoned it with a deadly poison and sent it as a present when the evening repast was being served to the prophet. Thankfully accepting the gift, the Prophet took the shoulder (the part which he loved most to eat) of the lamb for himself, took out another portion and gave it to Bishr, who sat next him, and likewise passed it on to others who were sitting with him, at the meal. As soon as the Prophet took a mouthful of the meat, he felt an unusual taste and at once spat it forth saying that it was poisoned. † Bishr had in the meantime swallowed some of it and at once fell down and expired, without even stirring his limbs. All was confusion now. On diligent inquiry it was found that the lamb was cooked by a female captive named Zainab, niece of Marhab, the great warrior slain by Ali. She was summoned and interrogated as to the motive of the crime. She avowed it, vindicating it as justifiable revenge for the loss of her father, brother and husband and other relatives and for the devastations the conqueror had brought upon her country. She said that she thought within herself that if Mohammed was a true Prophet he would discover the mischief before any harm was done to him, and if he was a mere pretender, he would fall a victim to her vengeance and the Jews would be delivered from the tyrant. She was put to death.

Fadak.

After the conquest of Al-Qamus, the remaining strongholds capitulated and their lands were subjected to a tax of half of the produce.

† Bishr b. al Bará b. Ma'rur, an Ansár of the tribe of Khazraj. He was present at Aqaba, Bedr and Ohod.

7 A. H.

* Ali was sent to Fadak, a Jewish town not far from Khaibar to take it. † But, before the use of any force, the inhabitants tendered their submission, ceding half of their property to the Prophet. When the Angel Gabriel revealed to the Prophet the Divine command as in verse 28 of *Sur. XVII*, "And give unto one who is of kin (to thee) that which is due," he asked as to who was meant as 'being of kin.' The Angel named Fátema and told the Prophet to give Fadak to Fátema, as the income from Fadak $ belonged wholly to him on account of its being ceded to him without use of force. The Prophet accordingly bestowed upon Fátema ‡ his estate of Fadak for the subsistence of herself and her children. They appropriated the income from the sale of its produce till the

---

* في الدرالمنثور للسيوطى اخرج البزار و ابو يعلي و ابن ابى حاتم عن ابي سعيد الخدري قال لما نزلت هذه الاية و آت ذا القربى حقه دعا رسول الله صلعم فاطمة فاعطاها فدک - و عن ابن عباس قال لمانزلت وات ذاالقربي حقه اقطع رسول الله صلعم فاطمة فدكا —

ترجمه — تفسير در منثور سيوطي مين هے كه بزار اور ابويعلي اور ابن ابى حاتم نے ابو سعيد خدري سے روايت كى هے كه جب آيه وات ذا القربي حقه نازل هوا تو رسول الله صلعم نے فدک كي جائداد حضرت فاطمه كو مرحمت فرمائي - نيز ابن عباس سے مروي هے كه جب آيه وات ذاالقربي حقه نازل هوا تو پيغمبر صاحب نے فدک كى جائداد حضرت فاطمه كو عطا كي — نيز ملاحظه هو معارج النبوة — روضة الصفا - حبيب السير وغيره

قال ابوالفدا و كان فتح خيبر فى صفر سنة سبع للهجرة و سال اهل خيبر رسول الله صلعم الصلح على ان يساقيهم على النصف من ثمارهم و يخرجهم متى شاء ففعل ذلک و فعل مثل ذلک اهل فدک و كانت خيبر للمسلمين و كانت فدک خاصة لرسول الله لانها فتحت بغير ايجاف خيل —

ترجمه — مورخ ابوالفدا اپنى تاريخ مين لكهتا هے كه خيبر ماه صفر

---

† Madárij-al Nabowat; Ma'árij-al-Nabowat; Maqsad-i-Aqsa.

$ Ibn Hishám; Tabari; Mawáhib Ladunnia; Zarqáni; Abul Fida.

‡ Kanzalámmál Ali Muttaqi.

time when it was confiscated by Caliph Abubekr, soon after the death of the Prophet. It remained as State property until it was granted ¶ to Marwán by Caliph Othman in 34 A. H., and it continued to be the Jaghyr of the Omyyads until it was || restored by Caliph Omar b. Abd-al-Aziz to Imám Mohammed Báqir, son of Ali b. Hosain, the then head of the Fátemites, as the rightful owner of the property. The other half of Fadak remained in possession of the Jews till Caliph Omar turned them out to Syria paying them compensation.

Arrival of Ja'far.

† While the Prophet was at Khaibar, Ja'far, Ali's brother, having returned from Abyssinia, went out together with his wife Asmá bint Omais and five other exiles to see the Prophet, and reached Khaibar on the day of its conquest. The Prophet was much pleased to welcome back his cousin after so long a separation, and joyfully exclaimed that he did not know which of the two incidents—Ja'far's arrival or the conquest of Khaibar—delighted him most. He proposed that the new arrivals should be treated as a party of the men of the Campaign and the army cheerfully accepted the proposal and they were admitted to share in the booty of the war.

Abu Horeira.

A young man apparently a mendicant, appearing before the Prophet at Khaibar, embraced Islam. He was named Abu Horeira. He never went back to his home; came back to Medina

---

سنه ۷ هجري مين فتح هوا اور اهل خيبر نے پيغمبر صاحب سے اس شرط پر صلح کرنی چاهي که اونکو اونکے باغات کے پهل نصف ملا کرين اور آنحضرت جب چاهين اونکو خارج البلد کردين چنانچه اونکی درخواست منظور کرلی گئی اور ايساهي معامله اهل فدک کے ساتهه بهی طے پايا خيبر کی آمدنی عام مسلمانون کيلے تهي اور فدک کی خاص رسول الله کيلے کيونکه وه بغير حرب و ضرب کے فتح هوا—(تاريخ احمدي ص ٦٥)

¶ Rawdzat-al Nátzirin Ibn Abi Shahna.

|| Sunan Abi Dáud.

† Rawdzat-al-Ahbáb; Zarqáni.

7 A. H.

when the Prophet returned thereto and was accommodated with the men of Suffa, *i.e.* the men who lived in the rooms alloted to the poor, adjoining the great mosque of the Prophet. Till the death of the Prophet he remained with him. Afterwards he was a favourite of the Caliphs till he became a courtier of Mo'áwiya, who at last appointed him a Governor. He is a great authority with the majority of the Sunni Moslems, being, it is said, a reporter of no less than 5,374 traditions, which he is accredited with having heard from the Prophet and committed to his memory, during about four years of his stay with him. In this respect Abu Horeira excels the men who lived throughout almost the whole prophetic career of the Prophet with him, but could not remember even a thousand traditions.

The Prophet at Wadi-al-Qora.

† After the conquest of Khaibar, the Prophet, proceeding to Wádi-al-Qora, laid siege to the Jewish town, which, after a resistence of one or two days in which eleven Jews were killed, surrendered. The Jews of Taimá also tendered their submission.

Having subjugated the Jews of Khaibar and its surrounding settlements the authority of the Prophet was established over all the Jewish tribes north of Medina and the cause of constant alarm was thus removed.

Return of the Sun for Ali's prayers.

* The following incident, which occurred during this period is noteworthy: While on his march to Wádi-al-Qora from Khaibar, the Prophet halted at Sahbá, where in his tent he reposed with his head on the lap of Ali. Suddenly he felt nervous and became senseless as in the state of receiving Revelations. Ali continued sitting motionless

---

* روي الطحاوي في مشكل الاثار عن اسماء بنت عميس ان النبي صلعم صلى الظهر بالصهباء ثم ارسل عليا فى حاجته فرجع و قد صلي النبى صلعم العصر فوضع النبى صلعم راسه فى حجر علي فلم يحركه حتى غابت

† Abul Fida.

7 A. H.

till the Prophet awoke and asked Ali if he had performed his afternoon prayers. The sun had just set. Ali replying in the negative, the Prophet prayed to God for the return

---

الشمس فقال اللهم ان عبدک علياً احتبس بنفسه علي نبيک فرد عليه شرقها قالت اسماء فطلعت الشمس حتي وقعت علي الجبال و على الارض ثم قام علي فتوضا و صلى العصر ثم غابت —

ترجمه—طحاوي نے کتاب مشکل الاثار مین اسماء بنت عميس سے روايت کي هے که جب پيغمبر خدا نے مقام صهبا مين پهونچکر نماز ظهر ادا فرمائي اوسوقت علي کو ايک ضروري کام کيلئے بهيجا تها جب وه واپس آے آنحضرت نماز عصر پره چکے تهے اور حضرت علي کے آتے هي اونکے زانوپر سر رکهکر آرام فرمانے لگے تا اينکه آفتاب غروب هوگيا - حب رسول الله بيدار هوے اور اونکو معلوم هوا که حضرت علي نے نماز نهين پڑهی تو دعا کي که الهي تيرے عبد خاص علي نے تيرے نبي کے لئے ايثار نفس کيا اوسکے لئے آفتاب کو بار دگر طالع فرما - اسماء کهتے هين که ناگهان آفتاب نکلا اور اوسکی شعاع زمين اور پهاڑونپر ضيا افگن هوئي اور حضرت علی نے وضو کرکے نماز عصر پڑهی اسکے بعد آفتاب پهر غروب هوگيا - محدث دهلوي در مدارج النبوة آورده که چون آنحضرت صلعم بعد از رجوع از خيبر بمنزل صهبا رسيد نماز عصر گزارد و بعد از گزاردن نماز سر مبارک در کنار علي نهاده بخواب رفت و آثار وحي برآنحضرت ظاهر شدن گرفت حضرت علی نماز ديگر نگزارده بود و زمان وحی چنان دراز شد که آفتاب غروب کرده چون وحی منجلی گشت حضرت صلعم از علی پرسيد که نماز عصر گذاردهٔ گفت لا يا رسول الله نه گزارده ام حضرت مناجات کرد و گفت خداوندا علی در طاعت تو و طاعت رسول تو بود آفتاب را براے وے باز گردان که نماز عصر بگذارد پس حقتعالي مسالت حبيب خود را اجابت کرد و آفتاب بعد ازان که بمغرب فرو رفته بود طالع شد چنانکه شعاع آن بر کوه وهامون بتافت و خلايق براے العين مشاهده کردند و علی وضوکرده نماز گزارد -(تاريخ احمدي ص ٦٣)

فی کتاب الشفا للقاضي عياض عن اسماء بنت عميس ان النبي صلعم کان يوحي اليه و راسه في حجر علي فلم يصلی العصر حتى غربت الشمس فقال النبي صلعم اصليت يا علي قال لا فقال اللهم انه کان فی

of the sun to enable Ali to offer his prayers. ‡ Instantly the sun returned to the horizon with his brightness and stayed affording sufficient time for Ali to perform the Prayers and then went down again.

Omm Habiba.

The Prophet returned to Medina in the month of Jamádi II, 7 A. H. where he completed his marriage with Omm Habiba, daughter of Abu Sofyán, which the King of Abyssinia had contracted for her, having paid her a dowry of four hundred Dinárs. She was over thirty years of age at the time.

The Prophet's Omrat-al-Qadza.

After his return from Khaibar, the Prophet passed four or five months in Medina, when the time came for fulfilling the Omrat-al-Qadza, *i. e.* visiting Mecca to perform the rites of Omra or lesser pilgrimage, which he was debarred from performing in the previous year. The Prophet, accompanied by about two thousand followers, including all those who had last year returned with him unsuccessful from Hodaibiya, proceeded to Mecca in the month of Zhil Qa'da, 7 A. H. The Qoreish, receiving

---

طاعتک و طاعة رسولک فاردد علیه الشمس قالت اسماء فرأیتها طلعت بعد ما غربت و وقفت علی الجبال و الارض و ذلک بالصهباء من خیبر

ترجمه— شفاے قاضی عیاض مین اسماء سے روایت ہے کہ جناب رسول خدا کا سر مبارک حضرت علی کے زانوپر تہا اوسی حالتمین رسول مقبول پر وحی کا نزول هوا جسکیوجهه سے حضرت علی نماز عصر نه پڑه سکے حتی که آفتاب غروب هوگیا پس جب وه حالت نزول وحی برطرف هوئی تو جناب رسالت ماب نے حضرت علی سے پوچها که تمنے نماز عصر پڑهی ہے اونهون نے کها که نهین پڑه سکا - آنحضرت نے مناجات کی که خداوندا علی تیرے اور تیرے رسول کی اطاعت مین مصروف تها اوسکے لئے آفتاب کو بار دگر طالع فرما - اسماء کهتے هین که ناگهان مینے دیکا که آفتاب نکل آیا جسکی شعاع زمین اور پهاڑونپر پڑی اور یهه واقعه مقام صهبا کا ہے جو خیبر کی راه مین ہے —(تاریخ احمدي ص ٦٤)

‡ Tárikh-al-Khamis; Rawdzat-al-Ahbáb; Habib-al-Siyar Rawdzat-al-Safá. Ibn Hajar; Ibn Magházili; Hamwini.

intelligence of his near approach, retired, according to the stipulation, from the town to the adjoining hills; and the Prophet entered the Holy City together with his followers undisturbed. They approached the Ka'ba going round it the seven circuits, kissed the Hajar-al-Aswad and then proceeded to Safá and Marwa, where the sacrifices were made. Having shaved their heads, the ceremonies of the Omra were finished. Next day the Prophet entered the Ka'ba, directed Bilál, who ascended the Holy House and said with his loud melodious tone the Call to midday Prayers; all the Moslems assembled and the Service was performed by the Prophet under the walls of the sanctuary. This was the first Grand Moslem Congregation within the holy precincts of Ka'ba.

Maimuna.

The Prophet remained in Mecca for three days. During these days Maimuna was betrothed to him at the recommendation of his uncle Abbás. She was a widow and an elderly woman of 51 years of age. She lived with her sister Omm-al-Fadzl, the wife of Abbás. Another of her sisters, Asmá bint Omais was married to Ja'far (Ali's brother); and a third named Selma was married to Hamza. Thus three sister girls were already married in the same family. On the fourth day the Prophet left Mecca and halted in the evening at Sarif, about eight Arabian miles from Mecca, where the marriage was consummated.

CHAPTER XIV.

The Muta Expedition. The Conquest of Mecca. The battle of Honein and other important events ending with the year 8 A. H.

Conversion of Khalid b. Walid & Amr b. As. 8 A. H.

As Maimuna was associated with high circles of Meccan nobility both by birth and by family connections, the Prophet, foreseeing the increase of his influence by marrying her, had readily assented to the proposal made by his uncle Abbás and he was not disappointed. Another sister of Maimuna was married to

Walid son of Moghira, a chief among the nobles of Mecca (but an accursed infidel as referred to in the Qurán, *Sur. LXXIV*). Khálid son of Walid, a cousin of Maimuna, after her marriage to the Prophet, repaired to Medina along with his friend Amr b. As in the beginning of the eighth year of Hegira, and entered into the new Faith.† Both these men had hitherto been bitter opponents of the Prophet and his faith. Khálid had taken an active part against the Prophet in the battle of Ohod, and was a leader of unsuccesful attempts to break the line of entrenchment in the Trench Campaign. Amr b. As had often used his poetic talents to the annoyance and detriment ‡ of the Prophet. Subsequent to their conversion to Islam, both these men were famous figures in the history of Islam.

The pulpit.

¶ Hitherto the Prophet delivered his Sermons leaning upon a palm trunk driven into the ground floor of the Mosque. During the year 8 A. H., a pulpit with three steps was prepared for this purpose. Seating himself on the third or the uppermost step and placing his feet on the first or the lowest step, he now delivered the Sermons. Abubekr, when Caliph, used to sit on the second or the step in the middle, placing his feet on the first step. When Omar succeeded him, he took his seat on the first step and placed his feet on the ground floor. His successor, Othmán, followed for six years the example of his predecessor, but after six years he lifted himself up to the place where the Prophet used to sit. Mo'áwiya raised the pulpit to six steps high and took his seat on the uppermost step.

---

† Tárikh-al-Khamis; Ibn Athir; Habib-al-Siyar.

‡ "When Mohammed first announced his Mission, this youth (Amr b. As) assailed him with lampoons and humorous madrigals, which falling in with the poetic taste of the Arabs, were widely circulated, and proved greater impediments to the growth of Islamism than the bitterest persecution." *W. Irvings's Life of Mohammad p. 49.*

¶ Tárikh-al-Khamis.

Muta Campaign. 8 A. H.

‡ After his return from the pilgrimage (Omrat-al-Qadzá) to Mecca, the Prophet had been at Medina for about six months, when he received the intelligence of the murder of his messenger Hárith b. Omeir, whom he had despatched to the Governor of Bostra, with a letter inviting him to Islam. The messenger, while halting at Mūta, was killed by Sharahbil, the Chief of Ma'áb or Muta. The sad news sorely grieved the Prophet and he resolved to punish the offending Chief in order to make his ambassadors respected in future. Collecting therefore, an army of three thousand men in the month of Jamádi I, 8 A. H. or September 629 A. D., the Prophet placed a white banner in the hands of Zaid b. Háritha, his freed man as Commander, and bade him to march fast so as to surprise the people of Muta, to invite them to Islam, and if they refused to embrace Islam, to fight against them in the name of the Lord. In case of Zaid being killed in battle, he directed that Ja'far (a brother of Ali) should assume the Command, and if Ja'far also fell then Abdallah b. Rawáha was to take his place, or if Abdalláh too was killed then the army were to choose their commander from among themselves. This order proved to be a prophecy.

On reaching Ma'án, Zaid received information that the Roman emperor Heraclius was camping at Ma'áb, in the territory of Belqá, with an army of one hundred thousand men. In fact it was Theodorus, brother of Heraclius, at the head of a formidable force along with the men whom Sharahbil, on receiving the tidings of the Mohammedan invasion, had summoned to his aid from the neighbouring tribes. Zaid halted at Ma'án and for two whole days the Moslem Chiefs discussed the difficulties of their position. Many of them suggested to give information to the Prophet and to wait his instructions. Abdalláh b. Rawáha, however, opposed the

‡ Tabari; Ibn Athir; Tárikh-al-Khamis.

suggestion and urged an immediate advance. He said, "Is it our number or the help of our Lord the Almighty on which we trust? We are fighting for the Lord and we can never be losers. Victory or Martyrdom! We shall have one or the other, we must not hesitate but step forward." Encouraged by this fervid speech, they all vociferated with one voice, "By God! The son of Rawáha has spoken the truth. Let us move forward." So the army advanced.

The Disastrous plight of the Moslem army.

Approaching Muta, they found themselves face to face with the enemy. The Roman army took the offensive and the battle began. Zaid leading forward his column with the Flag in his hand fought bravely, till he was killed at the age of fifty-five. The flag was soon taken up by Ja'far, who leaped down from his horse, which he at once maimed in token that he would either conquer or die. He led forward his men to the attack but his body was soon covered with wounds. He manfully kept up fighting till some Romans closed with him and his right hand was cut off. He took the Standard with his left and when that too was lost he held the flag with the mutilated remnants of his arms. Bnt at last he received a blow on his skull and fell dead. Next Abdalláh b. Rawáha raised the Standard aloft but he too soon met the same fate. Some ninety wounds, all in front of his body, were counted when Ja'far was buried along with Zaid b. Háritha and Abdalláh b. Rawáha in one and the same grave. Já'far was only 41 years of age when killed. Then the Moslem chiefs, following the instructions of the Prophet, assembled in a hasty council and elected Khálid, who assumed the command. But the chances of a drawn battle or of achieving any success had passed away, as the ranks were already thinned and the men had lost their courage; they had already taken to flight and "the Romans in full pursuit had made great havoc amongst the fugitives." *Wackidi p.* 125½ *Muir Vol. IV p.* 100. Khálid could do no more than to draw off the shattered remains of his army from the field with as little loss as possible and to save them from destruction. He therefcre led them back straightway to Medina.

‡ As the army approached the city, people came out to meet the returning men and cast handsful of dust at their faces crying out reproachfully: "Ye runaways! ye have fled from the enemy while fighting for the Lord." Khálid, however, is said to have received the title of Saifalláh or the Sword of God on this occasion.

Omm Selma wife of the Prophet once asked the wife of Selma son of Hishám b. Moghira as to why Selma, since his return from Muta, did not come out even to offer -s with the Prophet. She was replied that the people co tease him as a runaway from Muta, so he abstained going out of his house. *Tabari.*

e Prophet's nentations.

† The incidents occurring at the battlefield were instantly known by the Prophet at Medina, and he informed the men round about him of the details of the occurences at the moment. The same day when Ja'far was killed, the Prophet went to his house and calling his children embraced them tenderly and burst into a flood of tears. Asmá, the wife of Ja'far, guessed the truth and wailed loudly so that other women gathered round her. The Prophet then came to his own family and desired them to send food to Ja'far's house, because, he said, no food will be cooked there as they were sunk in grief at the loss of Ja'far. The Prophet then proceeded to the house of Zaid and, taking Zaid's little daughter into his arms, wept until he sobbed. The girl was crying bitterly and at this sight every one was overcome. A by-stander, however, said to the Prophet, "Why so! O Apostle of God"? "This," he replied, "is the fond yearning in the heart of a friend for friend." Next morning the Prophet entered the Mosque smiling, and when the people accosted

‡ Sirat-al-Nabi Vol. ii p. 372.

† Tabari; Ibn Khaldun; Ibn Athir; Tárikh-al-Khamis; Habib-al-Siyar.

him he said, "Yesterday what you saw in me was on account of grief for the massacre of my Companions, but later I saw them in Paradise comfortably lodged and I saw Ja'far with two wings like angels. Since then Ja'far is known among the Moslems as Ja'far Tyyár or Ja'far Zhul Janáhain, *i. e.* the winged martyr.

Infringement of the Hodaibiya treaty.

† By virtue of the Hodaibiya Treaty the Bani Khozá'a had declared themselves in alliance with the Prophet, while the Bani Bakar, acting under the same authority, had announced themselves partisans of the Qoreish. Both these tribes inhabited the adjoining valleys of Mecca; and an old standing feud existed between them. Each clan longed to avenge the murders committed on either side. The Hodaibiya treaty, which had now been nearly two years in force, provided that for the next ten years there shall be no aggression on the part of either party viz. the Prophet on one side and the Qoreish on the other. But some chief men of the Qoreish assisted in disguise their allies, the Bani Bakar, to attack by night an unsuspecting encampment of the Bani Khozá'a, killing some of them, The Khozáites sent a deputation of forty men to the Prophet, entreating him to avenge the treacherous murders. The Prophet resented it as an infraction of the Treaty at Hodaibiya, and promised to take up their cause as his own.

When the Qoreish knew of this deputation they were exceedingly alarmed and deputed Abu Sofyán, who proceeded to Medina to put matters right and to renew the compact of peace. ‡ On reaching Medina, Abu Sofyán first went to his daughter Omm Habiba, a wife of the Prophet, on whom he had counted. But his mortifications began from the very first place of seeking redress, for no sooner he wished to seat himself on a mat in her dwelling than she hastily folded it up exclaiming "It is a bed of the Apostle of God and too sacred to be molested by an impure idolator."

† Abul Fida; Ibn Athir.

‡ Ibn Hisham ; Tabari.

Abu Sofyán felt keenly the humiliation he was subjected to, and cursing his daughter left the place, and appearing before the Prophet offered some explanations wishing to renew the Peace Compact; but the Prophet would not vouchsafe to receive his explanations, and Abu Sofyán could not elicit any assurance from him. Then he sought intermediation of Ali and Abubekr but they too repulsed him. Next he tried to secure the favour of Fátema, the Prophet's beloved daughter and Ali's wife, entreating her to let her son Hasan be his protector. Fátema replied that Hasan was too young (being only about six years of age) to take any one under his protection, and added that no protection can avail against the will of the Apostle of God. Then he again turned to Ali, asking his advice in the awkward position of his mission. Ali told him that he (Abu Sofyán) could do nothing more than to proclaim on behalf of the Qoreish the friendly relations which they wished to maintain and a continuance of his own protection as the head of the Qoreish. Abu Sofyán, standing up in the courtyard of the Prophet's Mosque, proclaimed aloud as he was advised and then returned to Mecca and reported the affairs to the Qoreish, who received him with scoffs and observed that his Proclamation was of no avail without the concurrence of the Prophet. They said that Ali had made him only a plaything. Abu Sofyán replied that he knew that, but he knew not what to do. †

Preparations to invade Mecca. 8. A. H.

Abn Sofyán's unsuccessful attempts to get the Peace Compact renewed confirmed the report of the Khozáite deputation and left no room for doubt as to the guilt of the Qoreish. The infraction of the Hodaibiya peace terms having been proved, the Prophet resolved to take Mecca and the Meccans by surprise. He summoned his allies from all quarters to Medina, but did not give any intimation of the particular object he had in view. He kept it a secrect. One day Abubekr, entering his daughter Ayshá's house found her busy preparing the accoutrements of the Pro-

† Ibn Athir ; Habib al Siyar.

phet. Enquiring from her the reason, he was told that some expedition was soon to be undertaken, but she did not know in what direction. All the roads leading to Mecca were subsequently closed to prevent the intelligence of his movements being carried to the Qoreish.

When all the necessary outdoor arrangements were nearing completion, he ordered his followers in Medina to be ready for the expedition, enjoining them to utmost secrecy so that no hint in any way should leak out to Mecca. † In spite of all these precautions, the secret came very near being disclosed. Hátib son of Balta'a, one of the Mohájirs and a trusted follower of the Prophet, whose family remained behind in Mecca, wrote a letter to a friend in Mecca, revealing the intended expedition and despatched it through a woman named Sára. She was already on the road to Mecca, when the Prophet was apprised of the dispatch, through heavenly source, so he at once sent Ali and Zobeir with some other well mounted men in pursuit of the messenger. They overtook her and carefully searched her person but could not find the letter. All the men would have given up the search and turned back, but Ali was confident that the Prophet of God could not be mistaken nor misinformed. Enraged at being thus baffled, Ali drew his scimitar and, brandishing it over her, swore to strike off her head unless the letter was produced. The woman trembling with terror, drew forth the letter from the long tresses of her hair. Its contents ran thus: "Hátib son of Balta'a to the Meccans. Health! The Apostle of God is preparing to attack you unawares! To arms!" The writer of the letter having been discovered, was summoned before the Prophet. He asserted that he was a true believer, and excused himself by saying that he had his unprotected family at Mecca, whom he naturally desired to save by securing somehow the protection of some Meccans. Taking, however, his former services into consideration, the Prophet graciously accepted his plea and pardoned him. The opening nine verses of *Sur. LX* of

† Abul Fida; Ibn Athir, Tabari; Ibn Hishám.

the Qorán were subsequently revealed to warn others against doing likewise.

The March on Mecca.

On the 10th of Ramadzán, 8 A. H. or the 1st of January 630 A. D., the march began. While on the road, the Prophet asked for a cup full of water and broke his Fast in the presence of all his men who were also observing the rite, it being the Fasting month. * The example was followed by all with the exception of some, whom he declared sinful and disobedient to the Lord and His prophet if they persisted in maintaining their Fast.

It was the largest force Medina had ever put into the field. With the Mohájirs and the Ansárs were mustered the Ghifár, Aslam, Johaina and Ashja' bedouines. The Mozaina, Solaim and the Khozá'a joined the army on the road. Mozaina and Solaim bedouines contributed each a thousand men. The whole force numbered about ten thousand strong, at the head of which the Prophet was marching towards Mecca. Two of his wives, Omm Selma and Zainab bint Johash, accompanied the Prophet, as Ayesha after the affair in the expedition of Bani Mostaleq was never taken with him on an expedition. When they reached Johfa or Zhul Holeifa, Abbás, the uncle of the Prophet, together with his family who were migrating to Medina, met the Prophet, who detained Abbás to accom-

---

* اخرج مسلم فی صحیحه عن جابر بن عبدالله ان رسول الله صلعم خرج عام الفتح الي مكة فی رمضان حتی بلغ كراع الغميم وصام الناس ثم دعا بقدح من ماء فرفعه حتي نظر الناس ثم شرب فقيل له بعد ذلک ان بعض الناس قد صام فقال اولئک العصاة —

ترجمه — صحیح مسلم مین جابر بن عبدالله سے مروي هے که بزمانهٔ فتح مکه ماه رمضان مین رسول الله مع اصحاب بحالت صوم عازم مکه هوے حتي که مقام کراع غمیم مین پهونچے وهان آنحضرت نے قدح آب طلب کیا اور سب پر ظاهر کرکے روزه افطار فرمایا اسکے بعد لوگون نے آپ سے عرض کیا که بعض اشخاص نے روزه نهین کهولا آنحضرت نے ارشاد کیا که جنهون ایسا کیا وه گنهگار اور نافرمان هین-(تاریخ احمدي ص ٦٧)

pany him and despatched his family to Medina. The marches were made with all possible haste so that the army encamped on the seventh or eighth evening at Marr-al-Tzohrán on the borders of the holy land to the north west of the holy city. At this stage the army was allowed, for the first time during the whole journey, to kindle fires freely on the mountain tops of Marr-al-Tzohrán. Soon all the heights were ablaze with ten thousand fires, and the Meccans, who had not yet received any tidings of the impending danger, were struck with terror at this sight.

Submission of Abu Sofyan.

† Abu Sofyán, together with Hakim (the nephew of Khadija) and Bodail (a Khozáite Chief) set out to reconnoitre. Proceeding onwards to Marr-al-Tzohrán he fell in with Abbás, who within his heart sympathising with his townsfolk, had ridden forth from the army in the hope of meeting some wayfarer whom he might send back to the Meccans with the intelligence of the approach of the formidable army, and advising them to surrender if they wished to save themselves from destruction. Abbás, recognising Abu Sofyán's voice, accosted him, who impatiently asked Abbás as to what it was on the heights of yonder mountains. Abbás told him that Mohammed, with his ten thousand followers, was encamped to storm the city on the following morning. Abu Sofyán fell into a deep reverie at this news. Abbás then advised him to make immediately his submission to the Prophet. Seeing that all chances of opposition were hopelessly lost, he resigned himself to the dictates of Abbás, who, taking him up behind himself, brought him to the Camp, and informed the Prophet of the arrival of his distinguished friend. The Prophet directed Abbás to bring him in the morning.

While proceeding to the Prophet's tent, Abbas happened to pass by the tent of Omar, who, perceiving Abu Sofyán in company with Abbás, rushed out to kill him.

† Ibn Athir; Ibn Khaldun; Habib-al-Siyar; Hayat-al-Qulub, Ibn Hisham.

Though he was kept from this evil intent on being told by Abbás that he was for the time being under his protection, still Omar followed them with his drawn sword till they reached the Prophet. Omar withdrew only when he heard the Prophet granting Abu Sofyán shelter with Abbás for the night to be brought back to his presence the next morning. [Omar is not said to have killed a single person in any battle, but he was ever ready to unsheath his sword to put a prisoner to death.]

When Abu Sofyán appeared in the morning before the Prophet, along with Abbás, he was asked whether he believed that there was no god but the Almighty Lord alone. To this querry Abu Sofyán replied in the affirmative. Then he was asked whether he believed that Mohammed was the Prophet of the Lord. † Abu Sofyán hesitated and said that he had some doubts as to that. "Woe to thee," exclaimed Abbás, "it is no time for idle pride or scruples; testify and express at once in plain words thy belief that there is no god but One, and that Mohammed is His prophet, or else thy head shall be severed from thy body." Abu Sofyán immediately repeated the words, and thus the great leader of the Qoreish was at the feet of the Prophet as a convert. At the same time Hakim and Bodail also embraced Islam. The Prophet bade Abu Sofyán hasten back to the city, and tell the people that none who took refuge in the house of Abu Sofyán or in the Sanctuaty of Ka'ba would be harmed, and the inmates of those houses whose doors were closed would not be molested. It would not be out of place for the reader to remember the hostilities of Abu Sofyán against Islam and its founder. He was the bitterest of the enemies of the Prophet at whose life he never hesitated to make an attempt. Now Providence threw him at the mercy of the Prophet who could have avenged himself with a single word of command to behead him or to make an example of him by putting him in chains to the dread of the Meccans. But the contrast between

† Tabari ; Ibn Hishám ; Ibn Abi Shahna.

the noble Hashimite and the Omyyad is vividly noteable by the unparalleled magnanimity displayed by the Prophet towards his fallen foe. Our kind hearted noble Lord Mohammed (Peace be on him and his holy descendants) not only very graciously forgave Abu Sofyán but allowed him to maintain, rather raised, his position among his people by granting him the privilege of giving refuge to those who might seek shelter at his doors. Can any thing be more magnanimous?

‡Before Abu Sofyán could quit the Camp, the Forces were being marshalled. Standing by Abbás he watched each column and, being impressed by the sight, he exclaimed in astonishment, "Thy nephew is a mighty king, no doubt," Abbás reproachfully answered that he was more than a king, a mighty Prophet. Acknowledging the truth, Abu Sofyán hurried back to Mecca, where he shouted loudly that Mohammed was at their gates with a formidable force, that resistance and opposition would be of no avail, therefore the only wise course was an unconditional surrender, and that Mohammed had promised security to those who shut themselves up in their houses or who took refuge in the Sanctuary of Ka'ba, or in his house. The terrified people had no alternative but to follow the advice. So they fled in all directions to be shut up in their houses or to take shelter in the Ka'ba.

The Prophet's entry into Mecca. 8. A. H.

In the meantime, the army, receiving order for the march, proceeded to Mecca. On reaching Zhu Towa, near the city, and finding that no opposition for his further progress was organised, the Prophet in token of his gratitude to God, bowed low upon his camel and offered a prayer. W. Irving in his Life of Mohammed on page 150 gives the following account of the Prophet's entry in Mecca. "In the entry of Mecca, Mohammed, in the meantime, who knew not what resistance he might meet with, made a careful distribution of his forces as he approached the city. While the main body marched direct-

‡ Tabri ; Abul Fida ; Ibn Hishám.

ly forward, strong detachments advanced over the hills on each side. To Ali, who commanded a large body of Cavalry, was confided the sacred banner, which he was to plant on Mount Hajun, and maintain it there until joined by the Prophet."

"Express orders were given to all the Generals to practise forbearance, and in no instance to make the first attack; for it was the earnest desire of Mohammed to win Mecca by moderation and clemency rather than subdue it by violence. It is true, all who offered armed resistance were to be cut down, but none were to be harmed who submitted quietly. Overhearing one of his Captains †(Sa'd b. Obáda) exclaim, in the heat of his zeal, that no place was sacred on the day of battle, he instantly appointed a cooler headed Commander in his place. The main body of the army advanced without molestation. Mohammed brought up the reaguard, clad in a scarlet vest, and mounted on his favourite camel Al-Qaswa. He proceeded but slowly, however, his movements being impeded by the immense multitude which thronged around him. Arrived on mount Hajun, where Ali had planted the standard of the faith, he had a tent pitched for him. Here he alighted, put off his scarlet garment, and assumed the black turban and the pilgrims' garb."

"Casting a look down into the plain, however, he beheld with grief and indignation, the gleam of swords and lances, and Khálid, who commanded the left wing, in full career of carnage. ‡ His troops, composed of Arab tribes converted to the faith, had been galled by a flight of arrows from a body of the Qoreish; whereupon the fiery warrior charged into the thickest of them with sword and lance; his troops pressed after him, they put the enemy to flight, entered the gates of Mecca pell-mell with them, and nothing but the swift commands of Mohammed preserved the city from a general massacre". ***W. Irving's Life of Mohammed.*** Twentyeight Meccans were killed in the affray.

†Ibn Athir. ‡ Tabarl.

Not long afterwards the Prophet remounted his camel and proceeded direct to the Sanctuary of Ka'ba, saluted the sacred stone, performed the seven circuits round the Sanctuary and offered his devoutful prayers. At the sight of the haughty chiefs and the people, who had sought to destroy his religion, all the sufferings and injuries caused him by the people, their unrelenting persecutions, their brutal treatment of his followers and adherents, the privations caused him and the Háshimites by the interdict and ban at She'b Ali Tálib, their attempts at his life and the murderous pursuit which led him to make good his escape in the dead of night from his house, all must have flashed through his mind. It was now in his power to avenge himself for all the wrongs done to him. The city was at his mercy. But history does not afford a similar example of the magnanimous generosity and forbearance which was displayed by Mohammed. "What can you expect at my hands?" he asked them. "Mercy! Generous and Noble Sire!" they besought him. Tears came into the eyes of the Prophet when he heard them crying for mercy. "I will speak to you," he continued, "as Joseph spoke to his brethren. I will not reproach you today: God will forgive you, for He is merciful and Loving. اذهب انتم الطلقاء Go; ye are free!" Can anything be more sublime than this? (Eternal Peace be on him and his holy progeny.)

General amnesty announced by the Prophet.

There were 360 idols all around the Ka'ba. The Prophet pointed to each with his staff reciting the verse, "Truth has come and falsehood being perishable has vanished *Sur. XVII-82"*, and the idol fell down on its face. Pictures of Abraham and Ismael and of the Angels in female form, which covered the walls of Ka'ba were obliterated. The great idol named Hobal, treated as the deity of Mecca, was fixed on a high position beyond reach. To destroy it, the Prophet desired Ali to mount on his

Destruction of idols of the Ka'ba.

shoulders. † Ali mounted as was desired and standing over the shoulders of the Prophet wrenched the idol and threw it, to the ground. It crashed to pieces. A proclamation was made in the streets of Mecca that whoever believed in God and the Day of Judgment must destroy whatever images or idols he might have got into his house. Some persons were deputed to destroy the idols in the neighbouring habitations of Mecca.

Distribution of Offices connected with the Ka'ba.

Time for midday prayers having come, Ali, who had taken the key of the Sanctuary from its keeper Othmán b. Talha b. Abd-al-Dár presented it to the Prophet, who opening the door entered into and offered prayers. Bilál shouted his call to prayer from above the roof of the Sanctuary. After the prayers, the Prophet graciously gave back the key to Othmán b. Talha conferring on him the custody of the key as hereditary and perpetual office. Othmán was so affected with the justice of the Prophet that he readily embraced Islam on the spot in spite of his refusal at first to make over the Keys to Ali in order to prevent the Prophet's admission. Then turning to his uncle Abbás, the Prophet confirmed him in the office of giving drink to the pilgrims. These offices are still held by their respective posterity. He entrusted some Khozáites with repairs of the boundary pillars around the sacred territory, decreeing Ka'ba to be regarded hence-forward an inviolable sanctuary within which it should be unlawful to shed blood or even to fell a tree.

Homage done to the Prophet by the Meccans.

The Prophet then proceeded to the hill Al-Safá and summoned the people of Mecca to pay him their homage and fealty. Those very people who some eight years before abused, rejected and made him escape for his life, were now shamefully appearing with their heads down-cast, acknowledging Mohammed their master, their leader and the true Apostle of God. All the men first and then

† Madárij-al-Nabowat; Habib-al-Siyar; Zarqáni; Rawdzat-al-Ahbáb.

the women presented themselves and took the oath of fealty and allegience to the Prophet and to remain faithful Moslems, the men touching the hands of the Prophet and the women touching a piece of cloth covering his hand.

Proscribed persons.

† From the general amnesty extended to the Meccans, only eleven men and six women were excluded. They were proscribed and the Prophet ordered his Companions to kill them wherever they should find them. Howairith and Hárith, the two of the most inveterate enemies of Islam, were put to sword by Ali, instantly as he found them. "Among them was another apostate named * Abdalláh b. Sa'd (called Ibn Abi Sarh), whom Mohammed had employed at Medina for writing out passages of the Qurán from his dictation." (Note.—He used to change words, which being detected, he ran away from Medina as an apostate.) "His foster brother (Othmán b. Affán, after-

* قال ابوالفدا و اهدر دم ست رجال و اربع نسوة احدهم عكرمة بن ابی جهل و ثانیهم هبار بن الاسود و ثالثهم عبد الله بن سعد بن ابی سرح و كان اخا عثمان بن عفان من الرضاعة فاتی عثمان به النبی و ساله فیه فصمت النبی طویلا ثم امنه فاسلم فقال رسول الله لاصحابه انما صمت لیقوم احدكم فقتله فقالو اهلا اومات الینا فقال ان الانبیاء لا تكون لهم خائنة الاعین و كان عبدالله المذكور كتب الوحی و كان یبدل القران ثم ارتد و عاش الی خلافة عثمان فولاه مصر- و رابعهم مقیس ابن صبابة و خامسهم عبدالله بن الخطل و سادسهم الحویرث بن نفیل كان یوذی رسول الله و یهجوه فلقیه علی بن ابیطالب فقتله و اما النساء فاحدهن هند زوج ابی سفیان ام معاویه التی اكلت من كبد حمزة مع نساء قریش -

ترجمہ—تاریخ ابوالفدا میں ہے کہ پیغمبر صاحب نے بعد فتح مکہ چھہ مردوں اور چار عورتوں کا خون مباح فرمایا مردوں میں عکرمہ بن ابو جہل- ۲ ھبار بن الاسود - ۳ مقیس بن صبابہ - ۴ عبداللہ بن خطل ۵ حویرث بن نفیل - جو رسول کی تکلیف دھی اور ھجو میں مصروف

† Ibn Athir; Tárikh-al-Khamis; Rawdzat-al-Ahbáb.

wards third Caliph) sheltered him till quiet was restored, then brought him forward and implored forgiveness for him. The Prophet, unwilling to pardon so great an offender, for some time kept quiet but at last granted him quarter. When Abdalláh retired, Mohammed thus addressed his Companions who were seated about him: 'Why did not one of you arise and smite Abdalláh on the neck. I remained silent expecting this.' 'But thou gavest no sign unto us,' replied one of them. 'To give signs,' said Mohammed, 'is treachery; it is not fitting for a prophet in such a fashion to ordrain the death of any.' *W. Muir's Life of Mohamed.*"

رهتا تها اور حضرت علی نے اُوسکو دیکهتے هی قتل کر ڈالا - چهتا شخص عبد الله بن سعد بن ابي سرح جو حضرت عثمان کا رضاعی بهای تها - حضرت عثمان نے پیغمبر صاحب سے اُسکي جان بخشي چاهي - آنحضرت بهت دیر تک خاموش رهے بالاخر اُسکو امان دیدي اور اُوسنے اسلام لانیکا اظهار کیا - پیغمبر صاحب نے اصحاب سے فرمایا که مین دیر تک اسلئیے خاموش رها که تم مین سے کوئی شخص اُٹھے اور اوسکو قتل کردے - اصحاب بولے که اپنے ایما کیون نه فرمایا - آنحضرت نے کہا که انبیا کا یهه شعار نهین هے که وه کن آنکهیونسے اشاره کرین - عبدالله مذکور قران لکها کرتا تها اور اُسمین جهان چاهتا تها رد و بدل کردیتا تها بعد ازان مرتد هوگیا اور حضرت عثمان نے اپنے عهد خلافت مین اوسکو مصر کا حاکم کردیا تها اور جن چار عورتون کا خون پیغمبر صاحب نے مباح کیا اونمین سے ایک تو هند زوجه ابو سفیان مادر معاویه تهي جسنے حضرت حمزه کا کلیجه چبایا تها اور تین اوسکے ساتهه والی عورتین —

في الخميس قال اهدردم احد عشر رجال يوم فتح مكه الاول عبد الله بن خطل - والثانی عبدالله بن سعد بن ابی سرح الثالث عكرمه بن ابی جهل الرابع حویرث بن نفیل الخامس المقیس بن صبابه السادس هبار بن الاسود السابع صفوان بن امیه الثامن حارث بن طلاطله التاسع كعب بن زهیر العاشر وحشی قاتل همزه عم النبی والحادی عشر عبدالله بن زبعري — (تاریخ احمدي ص ۶۹)

8 A. H.

Of the eleven proscribed men only four were actually put to death; the rest escaped capital punishment, having somehow gained forgiveness. Four women were put to death while two were pardoned. With his singular magnanimity and unparalelled forbearance the Prophet won the hearts of the whole population of Mecca, so much so that within two days of his arrival almost all the inhabitants renouncing their deep rooted idolatory embraced his religion, acknowledging him as the Apostle of God.

Khalid's cruel conduct.

The Bani Jazhima, who lived at a day's march from Mecca, had already embraced Islam, but none of them had turned up to pay respects to the Prophet while he was so near. The Prophet deputed Khálid with a small detachment to enquire, with injunctions not to provoke a struggle. Khálid was secretly rejoiced to get this Commission, which afforded him a chance to revenge the murder of his uncle, as the Jazhimites some years ago had robbed a caravan from Yemen and in the affray Khálid's uucle Alfáka and Abd-al-Rahmán's father Awf were killed. † Khálid with his men proceeded to their abode and halted outside the habitation. *A party of the Jazhimites, taking their arms, came out to meet them, not knowing whether they were friends or foes. Khálid, hailing them with an imperious tone, demanded whether they were Moslems

* در مدارج النبوة محدث دهلوي آورده كه چون بني جذيمه از آمدن خالد خبر دار شدند بر غايت طريقه حزم و احتياط سلاحها پوشيده بيرون آمدند—خالد از ايشان پرسيد شما چه كسانيد گفتند ما مسلمانان ايم كه به محمد صلعم و شرايع دين وے ايمان داريم و نماز ميگزاريم و درميان خود مسجد بنا كرده اذان و اقامت گفته به جمعه و جماعت قيام مينمائيم - خالد كفت پس سلاح چرا پوشيده در برابر من آمده ايد گفتند ميان ما و قومے از عرب عداوت است بترسيديم كه شما از ايشان باشيد—خالد را عذر ايشان در محل قبول نيفتاد گفت سلاح خود بداريد ايشان بموجب فرموده عمل نموده سلاحها از خود دور كردند

† Abul Fida.

or infidels. In faltering tones they replied "Moslems." "Why then", asked Khálid, "have you come out to meet us with weapons in your hands." "Because," they said, "we took you to be some of the hostile tribes coming here to surprise us." Khálid sternly ordered them to lay down their arms. "They tendered an immediate submission, professed themselves converts and at the bidding of Khálid laid down their arms. But Khálid, actuated by the ancient enmity and thus eagerly giving proof of the unscrupulous cruelty which marked his subsequent career and gained for him the title of The Sword of God, made them all prisoners, and gave command for their execution." *W. Muir's Life of Mohammed page 135.*

Ali deputed to compensate the bloodshed.

‡ The Prophet, grieved at receiving the intelligence of this unprovoked outrage, raised up his hands to heaven and called God to witness that he was innocent of what Khálid had done. On his return, when Khálid was upbraided, he shifted the blame on Abd-al-Rahmán, but the Prophet indignantly rejected the imputation; and sent Ali with a sum of money for distribution among the people to compensate for the bloodshed, and to restore to them what Khálid had wrested from them.

The generous Ali excuted the Commission faithfully. Inquiring into the losses and sufferings of each individual, Ali paid them as much as they demanded. When all blood was atoned for and all the sufferers were satisfied, he distributed the remaining money among them, glad-

---

انگاه خالد گفت تا دستهاے یکدگر برشانه بر بستند و هر یک ازان اسیران را به یکے یاران خود بسپرد -وقت سحر ندا کرد که هر که اسیرے دارد به قتل آرد چنانچه به فرمودۀ او اسیران بیگناه را کشتند و در روایتے آمده که چون آنها سلاح انداختند خالد تیغ در ایشان نهاد قریب صد کس را ازآں قبیله بکشت پس یکے از بني جذیمه آمده انچه خالد بران جماعت کرده بود بعرض رسول صلعم برسانید - حضرت در غضب آمده سه بار فرمود خداوندا من بیزارم انچه خالد کرد —(تاریخ احمدي ص ۷۰)

‡ Abul Fida ; Ibn Athir ; Ibn Hishám.

dening every heart by his bounty. The Prophet applauded this generosity, praised and thanked Ali. Khálid was rebuked and reproved.

Khálid's cruel treatment of the Bani Jazhima, however, made such a bad impression upon the other Arab tribes who had not yet embraced Islam, that Bani Hawázin, Bani Thaqif, Bani Sa'd and several others, who already for some time were meditating to rise in opposition to the growing power of Islam, now anticipating an attack upon them, resolved to assume the offensive themselves. Under the leadership of their Chief, Málik b. Awf, the Bani Thaqif and the Bani Hawázin, along with the other tribes, assembled at Awtás valley between Mecca and Táef, to the number of four thousand fighting men, to oppose the forces of the Prophet, should they venture to approach them. They had brought with them their women, children, herds and flocks, which followed them in the rear. Doraid, a very aged and old warrior, who accompanied them in his litter, protested against this dangerous step, but the youthful Málik did not pay heed to his words, being of opinion that in the presence of their families, for their safety and honour, men will never turn their backs upon their foe, but will risk their own life fighting manfully till they achieved success.

The Battle of Honein. 8. A. H.

† The threatening intelligence from Táef compelled the Prophet to cut short his stay at Mecca, where he was busy in the arrangements of public affairs for about a fortnight since the Conquest on 20th Ramadzán. He left Mecca on the 6th of Shawwál, 8 A. H., with his ten thousand followers, who had come with him from Medina, and two thousand men from Mecca, who volunteered to fight by his side. Ali, as usual, held the sacred Standard of the Prophet. When the imposing force of 12,000 strong, composed of different tribes, each flying its own banner at its head, marshalled out, Abubekr joyfully exclaimed: "We shall not this day be worsted for want of our num-

† Tárikh al Khamis ; Rawdzat al Ahbáb.

bers." The army reached in the dead of night near the Honein valley, which lies about midway between Mecca and Táef.

In the meantime, the Bani Hawázin and their allies, under the directions of Málik b. Awf, having advanced upon the valley of Honein and taking their position in a secure place commanding the narrow pass, which formed an entrance to the valley, awaited quietly the approach of the Prophet's army.

The flight of the Moslems.

Early in the morning of 10th Shawwâl, the Moslem army began its move towards the Pass. The Prophet, on his white mule Duldul, rode in the rear of his forces. The foremost column, composed of the Bani Solaim and led by Khálid, was leisurely advancing up the steep and narrow Pass, when all on a sudden the Bani Hawázin sallied forth from their ambuscade and charged Khálid's column with impetuosity. † Khálid could not withstand the shock, and his column, staggered by the onslaught, broke and fell back. The shock was communicated from column to column. *All turned to fly, and panic seized the whole army.

* قال ابوالفدا فلما التقوا انكشف المسلمون لا يلوي احد علي أحد-

ترجمہ—تاریخ ابوالفدا مین ہےکہ جب دونون جانب کی فوجین باہم ملاقي اور مصروف جنگ هوئین تو مسلمانون کے پاؤن اوکھڑ گئے اور وہ ایسا بد حواس هوکر بھاگے کہ کوئی کسي کیطرت ملتفت نہ هوتا تھا—

فی حدیث البخاري عن ابي قتادة قال انهزم المسلون و انهزمت معهم فاذالعمر بن الخطاب في الناس فقلت له ماشان الناس قال امر الله ثم تراجع الناس الی رسول اللہ صلعم -

ترجمہ—صحیح بخاري کي ایک حدیث مین ابو قتادہ سے مروي ہے کہ بروز حنین مسلمان پسپا هوکر بھاگے تو مین بھی اونکے ساتھہ تھا-ناگاہ کیا دیکھتا هون کہ مفرورین مین حضرت عمر بن الخطاب بھی هین مینے اونسے عرض کیا کہ کیا حال ہے هم مسلمانون کا (کہ بھاگ کھڑے هوے) انھون نے فرمایا کہ خدا کي مشیت- بعد ازان هم سب لوگ رسول الله کے پاس واپس آے—

† Tárikh-al-Khamis; Rawdzat-al-Ahbáb; Habib-al-Siyar.

8 A. H.

As column after column in helter-skelter hurried past him, the Prophet called out, "Whither are you going? The Apostle of the Lord is here! Return! Return!" But no one paid heed to his words. ‖ The distinguished Companions of the Prophet including Omar b. Al Khattáb had also taken to flight. Only five men, all Bani Háshim, remained with the Prophet. ‡ The names of those who stood firm by him are:—Abbás and his son Fadzl, Ali, Abu Sofyán b. Hárith, and Rabi'a his brother.

فی سیرة الحلبیه للبرهان الدین الحلبي الشافعي و کان ابو سفیان بن الحارث اخذ برکابه صلعم و هو یقول حین رائي ما رائی من الناس الی این ایها الناس فلم ارالناس یلوون علی شيء فقال رسول الله صلعم یا عباس اصرخ یا معشر الانصار یااصحاب السمرة یعنی الشجرة التي کانت تحتها بیعة الرضوان—

ترجمه—سیرة الحلبیه برهان الدین حلبي شافعی مین هے که اوسوقت ابو سفیان بن الحارث پیغمبر صاحب کی رکاب تهامے هوئے تهے اور آنحضرت لوگونکو گریز کرتے هوے دیکهکر فرما رهے تهے که تم کهاں بهاگے جارهے هو مگر وه کسیطرح التفات نه کرتے تهے آنپے حضرت عباس سے فرمایا که انکو آواز دو که اے گروه انصار اے اصحاب سمره یعنے زیر درخت سمره بیعت رضواں میں شریک هونیوالو (کهاں بهاگے جارهے هو)—

قال الحلبی فی سیرة الحلبیه و في روایة لما فرالناس یوم حنین عن النبی صلعم لم یبق معه الا اربعة ثلاثة من بنی هاشم و رجل من غیرهم علی بن ابیطالب والعباس و ابو سفیان بن الحارث و ابن مسعود —

ترجمه—علامه حلبی سیرةحلبیه مین فرماتے هین که ایک روایت مین یوں آیا هے که جب بروز حنین لوگوں نے رسول الله کے پاس سے فرار کیا تو آنحضرت کے ساته صرف چار شخص باقي ره گئے تهے تین بنی هاشم یعنے علی بن ابیطالب اور عباس اور ابو سفیاں بن الحارث اور ایک غیر بني هاشم یعنے عبد الله بن مسعود—(تاریخ احمدي صفحه ۷۳)

‖ Tárikh-al-Khamis; Ibn Qaiyam's Zádal Ma'ád.

‡ Mawáhib Ladunnia, Tárikh-al-Khamis and Fathal Bári give names of only four persons who stood firm by the Prophet.

‡ Some of the Meccan Chiefs, gladdened by this reverse, opened their hearts making spiteful remarks against the Moslems; *e.g.* Abu Sofyán b. Harb said: "They will never stop till they reach the sea shore." Jabala or Kalda brother of Safwán said: "Mohammed's magic is this day broken." Sheiba son of Othmán b. Abi Talha (killed at Ohod) vowed that he would now slay Mohammed. Confusion was increasing.

Taunts of the Meccans.

At last the Prophet asked his uncle Abbás, who held his mule, to call aloud: O citizens of Medina! O men of the Tree of Fealty (alluding to those who took the oath under the tree at Hodaibiya)! O ye of the Sura Baqar (reminding them of their paying homage at the time of embracing Islam)! The stentorian voice of Abbás, when he repeatedly called aloud, was heard by the flying columns, and it was answered with Labbaik from all sides and the men began to return. About a hundred men, † all Ansárs, gaining the narrow Pass, checked the advance of the enemy. The standard bearer of the Bani Hawázin named Othmán or Abu Jarwal, who was a man of extraordinarily tall stature and stout built, came forward and challenged the Moslems to single combat. Ali stepped forward and engaged him. In the meantime the Moslem army gradually rallied round the Prophet. ¶ Ali succeeded in slaying his antagonist. Now both the parties closed with each other and hand to hand fight ensued. The conflict was terrible. The Prophet, who was watching the struggle from an eminence, taking a handful of gravel, cast it towards the enemy saying: "Ruin seize them." They wavered and in a short time finally took to flight. The Moslems hotly pursuing them slew many. For the mention of this battle in the Qurán see the following translation:—

Return of the Companions.

‡ Abul Fida; Ibn Hishám.

† Amir Hasan's Ayát Mohkamát Vol. II p. 411.

¶ Ibn Hishám; Rawdzat-al-Safá; Habib-al-Siyar; Tabari.

Sura IX-25 "Already hath God helped you in many engagements, and on the day of Honein when ye were priding in your multitude, but it availed not unto you at all, and the earth became too strait for you although it was widely large, then did ye turn your backs fleeing." (*i.e.* The earth seemed to you to be too narrow in your precipitate flight. *Savary*).

26 "Then God sent down His (Security) Sakina upon His apostle and upon the faithful and sent down hosts (troops of angels) invisible to you; and He punished those who disbelieved and this was the reward of the ungodly."

Khálid, as usual, pre-eminent in cruelty, was reprimanded for slaying a woman.

Defeat and flight of the infidels.

The battle was won. The enemy, † losing seventy of their bravest of whom forty fell under the sword of Ali, fled towards their camp at Awtás, followed immediately by a strong detachment from the Moslem army, under the command of Abu Amir Ash'ari, in their pursuit. They turned back to face the pursuers. Abu Amir, after killing several of them, was himself slain. Then his cousin Abu Musa Ash'ari, assuming the command, put them to flight. They fled towards Táef leaving their Camp, which fell into the hands of the Moslems. Six thousand captives including women and children, 40,000 sheep and goats, 4,000 okks of silver and 24,000 camels formed the booty of Honein and Awtás. The prisoners and the booty were removed to Je'rána valley and kept there in shelter awaiting the return of the army from Táef, where the Moslems were now pushing forward.

Siege of Taef. 8 A. H.

Soon after the return of the detachment from Awtás, the Prophet procceded with his armies through Nakhla and laid siege to Táef. The Hawázin and their allies in Táef,

† Amir Hasan's Ayát Mohkamát Vol. II p. 411; Sirat Ibn Hishám; Habib-al-Siyar.

anticipating the siege, had already undertaken defensive measures. The siege was prolonged for over twenty days without producing the slightest effect; and the Prophet, having a dream, concluded that the operations would not be successful, and determined to raise the siege. But his army, receiving orders for retreat, began to murmur, whereupon he permitted them to make a general assault the next day. The assault was made and the assailants were repulsed with loss. Abdalláh, a son of Abubekr, received a wound, which caused his death, though some years later. Abu Sofyán, the Meccan Chief, lost one of his eyes with an arrow shot. At last, the army marched back towards Je'rána, where the booty of Henein was kept pending distribution.

Distribution of Honein war booty.

Notwithstanding the long interval between the Honein battle and the distribution of its booty, none of the tribes turned up to open negotiations seeking to regain their captive families, as was expected by the Prophet. Now the army, fearing lest the tribes might turn up and the Prophet with his magnanimous nature might give them back their property, thronged round him and clamoured for the distribution of the spoils of the recent battles, and manifested impatience for the delay. Annoyed at their attitude, the Prophet said indignantly to them: "Have you ever found me false or dishonest?" And plucking a hair from the back of a camel and raising his voice, he added: "By Alláh! I have never misappropriated a single hair's value of a booty, nor have I ever taken on account of my share more than a fifth, and even that fifth I have spent for your good." The booty was, however, divided as usual—four-fifths was shared by the army and one-fifth was his own share. Thus four camels and forty sheep or goats fell to the lot of each soldier and thrice the amount to each horseman along with some captives.

From the exultations of the Qoreish nobles of Mecca in expectation of the Prophet's defeat at Honein, it was evident that, in spite of their conversion to Islam, they were dubious in belief. To win their hearts (*Sura IX*-60) and to rivet them more firmly to him and to his Faith, the Prophet offered them large gifts from his own one-fifth of the booty, in order to convince them that they were, with their conversion, gaining much and losing little. Thus to Abu Sofyán he gave one hundred camels and fifty okks of silver. To Yazid and Moáwiya sons of Abu Soyán, to Ikrima son of Abu Jahl and to his brother Hárith, to Safwán b. Omyya, to Hakim b. Hozám as well as to other men of distinction the Prophet granted gifts in due proportion, and all from his own share. The recipients of such gifts are known in the history of Islam as 'Conciliated Moslems.'

† "Among the lukewarm converts thus propitiated was Abbás b. Marwás, a poet. He was dissatisfied with his share, and vented his discontent in satirical verses. Mohammed overheard him. 'Take that man hence,' said he, 'and cut out his tongue.' Omar, ever ready for rigorous measures, would have executed the sentence literally, and on the spot," but ‡ Ali, who better understood the Prophet's meanings, "led the all trembling, Abbás to the place where the captured cattle were collected and bade him choose what he liked from among them. 'What!' cried the poet, joyously, relieved from the horrors of mutilation, 'is this the way the Prophet would silence my tongue? By Allah! I will take nothing.' Mohammed, however, persisted in his generosity, and sent him sixty camels. From that time forward the peot was never weary of chanting the liberality of the Prophet." *W. Irving's Life of Mohammed, p. 162.*

Discontent of the Medina men.

The men of Medina, who had borne the brunt of the conflict, felt themselves slighted by this petting of the Qoreish. They mistook it as a mark of the Prophet's esteem for his kinsmen and a disregard for the meritorious services

† W. Irving's Life of Mohammed p. 162.
‡ Rawdzat-al-Ahbáb ; Habib-al-Siyar.

rendered by them during the past years of struggle. They grumbled at the preference shown to the Qoreish. Abul Fida says: The distribution being finished, Zhul Khoweisara spoke out himself against the Prophet, who then declared Zhul Khoweisara as the man whose posterity would turn out dissenters or Khárijites; and it so happened that one Harqus son of Zhul Thaddiya, a descendant of Zhul Khoweisara, was the first who took the oath against Caliph Ali and turned out a Dissenter or Khárijite.

The Medina men reconciled.

Having realized the discontent of the men of Medina, the Prophet, accompanied only by Ali, entered into his tent, and, shortly after, he called for the leading men of Medina. In the words of *W. Irving:* "Hearken, ye men of Medina," said he; "were ye not in discord among yourselves, and have I not brought you into harmony? Were ye not in error, and have I not brought you into the path of truth? Were ye not poor, and have I not made you rich?" They acknowledged the truth of his words. "Look ye!" continued he, "I came among you stigmatised as a liar, yet you believed in me; persecuted, yet you protected me; a fugitive, yet you sheltered me; helpless, yet you aided me. Think you I do not feel all this? Think you I can be ungrateful! You complain that I bestow gifts upon these people, and give none to you. It is true, I give them worldly gear, but it is to win their worldly hearts. To you, who have been true, I give *myself*! They return home with sheep and camels; ye return with the prophet of God among you. For, by Him in whose hands is the soul of Mohammed, though the whole world should go one way and ye another, I would remain with you! Which of you, then, have I most rewarded?"

The Ansárs were so affected by the Prophet's speech that they sobbed aloud, their beards becoming wet with tears, and they exclaimed: "O Apostle of God! we are content with thy society and we are satisfied with our shares."

War Prisoners.

†Among the captives was an aged woman named Sheima, who said she was the daughter of Halima, the Prophet's nurse and thus his foster sister. She was brought before the Prophet, who recognizing in her the girl that used to tend and carry him when he was nurtured by Halima among the Bani Sa'd, held out his cloak towards her and seated her affectionately beside himself. He offered to take her to Medina, but she preferred remaining with her tribe. So she was allowed to go back with handsome presents, and was furnished liberally for her journey.

Encouraged by this kind tretment of their kinswoman, a deputation of the Bani Sa'd, Bani Hawázin and other tribes approached the Prophet, submitted to his authority and begged for the restoration of their women, children and the property. ‡ "Which is dearest to you," said he to the Hawázins, "your families or your goods?" They replied, "Our families." "Enough," rejoined he, "as far as it concerns Al-Abbás and myself, we are ready to give up our share of the prisoners; but there are others to be moved. Come to me after noontide prayer, and say, We implore the ambassador of God that he counsel his followers to return us our wives and children; and we implore his followers that they intercede with him in our favour." The envoys did as he advised. Mohammed and Al Abbás immediately renounced their share of the captives; their example was followed by all."

Ali inspired with Divine Secrets.

During the period when the army was sitting round the besieged town of Táef, the Prophet sent out a detachment under the command of Ali to invite the tribes, inhabiting the vicinity all around Táef, to Islam and to destroy the idols worshipped by them. Ali had some encounters; especially the Khoth'am clan offered opposition but their chief named Shaháb being slain by Ali, they submitted. Faithfully and successfully executing his mission, when Ali returned,

†Tabari.
‡W. Irving p. 161.

the Prophet on seeing him exclaimed Alláh-o-Akbar and *took him alone to his sacred apartments to have a long and confidential talk. His prominent †Companions, more especially Omar, began to murmur, wondering why the Prophet so long engaged his cousin in confidential conversation, not allowing others to interfere. Hearing this, the Prophet said that *God Himself had inspired Ali with Divine Secrets,* it was for this reason that he was engaged in confidential discourse so long.

To the Chief of the Bani Hawázin viz. Málik b. Awf, who had shut himself in his stronghold at Táef, the Prophet intimated that if he embraced Islam he

Malik b. Awf.

---

* اخرج الترمذي عن جابر قال دعى رسول الله صلعم عليا يوم الطائف فانتجاه فقال الناس لقد طال نجواه مع ابن عمه فقال رسول الله صلعم ماانتجيته و لكن الله انتجاه

ترجمه—ترمذي نے جابر سے روايت كي هے كه محاصره طائف كے زمانے مين جناب رسولخدا نے حضرت على كو بلاكر تخلئے مين بصيغه رازسرگوشى فرمائي تو لوگون نے كہا كه كيا هے جو پيغمبر صاحب نے بهت دير تک اپنے بهائى سے راز كى گفتگو كى آنحضرت نے يهه سنكر فرمايا كه على سے ميننے راز كى باتين نهين كين بلكه خدا نے كى هين—

محدث دهلوي در معارج النبوة آورده كه در هنگام خلوت و مشاورت نبى با على امير المومنين عمر رضى الله عنه با حضرت رسول صلعم گفته كه يا رسول الله با على راز ميگوي و باوے خلوت ميكني آن سرور فرمود ما انتجيته و لكن الله انتجاه
يعني من با او راز نميگويم بلكه خدايتعالي با او راز ميگويد—

محدث دهلوي در شرح مشكوة در معنى و لكن الله انتجاه فرموده كه يعنى خداے تعالي امر كرده است مرا كه راز گويم با او پس رازگفتم من بجهت فرمانبرداري كردن امر حق تعالي را و تواند كه معنى آن باشد كه من ابتداے راز گفتن باوے نه كرده‌ام وليكن خدايتعالي را ميگويد باوے و القاے اسرار ميكند در دل وے من نيز راز ميگويم باوے از جهت موافقت و متابعت فعل الهي—(تاريخ احمدي ص۷۴ و ۷۵)

†Habib-al-Siyar; Ma'árij-al-Nabawat; Kanz-al-Ommál.

would be given back his goods as well as his family and a present of one hundred camels besides. He accepted the offer and was, in addition to the presents, given command of all his country-men who should at any time embrace Islam. After his conversion to Islam he proved a useful and zealous Moslem.

Return of the Prophet.

The distribution of war spoils having finished, the Prophet took upon himself the pilgrim vows. On the 18th of Zhulqa'da, 8 A. H., dressed in pilgrim garb, he visited Mecca, where he performed the Lesser Pilgrimage.

Otáb b. Osaid and Mo'ázh b. Jabal, whom the Prophet had appointed Governor, and Imám or Chief Priest of Mecca respectively, at the time of his departure to Honein, were now confirmed in their respective offices. He returned the same night to Je'rána and the following morning marched homewards to Medina.

Ibrahim, son of the Prophet.

Upon his return to Medina, Mary, the Coptic girl, who had been sent to the Prophet by the Govèrnor of Egypt, gave birth to a son in the month of Zhilhajja, 8 A. H. The babe was named Ibráhim, but he lived only for fifteen months.

Drinking Prohibited.

In the year 8 A. H., the drinking of wine was absolutely forbidden; though the disapprobation commenced in 4 A. H., with the revelation of the Holy Quran's following verse:—

Sura II-216 "They will ask thee concerning wine and games of chance. Say: In both there is great sin and benefit unto men, but their sinfulness is greater than their benefit."

After this revelation some of the Moslems gave up drinking, while others continued drinking, till, in an entertainment given by Abd-al-Rahmán b. Awf, to which he invited several of the Prophet's Companions, one of them, after they had eaten and drank plentifully, raved shamefully during his evening prayer. This occasioned the following revelation in 6 A. H. *Al Beidzawi*:—

Sura IV-46 "O Believers! Come not to prayers when ye are drunk, until ye understand what ye say."

Still some Moslems did not give up the habit, till one of the most eminent Companions of the Prophet, being some day drunk to excess assaulted Abd-al-Rahmán b. Awf and fractured his skull with a camel's jaw-bone. Then sitting in a state of inebriety wailed over the loss of the Pagan Arabs slain by the Moslems in the battle of Bedr, reciting the elegy of Aswad b. Ya'far, which is given hereunder along with its translaiion:—

وكان بالقليب قليب بدر من الفتيان والعرب الكرام

Alas! In the well—the Qaleeb well of Bedr—lie some of the brave youths of noble Arabs.

ابو عدنى ابن كبشه ان سنحيا وكيف حياة أصداء و هام

Does † Ibn-i-Kabsha tell us that we shall be brought back , life; but how shall ‡ Asdá and Hám get back their lives?

ايعجزان يردالموت عنى وينشرنى اذابليت عظامى

Is he unable to ward off our death; though he is able to bring us to life after our bones have decayed.

الامن مبلغ الرحمن عنى بانى تارك شهرالصيام

Hallo! Who will carry my messege to God that I do not observe the month of Fasts;

فقل لله يمنعنى شرابى وقل لله يمنعنى طعامى

And tell God to prevent me from drinking and to stop my food.

The Prophet was very angry on receiving the report of this incident. He got up and proceeded at once, with his mantle dragging on the ground, to the spot where the Companion was wailing. Taking up something, which he held in his hand, he beat him therewith; whereupon cried

† Nick-name given to the Prophet by Pagan Arabs.

‡ Pagan Arabs believed that the soul of an unavenged victim was transformed into an owl, which wandered about his grave crying "Give me drink." After the murder was revenged, the soul vanished away and there was no cry at the grave.

9 A. H.

the Companion: "I seek shelter against the wrath of God and and that of His prophet." This incident is said to have occasioned the revelation of the following verses ordaining total abstinence from drink:—

Sura V-92 "O believers! Verily, wine, and games of chance, and images, and divining arrows are an abomination of Satan's work, therefore avoid them that ye may prosper.

93 "Satan only desires to sow enmity and hatred among you, by wine and games of chance, and keep you from remembering God and from prayer—Will ye not therefore abstain? Obey God and obey the Apostle and beware; but if ye turn back, know that Our apostle's duty is only to preach publicly."

'We will refrain,' 'We will refrain,' rejoined the offender. *Mustatraf Ch. 74, by Imam Sheikh Shahabbuddin Ahmad Abshahi.*

CHAPTER XV.

Wadi-al-Ramal or Zhat-al-Salasal expedition. Tabuk expedition. Announcement of Sura Bara'at. The Christians of Najran; and other important events ending with the ninth year of Hegirat.

Submission of the Bani Thaqif. 9 A. H.

After the submission and conversion of the Bani Hawázin and their chief Málik b. Awf, the Bani Thaqif found themselves surrounded on all sides by the followers of the Prophet, who looked upon them with scorn and treated them as infidels. They were compelled to keep themselves within their walls, as the Bani Hawázin, at the connivance of Málik, maintained an unceasing warfare against them. At length, in the month of Ramadzán 9 A. H., they sent an embassy to Medina to arrange for a compromise. The Prophet gladly received the deputation, and, refusing their solicitations for some concessions in their idolatrous practices, finally accepted their unconditional submission, on their confirming to the new religion and abandoning their idol worship. Abu Sofyán b. Harb and Moghira, both of whom exercised great influence over the tribe, were deputed to destroy their famous idol Al-Lát. They accompanied the retiring embassy. On reaching Táef, Moghira hewed the image to the ground and seized its ornaments and jewellery amid the cries and lamentations of the women.

Wadi-al-Ramal or Zhat-al-Salasal expedition.

†In the begining of the year 9 A. H., the Prophet received intelligence that the tribes inhabiting the Wádi-al-Ramal valley meditated a raid upon Medina, and that they were collecting arms and men for the purpose. He sent Abubekr at the head of an army to bring them to reason. The valley was surrounded on all sides by hills and thorny bushes and trees which served as ambuscade. Receiving the intelligence of the approaching force they sallied forth from their ambush and charged so fiercely that Abubekr and his army were forced to retreat, sustaining heavy loss. Next the Prophet sent an army under command of Omar, who also could prove no better than his predecessor. Amr b. As then offered his services, and was sent with an army, but he also fared no better and was beaten back to Medina.

At last, the Prophet despatched Ali at the head of an army consisting of Abubekr, Omar and Amr as Captains. Ali, at the start, took another direction and after some stages turned suddenly towards his destination through a rugged tract, marching by night and halting for rest in the day. Amr with Abubekr and Omar protested against the dangers of the route; but Ali paid no heed to the protests and proceeded on. At length one morning he reached over the head of the enemy and ravaged the valley, avenging the loss they had inflicted upon the preceding expeditions.

†Habib-al-Siyar; Rawdzat-al-Safá; Ma'árij-al-Nabowat.

9 A. H.

†The Prophet received a revelation as contained in Sur. C. of the Qurán and he announced the glad tidings of Ali's victory to his Companions. When Ali was coming back victorious, the Prophet went out with his followers to receive him. Seeing the Prophet, Ali got down of his horse. The Prophet bade him ride and told him that his services were approved by God and His prophet. Ali wept for joy at this intelligence. The Prophet continued: $"I fear lest the people should treat thee as Christ is treated by his followers, otherwise I would tell such things concerning thee that wherever thou goeth the people would take earth from under thy feet seeking cure therefrom."

This expedition is known as Zhát-al-Salásal expedition, which is related in the year 8 A. H. by some historians.

Tabuk expedition.

‡It was in the middle of 9 A. H. that Nabatæns, coming from Syria and visiting the markets of Medina, spread a rumour that the Roman Emperor Heraclius was moblising a huge army to surprise the Moslems at Medina. Receiving this intelligence, the Prophet resolved to meet the enemy on their way, and issued explicit orders to his men to make preparations for the expedition. The season was very hot and dry. People were unwilling to undertake the journey. Having collected, however, an army of ten thousand horse and twenty thousand foot, he formally appointed Ali, his vicegerent, as Governor of Medina and guardian of his family during his absence. ***W. Irving in his Life of Mohammed on page 170 says***: "Mohammed now appointed Ali governor of Medina, and guardian of both their families. He accepted the trust with great reluctance, having been accustomed always to accom-

† Kashfal Ghamma.

$ According to Yanábi-al-Mowaddat (Bombay Edition p. 107) this was said by the Prophet on the occasion of Ali's victory at Khaibar along with other praises. Habib-al-Siyar.

‡ Tárikh-al-Khamis; Rawdzat-al-Safá; Habib-al-Siyar; Rawdzat-al-Ahbáb.

pany the Prophet, and share all his perils. All arrangements being completed, Mohammed marched forth from Medina (Rajab 9 A. H.) on this momentous expedition. A part of his army was composed of Khazrajites and their confederates, led by Abdalláh son of Obay. This man, whom Mohammed had well denominated the Chief of the Hypocrites, encamped separately with his adherents at night, at some distance in the rear of the main army, and when the latter marched forward in the morning, lagged behind, and led his troops back to Medina. † Repairing to Ali, whose dominion in the city was irksome to him and his adherents, he endeavoured to make him discontented with his position, alleging that Mohammed had left him in charge of Medina solely to rid himself of an incumbrance. Stung by the suggestion, Ali hastened after Mohammed, and demanded if what Abdalláh and his followers said was true. "These men," replied Mohammed, "are liars. They are the party of Hypocrites and Doubters, who would breed sedition in Medina. I left thee behind to keep watch over them, and to be a guardian to both our families. ‡ *I would have thee to be to me what Aaron was to Moses; excepting that thou canst not be, like him, a prophet; I being the last of the prophets."* With this explanation Ali returned contented to Medina. Many have inferred from the foregoing, that Mohammed intended Ali for his Caliph or Successor; that being the signification of the Arabic word used to denote the relation of Aaron to Moses."

The army marched forward. The journey was very tiresome as water was scarce on the route. It being summer, the heat of the sun above and of the burning sand below was intolerable. After seven days' trying journey when they reached the fertile vale of Hejer, where lived in ancient times the impious and rebellious Thamud tribe, which was destroyed under the wrath of Heaven, the army commenced halting on the green pasture ground; and drawing water from the refreshing fountains

† Tabari; Abul Fida; Ibn Athir. ‡ Suyuti.

9 A. H.

began to prepare their food. But as soon as the Prophet, who usually marched in the rear, reached the spot, he forbade them from halting at the accursed place and ordered that none should drink of the water or use it for ablutions, that the dough which they had kneaded for their bread should be given to the camels. Instantly they obeyed and marched forward, halting at a place where they suffered considerably for want of water during the night. Next morning, however, to their great relief a plentiful shower of rain, prayed for by the Prophet, compensated the loss of wells at Hejer and gave fresh life to the men and animals. Resuming their march, they reached as far as Tabuk, a town situate about half way between Medina and Damascus, on the southern borders of ancient Edom ten stages from Medina, when the rumour, which necessitated this expedition, was found to be false. The Prophet ordered halt there, wishing no further advance. He deputed his Captains with small detachments to reconnoitre the surrounding country and to invite the ruling Chiefs and their people to Islam. For twenty days he halted at Tabuk. During this period several Jewish and Christian clans embraced Islam and professed adhesion to the Prophet. Some offered to pay annual tribute in token of their submission to him. Thus the expedition was not altogether fruitless. Almost the whole of the northern Peninsula was now subjugated. After twenty days' halt at Tabuk the Prophet marched back homeward and reached Medina in the month of Ramadzán.

Conspiracy to kill the Prophet

‡ On his return journey from Tabuk, the Prophet had to cross Aqaba Zhi Fetaq. He ordered his men not to take the route before his own passage thereon. During the night when the Prophet was crossing the Aqaba on his camel, led by Hozhaifa b. al-Yamán bridle in hand, and Ammár Yásir driving from behind, a sudden flash of lightning showed them fourteen or fifteen men advancing towards them. Hozhaifa raised an alarm and the Prophet harshly

‡ Durr Manthur; Tárikh-al-Khamis; Rawdzat-al-Ahbáb.

accosted the intruders, upon which they took to flight. "And they designed that which they could not effect." *Sura IX-75. Sale.* "The commentators tell us that fifteen men conspired to kill Mohammed in his return from Tabuk, by pushing him from his camel into a precipice, as he rode by night over the highest part of al Aqaba. But when they were going to execute their design, Hozhaifa, who followed, and drove the Prophet's camel, which was led by Ammár b. Yásir, hearing the tread of camels and the clashing of arms, gave the alarm, upon which they fled." *Sale.*

The Prophet asked Hozhaifa whether he could identify them. He replied in the negative. Upon this the Prophet said that those men had designed to kill him by frightening his camel to throw him down the steep cliff; and that those men were the people who would remain hypocrites till the Last Day. He named each and every one of them together with the name of their fathers, but with strict injunction to Hozhaifa not to disclose the secret. Hozhaifa desired him to have all of them beheaded, but the Prophet, not agreeing, said: "The people will say that Mohammed, having gained victories with their aid, is now going to kill them." Hozhaifa was known afterwards as "the Possessor of the Secret."

On being constantly importuned with solemn oaths by Caliph Omar, Hozhaifa, considering the advisability, appears to have given out the names of these hypocrites. But as the list included the most eminent Companions of the Prophet, the historians and commentators seem to have abstained from giving them publicity. Ibn Bábwaih, a learned Savant has, however, given the names, which I forbear to give for the sake of decency.

Destruction of the Dzerar Mosque. 9. A. H.

While it was yet an hour's journey to Medina, the Prophet received a deputation of the same men of Qobá, who had desired him, at the time of his departure to Tabuk, to consecrate their newly built mosque with his prayers and he had deferred to comply with their request till his return. They again approached the Prophet on the same errand. He now ordered to destroy the building and sent some of his men, who carried out the order.

† In fact this mosque was built with a sectarian or hostile bias as will appear from the following narrative :—There was one Abu Amir, a Khazrajite monk who was well versed in the Scriptures and knew that a Prophet was yet to arise. But still he denied to recognise in Mohammed the promised Prophet, and becoming jealous of his ever increasing influence and power in Medina, he fled to Mecca after the prophet's victory at Bedr. He joined the Meccans and accompanied them in the Ohod campaign against the Prophet. After the retreat of the Meccans, he fled towards the Roman territory. Certain malcontents communicated with him and invited him to his native town Qobá. He suggested to build a mosque in order to afford him shelter and to facilitate meetings of his associates to discuss measures against the Prophet. They built a mosque and to draw off men from the original mosque at Qobá, they desired the Prophet to come and consecrate it by himself praying in it. It was at the time when the Prophet was preparing to start for Tabuk; he therefore deferred to comply with their request till his return. In the meantime, he received the following revelation from Heaven : "And there are those who have built a mosque for mischievous purpose, and for (to propagate) infidelity and to make a division among the faithful, and for an ambush for him that hath fought against God and his apostle in time past; yet they will swear they intend nothing but good; but God beareth witness that verily they are liars." (*Sur. IX-108*). When they reappeared with the same errand before the Prophet on his return from Tabuk, he ordered the building to be pulled down.

Death of Omm Kulthum.

Omm Kulthum, wife of Othmán b. Affán (afterwards the third Caliph), breathed her last in the month of Sha'bán, 9 A. H.

† Rawdzat al-Ahbáb

9 A. H.

Death of Abdallah b. Obay, the Hypocrite.

About two months after the return of the Prophet from Tabuk, Abdalláh b. Obay, the leader of the Hypocrites in Medina, died in the month of Zhil-Qa'da 9 A. H. after a short illness. On the earnest entreaties of his son, a faithful Moslem, ready to strike off his own father's head for the sake of his devotion to the Prophet (see page 146), the Prophet consented to perform the customary burial service, and gave him his shirt to shroud the corpse, as he desired that his father's corpse might be wrapped up in the garment worn by the Prophet next to his body.

Soon after the prayers, he had the revelation: "Ask forgiveness for them or do not ask, even if thou ask forgiveness for them seventy times, God will by no means pardon them because they have no belief in God and His apostle and God guides not the ungodly (*Sur. IX-81*). The Prophet went behind the bier to the grave and watched his funeral. Some time after the occasion, he received the revelation, as contained in *Sur. IX-85*, forbidding him to pray over the corpse of any of the Hypocrites or disaffected persons nor to stand at their tombs.

Behaviour of Ayesha and Hafsa.

* The wives of the Prophet had formed two parties. † To one of them belonged Ayesha and Hafsa, the daughters of Abubekr and Omar respectively, Souda and Safiya; all others were in the other party. ‡ Taking advantage of

---

* فی ارشاد الساري لشرح صحیح بخاری عن عایشة ان نساء النبی كناحز بین انا و جفصه و سوده و صفیه في حزب و زینب بنت جحش و ام سلمه والباقیاته في حزب و هذا یرجح ان زینب هی صاحبة العسل وهذا غارت عائشه منها لكونها من غیر حزبها —

ترجمه — ارشاد الساري شرح صحیح بخاري مطبوعه نولكشور پریس لكهنو جلد ۷ ص ۳۱۴ پر هے كه حضرت عایشه كهتي هین كه هم ازواج نبي مین دو پارٹیان تهین - مین اور حفصه اور سوده اور صفیه ایک پارٹی مین تهین اور زینب بنت جحش اور ام سلمه اور باقي سب دوسري پارٹي

† Rawdzat-al-Ahbáb. ‡ Allàma Abbási.

9 A. H.

their fathers' position with the Prophet, Ayesha and Hafsa desired to exercise their influence over their husband, and sometimes their attitude towards the Prophet was not quite respectful. They made such demands as he could not provide for. Once on an accasion like this, both Abubekr and Omar happened to visit the Prophet, and finding him sitting among them sad and gloomy, each of them rebuked his daughter. At another time, when the Prophet's share of the spoils of some war was distributed, Ayesha demanded something which the Prophet could not, in justice, allot to her. She persisted in her demand so much so that the Prophet became sad and dejected. Ali tried to dissuade her but she lost her temper and spoke harshly to Ali. The Prophet was angry with her and he ‡ *authorized Ali to divorce in his behalf any of his (Prophet's) wives whenever he (Ali) so desired.* A revelation condemning such behaviour of the Prophet's wives was received as follows:

"O thou Prophet, say to thy wives, if ye desire the enjoyment of this world and its adornments, then come, I will make a provision for you, and I will dismiss you with an honourable dismissal." *Sura XXXIII-28.*

Some of the wives of the Prophet stooped to the level of common women and did not hesitate to adopt a diplomatic line of action. Some instances of their behaviour are:—(i) Zainab bint Johash, one of the wives, had received some good honey as a present. *When the Prophet visited her, she prepared a beverage of it for him, as he was known to have a liking for it. As it takes some time to dissolve honey into water, the Prophet's stay at Zainab's quarters was necessarily prolonged. This roused the jealousy of Ayesha. She consulted the members of her

*در روضة الاحباب چنین نوشته که عسل برای زینب بنت جحش بهدیه آورده بودند و وی برای آن سرور نگاه داشته بود چه عسل را دوست میداشت چون حضرت بنزد او میرفت شربت عسل برای وی میکرد بنابر آنکه عسل دیر آب میشود زیاده بر معهود در خانه او توقفی واقع

‡ Rawdzat-al-Ahbáb; Habib-al-Siyar; A'sam Kufi; Manáqib-Murtazawi.

party and managed to arrange for the disgrace of Zainab. When the Prophet came to Ayesha, she hinted that an obnoxious odour of Magháfir was emanating from his mouth. He felt it and replied that he had not eaten Magháfir, but that he had drunk a beverage prepared from honey. She then said that the bees might have sucked the juice of Magháfir flower, of which the honey was the produce. Leaving her, he came to Hafsa, only to hear the same story. Next day, when Zainab presented the beverage, he refused to drink it. (ii) † About the same period, it occurred that Hafsa had gone one day to her father's house, and in her absence the Prophet was with Mary, the Coptic girl, in Hafsa's quarters. In the meantime Hafsa came back, and seeing Mary in her quarters with the Prophet, she grew frantic and exhibited violent anger. To pacify her, the Prophet offered to give up Mary for ever. (iii) *The third is a case of breach of trust, and of disclosing a secret against the wishes of the Prophet. The Prophet usually foretold events and he related how trouble would spring up after his death. He said to Hafsa that it would be good tidings to her that on

---

میشد عایشه گوید من و حفصه باهم موافقت نموده با یکدگر گفتیم که حضرت بر هر کدام ازما که در آید باید که بگوید از تو بوے مغافیر میشنویم مگر مغافیر خوردۀ (مغافیر صمغ درختے است که بوے کریه دارد) القصه حضرت بر یکے از ایشان در آمد وے آن سخن را چنانچه مقرر بود گفت حضرت فرمود مغافیر نه خورده ام بلکه شربت عسل آشامیده ام پیش زینب بنت جحش آن زن گفت چریده است زنبور این عسل در درخت عرفط یعنے مغافیر فرمود چون چنین است دیگر هرگز ازان عسل شربت نیاشامم و لیکن این سخن را با هیچکس مگوي آن زن قبول نمود فاما وفا بقول خویش نکرده با آن دیگرے گفت جبریل آمد واین آیه آورد یا ایهاالنبی لم تحرم الخ—

* فی اعلام النبوة ص ۸۱ قال رسول الله صلعم الا ابشرک قالت بلي قال یلی هذاالامر من بعدی ابو بکر ثم یلیه بعدابو بکر ابوک فاکتمي هذا

† Zákir Hasain's History of Islam, Vol. II, p. 150.

9 A. H

his death, Abubekr would assume the Caliphate, and on his death her own father would be his successor. Hafsa was startled at this prediction but soon composed her demeanour. The Prophet strictly enjoined her not to disclose the secret. She agreed and consented, but, as soon as the Prophet was gone, she visited Ayesha and congratulated her on having got rid of her rival, the Coptic girl; continuing her discourse, she mentioned the secret against the injunctions of the Prophet. After these incidents the Prophet received the following revelation :—

Sura LXVI-1 O thou Prophet! Why holdest thyself to be denied that which thy Lord hath allowed thee (*i.e.* the giving up of Mary), seeking to please thy wives? Surely God is Forgiving, Merciful!

2 God hast permitted you to atone for your oaths, and God is your Master, and He is the Knowing, the Wise.

3 And when the Prophet told, as a secret, his prediction (about Caliphate) to one of his wives (Hafsa), and she betrayed it to another (Ayesha) and God informed him of it (the betrayal), he made her known part of it

---

فخرجت حتی دخلت علي عايشه فقالت الا ابشرک بابنه ابی بکر علی قالت بماذا فذكرت ذلک لها قالت قد استكتمهني فاكتميه فانزل الله تعالی يا أيها النبی لم تحرم الخ—

ترجمه—اعلام النبوة مين صفحه ۱۸ پر هے كه فرمايا رسول الله صلعم نے (حفصه سے) كه كيا تمكو مژده دون (حفصه نے) كها هان (حضرت نے) فرمايا كه ميرے بعد خلافت كو ابوبكر لے لينگے اور اونكے بعد تمهارے باپ (عمر) حاصل كرينگے - اس راز كو ظاهر نه كرنا-پهر حضرت حفصه حجره سے نكلين اور حضرت عايشه كے پاس آكر كهنے لگيں كه اے ابوبكر كی بيتی تمكو كوئي مژده دون حضرت عايشه نے كها وه كيا حضرت حفصه نے تمام راز كهولديا اور يهه بهی سمجهاديا كه مجه سے چهپانيكو كها گيا هے تم بهي چهپا ركهنا-اسپر سوره تحريم كی آيتين نازل هوئں —

(تذكرة الصحابيات ص ۱۰۰)

9 A. H.

and withheld a part, and when he taxed her
(Hafsa) with her betrayal, she asked, "Who
informed thee of this?" He said, "The All-
knowing, the All-informed has informed me."
4 *(It would be better) If ye both († Hafsa
and Ayesha) turn to God repentant, as
already your hearts have swerved (from
righteousness), but if you back each other
up against him (the Prophet) then verily,

* في الدرالمنثور للسيوطى اخرج البخاري و مسلم و ترمذي عن ابن عباس رضى الله عنهما قال لم ازل حريصا على ان اسأل عمر رضى الله عنه عن امرأتين من ازواج النبى صلعم اللتين قال الله لهما ان تتوبا الى الله فقد صغت قلوبكما حتى حج عمر و حججت معه فلما كان ببعض الطريق عدل عمر و عدلت معه بالاداوة فتبرز ثم اتي فصببت على يديه فتوضا فقلت يا اميرالمومنين من المراتان من ازواج النبى صلعم اللتان قال الله لهما ان تتوبا الى الله فقد صغت قلوبكما فقال و اعجبالک يا ابن عباس هما عائشه و حفصه—

ترجمه-تفسير در منثور سيوطي مين هے كه بخاري اور مسلم اور ترمذي (وغيره هم) نے ابن عباس سے روايت كى هے كه مين هميشه اس بات كو حضرت عمر سے دريافت كرنيكى خواهش ركهتا تها كه وه دو عورتين كون هين جنكى نسبت الله تعالى نے قران مجيد مين فرمايا هے كه تم توبه كرو تمهارے دل تيرهے هوگئے هين-مگر موقع دريافت كرنيكا نه ملتا تها-اتفاقاً ايكبار سفر حج مين ميرا اور حضرت عمر كا ساتهه هوا واپسى كيوقت اثناے راه مين حضرت عمر حسب ضرورت پيچهے پهرے تو مين بهى اونكے ساتهه ظرف آب لئے هوے پهرا حضرت عمر رفع ضرورت كيلئے گئے اور جب آے تو مينے اونكے هاتهون پر پانى دالا انهون نے وضو كيا اوسوقت مينے پوچها كه يا امير المومنين وه دو عورتين كون هين جنكے متعلق الله تعالے فرماتا هے كه توبه كرو تمهارے

† Sahih Bokhári Vol. III p. 168 Chapter on Divorce;
Do. Vol. IV p. 21 „ on Dress;
Fath-al-Bári ch. 22 p. 172
Tárikh-al-Khamis; Rawdzat-al-Ahbáb.

God his Protector and Gabriel and the Righteous of the Believers* (Ali) and the Angels will back him up besides.
5 Haply his Lord, if he (the Prophet) divorce you (Ayesha and Hafsa), will give him (the Prophet) in exchange wives better than you, Moslems, believing, devoutful, repentant, worshipping, given to fasting, widows and virgins.

These verses are a veritable threat to the wives that they shall be divorced, and one feels that the Prophet would have actually divorced his troublesome wives, but for a feeling of mercy that, if divorced, their lives shall be ruined, for they could not be re-espoused by any Moslem.

دل تیرھے ھوگئے ھین-حضرت عمر نے فرمایا که اے ابن عباس تعجب ھے که تم نهین جانتے وه دو عورتین عایشه اور حفصه ھین—

نیز ملاحظه ھوصحیح بخاري کتاب اللباس جلد ۴ ص ۲۱ -صحیح بخاری کتاب الطلاق جلد ۳ ص ۱۶۸ و فتح الباری جزو ۲۲ ص ۱۷۲

* سوره تحریم کی آیت فان الله ھو مولاه و جبریل وصالح المومنین مین صالح المومنین خاص حضرت علی کا نام ھے تفسیر درمنثور سیوطی مطبوعه مصر جلد ۶ ص ۲۴۴ سطر ۶ و ۷ و ۸ پر بروایت ابن عباس و بروایت اسماء بنت عمیس نیز بروایت علی بن ابیطالب تین روایتین مرقوم ھین جنکو علي الترتیب ابن ابي حاتم- ابن مردویه اور ابن عساکر نے اخراج کیا ھے سمعت رسول الله صلعم یقول و صالح المومنین علي بن ابیطالب یعنے پیغمبر اسلام علیه و آله السلام کو مینے فرماتے ھوے سنا ھے که قران مین صالح المومنین سے مراد علي بن ابیطالب ھے—

فخرالدین رازی اربعین مین اور حافظ ابو نعیم کتاب ما نزل في علی مین ابن عباس سے نقل کرتے ھین- في قوله تعالے و صالح المومنین قال ھو علي بن ابیطالب—

نیز ملاحظه ھو تفسیر ثعلبی اور کنزالعمال علی متقي—

الھم صل علے محمد و آل محمد

Separation of the Prophet from his wives for a month.

The Prophet, being thus informed about Ayesha and Hafsa, was very sorrowful and, in a gloomy mood, swore a separation for one month from his wives and confined himself to a lonely apartment of his mosque, appointing Ribáh, one of his slaves, on its door to watch against any intrusion. It was rumoured throughout the town that the Prophet had divorced his wives. All other wives were sad at this event. Omar was very anxious about his daughter Hafsa, who had caused all this trouble; he therefore tried several times to approach the Prophet, but the watchman would not allow him. †At last one day, Omar contrived means to get admission, by shouting loudly to the door-keeper (but meaning to be heard by the Prophet himself) to ask permission of the Prophet informing him at the same time that he (Omar) would not recommend forgiveness for Hafsa, whom he was ready to kill outright if the Prophet so desired. The Prophet heard the voice and directed the door-keeper to let Omar in. Having thus gained audience, Omar dwelt upon such topics as made the Prophet laugh. At length, finding the Prophet in a cheerful disposition, Omar asked him if he had really divorced his wives. Receiving answer in the negative, Omar came out and publicly declared the fact. One month having finished, the Prophet again visited his wives. Ayesha, on seeing him, remarked that his separation lasted only twenty-nine days and not a month as he had sworn. She was answered that the month consisted of only twenty-nine days and not thirty.

Announcement of Sura Bara'at.

‡The pilgrims at the annual pilgrimage of Mecca were for the most part heathens, who mingled idolatrous practices with the holy rites, but the Prophet had hitherto abstained from being present at the ceremonies; and contented himself with Lesser Pilgrimage or Omra in previous years. The sacred season of the year 9 A. H. was now drawing near. The Prophet, by this time, had received

† Rawdzat-al-Ahbáb. ‡ Abul Fida; Tárikh-al-Khamis.

9 A. H.

a revelation forbidding the idolators to perform the pilgrimage after this year, as contained in the openinng verses of *Sura IX* of the Qurán. The Prophet, therefore, deputed Abubekr to proceed on pilgrimage to Mecca, in order to promulgate the Revelation to the Pilgrims. Three hundred Moslems accompanied Abubekr and twenty camels were given him to be sacrificed on behalf of the Prophet.

* Shortly after the departure of Abubekr, the Prophet received Command from God and, in obedience thereto, he despatched Ali † on his swiftest camel the Al-Ghadzba, with injunctions to overtake the caravan and to take back the book (Verses of *Sura IX*) from Abubekr, and to proceed himself with it, to announce it to the pilgrims at Mecca.

---

*اخرج النسای عن انس قال بعث النبی صلعم براءۃ مع ابي بكر ثم دعاه فقال لا ينبغي ان يبلغ هذا الا رجل من اهلی فدعا عليا فاعطاه اياها ـ و اخرج ايضا عن علي ان رسول الله صلعم بعث براءۃ الی اهل مكة مع ابی بكر ثم اتبعه بعلی فقال له خذ هذا الكتاب فامض به الي اهل مكة قال فلحقته و اخذت الكتاب منه قال فانصرف ابو بكر و هو كئيب قال يا رسول الله انزل فی شئی قال لا الا انی امرت ان ابلغه انا او رجل من اهل بيتی و فی حديث آخر رواه النساي والترمذی (عن حبشی بن جنادة) قال رسول الله صلعم لا يودي عني الا انا او علي

ترجمه ـ نساي نے انس سے روایت کی هے که جناب رسولخداآ نے حضرت ابو بكر كو مع سوره براءت (اهل مكه كيجانب) بهيجا بعد ازان اونكو طلب كركے كها كه سوا ميرے يا ايسے شخص كے جو ميرے اهل سے هو اور كوی شخص امر تبليغ كو ادا نهين كرسكتا ـ پهر حضرت علی كو بلاكر اُنهين تبليغ سوره براءت كی خدمت عطا فرماي نيز

محدث موصوف نے حضرت علی سے روایت كی هے كه پيغمبر صاحب نے حضرت ابو بكر كو مع سوره براءت اهل مكه كی جانب بهيجا اسكے بعد هی اونكے عقب مين مجهكو روانه كيا اور فرمايا كه تم ابوبكر سے كتاب سورۂ براءت ليكر اهل مكه كی طرف جاو ـ چنانچه مينے اثناے راه مين ابو بكر سے ملكر كتاب موصوف ليلي پس ابو بكر نے واپس آكر پيغمبر

† Tirmizhi ; Ahmad Hanbal ; Tabari ; 'A'lám-al-wara ; Tafsir Mo'álim-al-Tanzil; Abul Fida.

9 A. H

Ali overtook the caravan at Araj and, taking the book from Abubekr, proceeded to Mecca; while Abubekr returned back dejected to Medina and asked the Prophet whether his (Abubekr's) dismissal from conveying the revelation to the people was based on any Command from God. The Prophet answered that he had a revelation to the effect (according to Hishámi) that none should deliver the Revelation to the people but he himself or a man of his family, or (according to Tirmizhi and Nasái) that none should deliver it to the people but he himself or Ali. Reaching Mecca, Ali read aloud, towards the close of the pilgrimage, on the great day of sacrifice, to the vast concourse of the pilgrims, the recitation of the Passage of the Qurán. Having finished it, he continued; "I have been ordered to explain to you, (1) That no one shall hence-forward make the circuits of the Holy House naked. (2) Any treaty, made by whomsoever with the Prophet, shall remain in force till its termination. That four months of liberty are allowed to all, after which the obligation devolving upon the Prophet will cease. (3) That no unbeliever will enter Paradise. (4) That the idolators must not come on pilgrimage after this year.

The Year of Deputations.

Towards the close of the ninth year of Hegira, embassies from all quarters of Arabia came uninterruptedly to the Prophet at Medina, to profess Islam and to declare the adhesion of their tribes to the Prophet. (*Sur. CX.*) Most of the princes and the chiefs of Omán, Bahrein, Yamáma and Bahra signified, by letter or by embassy, their submission to the Prophet and conversion to his faith.

صاحب سے بادل شکستہ و محزون عرض کیا کہ یا رسول اللہ کیا میری نسبت کوئي حکم نازل ھوا (جو آپنے کار تبلیغ سے مجھے معزول فرمایا) آنحضرت نے کہا کہ نہین بلکہ مجھے یہہ حکم الہي ھوا ھے کہ یا مین خود اُسکي تبلیغ کرون یا وہ شخص جو میرے اھلبیت سے ھو اور ایک دوسري حدیث مین جسکو نساي اور ترمذي نے حبشي بن جنادہ سے روایت کیا ھے یہہ الفاظ ھین کہ جناب رسولخدا صلعم نے فرمایا کہ میري جانب سے سوا میرے اور علي کے کوی شخص امر تبلیغ کو ادا نہین کرسکتا—

9 A.H.

The Prophet received the embassies with marked gentleness, entertained them liberally, dismissed them with handsome presents and furnished them generously for their return journey. He sent with them his men to instruct the people in the Qurán and the doctrines of the Faith, and to collect the public dues. One of the deputations from the Bani Hanifa, a Christian branch of the Banu Bakar, who inhabited Yamáma, was of Musailama the Imposter, who later on set himself up for a Prophet. So numerous were the embassies during the year that the ninth year of Hegira is known as "the Year of Deputations". This state of affairs continued till the next year.

The Christians of Najran.

*Still the Christians of Najrán held themselves away. The Prophet therefore sent them a letter inviting them to his Faith. Upon this they selected fourteen men—a Bishop and the Clergy—from amongst themselves, deputed them to see the Prophet at Medina and ascertain what Islam was, and to form a judgement of its merits. † Reaching Medina, these men, elegantly dressed in silk with gold rings on their fingers, saluted the Prophet, who turned from them and did not answer their salutation. They came back from the mosque and, complaining of

---

* در مدارج النبوة است که حضرت صلعم مکتوبے به نصارائے نجران نوشت و ایشانرا به اسلام دعوت نمود آنجماعت بعد از مشاورت یکدیگر چهارده کس را از قوم خویش اختیار کرده به مدینه فرستادند تا احوال رسول صلعم تحقیق کنند و خبر به ایشان رسانند و سه نفر درین بودند که کار و بار و اختیار بدست ایشان بود یکے عبدالمسیح ملقب به عاقب دیگر ابهم ملقب به سید و دیگر ابوالحارث - چون بمدینه رسیدند جامهاے راه از خود دور کرده حلهاے ابریشمین پوشیده و انگشتریهاے طلا دردست کرده به مسجد نبوی در آمدند و سلام کردند- حضرت جواب سلام ایشان نداد و روے مبارک از ایشان باز گردانید (الی ان قال) پس از مسجد بیرون آمدند به عثمان بن عفان و عبدالرحمن بن عوف

†Ibn Khaldum ; Ibn Athir ; Habib-al-Siyar.

the cold treatment, asked Othmán and Abd-al-Rahmán b. Awf to advise them what to do. They took them to Ali, who advised them to put off their silk dress and gold rings and to re-appear before the Prophet. They did so, and were received by the Prophet with kindness. They were given an opportunity for a conference, which turned entirely upon the Second person in the Trinity; concerning whom they cited passages from the Gospels, to which the Prophet gave answers and explained to them that Jesus Christ was no more than a Prophet. They left the Prophet promising to come over again after considering the arguments. In the meantime the Prophet received a revelation as follows:—

Sur. III—52 "Verily the position of Jesus with regard to God is like the position of Adam. He created him of clay, then said to him, Be, and he became."

54 "And he who disputes with thee concerning him after the truth had come to thee, say thou, Come, let us call together our Sons and your Sons, our Women and your Women, and our Souls and your Souls, then let us invoke and lay the curse of God on the liars."

گفتند پیغمبر شما مکتوبے به ما نوشت و ما را دعوت نمود چون نزد او آمدیم و سلام کردیم جواب نه شنیدیم و هر چند سخن کردیم از وے غیر سکوت چیزے ندیدیم اکنون راے شما درین باب چیست آیا باز گردیم بدیار خود یا توقف کنیم- عثمان و عبدالرحمن با علی گفتند راے تو درین مهم چیست گفت راے من آنست که این جامهاے فاخر و انگشتریهاے طلا از خود دور کنند و جامها بر رسم رهبانان پوشیده در مجلس شریف در آیند ان قوم بموجب فرموده علي عمل نموده به نزد آنحضرت صلعم رفتند و سلام کردند آنحضرت جواب سلام ایشان باز داد و فرمود که بان خداے که مرا براستي مبعوث فرمود که این قوم نوبت اول چون بمجلس من در آمدند شیطان با ایشان بود - بعد ازان سرور عالم ایشان را به اسلام دعوت نمود ایشان به آنحضرت گفتند چه میگوي در شان عیسي آنحضرت فرمود امروز جواب شما نمیگویم اقامت کنید درین بلده تا جواب این سوال بشنوید-گویا انتظار وحي کرد پس روز دیگر این آیت

9 A. H.

When they re-appeared before the Prophet, he informed them of God's decree, which was agreed upon as the means of settling the discussion. Time was appointed and an open place outside the city was fixed for the ceremoney to be held on 24th of Zhil-Hajja. Meanwhile they carefully meditated over the risk they were to undergo, and unanimously arrived at the conclusion that they should avoid it. They, however, kept the appointment. The Prophet taking with him Hasan and Hosain for his sons, Fátema his beloved daughter for his women and Ali, his devoutful vicegerent and son-in-law, for his soul, thus fulfiling the Heavenly dictates, appeared at the place of appointment.

‡ It is maintained by a large body of the Moslems that only these members of the Prophet's house composed of his permanent or unchangeable family, whom the Prophet loved dearly and who were distinguished from the rest of the Moslem world, on account of their having been declared purified by God,—sinless and faultless—in the Revelation

---

نازل شد - ان مثل عیسي عندالله کمثل آدم خلقه من تراب.........
......فقل تعالواندع ابناءنا و ابناوکم و نساءنا و نساءکم و انفسنا و انفسکم ثم نبتهل فنجعل لعنت الله علي الکاذبین—
سیدعالم ایشانرا طلبید و آیات را برایشان خواند مگر آنها اقرار نه کردند و بر اعتقاد خویش مصر بودند - حضرت فرمود چون باور نمیکنید بیائد تا با یکدیگر مباهله کنیم یعنی دعا کنیم درشان یکدیگر و گوئیم لعنت خدا بر دروغ گویان باد گفتند ما را مهلت ده تا درین باب تاملی کنیم و فردا بیائیم و در خلوت باعاقب گفتند رای تو درین باب چیست عاقب گفت که بخدا سوگند که شما میدانید که محمد پیغمبر مرسل است و در باب عیسي دلیل ظاهر آورده مباهله باوی نکنید ورنه هلاک خواهید شد چون خواهید که بر دین خود ثابت باشید باوی مصالحت کنید و جزیه قبول نمائید چنانچه روز دیگر صباح به نزد رسول صلعم آمدند - حضرت صلعم خود از حجرهٔ شریف بیرون آمده حسین بن علي در زیر بغل و دست حسن را گرفته فاطمه زهرا در عقب آنحضرت و علي مرتضي

‡ Habib-al-Siyar; Rawdzat-al-Safá; Tafsir Kashát.

contained in *Sura XXXIII-33* 'God desireth only to keep away from you the abomination, as (ye are) the members of the House (of the Prophet) and to purify you a (perfect) purification?

NOTE.—The pronouns in this part of the verse, being of the masculine gender, mean to indicate Ali, Hasan and Hosain whereas the pl. fem. used in the previous part of the verse, is directed to the wives.

Muslim in his Sahih records on the authority of Sa'd b. Abi Waqqás that when the verse "*Let us call together Our sons and your sons etc.*" Qurán *Sura III-54* was revealed, the Apostle of God summoned *Ali and Fatema and Al Hasan and Al Hosain and said, "O God these are my family." Suyuti's His. of Cal. by Major Jarrett, page 173*.

† The solemn appearance of the holy group overawed the Bishop and his people. They trembled at the consequences of the Ordeal, through fear of the terrible punishment that would fall upon them in case of failure, and expressed their unwillingness to undertake it. The Prophet then asked them to embrace Islam or to take up arms against him. They said that they were ready to pay

---

در عقب فاطمه و بایشان فرمود چون من دعا کنم شما آمین گوئید- سبحان الله این چه وقت و چه حالت است و چه شاهد و چه مشهود - گروه نصاراے نجران چون این پنجتن پاک را دیدند و حدیث دعا و آمین شنیدند بترسیدند ابوالحارث‌که در ایشان دانشمند بود گفت اے قوم بدرستیکه من روے چند مي بینم اگر بخواهند از خدا که زائل‌گرداند کوه را از جاے خود زائل میگرداند بخواهش ایشان زنهار مباهله نکید که هلاک شوید و هیچ نصرانی برروے زمین نماند..... پس گفتند یا ابالقاسم با تو مباهله نمیکنیم - فرمود پس مسلمان شوید گفتند این کار از ما نمي آید فرمود پس محاربه را آماده شوید گفتند مارا طاقت محاربه با تو نیست و لیکن مصالحت میکنیم با تو برآن که هر سال دو هزار حله که بهاے هر حله چهل درهم باشد دهیم و بروایتے آمده که سي اسپ و سي شتر و سی زره و سي نیزه نیز دهیم پس برین جمله مصالحت واقع شد—(تاریخ احمدي ص ۸۳)

† Ibn Athir.

him annual tribute in the shape of 2000 coats of mail, each coat costing about forty Dirhams. With these terms the Prophet graciously allowed them to return to their home.

History records many Ordeals similar to this, which were familiar to Christian people in Europe, centuries before and after this epoch.

In bringing forward Fátema, the Prophet showed to the people that she was the only woman who belonged exclusively to him and that none of his wives could be brought down to fulfil the execution of the Command; and none of his relations or Companions, but Ali, could stand for the Soul of the Prophet as ordained in the Command of God. Taking the children Hasan and Hosain with him, the Prophet pointed out to the people that they were his own sons, as he had already declared that God had decreed his lineal descendants to spring forth from Ali and Fátema and not direct from himself (see page 99). In short he, in practice, did show to the people that he himself, Ali, Fátema, Hasan and Hosain were the only persons who could stand to the Ordeal, as they were part and parcel of one and the same Celestial Light and whose appeals to God might instantly be answered.

CHAPTER XVI.

The Farewell pilgrimage of the Prophet. His Sermon at Ghadir-i-Khum. The meaning of Ahl-i-Bait explained.

The tenth year of Hegira commenced with the arrival of fresh embassies. Various tribes from the sea coast of Yemen, from Hadzramawt and from the Southern coast, sent their deputations signifying their submission to the Prophet and adhesion to his faith. Two chiefs of the Bani Kinda from Hadzramawt *viz.* Al Ash'ath and Wáil offered their personal allegiance and embraced Islam. This Al Ash'ath is the same who subsequently joined the rebellion, which broke out after the death of the Prophet, and offered strong resistance to the quelling party, which ultimately needed reinforcements. He was, at last, after much trouble, taken prisoner and sent to Caliph Abubekr, who pardoned him in spite of Omar's protests, on his renewing the allegiance, and gave his sister Omm Farwa in marriage to him. Subsequently he turned a Khárijite against Caliph Ali. His sons, Mohammed and Isháq, appeared notably in the army sent by Yazid for the massacre of Hosain b. Ali at Karbalá.

Ali's Missionary duties in Yemen.

† In the month of Rabi' II, of the tenth year of Hegira, Khálid b. Walid was deputed by the Prophet to propagate Islam among the people of Yemen. But, instead of satisfactory reports during the six months' stay of Khálid at Yemen, complaints against him were pouring in at Medina. ‡ The Prophet then deputed Ali, with three hundred of his followers, to replace Khálid. The youthful hero modestly expressed that he would have to deal with men far older than himself and well versed in old Scriptnres. The Prophet then putting his hand upon Ali's breast raised his eyes to heaven and exclaimed; "O God! Loosen Ali's Tongue and guide his heart." He then gave out a rule for Ali's guidance as a judge, saying, "When two parties come to thee, never pronounce in favour of one until thou hast heard the other." Then, arranging with his own hands Ali's head dress and giving into his hands the Standard of Faith, the Prophet bade him farewell. Ali proceeded to Yemen and there read the Prophet's letter to the people and delivered his sermons according to the dictates of the Prophet, preaching the doctrines of Islam to the multitudes, with the result that the whole tribe of Hamdánis embraced the Faith in a single day. (Ibn Athir, Kamil V. II). Ali reported the success of his mission to the Prophet, who on receiving the intelligence, instantly bowed low with his forehead on the ground, in humble reverence to God and offered Him

† Ibn Khaldun; Tabari.
‡ Abul Fida; Ibn Khaldun; Rawdzat-al-Ahbáb.

thanks. Other tribes, one after the other, followed the example of the Hamdánis. Some Chiefs did homage and made pledges on behalf of their people. Ali reported daily the progress of his mission. Now, receiving orders from the Prophet, he proceeded to Najrán, recollected the Dues from the people and then retraced his steps to Mecca, where he joined the Prophet in his last pilgrimage in the month of Zhilhajja 10 A. H.

In fulfilment of their pledge, some two hundred people from Yemen arrived at Medina, in the beginning of the 11th year of Hegira, (the year calculated to commence from Moharram) to tender their personal allegiance to the Prophet; and this was the last deputation received by him.

The Farewell pilgrimage of the Prophet.

† As the period for the annual pilgrimage approached, the Prophet made preparations for his pilgrimage to Mecca. He invited people from all quarters of the Peninsula to join him, in order to become acquainted with the proper performance of various rites attendant on the sacred ceremonies. Since his emigration to Medina this was the Prophet's first and the last Haj pilgrimage. Five days before the opening of Zhilhajja, the month of pilgrimage, the Prophet set out for Mecca followed by over a hundred thousand pilgrims. All his wives and his beloved daughter Fátema, the wife of Ali, accompanied him. During this journey, a son, who was named Mohammed, was born to Abubekr by his wife Asmá bint Omais.

The Prophet reached Mecca on Sunday the 4th of Zhilhajja 10 A. H. Soon after his arrival Ali, who hastened back from Yemen ahead of his men, joined the Prophet, who was very glad to see him and affectionately embracing him asked what vow he had taken for the pilgrimage. Ali replied, "I have taken upon me a vow to perform the same pilgrimage as the Prophet, whatever that might be, and I have brought thirty-four camels for the sacrifice." The Prophet joyfully exclaimed 'Alláh-o-

† Rawdzat-al-Ahbáb.

Akbar,' Great is the Lord, and said he had brought sixty-six. He added that in all the rites of the Pilgrimage, as well as in the sacrifice, he (Ali) would be his partner. Thus Ali also performed the Greater Pilgrimage along with the Prophet.

As the various ceremonies were to be treated as a model for future guidance, the Prophet observed rigorously each rite, whether in compliance with Revelations or in accordance with the patriarchal usage. Thus, when the camels were to be offered up in sacrifice, the hundred camels were sacrificed by himself and Ali conjointly. A repast, prepared from the meat of the sacrificed camels being served, the Prophet sat down with no other but Ali to partake of it. The ceremonies of the pilgrimage ended with shaving the heads and paring the nails after the sacrifice of animals. The pilgrim's garb was then put off and a Proclamation was made by Ali, who rode on the Prophet's Duldul, that the restrictions of Pilgrimage were over.

At the conclusion of the Pilgrimage, the Prophet reformed the Calendar, abolishing the teriennial intercalation; and appointing the year to be purely lunar consisting of twelve lunar months, thus fixing the month of Pilgrimage according to the changing seasons of the lunar year.

Sermon at Ghadir-i-Khum. 10 A. H.

Bidding farewell to his native city, the Prophet set out for Medina on the 14th of Zhilhajja from Mecca. *While on the way, at Ghadir-i-Khum, a barren tract on the outskirts of Johfa valley, three stages from Mecca, on the 18th of Zhilhajja, he ordered a halt, having received the following revelation :—

---

* في اسباب النزول للواحدی والدر المنثور للسيوطي و الفتح القدير للشوكاني و فتح البيان عن ابی سعيد الخدري قال نزلت هذه الاية يا ايها الرسول بلغ ما انزل اليک من ربک على رسول الله صلعم يوم غدير خم فی علي ابن ابي طالب رضی الله عنه —

10 A. H.

"O Thou Apostle! Proclaim what has been sent † down to thee from thy Lord; and if thou dost not, thou wouldst not accomplish thy Mission at all; and God will defend thee against men; verily God guides not the unbelieving people." *Sura V-71.*

‡ It is held that the Prophet had already been ordered to proclaim Ali his successor, but he had postponed the announcement for some suitable occasion to avoid misappreciation.

---

† It refers to the Commandment contained in *Sura XCIV* of the Qurán, which runs thus:

1 Have We not opened thy breast for thee?
2 And put off thy burden from thee,
3 Which galled thy back?
4 And have We not raised thy name for thee?
5 Then verily, with trouble cometh ease,
6 Verily, along with trouble cometh ease;
7 And when thou art eased, set up (thy successor),
8 And turn to thy Lord with fervour.

In the 7th verse, God has commanded the Prophet to appoint his successor.

‡ Tafsir Kabir; Tafsir Durr-al-Manthur; Tafsir Neshápuri; Sirat-al-Halabiya.

ترجمہ—کتاب اسباب النزول واحدي و تفسير در منثور سيوطي و تفسير فتح القدير شوکاني و تفسير فتح البيان علامہ صديق حسن خان مين بروايت ابن ابی حاتم وغيرہ ابو سعيد خدري سے مروي ھے کہ آيۂ يا ايها الرسول بلغ ما انزل اليک من ربک و ان لم تفعل فما بلغت رسالته روز غدير خم حضرت علی کی شانمين نازل ہوا—

في حديث نقله العينی فی عمدة القاري لشرح صحيح البخاري معناه بلغ ما انزل اليک الخ فی فضل علي بن ابيطالب فلما نزلت هذه الاية اخذ بيد علی و قال من کنت مولاه فعلی مولاه

ترجمہ—ايک روايت مين جسکو عينی نے عمدة القاری شرح صحيح بخاري مين نقل کيا ھے آيۂ يا ايها الرسول بلغ ما انزل اليک کے يہہ معنی مذکور ہين کہ اے رسول اوس حکم کو پہونچا دو جو تمہارے رب نے علی بن ابيطالب کے فضل مين نازل فرمايا ھے پس جب يہہ آيت نازل ہوی تو جناب رسالتماب نے حضرت علی کا ہاتھہ پکڑ کر ارشاد فرمايا

Now receiving this Command, he resolved to make the announcement without further delay. He therefore made a halt at the place where he received the reminder. The ground being cleared, a pulpit was formed of the saddles of camels, and Bilál, the Moazhin, shouted aloud,

---

کہ من کنت مولاہ فعلی مولاہ - یعنی جسکا مین مولا ہون علی بھي اُسکا مولا ھے—

فی تفسیر غرائب القران للنیشا پوری ان ھذہ الایۃ (یاایھاالرسول بلغ ماانزل الیک الایۃ) نزلت فی فضل علي بن ابیطالب رضي اللہ عنہ و کرم اللہ وجھہ یوم غدیر خم فاخذ رسول اللہ صلعم بیدہ وقال من کنت مولاہ فعلي مولاہ (الحدیث) —

ترجمہ—تفسیر غرائب القران علامہ نیشا پوري مین ھے کہ یہہ آیت (یا ایھاالرسول بلغ ما انزل الیک من ربک) حضرت علی کي فضیلت مین بمقام غدیر خم نازل ھوي اور جب اسکا نزول ھوا تو پیغمبر صاحب نے حضرت علي کا ھاتھہ پکڑ کر فرمایا من کنت مولاہ فعلي مولاہ—(تاریخ احمدي ص۹۰)

في الصواعق للشیخ ابن حجر المکي اخرج الطبراني وغیرہ بسند صحیح ان رسول اللہ صلعم خطب بغدیر خم تحت شجرات فقال ایھاالناس انہ قد نبانی اللطیف الخبیر انہ لم یعمر نبی الا نصف عمرالذی یلیہ من قبلہ واني لاظن ان ادعي فاجیب واني مسئول وانکم مسؤلون فماذا انتم قائلون قالوا نشھد انک قد بلغت و جھدت و نصحت فجزاک اللہ خیرا فقال الیس تشھدون ان لا الہ الا اللہ و ان محمداً عبدہ و رسولہ و ان جنۃ حق و ان نارحق و ان الموت حق و ان البعث حق بعدالموت و ان الساعۃ اتیۃ لاریب فیھا و ان اللہ یبعث من في القبور قالوا بلی نشھد بذلک قال اللھم اشھد ثم قال یا ایھاالناس ان اللہ مولای و انا مولی المومنین و انا اولي بھم من انفسھم فمن کنت مولاہ فھذا مولاہ یعنی علیا—

ترجمہ—صواعق محرقہ ابن حجر مکي مین بروایت طبراني وغیرہ بسند صحیح مروي ھے کہ جناب رسولخدا نے مقام غدیر خم مین درختون کے نیچے خطبہ ارشاد کیا اور فرمایا کہ خداے لطیف و خبیر نے مجھے خبر دي ھے کہ ھر نبی اپنے پہلے نبي کی نصف عمر پاتاھے چنانچہ مین گمان کرتا ھون

10 A. H.

"Hearken! Ye people, to the sacred service." The people having clustered round the pulpit, the Prophet stepped up,

---

که عنقریب بارگاه ایزدی سے میری طلبی ہوگی جسے مین قبول کرونگا (سنو) وہان مجھہ سے بہی سوال کیا جائیگا اور تم لوگون سے بہی پس تم کیا کہوگے سب نے کہا ہم گواہی دینگے اور دیتے ہین که آپنے احکام الہی کو کما حقه پہونچادیا اور حق کوشش و نصیحت ادا فرمایا خدا آپکو جزائے خیر عطا فرمائے آنحضرت نے ارشاد فرمایا که کیا تم لوگ اس بات گواہی نہین دیتے که سوا خدا کے کوئی معبود نہین - محمد اوسکا بندہ اور رسول ہے - جنت اور نار حق ہین - موت اور بعث بعدالموت حق ہے قیامت کے آنے مین کچھہ شبہہ نہین ہے اور خدا اون سب کو جو قبور مین ہین زندہ فرمائیگا - سب نے کہا بے شک ہم ان تمام باتون کا اقرار کرتے ہین - یہہ سنکر رسول مقبول نے فرمایا که بار الہا تو شاہد رہ پہر ارشاد کیا که ایہاالناس الله تعالے میرا مولا ہے اور مین کل مومنین کا مولا اور انکے لئے اونکے نفوس سے اولی ہون پس جسکا مین مولا ہون اسکا علی بہی مولا ہے - (تاریخ احمدی ص ۸۷)

در روضته الاحباب آمده که در اثنائے مراجعت چون آنحضرت بمنزل غدیر که نواحي جحفه است رسید نماز پیشین را در اول وقت گزارد بعد ازان رو بسوے یاران کردہ فرمود الست اولی بالمومنین من انفسهم یعنے آیا نیستم من اولی به مومنان از نفسہاے ایشان و روایتے آنکه فرمود گوئیا مرا بعالم بقا خواندند و من اجابت نمودم بدانید که من درمیان شما دو امر عظیم میگذارم که هر یکے از دیگرش بزرگتر است قران و اهلبیت من به بیند و احتیاط کنید بعد از من که بہ آن دو امر چگونه سلوک خواهید نمود و رعایت حقوق آنها بچه کیفیت خواهید کرد و آن دو امر از یکدیگر جدا نخواهند شد تا بر لب حوض کوثر بمن رسند آنگاه فرمود بدرستیکه خدائتعالي مولاے من است و من مولاے جمیع مومنانم - بعد ازان دست علی را گرفت و فرمود - من کنت مولاه فعلی مولاه اللهم وال من والاه و عاد من عاداه و اخذل من خذله وانصر من نصره و ادرالحق معه حیث دار -

taking on his right Ali, whose turban,* black in colour, with its ends hanging over both of his shoulders, was arranged by the Prophet himself. First the Prophet

---

* قال فی الاصابة اخرج البغوی و قال في كنزالعمال اخرج ابن ابي شيبة و ابو داؤدالطيالسی والبهيقي عن علی قال عممنی رسول الله صلعم يوم غدير خم بعمامة سوداء اطرق طرفيها علی منكبی—

ترجمه— اصابه ابن حجر عسقلاني مين بروايت بغوي اور كنزالعمال مين بروايت ابن ابی شيبه و ابو داؤد طيالسي و بهيقي حضرت علی سے مروي هے كه جناب رسولخدانے بروز غدير خم ميرے سر پر ايک عمامه سياه باندها اور اوسكے دونون كنارے ميرے دوش پر ڈالدے— (تاريخ احمدي ص ٩٠)

اخرج النساي عن ابي الطفيل عن زيد بن ارقم قال لما رجع النبی صلعم من حجة الوداع و نزل غدير خم امر بدوحات فقممن ثم قال كانی دعيت فاجبت وانی تارک فيكم الثقلين احدهما اكبر من الاخر كتاب الله و عترتي اهلبيتي فانظروا كيف تخلفوني فيهما فانهما لن يفترقا حتی يردا علی الحوض ثم قال ان الله مولاي وانا ولی كل مومن ثم انه اخذ بيد علی رضي الله عنه فقال من كنت وليه فهذا وليه اللهم وال من والاه وعاد من عاداه - فقلت لزيد سمعته من رسول الله قال ما كان في الدوحات احد الاراه بعينيه و سمعه باذنيه - و عن سعد قال كنامع رسول الله صلعم بطريق مكة فلما بلغ غدير خم وقف للناس ثم رد من تبعه و لحقه من تخلف فلما اجتمع الناس اليه قال ايها الناس من وليكم قالوا الله و رسوله ثلاثا ثم اخذ بيد علي فاقامه ثم قال من كان الله و رسوله وليه فهذا وليه اللهم وال من والاه و عاد من عاداه و من طريق اخر عن زيد بن ارقم قال قام رسول الله صلعم فحمد الله و اثنی عليه ثم قال الستم تعلمون انی اولی بكل مومن من نفسه قالوا بلي لشهد لانت اولي بكل مومن من نفسه قال فانی من كنت مولاه فهذا مولاه و اخذ بيد علی—

ترجمه—محدث نسای نے كتاب خصائص مين بروايت ابوالطفيل زيد بن ارقم سے روايت كی هے كه جب جناب رسولخدا نے حجة الوداع سے مراجعت كی اور مقام غدير خم مين نزول اجلال فرمايا تو حكم ديا كه

10 A. H.

praised God, then he addressed the multitudes thus: "Ye believe," said he, "that there is but one God, that Mohammed is His apostle and Prophet, that Paradise and Hell are truths, that death and Resurrection are certain." They all answered: "We believe these things." *He informed them that he was called to meet his Lord ere long, and then gave utterance to the solemn Adjuration: "I leave unto you two grand Precepts, each of which surpasses the other in its grandeur, *viz.* God's book (the Qurán) and my Progeny the family of mine—(consisting of the unchangeable members Ali, Fátema, Hasan and Hosain). Beware how you behave to them when I am gone from amongst you. Both of them will never

---

منبر تیار کیا جاے چنانچہ منبر تیار کیا گیا اور آنحضرت نے اُسپر رونق افروز هوکر فرمایا که مین جناب باري مین بلایا گیا هون اور مینے حکم الهي کو قبول کیا هے اب مین تم مین دو عظیم چیزین چهوڑتا هون ایک کتاب الله دوسرے اپنی عترت اهلبیت انمین سے هر ایک دوسرے سے بزرگتر هے اور یهه دونون ایکدوسرے سے جدا نهونگے تا اینکه میرے پاس حوض کوثر پر وارد هون پس دیکهنا که میرے بعد اونسے کیونکر برتاو اور تمسک کرتے هو- پهر آنحضرت نے ارشاد فرمایا که (سنو) میرا مولا الله تعالے هے اور مین کل مومنین کا ولي هون بعد ازان حضرت نے حضرت علی کا هاتهه پکڑ کر فرمایا که (دیکهو) جسکا مین ولي هون علي بهی اوسکا ولی هے خداوندا دوست رکهه اوسکو جو علی کو دوست رکهے اور دشمن رکهه اوسکو جو علی سے دشمنی رکهے -ابوالطفیل کهتے هین که مینے یهه حدیث سنکر زید بن ارقم سے پوچها که کیا تمنے اسکو جناب رسولخدا سے سنا هے زید بن ارقم نے کہا که ایک مینے کیا جو لوگ منبر کے گرد مجتمع تهے اون سب نے آنحضرت کو یهه ارشاد کرتے هوے دیکها اور اپنے کانون سے سنا—

نیز سعد بن ابي وقاص سے روایت کیگئي هے که هملوگ رسول الله کے ساتهه همسفر تهے جب آنحضرت غدیر خم مین پهونچے تو آپنے لوگونکو توقف کا حکمدیا چنانچه جو لوگ آگے نکل گئے تهے واپس آئے اور جو پیچهے ره گئے تهے وه پهونچ گئے پس جب کل لوگ مجتمع هوے تو

separate from each other until they reach me in Heaven at the Fountain of Kauthar;" continuing he said: "God is my Guardian and I am the guardian of all Believers."

آنحضرت صلعم نے تین بار استفسار فرمایا کہ ایہاالناس تمہارا ولی
کون ہے ؟ لوگون نے ہر بار عرضکیا کہ اللہ اور اسکا رسول - یہہ سنکر
جناب رسالتماب صلی اللہ علیہ و آلہ و سلم نے حضرت علی کا ہاتھہ پکڑ آ
اور اونکو بلند کرکے فرمایا کہ اللہ اور اوسکا رسول جسکا ولی ہے علي بھي
اوسکا ولی ہے الہی دوست رکھہ اوسکو جو علی کو دوست رکھے اور دشمن
رکھہ اوسکو جو علی کو دشمن رکھے—نیز محدث موصوف نے کتاب مذکور
مین بطریق دیگر زید بن ارقم سے روایت کی ہے کہ جناب رسالت ماب
کھڑے ہوے اور بعد حمد و ثناے الہی آپنے فرمایا کہ ایہاالناس کیا تم
نہین جانتے کہ مین ہر مومن کیلئے اوسکے نفس سے اولي ہون سب نے
جوابدیا کہ بیشک ہم گواہي دیتے ہین کہ آپ ہر مومن کیلئے اوسکے
نفس سے اولي ہین یہہ سنکر رسول مقبول نے حضرت علی کا ہاتھہ پکڑکر
فرمایا کہ (دیکھو) جسکا مولا مین ہون یہہ علی بھی اوسکا مولا ہے —

في المشكوة قال خرج احمد بن حنبل في مسنده عن البراء بن عازب
و زيد بن ارقم قال كنامع رسول الله صلعم فی سفر فنزلنا بغدير خم
فنودی فينا الصلوة جامعة و كسح لرسول الله صلعم تحت شجرتين
فصلی الظهر و اخذ بيد علي رضی الله تعالی عنه فقال الستم تعلمون انی
اولي بالمومنين من انفسهم قالو ابلی قال الستم تعلمون اني اولی بكل
مومن من نفسه قالوا بلي فقال من كنت مولاه فعلی مولاه اللهم و ال من
والاه و عاد من عاداه قال فلقيه عمر بعد ذلک نقال له هنيأً لک يابن
ابيطالب اصبحت و امسيت مولا كل مومن و مومنة—

ترجمہ—مسند احمد بن حنبل مین براء بن عازب اور زید بن ارقم
سے مروی ہے کہ ہملوگ جناب رسولخدا کے ساتھہ سفر مین تھے جب
غدیر خم مین وارد ہوے تو منادي نے ندا کی کہ الصلوة جامعہ
اور پیغمبر صاحب کے لئے درختون کے نیچے زمین صاف کیگئي پس
آنحضرت نے بعد نماز ظہر علی بن ابیطالب کا ہاتھہ پکڑ کر لوگون سے
ارشاد کیا کہ ایہاالناس کیا تم نہیں جانتے کہ مین مومنین کیلئے اونکے
نفوس سے اولی ہون سب نے کہا بیشک پھر آپنے فرمایا کہ کیا تم نہیں جانتے

10 A. H.

So saying, he took one hand of Ali into his own and lifting it upright solemnly proclaimed, "Whomsoever I own the guardianship, Ali too owns the guardianship of that. ‡ May God uphold those who befriend Ali and may He turn from those who turn enemy to him." † Announcing this thrice, he got down the raised platform and seated Ali in a tent, where the people did him homage. Omar bin Al Khattáb was the first to congratulate Ali and to acknowledge him "Guardian of all Believers."

Ali declared Successor.

* After the men, came all the wives of the Prophet and other ladies and congratulated Ali. ** At the conclusion of this Installation ceremony, the following famous verse of the Qurán was received by the Prophet from Heaven: "This day I have perfected your religion and accomplished you in my Grace. It is my good pleasure

---

که میں هر مؤمن کیلئے اوسکے نفس سے اولي هون سب نے عرض کیا که
در حقیقت یا رسول الله آپ هر مومن کیلئے اوسکے نفس سے اولی هین
تب آپنے ارشاد فرمایا که جسکا مین مولاهون علی بهی اوسکا مولا هے الهي
دوست رکهه اوسکو جو علی کو دوست رکهے اور دشمن رکهه اوسکو جو
علي کو دشمن رکهے - اسکے بعد حضرت عمر نے حضرت علی سے ملکر
فرمایا که مبارک هو تمکو اے فرزند ابوطالب که آج تم هرمومن و مومنه
کے مولا هوے

* در معارج النبوة گفته - گویند که بیشتر اصحاب حتي که امهات
المومنین امیر المومنین علی را تهنیت بجا آوردند —

** اخرج ابن مردویه و ابو نعیم عن ابو سعید الخدری قال لما
نزلت هذه الایة یا ایها الرسول بلغ ما انزل الیک من ربک الخ اخذ
النبي صلعم بید علی فقال من کنت مولاه فعلی مولاه الهم و ال من والاه
و عاد من عاداه فنزلت الیوم اکملت لکم دینکم و اتممت علیکم نعمتي
و رضیت لکم الاسلام دینا —

‡ Suyuti: 'O God! Befriend him who is a friend to Ali, and be an enemy to him who is an enemy to Ali.'

† Mishkát; Khasáis Nasái; Rawdzat-al-Ahbáb; Rawdzat-al-Safá.

that Islam be your Faith." *Sura V-5.* The Prophet bowed down in gratitute.

The meaning of Ahl-i-Bait explained.

* The 'Progeny or Family of mine' marked out in the Adjuration means the holy persons meant in the following verse of the Qurán: "Say thou, (O Prophet)! I ask not of you for it a reward, except the love of my kin." *Sura XLII-22.* † On revelation of this verse the Prophet was asked to name the persons whose love was thus ordained. He named Ali, Fátema, Hasan and Hosain.

حافظ ابن مردویہ اور حافظ ابو نعیم نے ابو سعید خدری سے روایت کیا ہے کہ جب آیۂ یا ایہاالرسول بلغ ما انزل الیک من ربک نازل ہوا تو جناب رسالت ماب نے حضرت علی کا ہاتھہ پکڑ کر فرمایا من کنت مولاہ فعلي مولاہ اللہم وال من والاہ و عاد من عاداہ-پس ارشاد نبوی کے بعد یہہ آیت نازل ہوی کہ

الیوم اکملت لکم دینکم و اتممت علیکم نعمتي و رضیت لکم الاسلام دینا-

یعنے آج ہمنے تمہارے دین کو کامل کیا تمپر اپنی نعمتین پوري کین اور تمہارے لئے دین اسلام کو پسند فرمایا—

* ملا محمد مبین در کتاب وسیلۃ النجات آوردہ قال اللہ تعالي قل لا اسئلکم علیہ اجرا الا المودۃ فی القربی بگو اے محمد کہ سوال نمیکنم بہ تبلیغ رسالت ہیچ مزدے مگر دوستی و محبت قربي— فی المدارک والبیضاوی والثعلبي والکشاف روي انہا لما نزلت قیل یا رسول اللہ من قرابتک من ہواءلاء الذین و جبت علینا مودتہم قال علی و فاطمۃ و ابنا ہما— در مدارک و بیضاوي و تفسیر کشاف و ثعلبی مذکور است کہ روایت کردہ شد ہرگاہ این آیہ نازل گشت سائلے از جناب حضرت رسالت صلی اللہ علیہ و آلہ و سلم سوال کرد کہ کدام اند از قرابت تو کہ دوستی و محبت ایشان بر ما واجب و فرض است فرمود رسولخدا صلی اللہ علیہ و آلہ و سلم کہ مفترض المحبت علی و فاطمۃ و ہر دو پسران حسن و حسین علیہم السلام اند—

ایضاً—رواۃ احمد و ابن حاتم والطبرانی والحاکم و صححہ و في الصواعق و نقل الثعلبی والبغوي عن ابن عباس انہ لما نزل قولہ تعالي قل لا اسئلکم علیہ اجرا الا المودۃ فی القربي قال قوم فی نفوسہم ما یریدون

10 A. H.

† The people suspected him to have named his dear relations in order that they may be regarded with awe and respect after his death. God informed His prophet of their suspicions and they were repentant.

* These are the persons, the fidelity to whose love and obedience will be the subject of interrogation on the Day of Judgment, when all persons will be questioned as to how they behaved to them and how they defended their cause and upheld their interests.

الا ان يخشينا على قرابته من بعد فاخبر جبريئل النبي صلى الله عليه و آله و سلم انهم اتهموه فانزل الله تعالى ام يقولون افترى على الله كذبا الاية فقال القوم يا رسول الله انك صادق فانزل و هو الذي يقبل التوبة عن عباده—

ترجمه—منقول است از ابن عباس هرگاه که این آیه مودت نازل شد قومے در دلهاے خود خیال فاسد آوردند که رسولخدا اراده کرد که از قرابت خود ما را بترساند تا ما بترسیم جبرئیل خبر داد و آگاه ساخت رسولخدا صلی الله علیه و آله را که این قوم تهمت میکنند ترا و آیه نازل کرد که میگویند در حق رسولخدا که این تاکید و ترغیب مودة قربی آیا افترا کرده است بر خدا و دروغ بسته یا مجنون است که در حالت جنون این چنین کلمات میگوید—بعد نزول آیه ام یقولون افتری الخ قوم گفتند یا رسول الله تو صادقی ما یان از خیالات خودها توبه کردیم پس نازل شد و هو الذي یقبل التوبة عن عباده —

* ملا محمد مبین در وسیلة النجات آورده که آیه کریمه وقفوهم انهم مسئولون دال است براینکه در روز حشر از همه بشر سوال خواهد شد که در حق امیرالمومنین علی بن ابیطالب صلواة الله علی نبینا و علیه و اهلبیت خیر البشر چه سلوک کردید و حقوق موالات ایشان کماحقه بجا آوردید یا نه و آنچه رسولخدا صلی الله علیه و آله و سلم در اداے حقوق و اطاعت و انقیاد و امر ایشان فرموده آن را سمعاً و طاعتاً امتثال کردید یا تخلف نمودید—

† Tafsir Tha'labi; Tafsir Kasháf; Beidzáwi; Madárik.

63

10 A. H.

* These are the personages declared in the Qurán as purified and freed from all impurities. When the verse, "Verily, God desireth to keep away from you the abomination, as (ye are) the members of the House (of the Prophet), and to purify you a (perfect) purification," (last portion of verse 33 of *Sura XXXIII*) was revealed to the Prophet, he sat under a blanket or mantle along with Ali, Fátema, Hasan and Hosain, and he declared that his House

---

* ابن مردویہ اور خطیب نے ابو سعید خدري سے روایت کی ھے کہ ام سلمہ کي باري کا دن تہا کہ جبریل رسول اللہ کے پاس آیت انما یرید اللہ لیذھب عنکم الرجس اھل البیت و یطھرکم تطھیرا لیکر نازل ھوے آنحضرت نے حضرت علی - حسن - حسین اور فاطمہ علیہم السلام کو بلایا اور اپنے پاس بٹہاکر انپر ایک کپڑا اوڑھایا - ام سلمہ کے سامنے پردہ پڑا تہا اوسوقت آنحضرت نے فرمایا - خدایا یہی لوگ میرے اھلبیت ھین ان سے برائي کو دور رکہہ اور انکو پاک پاکیزہ رکہہ جو پاکیزہ رکہنے کا حق ھے — ام سلمہ نے عرض کیا یا حضرت کیا مین بہي انکے ساتہہ ھوجاون حضرت نے فرمایا تم اپني جگہہ بیٹہی رھو اسمین شک نہین کہ تو نیکي پر ھے —

ترمذی نے حکم بہ صحت دیکر اور ابن جریر اور ابن منذر اور حاکم نے فصیح کرکے اور ابن مردویہ اور بیہقی نے چند طریقون سے ام سلمہ سے روایت کي ھے کہ وہ کہتی ھین کہ میرے گہر مین آیہ انما یرید اللہ الخ نازل ھوي اور میرے گہر مین فاطمہ حسن حسین اور علی بہی تہے آنحضرت نے جو چادر اوڑہے ھوے تہے ان لوگون پر ڈالدی اور فرمایا خدایا یہی لوگ میرے اھلبیت ھین —

صحیح مسلم جلد دوم شرح نووي ص ۲۸۰ پر ھے کہ زید بن ارقم سے پوچہا گیا کہ آیا اھلبیت رسول مین رسول اللہ کي ازواج بہی شامل ھین زید نے جوابدیا کہ خدا کی قسم ازواج رسول شامل اھلبیت ھرگز نہین ھوسکتین کیونکہ ازواج طلاق دینے کے بعد اپنے مان باپ سے ملحق ھوجاتي ھین اور نیز اھلبیت وہ ھین جنپر صدقہ حرام ھے —

ترمذي — ابن جریر - طبرانی اور ابن مردویہ نے عمر بن سلمہ سے روایت کي ھے کہ جب آیۂ - انما یرید اللہ الخ نازل ھوئی اُسوقت آنحضرت

10 A.H.

(family) consisted of only these persons. † Omm Selma, his wife, within whose quarters the Revelation came, asked permission to be included in the group under the blanket, but she was politely refused admission. The group is known ever since with the epithet 'Panjtan Pák' or the Holy group of Five.

* These are the persons who were compared by the Prophet with the Boat of Noah ¶ wherein those who embarked were saved, while those who sought shelter elsewhere were drowned.

ام سلمه کے گھر مین تھے - آنحضرت نے فاطمه - علي - حسن اور حسین پر اپنی چادر اوڑھاکر فرمایا خدایا یہی میرے اهلبیت هین ان سے هر برائي کو دور رکهه اور انکو اچهي طرح پاک و پاکیزه رکهه - یهه سنکر امسلمه نے کہا یا رسول الله مین بهی انکے ساتهه هوجاون - حضرت نے فرمایا تم اپني جگه پر رهو تم یقیني نیکی پر هو —

تفسیر در منثور ص ۱۹۹ سراج الوهاب شرح مسلم نواب صدیق حسن خان جلد ۶ ص ۴۶۶ قول مستحسن مولوی حسن الزمان ص ۴۰۲ پر هے که آیه تطهیر مین صرف محمد - علی - فاطمه - حسن اور حسین شامل هین اور کوي نهین هے —

ینابیع المودت مولفه شیخ الاسلام قسطنطنیه ص ۸۷ مسلم باب الفضائل مین هے که حضرت عایشه نے کہا که آیه تطهیر مین صرف رسول الله اور حضرت علی و فاطمه و حسن و حسین داخل هین ازواج مین سے کوی بهي نهین شامل هے ....

---

* تفسیر عزیزي شاه عبدالعزیز دهلوي - مین هے که فرمایا جناب رسولخدا نے که تم لوگون مین میرے اهلبیت کی مثال کشتی نوح کیطرح هے - جس کسی نے اُس کشتي مین پناه لی وه پناه پاگیا اور جس نے پناه نه لي وه غرق هوگیا —

تفسیر در منثور مطبوعه مصر جلد اول ص ۷۲ پر بروایت ابن ابي شیبه لکھا هے که فرمایا حضرت علی نے که امت محمد مین هماری مثال سفینه نوح اور باب حطه کی سي هے —

† Tirmizhi; Ibn Jarir; Sahih Muslim; Suyuti. ¶ Suyuti.

* These persons were the part and parcel of the Celestial Light of which the Prophet was created.

---

* احادیث متواترہ سے جوکہ بعض اس کتاب مین بھي مرقوم هوچکي هین ثابت هے که فرمایاجناب رسالتماب نے (۱) علي منی و انامنه و قال جبریل انا منکما (۲) انا و علی من نور واحد (۳) لحمک لحمی و دمک دمی ترمذي اور ابن ماجه نے یعلی بن مرہ سے روایت کی هے که فرمایا آنحضرت نے که حسین مجهه سے هے اور مین حسین سے هون —

قال احمد بن حنبل فی الفضائل قال رسول الله صلعم کنت انا و علی بن ابیطالب نوراً بین یدي الله تعالے قبل ان یخلق آدم باربعة الاف عام فلما خلق ادم قسم ذلک النور جزئین فجزوانا و جزو علي- و فی روایه خلقت انا و علی من نور واحد—

امام احمد حنبل نے فضائل مین لکها هے که فرمایا رسولخدا صلعم نے که مین اور علی ابن ابیطالب آدم کي پیدائش سے چار هزار برس پیشتر الله تعالي کے روبرو عالم نور مین تهے پس جبکه آدم پیدا هوے تو وه نور دو جزو پر تقسیم هوگیا—ایک جزو مین هون اور ایک جزو علی هے اور دوسری روایت مین یهه هے که مین اورعلی ایک نور سے پیدا هوےهین

علامه نطنزی نے خصائص علویه مین تفسیر فتلقي آدم من ربه کلمات کے ذیل مین لکها هے که خداوند عالم نے حضرت آدم سے فرمایا که اگر محمد و علي وفاطمه و حسن و حسین کا پیدا کرنا مقصود نهوتا تو تمکو پیدا نه کیا جاتا آدم نے عرض کیا که مجهے ان مقدس حضرات کي زیارت سے مشرف فرمایا جاوے — پس پرده هاے حجاب اٹهاے گئے اور آدم نے پانچ اشباح انوار دیکهے اور پوچها یهه کون هین-ارشاد باری هوا که پهلا نور میرا نبی محمد هے- دوسرا علی- تیسرا فاطمه- چوتها حسن- اور پانچوان حسین هے اور یهه پانچون تیري اولاد سے هونگے - آدم نے سجده شکر کیا— خلد سے نکلنے کے بعد جب آدم نے ان حضرات کے انوار مقدسه کا واسطه دیکر توبه کی تب توبه قبول هوي—

علامه سیوطي نے جمع الجوامع في باب جامع الدعا مین اور تفسیر در منثور مین اور دیلمی نے فردوس الاخبار مین طبرانی نے معجم صغیر مین حاکم اور ابن عساکر نے اپني اپنی مسانید مین-ابو نعیم اور بیهقی نے اور ابن مغازلی نے به اختلاف الفاظ اس روایت کو قلمبند کیا هے-

10 A. H.

These are the persons for whose virtuous deeds Mohammed was congratulated by God and *Sura LXXVI* of the Qurán was revealed to him in their praise.†

† Sale in his translation of Al Koran gives the following note on Verses 7—10 of Sura LXXVI:

Sale's translation of :—

Verse 5 "But the just shall drink of a cup (of wine), mixed with (the water of) Kafur,"

6* "A fountain whereof the servants of God shall drink; they shall convey the same by channels (withersoever they please)."

7 "(These) fulfil (their) vow, and dread the day, the evil whereof will disperse itself far abroad;"

8 "And give food unto the poor, and the orphan, and the bondman, for His sake, (saying,)"

9 "We feed you for God's sake only: we desire no recompense from you, nor any thanks:"

10 "Verily we dread, from our Lord, a dismal (and) calamitous day."

Sale's note from Al Beidzáwi on Verses 7—10:

"It is related that Hasan and Hosain, Mohammed's grand-children, on a certain time being both sick, the prophet, among others, visited them; and they wished Ali to make some vow to God for the recovery of his sons: whereupon Ali, and Fátema, and Fidza, their maid-servant, vowed a fast of three days in case they did well: as it happened they did. This vow was performed with so great strictness, that the first day, having no provisions in the house, Ali was obliged to borrow three measures of barley of one Simeon, a Jew of Khaibar; one measure of which Fátema ground the same day, and baked five cakes of the meal; and they were set before them, to break their fast with after sunset: but a poor man coming to them, they gave all their bread to him, and passed the night without tasting anything, except water. The next day, Fátema made another measure into bread, for the same purpose; but an orphan begging some food, they chose to let him have it, and passed that night, as the first: and the third day they likewise gave their whole provision to a famished captive. Upon this occasion Gabriel descended with the Chapter (Sura) before us, and told Mohammed that God congratulated him on the virtues of his family."

*As to God's promise in verse 6 read the account of Ali's miraculously disclosling a fountain for the supply of water to his armies in the sandy Mesopotamian desert, as given in the second volume.

No wonder that the Prophet balanced these sinless and faultless personalities with God's Book the Qurán and declared each higher in grandeur than the other. Ali was the only man who claimed a thorough knowledge of the Qurán. He proclaimed aloud, inviting all, to ask him when and where and on what occasion each and every verse of the Qurán was revealed to the Prophet, whose words, "I am the City of Knowledge and Ali is its Gate" testify to the fact. So were † Hasan, Hosain and Fátema.

These were the godly persons who were oft times attended upon by Angels.

* Still the people expressed their suspicions against the Prophet to have given Ali the lofty position of "the Guardian of all Believers" without any command from God; and he solemnly told them that it was from God's command.

---

† A noble instance of Hasan's generosity, and eagerness to attain God's pleasure, by fulfilling every virtue announced in His commands may be found in the following story, among thousands, relative to the Holy descendants of the Prophet :—

"A slave of Hasan the son of Ali, having once thrown a dish on him boiling hot, as he sat at table, and fearing his master's resentment, fell on his knees, and repeated these words: 'Paradise is for those who bridle their anger,' Hasan answered, 'I am not angry.' The slave proceeded: 'and for those who forgive men', 'I forgive thee,' said Hasan. The slave however finished the verse*, adding, 'for God loveth the beneficient.' 'Since it is so,' replied Hasan, I give thee thy liberty, and four hundred pieces of silver.'

* *Sura iii 127* And run with emulation to (obtain) remission from your Lord, and paradise, whose breadth (equalleth) the heavens and the earth, which is prepared for the godly;

128 Who give alms in prosperity and adversity; who bridle their anger, and forgive men: for God loveth the beneficient." Sale.

* قال العلامة محمد بن سالم الحفنى الشافعي في حاشية الشرح الجامع الصغير عزيزي جلد ٣ ص ٣٤٧ مطبوعه مصر-لما سمع ذلک بعض الصحابة قال اما تكتفي يارسول الله ان ناتي بالشهادة و اقام الصلواة و ايتاء الزكوة حتى ترفع علينا ابن ابيطالب فهل هذا من عندک ام من عند الله فقال صلى الله عليه و سلم و الله الذي لا اله الا هو انه من عند الله —

10 A.H.

† An incident which occured some time after the Prophet's declaring the Adjuration is worth noticing: A man, named Hárith son of No'mán Fihri (or Nadzr b. Hárith according to another tradition), disbelieved and suspected the Prophet to have made the announcement in his eagerness and love for Ali. He earnestly invoked the wrath of heaven upon himself if he was wrong in his suspicion. His prayer was at once answered with a stone falling over his head from above and killing him on the spot.

Inference drawn from the language of the Prophet in favour of Ali.

The reader might recollect to his memory the previous occasions on which the Prophet declared Ali his successor; firstly on the day of his proclaiming himself publicly the Apostle of God, when he said, "O sons of of Abd-al-Mottalib God hath never sent a Messenger, but that He appointed one, his brother, heir and successor to him from amongst his own relations (Vide page 41), and again when he declared Ali "to be to him what Aaron was to Moses," (Vide p. 214).

These utterances of the Prophet were not made of his own accord as the following verse of the the Qurán proves: "He speaks not for his own purpose; but gives utterance to the Commandments revealed to him." (*Sur. LIII-3 and 4*). It is inferred that the utterances under reference were in accordance with the Commandments of God. And the present announcement in the presence of thousands of people

---

ترجمہ—علامہ محمد بن سالم شافعی حفنی حاشیہ شرح جامع صغیر عزیزی جلد ۳ ص ۳۴۷ مطبوعۂ مصر مین لکھتے ھین کہ جب انحضرت نے خطبہ من کنت مولاہ فعلی مولاہ ارشاد فرمایا تو اوسے سنکر بعض صحابہ نے کہا کہ کیا ھملوگون کے لئے کلمہ شہادت کا ادا کرنا اور صلوۃ و زکوۃ کا پابند ھونا کافي نہین ھے۔ جو اب ھمپر ابو طالب کے بیٹے کو بلندی اور بزرگی دیجاتی ھے – آیا یہہ امر آپ کیجانب سے ھے یا خدا کیجانب سے آنحضرت نے فرمایا کہ قسم ھے اوسکي جسکےسوا کوی معبود نہین کہ یہہ امر خدا ھی کیجانب سے ھے (تاریخ احمدی ص ۹۱)

† Tafsir Tha'labi; Insán-al-Oyun; Nur-al-Absár; Arjah-al-Matálib; Nazhat-al-Majális from Qartabi.

was in confirmation of the previous declarations, which were never withdrawn during the interval of a score of years.

On the basis of the above, a large body of the Moslems hold that Ali was undoubtedly the chosen and declared successor of the Prophet from the very beginning of his prophetic career. Now he was distinguished to be to the Moslems what prophet was to them; which means that Ali was to be treated in place of (*i.e.* successor to) the Prophet after his death. Shah Ali Hasan Jaisi, a Sunni Sufi, has well expressed the meaning of *Mowla* in his stanza.

عبث در معنی من کنت مولا میروی هر سو
علي مولی به آن معنی که پیغمبر بود مولا

CHAPTER XVII.

Certain Imposters. The Prophet's last illness, last Prayer and Sermon in his Mosque. The death of the Prophet and his funeral ceremonies.

Distribution of Yemen.

Bázhán, the Governor of Yemen, having died, the Prophet, early in the eleventh year (calculated to commence from Moharram) of Hegira, divided among the different Governors the several provinces such as Hamdán, Márab and Najrán, which had hitherto combined under the authcrity of Bázhán. Shahr the son of Bázhán was allowed to retain the government of San'á and the surrounding territory.

Aswad, the Imposter.

Aswad, a chief of wealth and influence, gained over the nobles, who were dissatisfied of the distribution made by the Prophet, and drove out his officers, who fled to seek refuge with the nearest friendly tribes. He then subjugated Najrán. Having thus secured a large number of followers, Aswad proclaimed himself a prophet and marched upon San'á, where he defeated the army of Shahr, killed him and took his widow to wife. Some vague accounts of Aswad reached the Prophet, who despatched letters to his officers to put down the pretender. Aswad, however, was himself accelerating his own end by treating with contempt his officers, to whose bravery he was indebted for his successes. The widow of Shahr, now his wife, also waited an opportunity to avenge the death of her late husband. The officers of the Prophet opened up negotiations with the discontented people, with the result that the imposter Aswad was slain on the night preceding the death of the Prophet at Medina.

Musailama, the Imposter.

At about the same time, Musailama, a chief of the Bani Hanifa, proclaimed himself a prophet at Yamáma and deceived the people by giving forth verses professed to have been revealed to him from Heaven. None of his verses, however, are worth quoting. He pretended even to work miracles. One of his miracles was to slip an egg into a narrow-mouthed phial. The rumour reached Medina, and the Prophet sent him a letter reminding him of his homage (*See page 227*) and bade him to adhere faithfully to Islam. Musailama sent a reply purporting to say that he too was a Prophet like Mohammed and that he demanded therefore to divide the earth with him. The Prophet, having received the insolent answer, wrote to him: "I have received thine epistle with its lies and fabrications against God. Verily, the earth is the Lord's. He causeth such of his servants as He pleaseth to inherit the same. Peace be to him that treadeth the true path." The rebellion of Musailama was quelled in the time of Caliph Abubekr.

Tulaiha, the Imposter.

Another Imposter, named Tulaiha, a Chief of the Bani Asad, proclaimed himself prophet in Nejd. He was a warrior of some fame. After the death of the Prophet he revolted openly against Islam. He was defeated and subjugated in the time of Caliph Omar.

Syrian Expedition ordered.

At about the middle of the month of Safar, in the eleventh year (calculated to commence from Moharram) of Hegira, on Monday, the Prophet ordered his followers to make speedy preparations for an expedition against the people of Muta in the

Roman territory, to avenge the massacre there of his brave soldiers, who had fallen in recent skirmishes (*See page 183*). *The next day (Tuesday), he appointed Osáma to the command of the Army. Osáma was the son of Zaid, the Prophet's freed slave, who was slain at Muta, and was a youth of but seventeen or eighteen years. He instructed Osáma to hasten so that no tidings of the expedition might reach the enemy. "Fall suddenly upon them," he said, "and if thy Lord grant thee victory retrace thy steps without delay."

On Wednesday a violent attack of headache and fever seized the Prophet; but the next morning (Thursday) he found himself sufficiently recovered to prepare a flag-staff, with his own hands, which he made over to Osáma as the Standard for the Army. The camp was then formed at Jorf, three miles from Medina on the route to Syria. The Prophet ordered all his followers at Medina not excepting even Abubekr or Omar to join it at once. **Only Ali, who was required to remain with him at Medina, was excepted.

---

* قال ابن الوردی فی تاریخه و کان قد جهز جیشا مع مولاه اسامه بن زید واکد فی سیره فی مرضه

ترجمه—مورخ ابن الوردی نے اپنی تاریخ مین لکھا ھے که پیغمبر صاحب نے بحالت بیماری اپنے غلام اسامه بن زید کی افسری مین ایک لشکر تیار کیا اور اوسکی روانگی کیلئے تاکید فرمائی۔

**شیخ عبدالحق محدث دهلوی در مدارج النبوة آورده که در روز دیگر باوجود مرض لوائے برائے او بدست مبارک خود عقد نمود و فرمود اغز بسم الله و فی سبیل الله و قاتل من کفر بالله۔ پس اسامه لوا را گرفت و بیرون رفت و لوا را به بریده بن الحصیب داد تا دران لشکر صاحب لوا باشد و در جرف که نام موضع است قریب مدینه مطهره منزل ساخت تا سپاه آنجا جمع شد و حکم عالی چنان صادر شد که از اعیان مهاجر و انصار مثل ابوبکر صدیق و عمر فاروق و عثمان ذوالنورین و سعد بن ابی وقاص و ابو عبیده بن الجراح و غیر هم در آن لشکر همراه اسامه باشند الا علی مرتضی را که همراه نه کرد و این معنی بر خاطر بعضے مردم گران آمد که غلامے را برا کابر مهاجرین و انصار امیر گردانید و

Prediction about Ayesha.

The Prophet's malady was, however, developing; but for some days during his illness he maintained his custom of visiting his wives' apartments by turns. ‡One day, while passing the door of Ayesha, he heard her moaning: "My head! Oh, my head!". He entered and said: "Nay Ayesha, it is rather I who have need to cry, My head! My head! instead of thee." She continued crying, my head, my head! Then in a tender strain, he said: "Wouldst thou not desire, Ayesha, to die whilst I am yet alive, so that I might wrap thee up in a sheet, pray over thee and commit thee to the grave." Ayesha then archly burst forth: "Truly! I can understand thee, thou art desirous of living with another wife in my place, after having done all that thou hast spoken." He smiled at Ayesha's raillery and with a sad complaint of severe pain in his head he proceeded to the apartment of Maimuna.

According to another tradition Ayesha says: "As often as the Prophet passed my door, he used to speak a word to me. Now for two days he passed by without speaking a single word to me. So I made my maid-servant place my pillow at the door, and I reclined there with my head bandaged; when the Prophet passed by, he heard my moans and entered to speak to me as stated above."

Alas! Ayesha could not grasp the situation. She ought to have trembled at her fate thus predicted by the Prophet; she knew he was not in a hilarious mood to give utterance to such words, nor was there an occasion for

در مجلس ازین جماعت سخنان درین باب بظهور آمد چون این اخبار
به سمع شریف رسید خاطر مبارکش رنجیده شد و به غضب در آمد
و باوجود تپ و درد سر از خانه مبارک عصابه بسته بیرون آمد و
بر سر منبر رفت و خطبه خواند و فرمود اے معشر الناس این چه
سخن است که در باب امیر ساختن من اسامه را از شما سربر می زند
و در باب امارت پدرش در غزوه موته نیز سخن میکردید - بخدا
سوگند که وے سزاوار امارت است و پدرش نیز سزاوار امارت بود ―

‡ Rawdzat-al-Ahbáb.

such a grim jest to his beloved wife still in her youth, while he was himself at an advanced aged of sixty three not unconscious of the premonitions of his decay and badly suffering with headache and fever. The prophecy was fulfilled some forty seven years later, when in the time of Mo'áwiya she was buried alive. There was no bathing, no wrapping in the sheet, no coffin and no prayers over her. Simon Ockley in his History of the Saracens on page 375 has quoted from Price a footnote which runs thus: "There is a tradition that Ayesha was murdered by the direction of Mo'áwiya, and the following particulars are recorded: Ayesha having resolutely and insultingly refused to engage her allegiance to Yazid, Mo'áwiya invited her to an entertainment, where he had prepared a very deep well or pit in that part of the chamber, reserved for her reception, and had the mouth of it deceptively covered over with leaves and straw. A chair was then placed upon the fatal spot and Ayesha, on being conducted to her seat, instantly sank into eternal night, and the mouth of the pit was immediately covered with stones and mortar." Ayesha was thus unostentatiously buried as unostentatiously she was married.

The Prophet's last illness.

‡ His fever returned in Maimuna's apartment with increasing violence and occasional fits of swooning. All his wives and relations assembled to see him. It was advised that he should no more take the trouble of visiting his wives in rotation as was his wont, but to remain at one place peaceably during his illness. Ayesha's house was proposed and agreed upon unanimously for this purpose. The Prophet, with his head bandaged and his clothes loosely wrapped around him, shifted to the abode of Ayesha, supported by Fadzl son of Abbás on one side and by Ali, his cousin and son in law, on the other. † In the tradition related by Ayesha, she states that the Prophet was supported by Fadzl on one side and by another on the other side. She disliked to utter Ali's name through enmity which she bore towards him.

‡Tabari; Abul Fida; Ibn Athir. † Tabari; Rawdzat-al-Safá.

10 A. H.

Ayesha espying the Prophet's movement.

¶ One night, while in Ayesha's apartment, he softly rose from his bed and went out. Ayesha says she thought he was going to some other wife and she followed him stealthily till he reached the burial ground at Baqi', where he prayed forgiveness for those lying buried there. Before he turned, she hastened back to her house. Soon after, the Prophet came back, guessed the truth and questioned her. She had no alternative but to confess. He said, "Thou suspected me of having gone to some other wife while I went to the burial ground in obedience to God's command." In another tradition it is said that he was followed by a servant-maid Boreida sent by Ayesha to watch him. A third tradition says that Abu Ráfe', the Prophet's servant accompanied him. A fourth tradition names Abu Muwaiheba to have gone with him.

The Syrian Expedition urged.

The malady, although gaining ground, did not confine the Prophet entirely to his house. He used to move into the Mosque, through the door of his apartment opening into its courts, to lead the prayers every day. After about a week of his summoning the men to the Syrian Expedition, he perceived that the progress to join the camp at Jorf was very slow and he was angry to hear that the people said: "He hath put this stripling in command over the chief of the Mohájirs." After prayers he seated himself on the pulpit with his head bound with a napkin and addressed the people thus: "Ye people! What is this which hath reached me, that some of you murmur against my appointing Osáma to command the Syrian Expedition. Now, if ye blame me for his appointment, verily heretofore ye blamed me similarly for my appointing his father Zaid. I wish that ye treat him well, for he is one of the best amongst ye; †accursed is that whosoever keepeth back

¶Abul Fida; Ibn Athir.

†Milal and Nihal. Sharh Nahjal Balágha by Ibn Abi-al-Hadid; Sharh Mawáqif; Tárikh Muzaffari by Shahabddin; Ibn Abi'al Dam.

from * joining the force." Urging the early departure of the expedition, he left the pulpit and retired into his apartment.

Warnings to the Mohajirs and Ansars.

**Another day, after the prayers, he addressed the people thus: "Verily the Lord hath offered unto his servant the choice of continuance in this life and that which is nigh unto Himself, and I have chosen the latter. Verily all other Apostles died before me; ye should not expect me to live for ever." After a pause he continued, "Ye Ansárs! Treat them well to whom ye have given refuge; and ye Mohájirs, Verily the Ansárs are dear unto me, for among them I found a refuge, therefore honour them and treat them well." Then he recited *Sur. CIII.* ("By the declining day! Verily man's lot is one of loss, save those who believe, and do the things which be right, and enjoin truth, and enjoin steadfastness on each other." *Rodwell.*) † and verse 24 of *Sur. XLVII.* "Then, were ye near, if ye were in authority, to do evil in the earth and to cut asunder your ties of blood." Thus he warned his Companions against their malicious designs.

---

*فی الملل والنحل للشهرستانی و الحجج الکرامة للصدیق حسن خان
انه قال صلعم جهز و اجیش اسامة لعن الله من تخلف عنها —
ترجمه کتاب ملل و نحل شهرستانی اور حجج الکرامه نواب صدیق
حسن خان میں ہے کہ آنحضرت نے صحابہ سے ارشاد کیا کہ لشکر اسامہ کی
جلد تیاری کرو—خدا لعنت کرے اوسپر جو جیش اسامہ سے تخلف کرے-

**ملا محمد مبین در کتاب وسیلة النجاة آورده که آنحضرت صلعم
وصیت کرد مهاجرین را که با یکدیگر نیکی کنند -پس خواند سوره
والعصر تا آخر و این آیه بخواند- فهل عسیتم ان تفسد و فی الارض و
تقطعوا ارحامکم و این اشاره ایست بآنچه ملوک و اخراب مروانیه و
عباسیه باهل بیت نبوت کردند از جفا و ستم (عجب ! -وصیت بامهاجرین
و اشاره با ملوک و اخراب مروانیه و عباسیه ؟ مولف)

† Rawdzat-al-Ahbáb; Madarij-al-Nabowat.

10 A. H.

Some gold intended for alms.

‡ One day the Prophet asked Ayesha about some gold which he had given her to keep. It was seven Dinárs, the balance of an amount which he had received for distribution as alms. On her replying that it was by her, he desired her to distribute it among the poor. Then he fell into a half concious state. After a while when he gained consciousness, he again asked Ayesha to give the gold in charity. Thus thrice he vainly asked her. At last he took the money from her and made it over to Ali, who at once distributed it among indigent families.

The Prophet hindered to record his Will.

†On the Thursday preceding his death, when several of his chief Companions were present in the room, the Prophet, while lying on his bed, asked for writing materials saying :—*"Bring me paper and ink so that I may record for you a document which shall prevent your ever backsliding into error. Omar, the Discriminator, at once interposed thus: "The man wandereth in delirium, God's book ¶is sufficient for us." Some of those present said that the

---

‡ Rawdzat-al-Safa; Madárij-al-Nabowat.

†Ibn Khaldun; Tabari; Abul Fida.

¶A large body of the Moslems take this phrase of Omar's as a move of separation from the orthodoxy established by the Prophet, who directed all to follow the Qurán and his Progeny, declaring: "I leave unto you *two* grand Precepts, each of which surpasses the other in grandeur, God's Book and my Progeny; the twain will not be separated till they meet me in Paradise" (*see page 239*).

* اخرج مسلم عن عبيد الله عن ابن عباس قال لما حضر رسول الله صلعم و في البيت رجال فيهم عمر بن الخطاب قال النبي صلعم هلم اكتب لكم كتابا لا تضلون بعده فقال عمر ان رسول الله قد غلب عليه الوجع و عندكم القران حسبنا كتاب الله فاختلف اهل البيت فاختصموا منهم من يقول قربوا يكتب لكم رسول الله كتابا لم تضلوا بعده و منهم من يقول ما قال عمر فلما اكثروا اللغط والاختلاف عند رسول الله صلعم قال رسول الله قوموا عني قال عبيد الله فكان ابن عباس يقول ان الرزية كل الرزية ما حال بين رسول الله صلعم و بين ان يكتب لهم ذلك الكتاب من اختلافهم و لغطهم

writing materials should be furnished; others sided with Omar. A discussion ensued and the voices rose high to the annoyance of the Prophet. The ladies from behind the screens wished to provide the writing materials, but Omar chided them: "Quiet", he said, "Ye resemble the females in the story of Joseph, when your master falleth sick ye burst into tears, and the moment he recovereth a little ye begin teasing." The Prophet hearing this said:—"Chide them not: Verily they are still much better than ye are." Now some persons proceeded to ask the Prophet what his wishes were to be recorded.

ترجمہ— صحیح مسلم مین حضرت ابن عباس سے مروي ہے کہ جب جناب رسولخدا کا وقت احتضار ہوا تو دولتکدہ نبوت مین حضرت عمر بن الخطاب اور دیگر اصحاب مجتمع تھے-رسول مقبول نے ارشاد فرمایا کہ آو مین تمھارے لئے کچھہ (بطور وصیت) لکھدون تاکہ بعد ازان تم گمراہ نہ ہو-حضرت عمر بولے کہ پیغمبر صاحب غلبۂ مرض کیوجھہ سے ایسا کہہ رہے ہین تمھارے پاس قران موجود ہے اور وہی ہمارے لئے کافی ہے-اس بات پر حضار جلسہ مین اختلاف واقع ہوا-بعض تو یہہ کہتے تھے کہ رسول اللہ کے حکم کي تعمیل کرنا ضروري ہے تاکہ آنحضرت جو کچھہ چاہین تمھارے لئے تحریر فرمائن-اور بعض حضرت عمر کے ہمزبان تھے- جب اسبات پر بہت شور اور اختلاف ہونے لگا تو جناب رسالتماب نے فرمایا کہ میرے پاس سے ہٹ جاؤ-پس حضرت ابن عباس فرماتے تھے کہ مصیبت اور سخت مصیبت تھی وہ چیز جو لوگون کے شور و اختلاف کیوجھہ سے رسول اللہ کے ارادہ کتابت مین حائل ہوے اور جسکی وجہہ سے آنحضرت کچھہ نہ لکھہ سکے—(تاریخ احمدی ص ۹۷)

اخرج البخاري عن سعید بن جبیر عن ابن عباس رضی اللہ عنھما انہ قال یوم الخمیس ومایوم الخمیس ثم بکے حتي حضب دلعہ الحصباء فقال اشتد برسول اللہ صلعم وجعہ یوم الخمیس فقال ائتوني بکتاب اکتب لکم کتابا لن تضلوا بعدہ ابدا فتنازعوا و لا ینبغی عند نبی تنازع فقالوا ھجر رسول اللہ صلعم قال دعونی فالذي انا فیہ خیر مما تدعونی الیہ واوصاھم بثلاث اخرجوا المشرکین من جزیرۃ العرب و اجیز و الوفود بنحو ماکنت اجیزھم و سکت عن الثالثۃ او قال فنسیتھا—(تاریخ احمدی ص ۹۸)

But he angrily recited verse †2 *of Sura XLIX* (O Believers! Raise not your voices above the voice of the Prophet; neither speak loud unto him in conversation, as ye speak loud unto one another, lest your works become vain, while ye perceive not.) and said "Begone, let me alone, for my present condition is better than that

---

ترجمه ــــ صحیح بخاری مین بروایت سعید بن جبیر مروي هے که
کها عبدالله ابن عباس نے (آه) پنجشنبه کا دن کیسا دن تها اور یهه کهکر
اتنا روے که جو سنگریزے اوس جگه پڑے هوے تهے اونکے آنسوؤن سے تر
هوگئے بعد ازان کهنے لگے که جب بروز پنجشنبه رسول الله کے مرض کو
شدت هوی تو آنحضرت نے ارشاد کیا که مجهے کتابت کا سامان دو تاکه
مین تمهارے لئے کچهه (بطور وصیت) لکهدون جس سے تملوگ میرے بعد
کبهی گمراه نهو اسبات پر لوگون نے نزاع اور اختلاف کیا (آنحضرت نے فرمایا)
ف ــــ هو من جملة الحديث المرفوع و يحتمل ان يكون مدرجاً من قول
ابن عباس والصواب الاول و قد تقدم فی باب العلم بلفظه لا ينبغي
عندي التنازع - يعنی قال رسول الله قوموا عنی و لا ينبغی عندی التنازع
(فتح الباري شرح صحيح البخاري لابن حجر العسقلانی)
دیکهو نبي کے پاس جهگڑا نه کرنا چاهئے - لوگون نے کها رسول الله هذیان
بک رهے هین (يقال هجر الرجل اذا هذی فتح الباري) آنحضرت بولے که میرے
پاس سے هت جاو مین جس حالت مین هون وه تمهاري حالت سے بهتر هے
اسکے بعد آنحضرت نے تین وصیتین کین - ایک یهه که مشرکین کو جزیره
عرب سے نکالدو دوسری یهه که جو وفود تمهارے پاس آئین اونکي خاطر
و مدارات کرو - تیسری وصیت راوي نے بیان نهین کی یا بهول گیا ــ
تاریخ احمدی ص ۹۸)
روي الطبرانی عن عمر قال لما مرض النبی صلعم قال ادعوالی بصحيفة
و دواة اكتب كتابا لا تضلوا بعده ابدا فقال النسوة من وراء الستر الا

†This verse is said to have been occasioned by a dispute between Abubekr and Omar, concerning the appointment of a Governor of a certain place; in which they raised their voices so high, in the presence of the Apostle, that it was thought proper to forbid such indecencies for the future. *Sale*. Disregard of the Commandment necessitated the Prophet to repeat the warning, on this occasion.

which ye call me to". After a pause he continued, "But mind the three injuctions, firstly, Turn out every Infidel from the Peninsula, secondly, Receive the embassies hospitably and bid them farewell with largesses, as they were treated by me." The third injunction is said to have been forgotten by the tradition writer or its mention is omitted.†

تسمعون ما يقول رسول الله صلعم فقلت انكن صواحبات يوسف اذا مرض رسول الله عصرتن اعينكن و اذا صح ركبتن عنقه فقال رسول الله دعوهن فانهن خير منكم —

ترجمه—طبراني نے حضرت عمر سے روايت کی هے که جناب رسولخدا نے بحالت مرض ارشاد کیا که کاغذ اور دوات وغیره (سامان کتابت) میرے پاس لے آو تاکه مین ایک ایسا کتبه لکهدون جسکیوجهه سے تملوگ میرے بعد کبهی گمراه نهو مخدرات عصمت نے پردے کے اندر سے اصحاب کو مخاطب کرکے کہا که کیا تم لوگ رسول الله کا ارشاد نهین سنتے هو حضرت عمر نے اون بیبیون کو جواب دیا که تمهاري مثال صواحبات یوسف کي هے که پیغمبر صاحب کي بیماری مین روتی هو اور بوقت صحت اونکی گردن پر سوار هوتی هو- یهه سنکر آنحضرت نے فرمایا که ان عورتون سے معترض نه هو یهه تم سے پهر بهي غنیمت اور بهتر هین- تاریخ احمدي ص ۹۶

قال الخفاجی فی نسیم الریاض و فی بعض طرق هذالحدیث قال عمر ان النبی یهجر-

ترجمه— شهاب الدین خفاجي کتاب نسیم الریاض شرح شفاے قاضي عیاض مین لکهتے هین که اس حدیث کے بعض طرق مین هے که حضرت عمر نے فرمایا که پیغمبر صاحب هذیان بکتے هین — تاریخ احمدی ص ۹۹

اخرج احمد فی المسند و مسلم فی صحیحه عن سعید بن جبیر عن ابن عباس انه قال یوم الخمیس و ما یوم الخمیس ثم جعل تسیل دموعه حتي رأیت علي خدیه کانها نظام اللؤلو قال رسول الله صلعم ائتونی بالکتف والدواة او للوح والدواة اکتب لکم کتابالن تضلوا بعده ابدا- فقالوا ان رسول الله یهجر —

ترجمه— مسند احمد بن حنبل اور صحیح مسلم مین بروایت سعید

† Ibn Athir ; Bokáhri ; Muslim ; Mishkát etc.

Ibn Abbás lamented the irreparable loss sustained by the Moslems on this Thursday by the Prophet's being hindered to record what he wished for the guidance of his followers. Remembering the incident he wept till his tears made his cheeks and beard wet.

بن جبیر مروی ہے کہ حضرت عبداللہ بن عباس یہہ کہکر کہ روز پنجشنبہ کیسا دن تہا اتنا روے کہ موتیونکي لڑی کیطرح اونکے رخسارونپرآنسو جاری ہوگئے بعد ازان کہا کہ پنجشنبہ وہ دن تہا جب رسول اللہ نے ارشاد کیا کہ مجہے سامان کتابت دو تاکہ مین تمہارے لئے کچہ (بطور وصیت) لکہدوں جس سے تم میرے بعد کبہی گمراہ نہ ہو مگر افسوس لوگون کے کہدیا کہ آنحضرت ہذیان بک رہے ہین —(تاریخ احمدی ص ۹۸)

قال الشہرستانی فی الملل والنحل اول تنازع فی مرضہ علیہ السلام فیما رواہ محمد بن اسمعیل البخاری باسنادہ عن عبداللہ بن عباس قال لما اشتد بالنبی صلی اللہ علیہ و سلم مرضہ الذي مات فیہ قال ائتوني بدواۃ و قرطاس اکتب لکم کتابا لا تضلوا بعدي فقال عمر ان رسول اللہ قد غلبہ الوجع حسبنا کتاب اللہ و کثر اللغط فقال النبی علیہ السلام قوموا عني لا ینبغی عندی التنازع قال ابن عباس الرزیۃ کل الرزیۃ ماحال بیننا و بین کتاب رسول اللہ —

ترجمہ — علامہ شہرستاني کتاب ملل و نحل مین لکہتے ہین کہ پہلا تنازع و اختلاف جو رسول مقبول کے زمانہ مرض مین واقع ہوا وہ تہا جسکو بخاری نے کتاب صحیح مین اپنے اسناد کیساتہہ عبداللہ ابن عباس سے یوں روایت کیا ہے کہ جب رسول اللہ کے مرض موت مین زیادتی ہوئی تو آنحضرت نے فرمایا کہ مجہے دوات اور کاغذ دو تا کہ مین تمہارےلئے ایک نوشتہ (بطور وصیت نامہ) لکہدون جسکي وجہہ سے تم میرے بعد گمراہ نہو - یہہ سنکر حضرت عمر نے کہا کہ پیغمبر صاحب غلبہ مرض مین ایسا کہتے ہین ہمارے لئے کتاب خدا کافی ہے چنانچہ جب اسبات پر شور و غل ہوا تو آنحضرت نے فرمایا کہ میرے پاس سے ہٹ جاو تم لوگونکو لازم نہین کہ میرے حضور مین تنازع اور اختلاف کرو - اسي پر عبداللہ ابن عباس فرمایا کرتے تہے کہ مصیبت اور عظیم مصیبت تہا وہ اختلاف جسنے ہمارے اور پیغمبر صاحب کی تحریر مین حائل ہوکر آنحضرت کو کتابت سے باز رکہا — تاریخ احمدی ص ۹۹

The sickness of the Prophet was increasing every day and he felt its seriousness. The Syrian expedition, however, weighed upon his mind; he continued saying to those around him, "Send off quickly the Army of Osáma."

It is an admitted fact that till the evening (Maghrib) of the Thursday preceding his death the prophet continued moving into the Mosque to lead the prayers on each occasion; but at the bed time (Ishá) prayers, of that Thursday, it is said, he could not preside over the congregation.

Abubekr's leading the prayers.

There are several traditions about Abubekr's leading the prayers. It is said that on seventeen occasions, beginning with the night (bed-time or Ishá) prayers of Thursday preceding his death, the Prophet being unable to preside over the congregation in the Mosque, had commanded Abubekr to lead the prayers. It is, at the same time, admitted that at the morning prayers of the day on which his death took place, the Prophet moved into the Mosque, sat by the side of Abubekr, who was presiding over the assemblage, and that, when the prayers were finished, the Prophet delivered a Sermon from the pulpit with so powerful a voice that it reached beyond the outer doors of the Mosque to a considerable distance.

Some traditions are given below :—

† At the night prayer on Thursday, the Prophet ordered to tell Abubekr to lead the prayers. Upon this Ayesha said: "O Prophet, Abubekr is a man of tender heart, command that Omar should conduct the prayers." The Prophet consented, but Omar on receiving the order said that he could not supersede Abubekr while he was present among them. So Abubekr presided. In the meantime the Prophet, finding himself sufficiently recovered, came out to the Mosque. Abubekr, hearing the rustle of the Prophet's approach, wished to step back amongst the congregation, vacating the place for the Prophet, but

† Ibn Khaldun.

10 A. H.

the Prophet catching hold of his clothes bade him remain in the position and himself sat by his side and recited from where Abubekr had left.

Ibn Khaldun says that ***on all the seventeen occasions the Prophet*** in the same manner ***led the prayers*** of Abubekr sitting by his side, while the congregation was being led by Abubekr.

† Another tradition says that the Prophet ordered Abdalláh son of Zam'a to tell the congregation to read their prayers. While Abdalláh was proceeding into the Mosque, Omar met him first, so he told Omar to lead the prayers. Omar stood up and in his powerful voice commenced the *Takbir* 'Great is the Lord' preparatory to the service. The Prophet, hearing the voice of Omar from his apartment, called aloud No! No! No! Let no one lead the prayers but Abubekr." Omar withdrew and reproved Zam'a's conduct. He, thereupon, said that the Prophet did not name to him any particular person to lead the prayers.

‡ Another tradition runs thus:— When the hour of Public prayer came round, the Prophet called for water to perform the ablutions, but, on attempting to rise, his strength failed, so he commanded that Abubekr should read the prayers with the congregation, and having given this order he fell back in a fainting fit. Soon recovering, he enquired whether Abubekr had been informed of his order. Ayesha replied that Abubekr was a man of tender heart; he would weep and the people would, with difficulty, hear his voice, and that Omar, if ordered, would prove better. The Prophet again ordered that Abubekr should read the prayers with the congregation. Ayesha again recommended Omar but the Prophet would not allow any one but Abubekr. Then at the instance of Ayesha, Hafsa urged that Omar should be allowed to preside. Displeased and irritated, the Prophet exclaimed : "Truly, ye resemble the foolish women in the story of

† Madárijal Nabowat ; Rowdzat-al Ahbáb.

‡ Fathal Bári ; Bokhári ; Rawdzat-al Ahbáb ; Madárij-al Nabowat.

Joseph; give the command forthwith as I have desired." The command was given and Abubekr commenced the *Takbir* 'Great is the Lord.' Meanwhile the Prophet, recovering sufficient strength, came out to the Mosque, supported by Ali and Abbás. When Abubekr heard the rustle of the Prophet's clothes, he attempted to step backwards to join the row of the congregation, but the Prophet bade him remain in his position and himself took a seat by the side of Abubekr. So Abubekr was led by the Prophet and the congregation was led in prayers by Abubekr.

"There is a tradition in which Hafsa gives orders to Bilál to make her father (Omar) conduct the Public prayers, whereupon Mohammed chides her and says "she resembles the females in the story of Joseph"; adding these words, "speak to Abubekr that he lead the prayers; for verily if I make him not my deputy, the people will not be obedient unto him." *K. Wackidi p. 145 ½* from *W. Muir Vol, IV p. 266.*

"It is said that Abubekr led the prayers for three days before the Prophet's death. Another tradition makes him lead the prayers on seventeen occasions which would be equal to three days and part of a fourth." *K. Wackidi p. 145½, from W. Muir Vol. IV. p. 264.*

"In another tradition it is also said that *the Prophet throughout his illness came out to the prayers* whenever he could, and that if he came out late he made up at the end of the service what he had missed at the beginning of it." *K. Wackidi p. 145½, from W. Muir Vol. IV p. 264.*

From the varied traditions given above it is inferred that the Prophet to the last day of his life came out to the Mosque and led the prayers himself. It is reasonable too that, having already given Abubekr order to proceed with the army of Osáma and invoking curse upon the defaulter, it is improbable that the Prophet would give him (Abubekr) order to preside over the Public prayers in Medina, which meant his stay in Medina, quite contrary to his (the Prophet's) previous order, which was not withdrawn by him till his death.

10 A. H.

It is said that the right of presiding at the Public prayers was always recognised as the bare mark of chief secular power. Had Abubekr been appointed to preside at the Public prayers, the Ansárs, who are alleged to have assembled at Saqifa to choose a Caliph, while the Prophet's body was lying unwashed and unburied, would not have dared start so soon a movement in contravention of the Prophet's so recent a command, neglecting altogether that Abubekr's appointment by the Prophet to lead the prayers was intended to signify the delegation of the Supreme Authority to him.

A large body of the Moslems, conclusively infer that Abubekr's Imámat is an afterthought to justify his assumption of the Supreme Power after the Prophet's death.

† Another day the Prophet after prayers addressed the People thus:—"Brethren! if I caused any one of you to be unjustly scourged, I submit my own shoulders to the lash of retaliation. If I aspersed the good name of any one of you, let him proclaim my faults before the congregation. If I owe something to any one, he should come forward to make a demand against me; the little that I possess shall discharge the claim. I would rather blush in this world than in that to come." Continuing he said, "I have not made lawful anything excepting what God hath made lawful; nor have I prohibited aught but that which God in His Book hath prohibited.

From amongst the audience one man stepped forward and demanded three Dirhams, which were paid to him at once. After this the Prophet went to his apartment.

From Saturday night the sickness of the Prophet assumed a serious turn and till Sunday night, it is said, the fever continued unabated. On Sunday Osáma came from his camp to receive the blessings of the Prophet, preparatory to his departure to Syria, but at the time of his visit, the Prophet was unconscious in a fit of swooning. Osáma spoke to him but received no answer, except by the movement of his hand, which Osáma took between

† Madárij-al-Nabowat. Rawzat-al-Safá.

both of his own, and then kissing the hand and the forehead of the Prophet, he went back to his Camp.

The Prophet's last prayer and Sermon in his Mosque.

‡ Early in the morning on Monday (the day of death) the Prophet, with his head bandaged, came out to the Mosque supported by two men. After the prayers, he delivered a short Sermon, with a voice that reached beyond the outer doors of the Mosque, which was unusually crowded by the anxious people who had been seeking for the tidings of his welfare after the crisis of the preceding night. In this Sermon he also said that Evils were nearing and the darkest part of a dark and tempestous night was approaching, When the Sermon was ended, Abubekr said: "O Prophet, by the grace of God thou art better today." Osáma was also there to receive his blessings. The Prophet said to him: "Make haste with thy army; the blessing of the Lord be with thee." Osáma went back to his Camp and ordered march to be effected the same day. Abubekr departed to his house at al-Sonh, a suburb of the upper city.

Death of the Prophet.

The Prophet re-enterted his apartment and lay down exhausted on his bed. His strength was rapidly failing. ¶ Calling all his wives around him, he gave them necessary instructions and enjoined them to sit quietly in their homes and not to show themselves with the show of the Period of Ignorance. *Sur. XXXIII-33*. Fátema, his beloved daughter, was weeping. He called her and made her sit by his side and whispered something into her ear. She burst into tears. He then again whispered to her and dried her tears with his own hands. She then appeared comforted and † smiled. He then called Hasan and Hosain; his dear children, whom he fondled in his lap for years, to embrace them for the last time. Hasan put his face upon

‡ Tabari; Ibn Khaldun.

¶ Habib-al-Siyar; Madárij-al-Nabowat.

† Rawdzat-al-Ahbáb; Madárij-al Nabowat

10 A. H.

the face of the Prophet and Hosain threw himself upon his breast. *Both of them wept and cried so bitterly that the whole audience cried. The Prophet very affectionately embraced them, kissed them both and directed every one present to treat them and their mother with utmost love and respect, as they were treated by himself. (It was usual with the Prophet that when he saw Fátema approaching, he always stood up and, advancing a pace or two, received her with acclamations of joy. Then, kissing her hand, he used to seat her in his own place.) † Then he called Ali, who took his seat by the bed. The Prophet bade him repay the amount, which he said he had borrowed

* در روضة الاحباب است که جناب رسالت ماب با فاطمه فرمود که پسرانت را پیش آر فاطمه حسن و حسین را علیه‌التحیه والرضوان به نزدیک آن سرور آورد سلام کردند و در برابر جد بزرگوار بنشستند و چون اورا به آن حال دیدند گریه آغاز نهادند و چنان زار بگریستند که از گریه ایشان هرکه درآن خانه بود بگریست حسن روے خود را بر روے مبارک آنحضرت و حسین سر را بر سینه پرسکینهٔ آن سرور نهاد و حضرت چشمان نرگسین کشاد و در ایشان از سر لطف و شفقت نظر کرد و ایشانرا به بوسید و ببوئید و در باب تعظیم و احترام و محبت ایشان وصیت فرمود و در روایتے آنکه بعضے از خواص اصحاب بر در حجرهٔ حضرت حاضر بودند و از گریهٔ حسن و حسین بگریستند چنانکه آواز گریهٔ ایشان بگوش پر هوش آنسرور رسیده وے نیز بگریست (الي ان قال) انگاه فرمود بخوانید برادر من علي را-علی بیامد و بر بالین وے بنشست حضرت سر خود را از بستر برداشت جناب امیر در شیب بغل وے در آمد و سر مبارکش بر بازوے خویش نهاد- آنسرور فرمود اے علی فلان یهودي پیش من چندین مبلغ دارد که از وے براے تجهیزلشکر اسامه بقرض گرفته بودم زنهار که وے را از ذمهٔ من ادا کنی- اے علی تو اول کسے خواهی بود که بر لب حوض کوثر بمن رسي و بعد از من بسے امور مکروه بتو خواهد رسید باید که تنگدل نشوی و طریق مصابرت پیش گیري و چون بیني که مردم دنیا اختیار کنند تو باید آخرت را اختیار کني (تاریخ احمدی ص ۱۰۰)

† Rawdzat-al-Ahbáb ; Madárij-al-Nabowat ; Ma'árij-al-Nabowat.

from a certain Jew to defray the expenses of Osáma's Expedition and enjoined Ali to bear with patience and self control all the troubles which he would be subjected to after his death. He desired him to maintain with patience his right path of the next world when he would find the people going earnestly to that of this world. ‡ The Prophet took Ali's head inside his mantle, which covered both of them, till Ali took out his head and announced the death of the Prophet.

اخرج النساى في الخصائص عن ام سلمه قالت والذي تحلف به ام سلمه ان اقرب الناس عهدا برسول الله صلعم على قالت لما كان غدوة قبض رسول الله صلعم فارسل اليه رسول الله قالت و اظنه كان بعثه في حاجة فجعل يقول جاء علي ثلاث مرات فجاء قبل طلوع الشمس فلما ان جاء عرفنا انه اليه حاجة فخرجنا من البيت و كنا عند رسول الله صلعم يومئذ فى بيت عايشة و كنت فى آخر من خرج من البيت ثم جلست من وراء الباب فكنت ادناهم الى الباب فاكب عليه على فكان آخرالناس به عهدا فجعل يساره و يناجيه واللفظ حديث المستدرك فجعل يساره و يناجيه ثم قبض صلعم

ترجمه—خصائص نساي مين حضرت ام سلمه سے مروي هے كه قسم هے خدا كي قريب ترين مردم بوقت وفات سرور كائنات علي بن ابيطالب هين يعنے جسدن آنحضرت كا انتقال هوا اوسيكي صبح كو آپنے فرمايا كه علي كو بلاو جنهين شايد كسى كام كيلئے بهيجا تها اور جبتك وه نهين آے تين بار دريافت كيا كه على آے اتنے مين علي آفتاب نكلنے سے پهلے آگئے - پس هملوگ يهه گمان كرکے كه غالباً رسول الله كو علي سے كوي حاجت هے خانه عايشه سے باهر نكل آے اور مين سب كے بعد نكلكر دوسری عورتونكی نسبت دروازه سے قريب بيٹهي چنانچه مينے ديكها كه علي نے رسول الله كيجانب اپنا سر جهكايا اور آنحضرت اونسے بطور سرگوشي راز كی باتين كرتے رهے پس علي هی وه شخص هين جو رسول مقبول كے آخر وقت آنحضرت كے پاس تهے - نيز مستدرك حاكم مين

‡ Life of Ali by Dár Qutni wal Rázi p. 739; Life of Ali printed at Khádimal Tálim Press, Lahore; Madárij-al-Nabowat.

10 A. H.

* Ibn Sa'd and Hákim have recorded that the Prophet breathed his last with his head on the lap of Ali (*madarij-al-Nabowat*). The last words spoken by the Prophet, said Ali, were "The blessed companionship on high. Prayers, prayers," after which he stretched himself gently and then all was over. Eternal peace be on him and on his holy progeny, who sacrificed themselves to the cause of Islam and led us to the path of righteousness.

ھے کہ رسول اللہ صلعم وقت وفات تک حضرت علی سے راز کے امور ارشاد کرتے رھے اوسکے بعد انتقال فرمایا۔ (تاریخ احمدی ص ۱۰۲)

* روی ابن سعد فی الطبقات عن علي بن الحسین قال قبض رسول اللہ و راسہ فی حجر علی و فیہ ایضاً عن ابی عطفان قال سالت ابن عباس ارائت رسول اللہ توفی و راسہ فی حجر احد قال توفي رسول اللہ صلعم و ھولمستند الی صدر علی قلت فان عروۃ حدثني عن عایشہ انھا قالت توفی رسول اللہ صلعم بین سحری و نحری فقال ابن عباس اتعقل واللہ لتوفی رسول اللہ صلعم و ھو مستند الي صدر علی و ھوالذی غسلہ —

ترجمہ—ابن سعد نے طبقات مین حضرت علی بن حسین سے روایت کی ھے کہ جسوقت جناب رسالتماب نے وفات پائی اونکا سر مبارک حضرت علی کی آغوش مین تھا۔نیز کتاب مذکور مین ابو عطفان سے مروی ھے کہ مینے عبداللہ ابن عباس سے پونچھا کہ آیا آپنے دیکھا ھے کہ رسول اللہ کا سر مبارک وقت وفات کسکی آغوش مین تھا—عبد اللہ ابن عباس نے کہا کہ جب رسول اللہ نے انتقال فرمایا تو آنحضرت کا سر علی بن ابیطالب کے سینہ سے لگا ھوا تھا۔ مینے کہا کہ عروہ تو مجھ سے حضرت عایشہ کی یہہ حدیث بیان کرتا ھے کہ جب پیغمبر صاحب نے انتقال فرمایا تو آنحضرت اون ھی کی گود مین تھے۔ عبد اللہ بن عباس بولے کہ کچھ سمجھتے بھی ھو خدا کی قسم جب رسول اللہ نے وفات پائی تو وہ علی کے سینہ پر تیک لگائے ھوے تھے اور علی ھي نے آنحضرت کو غسل بھی دیا

در روضۃ الاحباب روایت جابر بن عبداللہ انصاري ملخصاً منقول است کہ گفت در زمان خلافت عمر بن الخطاب کعب الاحبار بنزد وے آمد و گفت یا امیرالمومنین آخر کلمہ کہ رسول صلعم بان تکلم فرمودچہ بود۔ عمر گفت ازعلی بن ابیطالب بپرس کعب از علي پرسید جناب امیر فرمود الصلوۃ الصلوۃ

Fátema beating her face in bitter lamentation joined the other women wailing aloud. It was but a little after midday on Monday, the † 2nd of Rabi' I, of the eleventh year (calculated to commence from Moharram) of Hegira, when the Prophet breathed his last at the age of sixty-three years. Other dates assigned are the †† 28 of Safar and the ¶ 12th Rabi' I. The day of death, is however, unanimously admitted as Monday.

* A tradition says that before his death some one asked permission to visit the Prophet, who was at the time in an unconscious state. Fátema replied to the stranger that it was not time for such an intrusion. Not

* از روضة الاحباب محدث جمال الدين و مدارج النبوة شيخ عبدالحق محدث دهلوي - ملا محمد مبين در وسيلة النجاة نقلكرده - از ابن عباس منقول است که روز وفات آنحضرت صلعم حق تعالے امر کرد ملک الموت را که بر زمین ا نزدیک حبیب من محمد برو و بپرهیز از آنکه بے اذن بروے در آئی و از آنکه قبض روح وے بے اذن کنی - پس قابض ارواح از بیرون خانه برصورت اعرابی بایستاد و گفت السلام علیکم یا اهل بیت النبوة و معدن الرسالت و مختلف الملائکه اذن میدهید مرا تا در آیم رحمت خدا بر شما باد - فاطمه زهرا بر بالین رسولخدا بود جواب داد که پیغمبر بحال خود مشغول است حالا وقت ملاقات نیست دیگر اذن طلبید و همان جواب شنید - بار سوم اذن باواز بلند طلبید چنانچه هرکس که در آن خانه بود از هیبت آواز برخود لرزید - حضرت بهوش باز آمد و چشمان مبارک بکشاد و پرسید که چه میشود - صورت حال را بعرض رسانیدند - فرمود اے فاطمه دانستی که این کیست این شکننده لذات و قطع کننده آرزوهاے و شهوات است و متفرق کننده جماعات و بیوه گردانندهٔ زوجات و یتیم کننده بنین وبنات است —
فاطمه چون این سخن بشنید بگریست - فرمود حضرت صلعم اے دختر من گریه مکن که جمله عرش بر بکاے تو گریه میکنند و بدست مبارک خود اشک از چهره مبارک فاطمه پاک کرد و دلداریها و تسلی ها داد - و در

† Kashf-al-Ghamma (Shia); Ibn Hajar-al-Asqaláni; Tabari; Abul Fida; Ibn Athir; Ibn Khaldun; Tárikh-al-Khamis (Sunni.)

†† Hayát-al-Qulub (Shia.)

¶ Wáqidi; Sirat-al-Halabia (Sunni).

10 A.H.

heeding the answer, permission was again sought for and again Fátema replied in the same manner. Third time the permission was asked in a horrible voice, so that Fátema was terrified to hear it. Gabriel, who had by this time come down to visit the Prophet, said to him: "This, O Prophet! is the angel of death. He asketh of thee permission to enter. Never before hath he asked permission of any man, neither shall he be so solicitous hereafter." The Prophet then asked Fátema to let him in,

---

بعضے روایات حدیث خبر موت آنحضرت صلعم و گریه فاطمه و تسلیه آنحضرت اورا که تو پیشتر لاحق میشوي بمن و تو سید نساء جنت خواهي بود درین وقت آمد و گفت بار خدایا ویرا در مفارقت من صبر کرامت فرما-فاطمه زهرا سلام الله علیها گفت و اکرباه فرمود آنحضرت صلعم نیست هیچ کرب و اندوه بر پدر تو بعد"از امروز.......... انگاه فاطمه را فرمود که پسران خود را پیش آر پس فاطمه حسن و حسین را علیهم السلام پیش آنحضرت صلعم آورد چون اورا بدین حال دیدند گریه آغاز نهادند و چندان گریه و زاری کردند که از گریه ایشان هرکه در خانه بود بگریست-آنحضرت صلعم ایشان را ببوسید و ببوئید و در باب تعظیم و احترام و محبت ایشان صحابه و تمامه امت را وصیت فرمود و در روایتے آمده که آنها که در حجره بودند نیز گریستند و چون آواز گریه ایشان بگوش حضرت رسید آنحضرت صلعم نیز بگریست ام سلمه گفت یا رسول الله موجب گریه چیست فرمود صلعم گریه من برایے رحم و شفقت بر امت است که آیا بعد از من حال ایشان بکجا خواهد رسید-بعد ازان عایشه رضی الله عنها پیش رفت و کفت یا رسول الله چشم بکشایے و در من نگاهے کن و وصیتے فرمای حضرت چشم بکشاد و گفت اے عایشه بمن نزدیک شو فرمود که دیروز که وصیت کرده ام وصیت همان است باید که بموجب آن عمل کني و حفصه نیز پیش برفت و بدستوریکه باعایشه مکالمه فرمود با حفصه نیز گفت و تمامه ازواج را وصیت کرد بعد ازان فرمود برادر من علی را بیارید علی بیامد و بر بالین آنحضرت بنشست و سر مبارک را بر زانوے خویش نهاد آن سرور صلعم فرمود اے علی فلان یهودی پیش من چندان مبلغ دارد که

so the angel of death came in, stood before the Prophet and said: "O Prophet of the Lord! Verily God hath sent me unto thee and hath directed me to act according to thy wish. Bid me to take thy soul and I will take it, or bid me to leave it and I will obey thee." Upon this Gabriel

---

از وے براے لشکر تجهیز اسامه بقرض گرفته بودم زنهار که قرض اورا از ذمه من ادا کنی و فرمود اے علی تو اول کسے خواهی بود که درلب حوض کوثر بمن برسي و بعد از من مکروهات بتو خواهد رسید باید که دلتنگ نشوی و صبر کني و چون بینی که مردم دنیا اختیار کنند باید که تو آخرت اختیار کني- و در روایتے آنکه فرمود دوات و صحیفه بیار تا براے تو وصیتے بنویسم علی گوید ترسیدم که تامن اسباب کتابت را مهیا سازم آنحضرت از دنیا نقل کند و من بدولت وصیت وے نرسم گفتم یا رسول الله وصیتے که میخواهي بکن که یاد گیرم فرمود-الصلوة و ما ملکت ایمانکم - در روایتے آنکه گفت الله الله فیما ملکت البسوا ظهورهم و اشبعوا بطونهم و لینوا الهم القول - علي مرتضی گوید که حضرت با من سخن میگفت و آب دهن وے بمن میرسید پس حال بروے متغیر شد و زنان از پس پرده بیطاقتي مینمودند و من نیز تحمل آن نداشتم که وے را بۂ این حال به بینم گفتم اے عباس مرا دریاب عباس آمدو با یکدیگر وے را بخوابانیدم ذکر هذا کلهه فی روضة الاحباب و مدارج النبوة و هر گاه کۂ ملک الموت روح اطهر ویرا صلعم قبض کرد و با علی علئین برد - گفت وا محمداه وا رسول رب العالمین

از علي بن ابیطالب منقول است که گفت از جانب آسمان اواز وا محمدا می شنیدم - و روایت کرده شده است از ام سلمه که گفت آمدم من و دست بر سینۂ آنحضرت روزیکه وفات یافت نهادم پس گذشت بر من چند جمعه که طعام میخورم و وضو میکنم و نمیرود بوے مشک از دست من- و بصحت رسیده که چون آنحضرت رحلت کرده فاطمه زهرا گریۂ کرد و زاری نمود و گفت-یا ابتاه - دعوت حق را اجابت فرمودي وا ابتاه بجنت الفردوس نزول نمودي - وا ابتاه خبر مرگ ترا بجبریل که رساند وا ابتاه بعد از تو وحی برکه فرود آید و جبرئیل برما کے آید خداوندا روح فاطمه را بروح او صلعم برسان بار خدایا مرا بدیدار

10 A. H.

interposed thus:–"O Ahmad! verily the Lord is desirous of thee." "Proceed then," addressed the Prophet to the Angel of Death, "and do thy work". Gabriel now bade adieu to the Prophet: "Peace be on thee," he said, "O Prophet of the Lord! my descent to the earth ends with thee." So the Prophet died, and there rose a wailing of celestial voice from unvisible mourners.

The news of the Prophet's death soon spread all over Medina and the people flocked to the Mosque to learn the truth. Abubekr was at his house in Al Sonh, a suburb of the upper city. Ayesha sent Sálim b. Abid to fetch him at once.

Omar enacting a strange scene.

Meanwhile a strange scene was being enacted at the Mosque. Shortly after the Prophet's death, Omar entered the apartment and raising the sheet which covered the body, gazed earnestly on the Prophet's features, which looked as of one quite peacefully sleeping. Softly replacing the covering, he started up and exclaimed: "The Prophet is not dead, he hath gone to His Lord as aforetime Moses did and remained forty days absent. He will yet return among us again." Brandishing his sword he exclained, "I will cut off the head of him who dares say

---

رسول خویش قرین گردان بار خدایا مرا از ثواب حبیب خویش بے نصیب مدار و در روز قیامت از شفاعت او محروم مگردان و گویند بعد گذشتن آنحضرت صلعم فاطمه زهرا را کسے خندان ندید-آورده اند که صحابه بعد از وفات آنحضرت صلعم سرا سیمهٔ و حیران گشتند و برعلي مرتضی حالتے طاري گشت که طاقت جنبیدن نداشت-و ابو بکر درخانه خود بود در محله سنح از عوالي مدینه بعد از وفات رسولخدا صلعم آمد و تعزیه تسلیه اهلبیت بجا آورد و گفت کار غسل و تجهیز و تکفین تعلق بشما دارد شمایان قیام نمائد و خود با اکابر مهاجرین و اشراف انصار بهٔ سقیفهٔ بني ساعده بقرار دادن امر خلافت رفت و مشغول به خلافت شد-

انا لله و انا الیه راجعون

اهل دنیا حب دنیا داشتند مصطفی را بیکفن بگذاشتند

that the Prophet is dead." He was haranguing the people in a similar strain when Abubekr appeared. He listened to the words of Omar for a moment and then passed on to the door of Ayesha's apartment. He entered, and, lifting the sheet which covered the body of the Prophet, stooped down and kissed the forehead. Then taking the head upon his hands, he slightly lifted it and minutely scanned the features. Replacing the head gently on its pillow, he exclaimed:—"Yes! sweet thou wert in life and sweet thou art in death. Alas, my master! thou art dead indeed." Covering the body, he issued forth and proceeded at once to the spot where Omar was brandishing his sword and haranguing the people. "Be quiet Omar! sit thee down," cried Abubekr. But Omar would not listen to him. Turning therefore to the assemblage, he addressed them thus:—"Do ye forget already the verse which was revealed to the Prophet after the day of Ohod,—" Mohammed is but a man with a Mission, verily other Apostles died before him; what then! If he were to die or to be killed, would ye turn upon your heels?" *Sur. 131-138.* Again, know ye not the verse revealed to the Prophet, 'Verily O Mohamad! Thou shalt die, and verily they shall die; *Sur. XXXIX-31*;' continuing, he said: "Whosoever worshippeth Mohammed, let him know that Mohammed is indeed dead; but whosoever worshippeth God, let him know that God is immortal, He liveth and dieth not." The truth now being known, the audience, sobbed aloud. The verses of the Qurán having been repeated to them, it appeared as if they had never heard them. Omar, on hearing these verses recited, was struck with horror. In after times he himself related that hearing Abubekr reciting the verses, he trembled and dropped down, and then he knew of a certainty that the Prophet was indeed dead. Omm Aiman had sent word to his son Osáma at Jorf, informing him of the critical condition of the Prophet. Osáma had given to his army the order for immediate march and his foot was already in the stirrup when the messenger from his mother arrived. Stunned by the news, the army was broken up, and he returned to Medina preceded by Boreida b. Al Hasib his standard bearer, who proceeding direct to the Mosque planted the banner at the door of the apartment wherein the Prophet lay dead.

Shortly after the above incidents, towards the afternoon, there appeared in the Mosque a friend who came running hastily to Abubekr and Omar and informed them that many a chief of Medina had assembled at Saqifa Bani Sá'da and were proceeding to choose Sa'd b. Obáda as their leader. "If ye have a desire to secure the Supreme Authority," said he, "ye should not lose a minute to reach thither before the matter is settled and opposition becomes dangerous." Receiving the intelligence, Abubekr and Omar hurried to the Saqifa, in company with Abu Obeida and several others.

Wash & burial of the Prophet.

Meanwhile Ali, unaware of the movement outside, was busy inside the apartment in the preparations for washing the Prophet's body, in company with Abbás, his two sons Fadzl and Qutham, Osáma and Sáleh or Shaqrán. Having closed the door of the apartment and drawing a curtain of a sheet of Yemen stuff, they took the body in for washing. * Ali was the only man named by the Prophet to wash his body, (as was also predicted by him while he

---

* اخرج ابن سعد في الطبقات عن علي قال اوصانى النبي صلعم لا يغسله احد غيرى فانه لا يرى عورتي احدا لا طمست عيناه -

ترجمه- ابن سعد نے طبقات مین حضرت علي سے روایت کی ہے کہ پیغمبر صاحب نے مجہے وصیت فرماي تہی کہ میرے سوا کوئی دوسرا شخص آنحضرت کو غسل ندے ورنه وه نا بینا هوجائگا -(تاریخ احمدی ص ۱۰۳)

قال ابن الوردي في تاريخه تولى غسله علي و العباس والفضل وقثم ابني العباس و اسامه بن زيد و شقران مولي النبى صلعم فكان العباس و بنوه يقلبونه و اسامه و شقران يصبان الماء و علي يغسله -

ترجمه— مورخ ابن الوردی اپني تاریخ مین لکہتا ہے کہ رسول الله کے غسل کے متولی علی اور عباس اور فضل اور قثم اور اسامه اورشقران

was giving the first wash to Ali at the time of his birth) as he had said that any one, other than Ali, that looked upon his nakedness, would forthwith turn blind. So Ali washed the body and the others aided him. After washing the body they laid it out, putting on it the garments in which he died. Two sheets of fine white cloth were wound around the garment, and above all was cast a sheet of striped Yemen stuff. Then came the parties for praying over him. First the relations and next to them the followers and the Companions of the Prophet entered the apartment in batches of ten at a time and prayed over him. Thus the body remained till the time of burial.

* The people differed as to the place for the burial of the Prophet. The matter was settled by Ali, who said that he heard the Prophet saying, that in whatsoever spot a prophet dies he should be buried there. In Medina there were two grave-diggers *viz.*, Abu Obeida b. Al-Jarráh, who dug the grave for the Meccans, and Abu Talha Zaid b. Sahel, who dug the graves for the Medinians. Abbás

---

تھے - عباس اور فضل اور قثم آنحضرتکو پھیر تے تھے اور اسامہ اور شقران پانی ڈالتے تھے اور حضرت علي غسل دیتے تھے —

فی تاریخ الخمیس کان العباس والفضل والقثم یقلبونه و کان اسامة و شقران یصیب الماء علیه و اعینهم معصوبة —

ترجمہ — تاریخ الخمیس مین ھے کہ عباس اور فضل اور قثم آنحضرت کو کروٹ پھراتے تھے اور اسامہ اور شقران پانی ڈالتے تھے اور ان سب کي آنکھون پر پٹیان بندھی ہوئی تھین — (تاریخ احمدی ص ۱۰۳)

* ملا محمد مبین در وسیلة النجات آوردہ کہ اختلاف واقع شد کہ آنحضرت را کجا دفن کنند علي مرتضی فرمودہ در روے زمین ھیچ بقعہ نیست گرامی تر نزد خداے تعالي از بقعۂ کہ روح پیغمبر در آن قبض کردہ شد پس فراش وے برداشتند و حفر قبر در موضع معین و مقرر کردند و در مدینہ حفارے کہ لحد میکند نامش ابو طلحہ انصاری بود آمد پس حفر کرد قبر بطریق لحد و شب چھارشنبہ وقت سحر بود کہ آنحضرت را طرف پائین در قبر آوردند واصح آنست کہ علی و عباس و فضل و قثم در قبر در آمدند —

sent a man to each of the two to fetch them. Abu Obeida was not at his house, as he was with Abubekr and Omar at Saqifa, busy in the Caliphate affairs, so his services could not be availed of. Abu Talha came in and dug the grave for the Prophet. The burial took place in the night after Tuesday or early in the morning of Wednesday. The body was lowered into its last resting place by the same near relations, who had washed and laid it out. Ali was the last person to leave the interior of the tomb. The Lahad or Vault being shut up, the grave was filled with earth, and some water was sprinkled over. * The people then left the tomb and proceeded to the house of Fátema to condole with her in her bereavement. Ayesha continued to live in the room adjoining the one which contained the tomb.

---

* ملا محمد مبین در وسیلة النجات نقلکرده که پاشید بلال آب بر قبر شریف بقربهٔ ابتدا کرد از جانب سر و بلند کرده شد قبر شریف وے از مقدار یک شبر و در روایتے چهار انگشت آمده — و چیده شد بر قبر از سنگریزه هاے سرخ و سفید — و آمدند صحابه بعد از دفن نزد فاطمه گفت چگونه بود داد دل شما که ریختید خاک بر رسولخدا گفتند بلے یا بنت رسول الله یا زهرا ماهم درین خیال رفته بودیم و اندوهناک بودیم لیکن چه توان کرد از حکم شرع چاره نیست

قال ابوالفدا و ابن الوردي قبل دفن رسول الله يوم الثلاثاء ثانى يوم وفاته و قيل ليلة الا ربعاء و هو الا صح و قيل بقى ثلاثا لم يدفن

ترجمه — ابوالفدا و ابن الوردي لکهتے هین که آنحضرت نے دوشنبه کو انتقال فرمایا اور اوسکے دوسرے دن منگل کو اور بروایتے شب چهارشنبه کو مدفون هوے اور یهی صحیح تر هے نیز بعضونکا قول هے که آنحضرت تین دن تک دفن نهین هوے — (تاریخ احمدي ص ۱۰۴)

فى تاريخ الخميس روى عن محمد بن اسحق انه قال قبض رسول الله صلعم يو الاثنين فمكث ذلک اليوم و ليلة الثلاثاء و يوم الثلاثاء و دفن في ليلة الاربعاء

ترجمه — تاریخ الخمیس مین بروایت محمد بن اسحق منقول هے که جناب رسالت ماب نے دوشنبه کو وفات پائی اور شب چهار شنبه کو مدفون هوے —

The First Four Successors of The Holy Prophet Mohammed

The Prophet's successors. Abubekr, the First Caliph.

"Ali was cousin-german of Mohammed and husband of Fátema, his beloved daughter. The right of succession, in order of consanguinity, lay with Ali; and his virtues and services eminently entitled him to it. On the first burst of his generous zeal, when Islamism was a derided and persecuted faith, he had been pronouuced by Mohammed his brother, his vicegerent; he had ever since been devoted to him in word and deed, and had honoured the cause by his magnanimity as signally as he had vindicated it by his valour." *W. Irving.*

"The birth, the alliance, the character of Ali, which exalted him above the rest of his countrymen, might justify his claim to the vacant throne of Arabia. The son of Abu Tálib was, in his own right, the Chief of the family of Háshim, and the hereditary prince or guardian of the city and temple of Mecca. The light of prophecy was extinct, but the husband of Fátema might expect the inheritance and blessing of her father: the Arabs had sometimes been patient of a female reign; and the two grandsons of the Prophet had often been fondled in his lap and shown in his pulpit, as the hope of his age, and the Chief of the youth of paradise. From the first hour of his Mission to the last rites of his funeral, the Apostle was never forsaken by a generous friend, whom he delighted to name his brother, his vicegerent, and the faithful Aaron of a second Moses." *Gibbon abridged by W. Smith, p. 466.*

The merits of Ali and the language of the Apostle of Alláh in his favour had roused the envy of his contemporaries; and the hereditary claims of the youthful hero, over and above the Prophet's declarations appointing him his vicegerent and proclaiming his position as that of Aaron to Moses, were not agreeable to an aristocracy of the elders desirous of securing the sceptre for themselves. The preeminence of the Háshimites, which had reached its zenith with the advent of Mohammed (Peace on him and his holy progeny), was anxiously longed for to be crushed. The death of the Prophet restored, at length, their liberty and the ancient discord of the tribes was rekindled. In after days Omar confessed that the Qoreish could never be reconciled to the proud † pre-eminence of the line of Háshim. So they were all bent upon wresting from Ali the chance of his succession to the Apostle of Alláh, thus destroying the pre-eminence of the Háshimites. As soon as the Prophet's eyes were closed, without even waiting to commit him to the grave, they convened a meeting at Saqifa Bani Sá'da to deliberate on the election of one to assume the authority in place of the Prophet, and thus to deprive Ali of his right of succession.

The election at Saqifa Bani Sa'da.

While the unsuspecting vicegerent of the Apostle of Alláh was busy with the arrangements for his burial, the Mohájirs of Mecca and the Ansárs of Medina were parading their respective merits at the Saqifa. The Mohájirs claimed preference in view of their priority in Islam, their kinship with the Prophet, and their immigration with him at the manifest hazard of their life and property. The Ansárs urged that they had as much right as any others whatsoever, on account of their receiving the Prophet in his escape from his Meccan enemies, of protecting him in the time of adversity, and of helping him in making head against his powerful foes, resulting ultimately in the establishment of his paramount power and authority. They even ‡ alleged that they apprehended revenge* if authority

† Ibn Athir Kámil vol. iii p. 25.

‡ Ibn Qoteiba; Ibn Athir; Tabari; Rawdzat-al-Safá.

* "Revenge was almost a religious principle among the Arabs. To revenge a relative slain was the DUTY of his family, and often involved the honour of his tribe; and these debts of blood sometimes remained unsettled for generations, producing deadly feuds.." *W. Irving*.

Gibbon points out that the Arabs led a life of malice and suspicion while fifty years sometimes elapsed before the account of vengeance was finally settled.

went to the people whose fathers and brothers they had killed in defending the Prophet. [It may be noted here that this is the secret of the Karbala tragedy, which was spoken out by Hobáb, a quick-witted and prudent spokesman of the Ansárs. His fears proved correct with the revengeful massacre of the Prophet's or Ali's posterity at Karbala condemning even a six months' babe, and with the hideous crimes perpetrated in the outrages and the massacre of the Ansárs at Harra.] When Hobáb expressed this view, Omar indignantly retorted: "Thou shouldst die if the Caliphate settled with such people as whom thou fearest."

To refute ‡ the claims of the Ansars, said Omar, I myself wished to deliver a speech which I had particularly planned in my mind—because I presumed ¶ Abubekr would fall short of the occasion—but Abubekr stopped me and I thought it not proper to disobey the Caliph twice* in a day. However, to my great relief, I found him equal to the task. He argued that the Qoreish did not deny the services rendered by the Ansárs to promote the cause of Islam, but with all their meritorious services they should not deem themselves entitled to aspire to the sole authority over the Qoreish. As to the apprehensions spoken out by Hobáb, he added that they need not entertain any such fear, especially when they were offered a hand in the government with their assistance as minister or Wazeir. The Ansárs then said that they would be content to have one Caliph from each of the two parties to exercise † joint authority, and even nominated Sa'd b. Obáda, their leader, to be elected from amongst them. But Abubekr and his party would, by no means, approve of such a proposal, persisting that the government must

‡ Tabari; Ibn Athir; Sirat-al-Halabiya.

¶ Ibn Qoteiba.

*i.e. Once, the same day on the occasion of Abubekr forbidding him to harangue the people at the doors of the Prophet, when he lay dead (see page 274) and again on this occasion.

† Ibn Qoteiba; Rawdzat-al-Ahbáb; Rawdzat-al-Safá.

remain in the hands of the Qoreish, while the Ansárs should content themselve with the Wazirate or Ministry.

Abubekr elected to succeed the Prophet.

The Ansárs not yielding, the contention grew so hot that they were just upon falling to ‡ blows when Abubekr intervened and asked them if they had not heard the Prophet say that 'NONE was apt to exercise authority over the Qoreish BUT one from amongst themselves.' Bashir b. Sa'd, one of the Ansárs who shared the views of the Mohájirs, at once answered in favour of the Mohájirs. Thus encouraged, Abubekr resolutely exclaimed that the Qoreish would not accept any one but a Qoreish to rule over them; and stepping forth, he pointed out Omar and Abu Obeida to the Ansárs to choose either of them as the Caliph. Now the Ansárs began to say that they would prefer paying homage to ¶ Ali, the best of the Qoreish. At this juncture, Omar impatiently cried out: 'Stretch forth thy hand O Abubekr! Verily, I will swear thee allegiance.' Abubekr replied: 'Thou art firmer than I,' and again he repeated it. Omar, † then seizing the hand of Abubekr, said: 'Thou art better fitted than I, and verily thou hast my firmness together with thine own merits, I swear thee allegiance.' Thus Omar declared in a loud voice that he recognised Abubekr as Chief, and took the oath of fealty to him. Abu Obeida and some other Mohájir, who had accompanied them to Saqifa, followed his example. Bashir and another Ansár of his party swore allegiance to Abubekr, and the confusion was now over. Hobáb * had an altercation with Bashir for his traitorous conduct in preferring Abubekr over Sa'd b. Obáda, but at the intercession of certain other Ansárs their warm contention was abated.

Sa'd b. Obáda, the head of the Ansárs, was deeply

‡ Ibn Athir; Tabari.

¶ Ibn Athir; Tabari (Persian Edn.) Habib-al-Siyar; Rawdzat-al-Safá.

†Tabari; Suyuti.

*Ibn Qoteiba.

chagrined at being thus superseded. He did not pay homage to Abubekr. He subsequently left Medina and retired in disgust to Syria, where, it is said, he was foully ‡ murdered in the time of Omar in *15 A. H.*

Inauguration of Abubekr.

Having received the covenant of allegiance in the Saqifa, Abubekr, when the morrow came, seated himself on the pulpit in the Mosque where the people were made to assemble to swear him a general allegiance and to ratify the allegiance sworn at the Saqifa, in order to preclude a reversion. At the sight of the assemblage, Omar was convinced of Abubekr securing his succession on a firm footing. The next thing was to guard against any serious rupture, which he apprehended on the part of Ali if he presumed to anticipate the suffrage of his brethren in the manner * as Abubekr had his choice at Saqifa. Therefore, before Abubekr would begin his address, Omar was prudent enough to adopt measures to check the rupture—if any—by penalizing with capital punishment each and every one who should do such a thing as Abubekr had yesterday done *i.e.*, suffrage without the consent of all the Mussalmans. Standing by the pulpit, Omar † first addressed the assemblage :

"Notwithstanding that Omar was the first to propose Abubekr to the assembly, and to acknowledge him as Caliph, he did not afterwards approve of that choice, which necessity had suggested at that critical juncture.

---

‡Mas'udi ; Aqd-al-Farid ; Rawdzat-al-Safa

*1. "The two Sheykhs (Bokhari and Muslim) record that Omar said...........Let not any man deceive himself so as to say that fealty to Abubekr was hastily given—although it was even so—yet the Lord prevented the evil consequences thereof..........." *Major Jarret's trans. of Suiyuti's His. of Cal.*

2. "The urgency of the moment aud the acquiescence of the people might excuse this illegal and precipitate measure but Omar himself confessed from the pulpit, that if any Mussalman should hereafter presume to anticipate the suffrage of his brethren, both the elector and elected would be worthy of death." *Gibbon.*

† Tabari ; Suyuti.

This appears from what he said: That he prayed to God to avert the ill consequences which it was to be feared would follow upon such an indiscreet choice. That the man who should do such a thing would deserve death ; and if any one should ever swear fealty to another without the consent of the rest of the Mussalmans, both he that took the government upon him, and he that swore to him ought to be put to death." *S. Ockley's His. Sar. p. 82 from Abulfaragius.*

Omar's address to the assemblage in the Mosque concluded thus: In the words of *Sir W. Muir*: "O ye people! That which I spoke unto ye yesterday was not the truth. Verily I find that it is not borne out by the Book which the Lord had revealed, nor by the Covenant we made with His apostle. As for me, verily, I hoped that the Apostle of the Lord would continue yet a while amongst us and speak in our ears a word such as might seem good unto him and be a perpetual guide unto us. But the Lord hath chosen for His apostle the portion which is with Himself, in preference to that which is with you. And truly the inspired word which directed your Prophet is with us still. Take it therefore for your guide, and ye shall never go astray. And, now, verily, hath the Lord placed the administration of your affairs in the hands of him that is the best amongst us, the Companion of His prophet, the sole companion, the second of the two when they were in the cave alone. Arise! swear fealty to him." *W. Muir's Life of Mohammad.*

NOTE—I. Ibn Abi'l Hadid says: It is held by a large body of the Moslems that the whole policy and the illegal and seemingly precipitate measures adopted by Abubekr and Omar for securing the Caliphate, were a pre-meditated and well formed plan, moulded during the the Prophet's illness when his *bed was besieged by the artful Ayesha, the daughter of Abubekr and the enemy of Ali. Gibbon.* Abubekr was well stricken in years; being about the same age as the Prophet, it was not probable he would long survive. Omar was much younger than Abubekr, he trusted therefore that ere long he would succeed him. It is thus hinted that they had settled between themselves the order in

And the people swore unto Abubekr a general allegiance. Those who had sworne allegiance at the Saqifa ratified their oath.

Abubekr's first address to the people from the pulpit.

"Ibn Sa'd records on the authority of Al-Hasan of Basrah that when allegiance was sworn to Abubekr, he stood up and preached saying: And now, verily, I have been placed in this authority, though I am averse to it, and by Allah, I would have been pleased if any of you had sufficed for it in my stead, but if you charge me to act unto you as did the Apostle of God, I could not undertake it, for the Apostle of God was a servant whom the Lord honoured with His inspiration and preserved him thereby from error, and surely I am a mortal and am not better than any one of you—therefore watch over me, and when you see that I am steadfast then obey me, and when you see that I turn aside from the right path, set me aright. And know that I have a devil that seizes upon me, therefore when you see me enraged, avoid me, for at that time I cannot be influenced by your counsels or your good salutations." *Major Jarret's trans. of Suyuti's His. of Cal. p. 72.*

Absence of Abubekr and Omar

From the time of the death of the Prophet on Monday noon till the last portion of the night preceding Wednesday, Abubekr and

---

which they should come to power, and in accordance with this settlement Abubekr on his death-bed did not content himself with the election of his successor but nominated Omar in black and white—to avoid the risk of election—to succeed him.

2. The reply of Omar to Hobab, as observed in a previous paragraph above, also suggests that he was confident of the Caliphate settling with his partisans.

3. Omar's statement that he thought it not proper to disobey the *Caliph* twice in a day (as already observed in a paragraph above) also goes to show that he had already taken Abubekr as Caliph before the election; or else how could he say so, as it is strongly professed that the Prophet had not nominated his successor wnich necessitated the election.

from the funeral ceremonies of the Prophet.

Omar were busy* with the election affairs and could not †attend the funeral ceremonies of the Prophet, who was buried before they could come to join the ceremony. In fact they avoided to fall in with Ali before achieving complete and sure success in securing the Caliphate. After their success beyond the possibility of a reversion they came, but the funeral ceremonies were all finished.

Father wondering at his son's election.

"Al Hákim records in his Mustadrak (Supplement) from Abu Horeira that when the Apostle of God died, Mecca was convulsed by an earthquake, and Abu Qoháfa (father of Abubekr) noticed it and said, 'What is this?' They said, 'the Apostle of God is dead.' He answered, 'It is a momentous event, who then hath risen up in authority after him?' They said, 'Thy son.' He replied, 'Will the Banu Abd Manáf and the Banu Al-Moghira consent to this?' They answered, 'Yes.' He exclaimed, 'There is no overthrower of that which hath been exalted, and no exalter of that which hath been humbled!' *Jarret's translation of Suyuti's History of the Caliphs page 188.*"

Ali's attitude after the election of Abubekr.

Though the Caliphate was actually settled on Abubekr, there was still dissatisfaction among the people. None of the Háshimites was present at the Saqifa, or in the general allegiance sworn in the Mosque. Al Zobeir, Miqdád b. Aswad, Salmán Farsi, Abu Zharr Ghifári, Ammár Yaser, Barra b. Azheb, Khálid b. Sa'id, Abu

---

* With the experience of Saqifa fresh in memory, Omar on his death-bed, gave three days' time for the election of his successor, although it was to be made from amongst only six men of his own nomination, who were the only electors. It is evident that the election, at the Saqifa from amongst the contesting parties of the Ansárs and the Mohájirs would have occupied much more time but for the crafty measure taken by Omar to finish the whole affair.

† Kanzal Ommál; Arjah-al-Matáleb.

Ayyub Ansári, Khazima b. Thábit and others, as well as the Hashimites, kept themselves † aloof, not liking to pay homage to Abubekr, as they were of opinion that the right of succession belonged to Ali b. Abi Tálib alone.

Ali felt naturally grieved at the course the events had taken, but he made no stir. Had he made an attempt at arms against the people—the same who never dared to face the Champions of the Infidels, who were always overpowered by Ali—he would certainly have proved victorious as he proved himself throughout his life; but the victory would have been gained at the cost of the religion, which at this early stage of its life would have been strangled by the civil war. He, therefore, patiently shut himself up in his house, in the interests of Islam, which he had so long helped to establish at the risk of his life; and he turned his attention to the collection of the Qurán, which they think he wrote according to the order of its revelations. "Mohammed bin Sirin adds, if that Book were to be met with, there would be found in it much instruction." *Jarret's trans. of Suyuti's Hist. Cal. p. 188.*

Original name and titles of Abubekr.

At the time of his election Abubekr was about sixty years of age. He was the son of Abu Qoháfa, a Qoreishite, separated in parentage from the seventh forefather of the Prophet's lineage of ancestors. Abubekr was the seventh in descent from Tym the son of Morra, the seventh fore-father of the Prophet (vide the Genealogical Table.) The clan to which Abubekr belonged was denominated Bani Tym after the name of Tym. His mother Selma was a daughter of his father's uncle Sakhr. Though Abubekr is reckoned as one of the early converts to Islam yet his father Abu Qoháfa embraced the Faith after two decades of the Prophet's mission. Abubekr's original name was Abd-al-Ka'ba. He was also named Atiq. "His mother had no son surviving, and when she gave him birth, she took him to the temple and exclaimed, 'O Deity! If this one is granted immunity from death, then bestow him

† Abul Fida; Habib-al-Siyar etc.

upon me.' Afterwards he was named Atiq, *i. e.*, Liberated." *Jarret's trans. of Suyuti's Tarikh-al-Kholafa, p. 27.*

"As regards the title of As-Siddiq, it is said that he was so called in the Period of Ignorance, because he was distinguished for the love of truth. (Ibn Mondah)." *Ibid. p. 28.* "Mos'ab b. Al-Zobeir and others say that the people concurred in naming him (Abubekr) As-Siddiq (witness to the truth) because he hastened to testify to the Apostle of God, and steadfastly adhered to the truth......" *Ibid p. 25.*

On his conversion to Islam at the age of 38, Abubekr was named Abdalláh. After the marriage of his virgin daughter Ayesha he was called Abubekr (the father of the virgin), as she was the only one of the Prophet's wives that came a virgin to him, the others being widows.

Abubekr's habits and Profession.

Abubekr was a Genealogist, well versed in counting the pedigrees of the Arabs, more specially that of the Qoreish. "Ibn Asákir records from Al-Miqdám that.........Abubekr used to be a great reviler as well as a great genealogist." *Jarret's Trans. of Suyuti's Tarikh-al-Kholafa p. 54.*

Abubekr had taken to trade in cloth. Next morning after allegiance had been sworn unto Abubekr, he arose and was going to the market place with some mantles upon his arm, when Omar said to him: "Whither art thou going?" He replied: "To the market." Omar said: "Dost thou do this although thou hast been given to rule over the Moslems?" He answered: "Whence then shall my family be fed?" Omar replied: "Come, Abu Obeida shall provide for thee;" and they went to Abu Obeida (the Treasurer of the Bait-al-Mál, public treasury.) They assigned him two thousand dirhams and he said: 'Increase the sum for me, for I have a family and you have employed me on other work than my own trade.' So they gave him an increase of five hundred dirhams." *Jarret's trans. of Suyuti's Tarikh-al-Kholafa, p. 79.* But this amount being still insufficient for the maintenance of himself and his family, a yearly allowance of six thousand dirhams was fixed for his household charges, † Some say eight thousand dirhams.

Ali subjected to humiliation.

"Abubekr sent Omar to Fátema's house, where Ali and some of his friends were gathered, with orders to compel them by force to come in and do fealty to him, if they would not be persuaded by fair means. Omar was just going to fire the house, when Fátema asked him what he meant. He told her that he would certainly burn the house down unless they would be content to do as the rest of the people had done‡..............." *S. Ockley's His. Sar. p. 83.* Knowing, as they did, the temper of Omar, the men came out of the house. They were Ali, Abbás and Zobeir. Ali reproached them saying: 'O ye Mohájirs! Ye claimed the succession to the Apostle of God preferring your priority in Islam and your kinship to him before the Ansárs. Now I put forward the same arguments in preference to you. Am I not the first who believed in the Prophet before any of you embraced his faith? Am I not the nearest in relation to the Prophet than any one of you? Fear God, if ye are true Believers, and do not snatch away the Prophet's authority from his house to your own.' Standing behind the door, Fátema reproachfully addressed the raiding party thus: 'O people! Ye left behind you the Prophet's dead body to us and proceeded to wring out the Caliphate for yourselves, extinguishing our rights.' Then she burst into weeping and cried: 'O father! O Apostle of God! How soon after thee troubles are pouring on us at the hands of the son of Khattáb and the son of Abu Qoháfa. How soon they have ignored thy words of Ghadir Khum and thy saying that Ali was to thee as Aaron was to Moses.' Hearing Fátema's wailings, most of the people in Omar's party could not keep themselves from weeping and turned ¶ back. Ali was, however, taken to Abubekr and was asked to swear him allegiance. He

†Ibn Athir.
‡Also Abul Fida; Aqdal Farid.
¶Ibn Qoteiba.

said, 'what if I do not do him homage?' He was answered, 'By Alláh, we shall kill thee if thou dost not do as others have done.' Upon this Ali said, 'what! will ye kill a man who is a servant of the Lord and a brother of the Apostle of the Lord?' Hearing this, Omar exclaimed, 'We do not admit that thou art a brother of the Apostle of the Lord;' and addressing Abubekr, who was silent all the time, he desired him to speak out his (Ali's) fate. But Abubekr said that so long as Fátema was alive, he would not compel her husband anywise. So Ali departed and proceeded direct to the tomb of the Prophet ‡ where he cried out, "O my brother! thy people now treat me with contempt and are bent upon killing* me."

Fatema's claim to inheritance.

Fátema—the only surviving child of the Prophet, his best beloved—claimed inheritánce of the property which could be apportioned to her in the tithe lands of Medina and in Khaiber, as also Fadak, which, having been acquired without the use of force, the Prophet (her father) had given her for her maintenance in accordance with the commands of God (*as in Verse 28 of Sura XVII*). Abubekr refused to acknowledge her claim saying: "but the Prophet hath said, We the group of prophets do not inherit, nor are we inherited; what we leave is for alms". Hearing this saying ascribed to the Prophet, contrary to the versions of the Qurán, Fátema felt grieved and was so much displeased with Abubekr that she never again spoke to him as long as she lived; and when she died after six months of the death of her father, Abubekr was not

‡ Ibn Qoteiba.

*It is contended by a large body of Moslems that according to their speculated terms, Omar was to succeed Abubekr on his death, but he naturally feared lest in the uncertain interval there might occur an outbreak on the part of the rightful claimant Ali, which would possibly destroy his ambitious dreams, he therefore anxiously wished and tried to get rid of Ali any how. But Ali was wise enough to bear with patience all the gravely insulting provocations and avoided any out break which would have endangered the safety of Islam.

allowed, in compliance with her will, to join her funeral. †It is significant that Abubekr was the single narrator of the tradition above referred to.

"He (Abubekr) was a man of great judgement and discretion, whose wariness and management at times almost amounted to craft, yet his purposes appear to have been honest and unselfish, directed to the good of the cause, not to his own benefit." *W. Irving.*

"Abu No'aim in his Hulyah writes on the authority of Abu Sáleh that when the people of Yemen came in the time of Abubekr and heard the Qurán, they began to weep, and Abubekr said: Thus were we, but afterwards our hearts became hardened." *Jarret's trans. of Suyuti's His. Cal.*

Offers of hostility rejected by Ali.

"Abu Sofyán b. Harb went to Ali and said, 'How is it that the authority is with the least of the Qoreish in insignificance and the meanest of them? (i. e. Abubekr); by Alláh I would like to pour the Qoreish upon him, horse and foot.' Ali replied, 'Verily it is long since that thou hast been hostile to Islam, O Abu Sofyán, but that hurts it not at all....................' *Major Jarret's trans. of Suyuti's His. Cal. p. 66.*"

According to Dr. Weil, Abu Sofyán and some relations of Ali offered to assist him in maintaining his rights by the sword. But Ali had the safety of Islam at his heart, therefore he flatly rejected their offers. Abu Sofyán, being the most powerful, was won over with promises of good prospects for his sons; and subsequently his son Yazid was created General of a Division of Abubekr's forces, and thus he became a warm adherent of the Caliph.

Abubekr pretending to relinquish the Caliphate.

After the death of Fátema, when Abubekr came to see him, Ali upbraided him with want of openness and good faith in conducting the election affairs without his knowledge. Abubekr, disavowing all intrigue, said, that the exigencies of the situation prompted him to do

† Bokhári; Muslim; Masnad Ahmad Hanbal.

what he did, and, that had he been late the government would have been wrung out of his hands by the Ansárs. However, in order to pacify Ali, he expressed his willingness to relinquish his charge in his favour. The public declaration of the Relinquishment was fixed to be made in the Mosque at the noon day prayers. † At the appointed time Abubekr ascended the pulpit in the Mosque and addressing the congregation, he asked the leave of the congregation to resign and transfer the charge to a worthier person. Concluding he said: "Break off your homage to me as I am not the best whilst Ali is amongst you." The people, of course, would not listen to such a proposal mooted so abruptly. Ali was loth to create any disturbance and retired to his quarters. It is, however, certain that he did not do fealty to Abubekr, at least, as some assert, till the death of his wife Fátema.

Remonstration of Al-Hasan.

There is a tradition that Al-Hasan, the son of Ali, one day went to Abubekr, who was then on the pulpit of the Apostle of God, and said, "Come down from the seat of my father." Abubekr, answered, "Verily thou speakest the truth, for this is thy father's seat," and he seated him in his lap and wept. Ali said, "by Alláh, this was not said by my command." Abubekr said, "thou speakest truly, by Alláh, I did not suspect thee." *Jarret's trans. of Suyuti's Tarikh-al-Kholafa, p. 81.*

Some accounts of Abubekr's Caliphate.

Abubekr, not being a legal heir to the Prophet, nor even a Háshimite to be considered as a member of the clan to which the Prophet belonged, was not recognised universally as a rightful successor to the Prophet. Consequently most of the tribes throughout the Peninsula stopped payment of the tithes payable to the government. The legates of the Prophet, the collectors of tithes, were expelled. From every quarter in rapid succession reached the news of spreading disaffection to the Caliph. To this may be

† Fawáteh Meibizhi p. 128; Abtál-al-Bátil from Fadzal b. Rozbhán.

added the dangerous attitude of the imposters Musailama and Tulaiha, who were threatening the safety of Islam in the centre of the Peninsula and at the North-east of it respectively.

Summoning therefore the whole available forces, Abubekr divided them into eleven independant columns, with a distinguished leader to command each. The Commanders were instructed to reclaim the provinces alloted to them. On reaching their destinations they were required to summon the apostates and to ask them to repent and to acknowledge their submission to the Caliph. Should they accept these terms they were to be pardoned and received back into Islam. If they refused, they were to be attacked, their fighting men cut to pieces and their women and children taken prisoners. The Azhán or Call to Prayers was to be the test of faith; if that were heard and responded to by the people, they were not to be molested; if not, they were to be treated as apostates and as such to be attacked. Thus instructed, Khálid b. Walid was sent against Tulaiha; Ikrima and Sharahbil were appointed to punish Musailama; Khálid b. Sa'id was named for the Syrian border; Mohájir was deputed to Yemen; Alá to Bahrein; Hozhaifa b. Mohsan and Arfaja to Mahra.

Tulaiha, the Imposter. 11-12. A. H.

Deputed by the Caliph, Khálid advanced against Tulaiha, the Imposter. His column, by far the greatest of the eleven, was composed of a large number of the Prophet's Companions, the flowers of the Mohájirs. Later on, the Bani Tay, persuaded by Adi, also joined Khálid with one thousand horse. Thus strengthened, Khálid marched forward. The armies of the opponents met at Bozákha, where after a hard and long contest Tulaiha took to flight and escaped with his wife to Syria. Khálid stayed for a month at Bozákha, where the Bani Asad, Bani Solaim, Bani Amir and the Bani Hawázin came in, tendered their submission and paid the Tithes.

Having subdued the tribes inhabiting the hills and

Malik b. Nowaira. His cruel fate. 12. A. H.

desert to the North-west of Medina, Khâlid bent his steps Southwards against the Bani Yerbo'. Málik b. Nowaira, their Chief, was a man of noble mien, great valor, an exellent horseman, renowned for his generosity and princely virtues as well as for his poetic talents—all great claims on Arab admiration. To these may be added the enviable fortune, which proved fatal to him, of having for wife the most beautiful woman in all Arabia, famous for her queenly grace, named Omm Tamim or Omm Motamim or Lailá. The men of Medina at first opposed the scheme, as they alleged that Khálid had no authority for attacking the Bani Yerbo'. But for some reason Khálid was bent upon it;so he haughtily replied, "I am the Commander, in the absence of orders it is for me to decide. I will march against Málik b. Nowaira with the men of Mecca and with such others as choose to follow me. I compel no man." And he advanced forward.

† Hearing of the approach of Khálid, at the head of a large force, four thousand five hundered strong, Málik resolved on immediate submission. He knew the ordinance of Abubekr that none, who readily responded to the Call to Prayers or who did not offer resistance, was to be molested. Khálid, however, treated the tract as an enemy's lands, sent forth bands everywhere to slay, plunder, and take captives all those that hesitated in tendering submission. Amongst others, Málik was brought along with his wife as captive. The beauty of the latter dazzled the eyes of the rough soldier and hardened his heart against her husband. "Dost thou refuse to pay the Tithes,?" demanded Khálid harshly of Málik. "Can't I pray without these exactions?" was the response. "Prayer without alms is of no avail," rejoined Khálid. "Is this thy master's bidding?" asked Málik haughtily. "Yes! My master and not thine!" roared Khálid furiously. "By Alláh thou deserveth death." "Is this also the order of thy

†Tabari; Ibn Athir; Abul Fida.

master?" rejoined Málik with a sneer "Again!" cried Khálid scornfully, "Strike off the head of this rebel." His officers interfered. Abu Qatáda and Abdalláh b. Omar stated that Málik had at once responded to the Call to Prayers and that he was a Moslem. Málik's wife threw herself at Khálid's feet, with her face unveiled and her hair dishevelled, imploring mercy for her husband, who noticing the admiring look of Khálid on the charming beauty of his wife cried out, "Alas! Alas! here is the secret of my fate. Her beauty is the cause of my death!" "Nay!" cried Khálid, "it is because of thine apostasy that God killeth thee." "I am not an apostate," answered Málik, "I profess the true faith." But the assumed rage of Khálid was not to be appeased. The signal of death was given. Scarce had the profession of faith passed on the lips of the wretched man when his head fell under the scimitar of Dzarár b. Azwar, a brute after Khálid's own heart.

‡ Khálid, not content with so much brutality, ordered the heads of the slain to be cast into fire under the cooking pots. Málik's head had a mass of hair with flowing locks, so his skull could be burnt with great difficulty. †The same night, while yet the ground was wet with the blood of Málik, his wife was dragged to the lustful embrace of Khálid. She was wedded formally at the same spot a day or two after, in spite of the time-limit fixed by the Prophet for marrying a widow.

Complaint to the Caliph against Khalid.

The men of Medina, who had first opposed Khálid for his advance on the Bani Yerbo', and again remonstrated with him at the murder of Málik, were shocked at his cruel fate and despised Khálid's conduct after the murder. Abu Qatáda swore that he would never serve under his banner. He left the Camp and set out at once for Medina, along with Motammim, Málik's brother, who laid a formal complaint before the Caliph. Omar, hearing all about the affair from Abu Qatáda and others, took up the cause of

‡ Abul Fida.

† Tabari; Tárikh-al Khamis; Sawáeq.

the murdered Chief. ‡ He desired Abubekr to have Khálid stoned to death for adultery or executed for the murder of a Moslem. But Abubekr would not listen to such proposals. Then Omar suggested that the offender should be degraded and put in chains, saying that the sword dipped in violence and outrage must be sheathed. Abubekr, however, observed that Khálid had sinned through error rather than intention. He also remarked that Wahshi, who killed Hamza, the uncle of the Prophet, was pardoned by him. Nevertheless he summoned Khálid to answer for the charge.

Abubekr's Judgment.

¶ Khálid came to Medina and was proceeding to the Caliph in his field costume with his turban wound roughly round his head, with arrows stuck in it as the distinctive ensign of a General, when he met Omar, who chided him calling him a murderer and an adulterer, and seizing the arrows from his turban broke them over his shoulders. Khálid, not knowing whether he would be received by the Caliph in the like manner, kept quiet and proceeded to Abubekr. † He paid two Dinars to the door-keeper and asked him to be presented to the Caliph when alone and in good humour. Being thus presented, he told his story, which was accepted by Abubekr. He was chided only for having wedded his victim's widow on the field and under such circumstances which were so disgusting to the customs and feelings of the Arabs. When he came out, he showed to Omar by his attitude that he had been exonerated. Omar remained silent, but unconvinced of his innocence. He neither forgave nor forgot the atrocity ; and, when he came to power, the deposition from his office was the first order which Omar passed and issued against Khálid.

Fujat Salmi.

Fuját Salmi, a chief of the Bani Solaim (and according to Ariza-i-Kháwar and Tahzib-al-Matin, a Companion of the Prophet who had taken part

‡ Kanzal Ommál.

¶ Tabari ; Abul Fidá; Khamis ; Ibn Wázeh ; Ibn-al-Wardi.

† Tabari Persian Edition ; Rawdzat-al-Safá.

in Bedr), appearing before Abubekr, offered his services to subdue his neighbouring disloyal tribes; and asked to be furnished with the necessary arms and accoutrement for his followers. Being equipped by the Caliph, he is said to have abused the trust, by carrying out marauding expeditions wherever there was a chance of plunder, indiscriminately against loyal and disloyal tribes. The Caliph, receiving the intelligence, deputed Tariqa b. Hájiz to bring him to his senses. Fuját challenged his adversary to a parley and asserted that he himself held a commission similar to his from the Caliph. They, at length, agreed to appear before the Caliph to explain.

Thus Fuját, laying aside his arms, proceeded to Medina along with Tariqa. But no sooner had he appeared before the Caliph than he was ordered to be seized and burnt alive. He was immediately dragged away to Baqi' where a large fire was kindled and the doomed man thrown into the flames†.

Abubekr, who is said to have been a man of tender heart, mild in his judgments, and generous to a fallen foe, was afterwards sorry for this savage act of his. It is one of the three things which haunted him most and of which he used to say in his last days of life "I would I had not done‡."

Rebellion in Hadzramaut under Ash'ath b. Qais. 12. A. H.

Ziyád b. Lobid, the Governor of Hadzramawt, had roused the hatred of the Bani Kinda by his harshness in collecting the tithes. Once he took hold of a camel, belonging to one Yazid b. Mo'áwiyat-al-Qora, and refused to give it back in exchange for a better camel, which was offered by Yazid. He appealed to Hárith b. Soráqa, a powerful Chief of the place, who supported Yazid and asked Ziyád to restore the camel in exchange. Still Ziyád refused to give back the camel. This enraged Hárith, who himself released it from the shed where the camels were herded, and spoke out; "So

†Ibn Athir; Ibn Khaldun.

‡Aqdal Farid; Murawaj-al-Zahb; Kanzal Ommál.

long as the Prophet lived, we obeyed him; he is now dead, we are not bound to obey any one else than his successor from his own family. The son of Abu Qoháfa has no right to govern us. We have no concern with him." He composed a poem in praise of the Prophet's family and in scorn of Abubekr and sent it to Ziyád. Noticing the contemptuous attitude of the people, Ziyád fled for his life and sought shelter with Bani Zobid, a neighbouring tribe. But they received him coldly and expressed themselves in symathy with the views of Hárith. They said that they believed that the Mohájirs and the Ansárs had deprived the rightful heir of his rights through their envy for the superiority of the Háshimites and that it was quite improbable that the Prophet, before his death, should not have nominated his successor from amongst his own family. Finding himself unsafe with such people, Ziyád fled for shelter with other tribes, but everywhere he met a similar treatment. At last he took his way to Medina, where he reported the details to the Caliph, who, alarmed at the intelligence, furnished him with four thousand fighting men to subjugate the revolting tribes.

Ziyád came back to Hadzramawt and tried, for a considerable time, in vain to reclaim the people and the country. Ash'ath b. Qais, Chief of the Bani Kinda, offered strong resistance. Ash'ath had embraced Islam and paid homage to the Prophet in 10 A. H. (see page 231). At the same time he was betrothed to Omm Farwa, sister of Abubekr. Learning the difficulties of Ziyád, Abubekr directed Mohájir b. Abi Omyya and Ikrima b. Abu Jahl to proceed at once from San'á and Aden respectively to reinforce Ziyád.

"Surrounded by the enemy Ziyád despatched an urgent summons to Mohájir to hasten to his deliverance. By this time Mohájir and Ikrima, marching respectively from San'á and Aden, had effected a junction at Marab, and were crossing the sandy desert of Sayhad, which lay between them and Hadzramawt. Learning the critical position of Ziyád, Mohájir set off in haste with a flying squadron, and joining Ziyád, fell upon Ash'ath, and discomfited him with great slaughter. The routed enemy fled for refuge to the stronghold of Nojair which Mohájir immediately invested. Ikrima soon came up with the main body, when there were troops enough both to surround the city and also to ravage all the country round about. Stung by witnessing the ruin of their kindred, and preferring death to dishonour, the garrison sallied forth and fought at every point about the fortress. After a desperate struggle, in which all the approaches were filled with the dead, they were driven back. Meanwhile Abubekr, apprised of the obstinate resistance, sent orders to make an example of the rebels and to give them no quarter. The wretched garrison, with the enemy daily increasing, and no prospect of relief, were now bereft of hope. Seeing the position desperate, the wily Ash'ath made his way to Ikrima and treacherously agreed to deliver up the fortress if nine lives were guaranteed. The moslems entered, slew the fighting men, and took the women captive. The list of the nine to be spared was presented to Mohájir. "Thy name is not here," cried the conqueror exultingly to Ash'ath, for the craven traitor had forgotten, in the excitement of the moment, to enter his own name; "The Lord be praised, who hath condemned thee out of thine own mouth." So, having cast him into chains, he was about to order his execution, when Ikrima interposed and induced him, much against his will, to refer the case to Abubekr. The crowd of captive women, mourning the massacre of their sons and husbands, loaded the recreant, as he passed by, with bitter imprecations. (A thousand women were captured in the fortress. They called after Ash'ath as he passed, "he smelleth of burning," *i.e.* he is a recreant traitor.)

Abubekr's judgment.

"Arrived at Medina, the Caliph abused him as a pusillanimous wretch who had neither the power to lead nor yet the courage to defend his people; and he threatened him with death. But at last, moved by his appeal to the terms agreed upon by Ikrima, and by his protestations that he would thenceforth fight bravely for the Faith, Abubekr not only forgave him, but allowed him to fulfil the marriage with his sister (Omm Farwa). Ash'ath remained for a while in idleness at Medina, and the Caliph was heard to say that one of the three things that he repented having done during his Caliphate was his weakness in sparing the rebel's life." *Muir's Annals, p. 57.*

† Omm Farwa bore Ash'ath one daughter and three sons. The daughter (Jo'da) poisoned Hasan son of Ali which caused his death. Two sons, Mohammad and Isháq figured in the armies of Yazid against Hosain son of Ali at Karbalá. Mohammed, later on, was killed fighting in the army of Mos'ab against Mokhtár, the avenger of Hosain's murder.

Expeditions to foreign countries.

The apostates having thus been subjugated and reclaimed and the revolts being suppressed, conquests in foreign territories were contemplated and expeditions were despatched to Syria and Iráq. The Romans were discomfited in the battle of Yermuk which brought a considerable part of Syria under the sway of Islam in 12–13 A. H. In the same period great progress was made towards the Persian borders.

Appointment of Yazid.

Towards the the close of 12 A. H. (Spring of 634 A. D.) Yazid, son of the famous Omyyad chief Abu Sofyán, was despatched to Syria in command of a battalion with a great levy from Mecca including many Omyyads and famous chiefs of the Qoreish. His brother Mo'áwiya, shortly after, joined him, along with his father Abu Sofyán and his sister Howairiya and other members of the family.

Here it will not be out of place to remark that the ascendency over the Háshimites coveted for generations and already almost gained by the Omyyads after the death of Abd-al-Mottalib (vide p. 12) was finally crushed by the Prophet with his conquest of Mecca. Now Abubekr turned the tables. He offered the Omyyads a chance to regain and improve their position by appointing

† Rawdzat-al-Ahbáb; Ibn Khaldun; A'tham Kufi.

Yazid as a General of a Division of his Forces; thus furnishing them with ample opportunities to re-establish their power, which they were only too glad to seize. Nor were they slack in attaining their object. Very soon Yazid secured for himself the high position as Governor of Damascus (14 A.H. Summer of 634 A.D.) in the time of Caliph Omar. Some four years later (18 A. H. Autumn of 639 A. D.) when both Yazid, the Governor of Damascus and Abu Obeida, the Commander-in-Chief in Syria, had perished in plague, "Omar appointed Mo'áwiya, son of Abu Sofyán and brother of Yazid to the Chief Command in Syria, and thus† laid the foundation of the Omyyad dynesty." Abubekr in his own interests (as observed on page 291) disregarded the consequences detrimental to the Háshimites, the descendants of the Prophet; and Omar promoted the Omyyads' cause, neglecting the old standing rivalry and wilfully ignoring the enmity which the Omyyads bore towards the Háshimites after the battle of Bedr in which Otba, Sheiba and Walid, the forefathers of Yazid and Mo'áwiya and the eminent leaders of the Qoreish, had fallen under the sword of the Háshimites. The result of raising the Omyyads was too obvious, as it was foreseen and spoken out by Hobáb in the Saqifa election—the destruction of those who killed the Qoreish—(vide page 281). Mo'áwiya tactfully established his authority in the long run over all Arabia. After his death, his son Yazid avenged his slain relatives and collected the debts of blood, which remained unsettled for two generations, from the Prophet's family at Karbalá,.

Abubekr's knowledge of the Quran.

Abu Obeida from Ibráhim-at-Tymi relates that Abubekr was asked regarding the saying of the Most High, "Grapes and Clover" (*Sur. LXXX-28* عنبا و تضبا) and he said, "what sky would overshadow me and what earth would sustain me, if I speak regarding the Book of God that which I know not." ***Jarret's Trans. of Suyuti's His.***

"Al Baihaqi and others relate from Abubekr—that he

† Muir's Annals, p. 237,

was asked regarding the meaning of Al-Kalálah (*Sura IV-175*) and he said: "I will presently give an opinion regarding it, and if it be just, it is from God, but if it be faulty, it cometh from me and from the Evil one. I think it to mean lacking parent and off-spring;" and when Omar became Caliph, he said, "Verily, I forbear from setting aside a thing that Abubekr hath spoken." [Al-Kalálah translated by Sale: "a distant relation." Zamakhshari in his great Commentary gives it three meanings, 1. One who has neither son nor father alive; 2. One who has neither father living nor any issue; 3. One who has no living relative in the direct paternal line, nor through his own children]. *Major Jarret's Trans. of Suyuti.*

Al-Lálakai (Abul Qásim Hibatalláh b. Hasan b. Manthur-al-Rádzi) records in his Sunnat on the authority of Ibn Omar, that a man went to Abubekr and said, "Dost thou think that fornication in a man is predestined?" He answered, "Yes." Then, he said, "if God hath predestined it concerning me, will He punish me, for it?" He replied, "Yes, thou son of an uncircumcised woman, and by Alláh, were a man by me, I would command him to bring thee to reason." *Ibid.*

Málik and Dár Qutni from Al-Qásim b. Mohammed relate that two grand-mothers went to Abubekr demanding their inheritance, the mother of a mother, and the mother of a father, and he accorded the inheritance to the mother of the mother. Thereupon Abd-al-Rahmán b. Sahel, the Auxiliary who had fought at Bedr and was an associate of the Banu Hárith said to him, "O Vicegerent of the Apostle of God! Dost thou bestow it upon her, who, if she died, would not be inherited of?" (According to the Mohammedan Law a grand-son does not inherit from his maternal grand-mother). So he divided it between the two. *Ibid.*

Some traditions concerning Abubekr.

Al-Bazzár, (As Sirár) relates the tradition: when there was revealed, "Lift not up your voices above the voice of the Prophet" *Sur. XLIX-2*) Abubekr said, "O Apostle of God, I will not address thee save in the voice of one who is decrepit." *Major Jarret's Trans. of Suyuti.*

(This verse is said to have been occasioned by Abubekr and Omar having raised so high their voices in addressing the Prophet concerning the appointment of a governor of a certain place that it was necessary to forbid it for the future—*Sale.*)

Al Dár Qutni relates the tradition that Abubekr kissed the Black Stone and said, "Were it not that I have seen the Apostle of God kiss thee, I would not have kissed thee." *Ibid.*

Ahmad in the Zohd relates the tradition from Abu Imrán-al-Juni, that Abubekr as-Siddiq said, "I would I were a hair in the side of a servant, a true believer." *Ibid.*

† The Prophet said to Abubebr: "*Scepticism* (Shirk) moves more stealthily among you than the creeping of an ant."

Abubekr narrated 142 traditions from the Apostle of God. Some of them are as follows:—

Some traditions on Abubekr's authority.

"Infidelity (Shirk) moves more stealthily among my people than the creeping of an ant." *Major Jarret's trans. of Suyuti.*

"We (the Prophets) are not inherited of; that which we leave is the portion of the poor." *Ibid.*

Abubekr's illness. Nomination of successor.

In the month of Jamádi II, 13 A. H. (Aug. 634 A. D.) Abubekr, having bathed incautiously on a cold day, was seized with fever. After a fortnight's illness, when he felt himself too weak and exhausted, he became hopeless of his recovery, and desired to put Omar in authority by nominating him as his successor, thus to avoid the risk in his election. To break the resolve to the people, he first made its disclosure in a sort of consultation with Abd-al Rahmán, who on receiving the intelligence praised Omar but added that he was too harsh. Next he consulted Othmán, who said, "Omar with his inward heart is better than what he is with his outward appearance." Upon this

† Izálat-al-Khifá Urdu Vol. II p. 214.

Abubekr said, "The Lord bless thee Othmán! If I had not chosen Omar, I would have not passed thee over." Knowing this resolve, (according to Tárikh-al-Khamis and Rowdzat al Safá) Talha and several other Companions of the Prophet approached Abubekr and protested against the nomination. Talha expostulated thus: "How would thou answer to thy Lord to have left his people to the care of so hard a master as Omar." Hearing this, Abubekr seemed much excited and he cried, "Set me up," and, calling Othmán, he at once dictated an ordinance as follows: "I, Abubekr son of Abu Qoháfa, at the eve of my approaching end, do make this declaration of my will to the Moslems. I nominate as my successor—." At this point Abubekr fainted and could not speak. Othmán, who knew whose name Abubekr would dictate, added 'Omar b. Al-Khattáb.' When Abubekr became again conscious, he asked Othmán to read what he had written. When Othmán read the name of the successor as written by him on the ordinance, Abubekr said, "Alláh-o-Akbar! God bless thee for thy foresight. If in the swoon I had passed away the people would have been left in the dark without the addition thou hast made." Then he continued the dictation: "Listen to him and obey him: for he will rule with justice, if not, God, who knows all secrets, will treat him likewise. I mean all for the best, but I do not know the hidden hearts. Fare ye well." The ordinance having been sealed with his seal, the Caliph desired that it should be read over to the people in the Mosque. Omar himself was present and he hushed the noise and made the people keep quiet that they might hear.

†Ibn Qoteiba in his book 'Imámat' writes: "when the ordinance was being taken by Sháhid a slave of Abubekr, for being read over to the people, somebody asked Omar, who accompained the bearer, "what is it about?" Omar replied that he knew nothing but that he was concerned with it more than any other. The man then said, "if thou knowest not, I do know that last time thou made

†Zakir Hosain's History of Islam vol. iii p. 54.

Abubekr Caliph, now in his turn he hast made thee Caliph in his place."

"It was said to Abubekr in his illness, "what wilt thou say to thy God, now that thou hast appointed Omar to rule?" He replied, "I will say to Him, I have appointed over them the best of them." (Ibn Sa'd). *Jarret's trans. of Suyuti's Tarikh-al-Kholafa, p. 122.*

Abubekr As-Siddiq said, "there is not upon the face of the earth a man dearer to me than Omar." (Ibn Asákir). *Ibid.*

Abubekr's death bed.

‡During his illness, Abubekr lamented three of his acts, which he said: "I would I had not done." (1) The raiding of Fátema's house, notwithstanding the conspiracies which, he said, were held there against him. (2) The burning alive of Fuját Salmi. He said the man should have been released or put to sword but not burnt. (3) To have spared the rebel Ash'ath to whom Abubekr subsequently gave his sister Omm Farwa in marriage. The man, he said, was always forward in wickedness.

"An-Nasái records from Aslam, that Omar beheld Abubekr, who seized hold of his own tongue and said, 'this it is that hath brought me to that to which I have come'. *Jarret's trans. of Suyuti's Tarikh-al-Kholafa, p. 104."*

Some time before his death Abubekr asked, 'on what day did the Apostle of God die', and he was answered that he died on a Monday.

Abubekr's death.

¶Abubekr died, at the age of 63 years, on Tuesday the 22nd of Jamádi II, 13 A. H. or 22nd of August 634 A. D. having reigned two years three months and ten days. His wife Asmá bint Omais, helped by his son Abd-al-Rahmán, gave him his last wash. Omar read the prayers reciting the Takbir four times. Grave was dug for him by the side of the grave of the Prophet, and the niche of his grave touched the grave of the Apostle of God. He was buried with his head in a

‡Tabari; Aqd-al-Farid; Kanz-al-Ommál etc.

¶Jarret's trans. of Suyuti, p. 86.

level with the Prophet's shoulder.

Abubekr and his family's concerns with the Prophet's family.

Abubekr had four wives, one of whom died in his life-time. His surviving issues from each wife are named in the Table given below:—

Wedded before Abubekr's conversion to Islam.

1. Qatila, daughter of Abd-al-Uzza.
   - Asmá, d. 76 A. H. wife of Zobeir b. Al-Awám d. 36 A. H.
     - Abdalláh d. 64 A. H.

2. Omm Román, daughter of Hárith, d. 7 A. H.
   - Abd-al-Rahmán d. 53 A.H. His original name was Abd-al-Uzza. Embraced Islam after the Hodaibiya Treaty.
   - Ayesha d. 58 A.H.

Wedded after Abubekr's conversion to Islam.

3. Habiba, daughter of Khárja Ansár
   - Omm Kulthum, wife of Talha d. 36 A.H. (a cousin of Abubekr, and son of Obeidalláh.)
     - Mohammed d. 36 A.H.

4. Asmá, daughter of Omais.
   - Mohammed b. 10 A.H. d. 38 A. H. After Abubekr's death Ali married Asmá, thus Mohammed was brought up by Ali.

History shows that Abubekr himself and his whole family (excepting Asmá and her son Mohammed) were hostile to the Prophet's family, in utter disregard of what the Qurán ordained (see page 242) or what the Prophet said (see page 239) relating to the respect and love for his family. The following is the list of those whose hostility was distinctively marked:—

1. Abubekr, on his accession to the Caliphate, sent Omar to Fátema's house to compel Ali by force to come

in and do fealty to him. Omar threatened to burn the house down upon Fátema, and brought Ali under escort to Abubekr where he was so humiliated and insulted that he cried bitterly at the tomb of the Prophet complaining against the treatment he had received. Subsequently Fátema was so much grieved by Abubekr that, so long as she survived her father, she never spoke a word to Abubekr, and on her death-bed she forbade his joining her funeral. (*See page 290.*)

2. Abubekr's daughter Ayesha revolted against Ali the Caliph, and at the head of 30,000 soldiers she fought the battles of Jamal. But she was discomfited with heavy loss.

3. Abubekr's son Abd-al-Rahmán was also fighting for her sister's cause in the same battles.

4. Abubekr's son-in-law Zobeir b. Al-Awám, the husband of Asmá the eldest daughter of Abubekr, was the Commander of Ayesha's armies. During the heat of the battle he withdrew and took the road towards Mecca, but was slain only at a short distance from the field of battle.

5. Abubekr's grand-son Abdalláh the son of Zobeir by Asmá, was the Commander of Ayesha's infantry. He was the adopted son of Ayesha. After the battle he was traced out from under a heap of the slain lying in the battle-field.

6. Abubekr's cousin, Talha, as also the husband of Abubekr's daughter Omm Kulthum, was a Commander of Ayesha's Troops. In the heat of the battle, Marwán (the Secretary and the evil genius of Caliph Othmán), an officer in the same forces, seeing Talha busily engaged, said to his slave: "It was but the other day that Talha was busily instigating the murderers of Othmán and now he is so busily seeking to revenge his blood. What a hypocrisy to gain worldly grandeur!" So saying he shot an arrow, which pierced through Talha's leg and struck his horse, which flew wildly off the ranks and Talha fell to the ground. He was instantly taken to Bussorah where he died after a while.

7. Abubekr's cousin Abd-al-Rahmán, a brother of Talha, also fell fighting in the same battle.

8. Mohammed, the son of Talha, also fell in the same battle.

9. Abubekr's sister Omm Farwa's daughter, Jo'da bint Ash'ath poisoned Al-Hasan, the son of Ali, to death. She was suborned, to commit the wickedness, by Yazid the son of Mo'áwiya or by himself.

10. Abubekr's sister Omm Farwa's son Mohammed.

11. Abubekr's sister Omm Farwa's son Isháq, both brothers, the sons of Ash'ath, appeared among the armies of Yazid, fighting against Hosain, the son of Ali, at the Karbalá tragedy. Later on, the former was killed fighting against Mokhtár, who was avenging the murder of Hosain; while the latter, who had taken off the dead body of Hosain some of his clothes, was torn to death by dogs.

12. Mos'ab, a son of Zobeir the son-in-law of Abubekr, fought against Mokhtár, who was killed avenging the murder of Hosain.

CHAPTER—XIX.

Omar, the second Caliph.

Omar's succession to the Caliphate.

Omar assumed the Caliphate, according to the bequest of Abubekr, on Tuesday the 22nd of Jamadi II, 13 A. H. or 634 A. H. The morning following the death of Abubekr, Omar ascended the pulpit to address the people. The first sentence which he uttered on the pulpit was, 'O God! verily I am rough in temper, therefore soften me; and verily I am weak, therefore strengthen me; and verily I am avaricious, therefore make me generous. *Jarret's Trans. of Suyuti's Tarikh-al- Kholafa, p. 144.*

The first act of the new Caliph was to issue a dispatch deposing Khálid from his chief Command in Syria, allowing him, however, to continue his services in subordination of Abu Obeida. The second act was in fufilment of Abubekr's dying behest to raise a fresh levy for Mothanna, for the reinforcement of the Iráq campaign. A new standard was planted in the court of the Great Mosque and urgent proclamation was made that soldiers were to rally round it. Then followed the oath of fealty, which occupied more than three days to accomplish.

Omar's ancestry and Antecedents.

Omar was a Qoreish, remote from the ancestry of the great Prophet by eight generations. He was eighth in descent from Adi, the son of Ka'b the eighth forefather of the Prophet (vide the Genealogical Table). The clan to which Omar belonged was denominated after the name of Adi. The Bani Adi originally lived at Safá in the suburbs of Mecca, but, on account of the hostile attitude of certain Qoreish clans, they shifted to the Dzajnán valley about 25 miles North-west of Mecca under the protection of Bani Sahm. Omar's father was Al-Khattáb, whose original occupation was fuel wood selling.† His mother Hantama was a daughter of Hishám and sister of Abu Jahl. Khattáb

† Aqd-al-Farid; Izálat-al-Khifa.

and Amr were the sons of Nofail, whose widow Jáida, the mother of Khattáb, was taken by Amr to wife and bore to him Zaid, who thus stood, at the same time, the cousin and uncle of Omar. During the period of his Caliphate, when Omar happened to pass through the valley of Dzajnán, he remembered with wonderment the vast difference between his present position and the circumstances of his boy-hood when, with a shirt of coarse wool upon his body, he said, he used to tend the sheep of his father there in that valley and collected the dry leaves and fuel wood, which he carried upon his head in the evening to his father, on pain of being beaten or rebuked for negligence. But now, he said, there was none to mediate between himself and God.‡

AN-Nawáwi says that Omar was born thirteen years after the year of the Elephant. He embraced Islam at the age of 33 years, and assumed the Caliphate at the age of 52. Before his conversion to Islam, he was as deadly hostile to the Prophet as his maternal uncle Abu Jahl—the Pharaoh of the Qoreish—who fell slain in the battle of Bedr.

Mohammad b. Sa'd, the Secretary of Wackidi, on the authority of Zohri states that the Epithet Al-Fáruq, an addendum to the name of Omar was introduced by Ahl-i-kitáb (*i.e.* the Jews or Christians) and afterwards adopted by the Mussalmans, who have received nothing on this account from the Prophet.†

Omar was the first Caliph who assumed the title of Amir-al-Mominin, *i. e.* the Commander of the Faithful. Abubekr used to write, "From the Caliph of the Apostle of God." Omar, on his accession to the office, used to write, "From the Caliph of the Caliph of the Apostle of God." Subsequently the title Amir-al-Mominin was adopted in place of the too long and cumbersome phrase hitherto used. This title was ever afterwards used by all the succeeding Caliphs. *Jarret's Trans. of Suyuti's His p. 143.*

‡ Ibn Athir ; Izálat-al-Khifa.

† Tabari; Ibn Athir; Rawdzat-al-Ahbáb.

Omar was preaching from the pulpit one day, when Al-Hosain, the son of Ali stood up against him and said: "Come down from the pulpit of my father." Omar replied: "It is the pulpit of thy father, not the pulpit of my father; who hath counselled thee to this?" Then Ali rose and said: "By Allah! no one counselled him to this." *Ibid p. 148.*

Remonstration of al-Hosain.

In the year 14 A. H. Omar introduced the Special Service of reciting the Qurán in the month of Ramadzán, and, for the first time, he assembled the people for the prayers which he named At-Taráwih." *Ibid p. 135.*

Introduction of Tarawih.

Numerous conquests of foreign lands and victories are the especial feature of Omar's reign.

In the year 14 A. H. Damascus was taken, partly by force of arms and partly by Convention; and Yazid, the son of the Omyyad chief Abu Sofyán, was made Governor of Damascus. Yazid subsequently extended his authority from Damascus towards the desert as far as Tadmor; and he deputed his brother Mo'áwiya westward, who, meeting little opposition, reduced Sidon and Beyrout and pushed his conquests as far north as Arqa.

Some accounts of Omar's Caliphate.

In the year 15 A. H. the whole of the country of Jordon was conquered.

In the year 16 A. H. Omar went to Jerusalem and concluded a Treaty. Takrit was captured. Khálid defeated the Romans near Kinnisrin or Chalcia. He was consequently received back into the Caliph's favour and made governor of Kinnisrin. Next fell Aleppo, then Antioch—the third metropolis of the world. Syria, from the farthest north to the borders of Egypt, was brought entirely under the sway of Islam, and the Roman Emperor Heraclius gave up Syria as lost. Only Cæsaria remained with the Romans. Al Ahwáz and Madáen were taken the same year. In the battle of Jalolá, the Persian Emperor Yazdjird, being defeated, fled to Rai, the northern capital of Persia in the direction of the Caspian sea. The ruins of Rai are still to be found 5 or 6 miles south-east of Tehran, of considerable extent. The Royal city was captured and demolished by No'aim, who laid the foundation of a new city in 22 A. H.

Ziyad.

Among the captives taken at Jalolá was a youth named Ziyád, who was distinguished for his singular readiness and address. He was sent to Medina along with the fifth of the spoils to the Caliph. His parentage was doubtful. His reputed father was the Omyyad Abu Sofyán, who in a state of intoxication is said to have enjoyed the society of his mother, who was a slave kept by another person at Táef—Ziyád was a fruit of this love-affair. Subsequently he foreshadowed the greatness of his administrative talents. Abu Musa Ash'ari, Omar's governor of Bussorah, had made over the seals of his office to the youth. He was eventually acknowledged by Mo'áwiya (son of Abu Sofyán) as his brother, much to the scandal of the public. He was destined to play a prominent part in the history of Islam.

Mohammedan Era.

In the month of Rabi I of the same year, the Era of Hegira commencing with Moharram as the first month was adopted by the advice of Ali b. Abi Tálib.†

Khalid's deposition.

In the year 17 A.H. Bussorah and Kufa were founded. Khálid again incurred the displeasure of Omar. He was greatly enriched with the spoils of the wars in the Archipelago. Most of his old friends from Iráq flocked to him in expectation of his bounty. He gave 1000 pieces of gold to Ash'ath, chief of the Bani Kinda; and friendly largesses to many others. This extravagance of Khálid invoked the anger of Omar more than his indulgence in wine, though Omar was much displeased to learn that Khálid had bathed himself in wine at Amida, so that the odour thereof clung strongly about him when he came forth. ‡ Khálid was arraigned by the Caliph on both these charges, but when he appeared at Medina to answer for the charges he was required to account for only his

† Suyuti.

‡ Muir's Annals, p. 219.

extravagance. In reply, he said that his whole fortune amounted to not more than 60,000 pieces which, he said, he had gained from war spoils mostly in the days of Abubekr; and he offered that any thing found in excess of the sum named, might be confiscated to the State. So his affects were valued, and the estimate reaching 80,000, Omar confiscated the difference and deposed Khálid, who retired to Hims, where he died in the eighth year of Omar's Caliphate. The man to whom Abubekr owed all his success in his Caliphate and who, with his victories and conquests, had raised Omar aloft to the position of an emperor, ended his days in penury and neglect.

Famine.

In the year 17-18 A.H. famine broke out in Hejáz. It was named the Year of Ashes, because of the land being so charged with the parched and sandy soil as to obscure the light by a thick and sultry haze. The air was dry and dusty and there was nothing green on earth.

Plague.

In the year 18 A. H. plague ravaged in Syria, made a great havoc at the head quarters of Arabs at Hims and Damascus; 25,000 perished of the pestilence. Abu Obeida, who held the chief command in Syria, together with his son, fell a victim to the pestilence. Yazid the governor of Damascus also fell a prey to the virulence of plague. It spread to Iráq as far as Busscrah.

Mo'awiya's appointment as governor of Syria.

Both Abu Obeida and Yazid being dead, Omar appointed Mo'áwiya b. Abu Sofyán governor of Syria to hold the chief Civil and Military control over the province, and laid the foundation of the Omyyad dynasty.†

Mo'áwiya was a man of unbounded ambition, and he turned to good account his new position. He busily consolidated the administration of Syria, and with a clever foresight strengthened his hold upon the province against the contingencies of the future. His factious spirit, inherited by him from his parents (his father Abu Sofyán,

†Muir's Annals, p. 237.

the bitter opponent of the Háshimites like his father Harb and grand-father Omyya; his mother Hinda, who, tearing open the dead body of the Prophet's uncle Hamza, had chewed the liver and sucked the blood from it), was, though yet in embryo, spurning the divine claims of Ali, the proclaimed vicegerent and cousin of the Prophet and the husband of his favourite daughter Fátema, and the father of the Prophet's holy progeny. Ali was neither ambitious nor an envious man. He had only the interest of Islam at his heart. He readily counselled the Caliph with his sagacious advice in solving difficult problems for which he was often praised by the Caliph with such phrases:† "If there were no Ali, Omar were dead"; "May God lengthen thy life"; "May God strengthen thee"; "May God preserve him (Omar) from a perplexing case which the father of Al-Hasan was not present to decide." Though honoured to all outward appearances and eulogized for his wit and judgment yet Ali was never given a chance to rise to power. The contrast is concievable. Mo'áwiya attained at length the aims of his foresighted policy, as will be seen from the history that follows.

In the year 19 A. H. Cæsaria was over-powered and captured, bringing the Syrian territory completely under the sway of Islam.

The year was also distinguished by the bursting forth of volcanic fires from a hill called Leilá in the neighbourhood of Medina. A naval expedition sent to Abyssinia met a disaster, all the vessels being wrecked.

In the year 20 A. H. Tustar was taken possession of. The Roman Emperor Heraclius died in the same year.

In the year 21 A. H. the battle of Naháwand took place, after which the Persians were unable to hold out any longer.

In the year 22 A.H. Azharbaiján and Rai were carried by force. Also Hamdán.

In the year 23 A. H. took place the conquest of Kirmán, Sujestán, Mekrán and Ispehán. Towards the

†Jarret's trans. of Suyuti's Tárikh-al-Kholafa, p. 142 and p. 175.

close of this year, Omar was stabbed, receiving mortal wounds.

Omar's knowledge of the Quran.

While at Jerusalem in the year 16 A. H., Omar delivered a Sermon. In the course of his address he quoted from the Qurán the passage: "whom God guides, he is guided indeed, and whom He misleadeth thou shalt not find for him a patron to guide," *Sur. XVIII-16*; as also in *Sur. IV-90, 142*; and *Sur. XVII-99*). A Christian priest who sat before him stood up and cried; "Nay! God misleadeth no one" and he repeated it. Omar, instead of explaining to the priest the correct version of the text, bid those who stood by him to strike off his head if he interrupted any more. The man understood what was ordered and held his peace.†

Al Baihaqi and others report from Abubekr, that he was asked regarding the meaning of Al-kalálah' (*Sur. IV-*15, 175) and he answered: "I will presently give an opinion regarding it, and if it be just, it is from God, but if it be faulty, it cometh from me and from the Evil one. I think it to mean lacking parent and offspring"; and when Omar became Caliph, he said, "Verily I forbear from setting aside a thing that Abubekr hath spoken."‡

Whip in hand Omar used to perambulate the streets and markets of Medina, and often in the nights he went on rounds through the city. One night while going on his usual round in the town, Omar passed by a house wherein some-body was singing. The door being bolted, he jumped over the back wall, and found there a man and a woman having a good time with a bottle of wine. Omar, addressing the man in an angry tone exclaimed; "O enemy of God! didst thou think that thy sin shalt pass unnoticed?" The man, recognizing in the intruder the Caliph, cried: "O prince of the Faithful! Give me a patient hearing. If I am guilty of one sin, thou art guilty

---

† Fatuh-al-Shám; Wáckidi; Muir's Annal's, p. 211.

‡ Jarret's trans. of Suyuti's Tarikh-al-Kholafa p. 97.

of three with thine acts contrary to the dictates of the Holy Book, which (a) enjoins thee not to be inquisitive. *Sur. XLIX-12.* (b) requires thee not to enter a house but from its doorway, especially prohibiting entry from behind the house as thou hast done. *Sur. II-185*, (c) ordains thee not to enter a house without leave of its occupants, and when so entered requires thee to salute them. *Sur. XXIV-27.*" Omar feeling ashamed of his ignorance of the Qurán, asked forgiveness of them for his intrusion in return for a forgiveness which, he said, he would accord to them for their sin. The man with repentance, promised never again to do it, and the Caliph, obtaining their forgiveness, departed.†

One day while walking through the city, Omar happened to see a robust good looking youth of the Ansárs. Wishing to be in touch with the youth he asked of him some water to drink. He presented a cup-ful of syrup prepared from honey. Omar professed his indignation at indulging in such a luxury and mooted out the verse, "Ye have already enjoyed good things in your life of this world." The youth at once rejoined, "And (on) the Day when they shall be set at the Fire—(they will be told) ye have already enjoyed good things in your life of this world." *Sur. XLVI-19.* Thus adding the first half of the verse recited by the Caliph, he said that the verse related to the Infidels, not to the Believers. Omar, there-upon, drinking the beverage exclaimed: "The people are better acquainted with the Ordinances of the Qurán than myself."‡

One day from the pulpit, Omar ordained that the people must not raise the wife's dowry beyond four hundred Dirhams, on penalty of forfeiture to the State of the amount in excess. A woman got up at once and protested against the ordinance, saying; "O son of Khattáb! Is the word of the Lord to be followed or thy word?" Omar replied, "Nay, not my word, but God's". Whereupon she recited: "And if ye desire to change a wife in place of

† Izálat-al-Khifá from Ahyá-al-ulum.
‡ Ibn Abi-l-Hadid.

another, and have given the one of them a cow's skinful of riches, take not back from her any thing of it." *Sur. IV-24.* Thereupon, Omar, acknowledging that not only the men but even women had better knowledge of the ordinances of the Qurán than himself, withdrew his order.†

Omar's wit of Judgment.

Abdal Razzáq records that a woman went to Omar and said: "My husband rises in the night to pray and fasts all day," and Omar said, "Verily thou hast praised thy husband highly," whereon Ka'b b. Siwar exclaimed, "But she complains of him!" And Omar said, "how?" He replied, "she means that she has not her share of her husband's society." He answered," "then if thou thinkest that, judge between them." He said, "O prince of the Faithful ! the Lord hath permitted to him four wives, and to her of every four days, one day, and of every four nights, one night. *Jarret's Trans. of Suyuti's His. p. 147.*

Jábir b. Abdalláh went to Omar and complained to him of the treatment he had met with from his women, and Omar said: "verily, I find the same, so much so that when I ask for anything I want, my wife says to me, "thou goest only after the girls of a certain tribe, watching for them. *Ibid.*

Omar's miscarriage of Justice.

"On the death of Otba, the Governor of Bussorah, Omar appointed Moghira b. Sho'ba (one of those who were of great assistance to Omar and Abubekr at the Saqifa election) in place of the deceased in 15 A.H. He was a man of repulsive aspect, one-eyed, red-haired and rude in manners. In his youth he had committed a murder at Táef. His harem consisted of no less than eighty women, still his vagrant passion was not satisfied. One Omm Jamil, wife of Hajáj b. Atik and a daughter of Afqam of the Bani Amir used to visit Moghira in private. She was a woman of loose character and was known to have illegal intercourse with some other chief men of Bussorah. As Moghira was not liked by the people on account of his bad morals and vicious habits,

†Ibn Abi-l-Hadid; Kanzal Ommál.

he was scorned and hated by the gentry, who watched his conduct. Abu Bekra, a leading chief of Bussorah, who lived opposite the house of Moghira, was one day sitting with his friends when the wind blew open the window, which he rose to shut; but all of a sudden he caught sight of the revolting scene which was being enacted in the opposite room by Moghira with Omm Jamil.

He called his friends Náfe', Ziyád and Shibl, who also witnessed the adultery and identified Omm Jamil when she got up. Soon after, Moghira issued forth to lead the public prayer, as usual. They shouted him off as an adulterer and immediately sent the information to Omar, the Caliph at Medina, who summoned Moghira to his presence to answer the charge. Before the Caliph, Moghira denied the accusation and said that it was his wife whom the accusers mistook for Omm Jamil. The witnesses, AbuBakra, Náfe', and Shibl deposed so that by any reasonable law of evidence the crime had been established, but there remained still one witness to give evidence.

It was Ziyád, who (according to Ibn Khallakán) when made his appearance, the Caliph said, "here is the man who can save a Mohájir." So it happened that there was a flaw in the deposition of Ziyád the fourth witness.†" And the Caliph, with an ill-concealed groan at the miscarriage of Justice, ordered the witnesses, who had brought the charge, to be scourged according to the law and the accused released. "Strike hard," cried the bare-faced culprit, addressing the unwilling minister of the law, "strike hard, and comfort my heart thereby." "Hold thy peace," said Omar, "it wanted little to convict thee; and then thou shouldst have been stoned to the death as an adulterer." "The guilty chief was silenced but not abashed." *Muir's Annals, p. 265.*

In afterdays Omar said to Moghira, "whenever I happen to see thee, I fear lest some stone may fall upon me from the sky. ‡ In 21 A. H. (642 A. D.) Moghira was

† Ibn Athir,
‡ Ibid.

again appointed by Omar as Governor of Kufa.

Omar's watch over the citizens.

One night when Omar went forth on his usual round in the city; he heard an Arab woman singing:

This night when stars wander in their mighty journey, is wearisome.
And keeps me sleepless, for I have none with whom I may be merry;
And, by Alláh, were there no God whose issues were to be feared!
But I fear a Watcher, who keepeth ward
Over our souls, and whose recorder never is negligent.
The fear of the Lord and shame hindereth me.
And my husband, too worthy of honour that his place should be taken.

Omar kept hearing. At last he exclaimed, " what is the matter with thee?" She replied: "Thou hast sent my husband on service for some months and I pine for him." He said: "Dost thou desire to do evil?" She replied: "God forbid." Then he said, "restrain thyself, for verily a messenger shall go to him." When Omar came back to his house, he enquired of his daughter Hafsa, after how long a woman begins to pine for the society of a man? She hinted at four months. So the Caliph issued orders that the troops should not be kept on service for more than four months.‡

Omar's Innovations.

Omar was the First who adopted the use of the Scourge. *Jarret's Trans. of Suyuti's His.*

Omar was the first who assembled the people to prayers over the dead with only four Takbirs. *Ibid.*

Omar was the first who prohibited (Mutá') marriage limited to a term. *Ibid.*

Omar was the first who instituted Al-Taráwih of the month of Ramadzán. *Ibid.*

Omar was the first who adopted the title "Commander of the Faithful." *Ibid.*

‡ Suyuti.

Omar's death account.

"† Al-Zohri states that Omar used not to suffer a captive, who had reached the age of puberty, to enter Medina, but al-Moghira b. Sho'ba, the governor of Kufa, wrote to him and mentioned to him that he had with him a youth, a cunning workman, and asked his permission that he might enter Medina; and added that he was a master of several arts profitable to the people, for he was a blacksmith, an engraver and a carpenter. Omar therefore gave him permission to send him to Medina; and al-Moghira put a tax upon him of one hundred dirhams a month. He, however, went to Omar and complained of the severity of the tax, but Omar replied that the tax was not excessive. He therefore departed indignantly murmuring. Omar waited some days and then sent for him and said, "Was not I informed that thou sayest that if thou wouldst thou art able to make a mill that will grind by means of the wind"? He looked upon Omar sullenly and said, "Verily I will make a mill for thee that men shall talk about." When he retired, Omar said to those that were about him, "the slave but now threatened me." After a little, Abu Lulu took a double bladed dagger, having its haft in the middle, and hid in a corner of one of the recesses of the Mosque before day-break and remained there until Omar came forth, rousing the people for prayers, and when he drew near him, he stabbed him with three blows (Ibn Sa'd)." Of the wounds he received, the gash at the centre of Omar's abdomen below the navel was fatal.

"The wounded Caliph was carried to his family, and the sun being about to rise, Abd-al-Rahmán b. Awf read prayers before the people with the two shortest Suras. They brought Omar date-wine, and he drank of it and it came out of his wound, but it could not be distinguished from the blood; they therefore gave him milk, and it came out of his wound, and they said: "there is no harm to thee," and he answered, "if there be harm in being slain,

† Major Jarret's trans. of Suyuti p. 138.

why then I am slain." *Jarret's trans. of Suyuti's Tarikh-al-Kholafa, p. 138.*

Omar summoned Abd-al-Rahmán, who stanched the wounds. Then he summoned Ali, Othmán, Zobeir and Sa'd b. Abi Waqqás and told them that he chose six of the Companions of the Prophet to be the electors of his successor from amongst themselves. He ‖ named Abd-al-Rahmán b. Awf, Othmán b. Affán, Ali b. Abi Tálib, Sa'd b. Abi Waqqás, Zobeir b. Al-Awám, and Talha b. Obeidalláh. The last named being out of Medina at the time, he asked the others to wait three days for him or if he did not come within three days, the electors were enjoined to decide the matter without him † Meanwhile, he said, ‡ Sohaib shall lead the public prayers. When they had departed, he called ¶ Miqbád b. Aswad Kindi, a veteran Companion of the Prophet, and desired him to assemble the electors after his death in one place, at the same time directing Abu Talha Ansár, a warrior of some note, to take his stand at the door with a guard of fifty men and to allow no one beside the electors, excepting his son Abdalláh, and ordered that the selection should not be prolonged beyond three days. Then addressing his son, the Caliph said, "And list thee, Abdalláh, thou shouldst have a voice in the election. In case they disagree, then be thou with the majority, or if the votes be equal, then choose thou that side on which is Abd-al-Rahmán; and if the minority then resisted, they should be beheaded on the spot." ††

Nomination of electors and the mode of election of the successor.

[Note. A wonderful plan of the dying Caliph Omar to dispose of Ali! Sa'd and Abd-al-Rahmán were cousins, and the last named, having married a sister of Othmán, was in close touch with him. These three were sure to support each other. Abdalláh b. Omar, siding Abd-al-

‖ Sharh Fiqah Akbar by Mulla Ali Qári.
† Muir's Annals. p. 280. ‡ Kámil Ibn Athir.
¶ Tabari; Ibn Athir.
†† Tabari vol V p. 34 & 35; Kámil Ibn Athir.

Rahmán, was to form the majority. Of the minority, Ali, being the only discomfited claimant, was expected naturally to resist and therefore to be beheaded on the spot].

¶ Ali complained to Abbás, his uncle, that he was sure to be outvoted in the conclave. Abbás advised him not to join the bogus election, but Ali would not listen to him, thinking thus to avoid being blamed of absence and neglect in putting forward his claim at the right moment.

Crowds had assembled at the doors and now they were permitted to come in and see the wounded Caliph. There is the tradition that Ibn Abbás had a long conversation with Omar, pressing forward the rights of the Prophet's family to the Caliphate, but Omar answered attributing the claim to envy ‡. This shows that the inclusion of Ali's name in the conclave was not genial but with the policy of creating a chance to do away with him for good.

Omar was noted as a stern advocate of vengeance, and of a fiery and impatient temper. He was ever ready to unsheathe his sword to put a prisioner to death. ††

The people began to praise the wounded Caliph, saying "thou wert such and such," but he said, "yet by Alláh, I would that I might escape from Judgment with these as a sufficiency, nothing due by me nor to me, and that the companionship of the Apostle of God were a security unto me." Then Ibn Abbás praised him, but he said—"if the fulness of the earth in gold were mine, assuredly I would ransom myself therewith from the terror of the Day of Resurrection.." ***Jarret's Trans. of Suyuti's His. p. 139.***

At times he would exclaim, "O that my mother had not borne me"; "would that I had been a stalk of grass instead ||,"

¶ Abul Fida; Tabari; Ibn Athir.

‡ Muir's Annals p. 282.

†† Ibid p. 284.

|| Ibn Athir.

Omar was stabbed on Wednesday the 26th of Zhul Hajja, 23 A. H. and was buried on Sunday the 1st of Moharram, 24 A. H. He was about 63 years of age at the time of his death. Sohaib prayed over the bier with four Takbirs. He was buried by the side of his friend Abubekr near the Prophet's tomb. He reigned ten years six months and four or eight days. He reported 539 traditions from the Apostle of God.

Omar's appearance after death in dreams.

Ibn Sa'd records on the authority of Sálim bin Abdalláh b. Omar, that he said, I heard a man of the Auxiliaries say, I prayed to God that he would show me Omar in sleep, and I saw him after ten years and he was wiping the sweat from his forehead, and I said, O prince of the Faithful! What hast thou been doing? He replied, I have but now been freed from judgment, and had it not been for the mercy of my God, I had perished." *Jarret's Trans. of Suyuti's His. p. 152.*

And from Zaid b. Aslam that Abdalláh b. Amr b. As saw Omar in sleep and he said: "How hast thou fared?" He replied, "How long is it that I left you?" He answered, "Twelve years." He said, "Verily, it is even now that I am free from Judgment†." *Jarret's Trans. of Suyuti's His. p. 162.*

CHAPTER XX.

Othman, the third Caliph.

The Conclave 24. A. H.

In the death account of Caliph Omar, it has been already narrated how, on his death-bed, he nominated six electors, the Companions of the Prophet, to choose from amongst themselves his successor; with injunctions to assemble after his death for the purpose, and not to delay the choice, beyond the third day of their deliberations. After Omar's death, when his burial was over, Miqdád assembled the electors *viz.* Abd-al-Rahmán, Othmán, Sa'd, Zobeir, and Ali according to the dictates of Omar. Talha was not yet come. The conclave was held in the house of Miswar, a nephew of Abd-al-Rahmán, the door of which was guarded by Abu Talha Ansár with fifty soldiers against intrusion by any one else, excepting Abdalláh, the son of Omar, who was to have his casting vote in case of necessity. Moghira b. Sho'ba and Amr b. As, however, stationed themselves at the door to make it appear that they too had a hand in the affair.†

Though now every body, however insignificant in his antecedents, had a right, from the example of the two Caliphs, to aspire to claim the Caliphate; but amongst these six electors Ali was the only one who had by far the strongest claims to it in view of his being noble by birth, of his being the nearest in kinship with the Prophet and being the closest in touch with him from his childhood, of his priority in Islam, of his knowledge of the Qurán, of his valour, of his judicious reasonings and, last of all though not the least, of his having been proclaimed by the Prophet his vicegerent and to stand in relation to him as Aaron was to Moses. Omar, however, raised five open claimants to compete with him and they wasted two days in unprofitable wrangling, each pressing his own claim.

---

†Tabari Vol. V p. 36.

At length Abd-al-Rahmán offered to forego † his claim to the Caliphate, if the rest would consent to abide by his decision in electing a Caliph of his choice. Othmán was the first to give his consent, then the others but Ali, who kept silent. When asked by Abd-al-Rahmán to give his consent, he said, 'First promise me that thou wilt not have any consideration for kith or kin, but will regard right alone.' Abd-al-Rahmán replied, 'I ask of thee to pledge thyself that thou wilt accept the choice made by me and against all dissentients will support the same;' continuing he said, 'I on my part, pledge myself not to be governed by self interest or regard for kith or kin.' Ali then assented as the rest and thus the election of the Caliph rested with Abd-al-Rahmán alone. ††

Then Abd-al-Rahmán had a long consultation with each of the electors separately in turn. Zobeir was in favour of Ali, how Sa'd voted, is not certain; Othmán pressed his own claim and so did Ali. The election was now narrowed between the two and it was on the last night of the third day's deliberations.

The Election. 24 A. H.

At the dawn of the morning, the Mosque was unusually crowded with the governors and chiefs of different provinces, as well as the citizens of Medina, who attended to join the morning Service and waited to learn who was to become their Amir. Abd-al-Rahmán, ascending the pulpit, addressed the people to advise him in the matter of election. Ammár Yasir, a veteran Companion of the Prophet and late Governor of Kufa, stood up and spoke, 'If thou earnestly desireth that there shouldst be no division in the land then salute Ali as Caliph.' Miqdád seconded him. But soon arose another voice crying, 'Nay! If it is thy desire that there be no division among the Qoreish, then salute Othmán.' It was from Abdalláh b. Abi Sarh, who, on being seconded by Ibn Rabi'a, smiled. Whereupon the venerable Ammár turned contemptuously on Ibn Abi Sarh and exclaimed, 'O apostate! hast thou ever

† Ibn Athir; Ibn Khaldun; †† Tabari Vol. V. p. 36.

before counselled the Moslems that thou || darest interfere today?' Addressing the audience, Ammár continued, † "O people! The Apostle of God was the honoured one who raised us to the pinnacle of honour with Divine Faith, wherefore let not the honour of his house pass out of his House." ‡ Upon this one of the Bani Makhzum (the tribe to which Khálid b. Walid belonged) cried angrily, "Thou passeth beyond thy bounds, O son of Somyya! who art thou to meddle with the affairs of the Qoreish in choosing their own Amir?"

The contention was growing hot when Sa'd interfered calling out to Abd-al-Rahmán, "Finish thy work before a tumult bursteth forth, elect whomsoever thou liketh to choose." "Yes, I have made up my mind," said Abd-al-Rahmán, and addressing the crowd: "Silence ye people," he called Ali to the front and addressed him thus: "If I elect thee to the Caliphate, thou must bind thyself by the Covenant of the Lord to act according to the Book of God, to the example of the Prophet and to the precedents of his successors." "I hope," responded Ali, "that I should do so. I shall act according to the best of my knowledge and judgment." Then addressing Othmán, Abd-al-Rahmán put the same question to him, who promptly answered uncondtionally, "Yea, I will."

Whereupon, either dissatisfied with Ali's answer or having already made up his mind against him, Abd-al-Rahmán, taking Othmán's hand in his own, turned his

---

|| Ibn Abi Sarh was a foster brother of Othmán. He is alluded to in *Sura VI-93* 'Who is more wicked than he who inventeth a lie against God and sayeth, it is revealed to me, and I will produce a Revelation like unto that which the Lord hath sent down'. He was employed by the Prophet as amanuensis, had interpollated passages of his own of a ludicrous nature, which being discovered, he fled to Mecca and turned apostate. When proscribed by the Prophet, Othmán gave him shelter and subsequently begged and obtained forgiveness of the Prophet. He was made Governor of Egypt by Othmán during his reign.

† Ibn Jarir

‡ Zákir Hosain's History of Islam, Vol. iii p, 118.

face upward looking towards the heavens and prayed thus aloud, 'O Lord hear me and bear me witness, verily what it was around my neck, I place the same around the neck of Othmán.' Forthwith he saluted Othmán as Caliph and the people followed his example.

†"It is not the first occasion that I have been deprived of my legitimate rights, but thou hast not been free of self-interest and partiality," said Ali to Abd-al-Rahmán, who was keen enough to warn Ali sharply with these words: "Beware, lest thou makest a way against thy own self", hinting at Omar's order to behead those who resisted. So Ali passed out with these words upon his lips. ¶"Surely patience becometh me; the help of God is to be implored against that which ye devise". *Sur. XII-18.*

Sir W. Muir in his Annals of the Early Caliphate, says:—

Everlasting disastrous effects of the choice.

"The choice of Abd-al-Rahmán laid the seeds of disaster for Islam at large, and for the Caliphate in particular. It led to dissensions which for years bathed the Moslem world in blood, threatened the very existence of the Faith, and to this day divides believers in a hopeless and embittered schism."

Inauguration of Othman and his first Address. 24 A. H.

It was the 3rd, || 4th or 5th* of Moharram, 24 A. H. in November, 644 A. D., that Othmán was inaugurated as Caliph. **On Friday following the inauguration, he ascended the pulpit to deliver his inaugural address to the public. But he was impeded in his speech in preaching, whereupon he exclaimed, "O ye people! the first attempt is a hard task, but after today, there are yet days, and if I live, the discourse will come to ye after its wont, for we were never preachers, but the Lord will teach us." (Ibn Sa'd). *Jarret's Trans. of Suyuti's His. p. 169.*

Othman's first court of justice.

Scarcely was Othmán established in office when a perplexing case was brought to him for decision against a son of Omar, the late

† Tárikh Kámil; Abul Fida. ¶ Tabari; Ibn Athir; Abul Fida. || Abul Fida. *A'sam Kufi. **Rawdzat-al-Ahbáb.

Caliph. The facts of the case were as follows :—

† Obeidalláh, the son of Omar, was told by Abd-al-Rahmán son of Abubekr that the day before Omar's assassination he had seen Abu Lulu, the assassin, in private discourse with the Persian prince named Hormuzán and a Christian slave of Sa'd named Jofina, and that, on being surprised by him, the three separated dropping in their confusion a double bladed dagger with its haft in the middle. The description of the dagger answered that with which Omar was wounded ; therefore Obeidalláh, suspecting a conspiracy, grew infuriated, rushed with a drawn sword to avenge the death of his father, and rashly fell upon Hormuzán whom he slew. Proceeding on to the place of the slave, he slew Jofina and then the daughter of Abu Lulu. He was seized at last by Sa'd b. Abi Waqqás and kept a prisoner pending the conclusion of the conclave, which was then in progress. The next day after the inauguration of Othmán, Sa'd brought Obeidalláh to Othmán demanding retaliatory punishment in accordance with the law for the murder of a Believer; for Hormuzán professed the Moslem faith, received stipend of 2000 dirhams from the Exchequer and was under the protection of Abbás, the uncle of the Prophet.

Othmán was perplexed between the letter of the law and the odium of following the murder of the father (Omar) by the execution of the son (Obeidalláh). There was not a bit of evidence or even presumption against the prince. Summoning a Council, Othmán asked their advice. Ali and several others declared that the law must be satisfied by the execution of the culprit. Several others said that they were shocked at the idea that the Commander of the Faithful was slain but the other day and today his son be put to death. At length to the great relief of Othmán, Amr b. As hit upon a stratagem suggesting that as the act of Obeidalláh took place in the interregnum between the Caliphates of Omar and Othmán, it did not come under the cognizance of either. Othmán

† Tabari; Ibn Athir ; Rawzat-al-Ahbáb ; Habib-al-Siyar.

gladly availed himself of the quibble and ordered the release of Obeidalláh. He desired to compensate the murder by payment of a sum of money from the public treasury, but Ali protested against the process. So Othmán paid the ransom money from his own pocket.† Obeidalláh escaped unpunished and the murder of the once magnificent Hormuzán, the Persian prince, remained unavenged. Some feeling was excited and the people said that the Caliph was already departing from the Law. Ziyád b. Lobid, a poet of Medina, satirised both the murderer and the Caliph who had let him off, in stinging verse. But he was silenced and the matter dropped.

On the third day of his Caliphate (Moharram, 24 A.H.) Othmán deposed Moghira b. Sho'ba from the government of Kufa and appointed Sa'd b. Abi Waqqás in his place. *Rawdzat-al-Ahbab.*

The year of Hæmorrhage 24 A. H.

In this year (24 A. H.) the people were attacked by a malady in which blood issued from the nose, and it was therefore called the "year of the hæmorrhage". *Ibid.*

This hæmorrhage seized Othmán, so that he was detained from the Haj Pilgrimage and deputed another in his stead. *Jarret's Trans. of Suyuti's His. p. 159.* ‡There is the tradition related by Ibn Hejer in his work Tathir al Jinán, on page 141, that the Prophet said: "One of the oppressors from the Omyyads shall step upon my pulpit and he will be seized with bleeding from his nose."

Appointment of Walid as Governor of Kufa.

In the year 25 A. H. Othmán appointed his uterine brother Walid b. Oqba b. Abi Mo'ait to the government of Kufa, deposing Sa'd b. Abi Waqqás. Walid ¶was a drunkard, a notorious debauchee and a man of scandalous fame. His father Oqba was taken prisoner in the battle of Bedr and when he was about to be put to

† Tabari; Ibn Athir; Rawdzat-al-Ahbáb.

‡ Zákir Husain's History of Islam Vol. III p. 124.

¶ Mas'udi.

death, he despairingly said, "who will take care of my children," and the Prophet replied, "Hell fire." Walid was one of the same children. The Caliph got a bad name for favouritism to his unworthy relations.

Extension of Ka'ba boundries.

In the year 26 A. H. while on pilgrimage at Mecca, Othmán, desiring an extension of the enclosure of the Ka'ba edifice, ordered the purchase of the houses adjoining the existing boundary walls. Some owners refused to sell their houses, which he ordered to be forcibly acquired. They proceeded to Medina and lodged their grievances before the Caliph against the acquisition by force. They were arrested and imprisoned, but afterwards released on the recommendation of Abdalláh b. Khálid b. Osaid. *Ibn Athir.*

Appointment of Abdallah b. Abi Sarh as Governor of Egypt.

† In the same year, Othmán removed Amr b. As, the conqueror of Egypt, from his government of Egypt and appointed his own foster brother Abdalláh b. Abi Sarh in his place. This Abdalláh was the same who is alluded to in *Sur. VI-93*. Amr came back to Medina and took his abode, as Sa'd b. Abi Waqqás the ex-governor of Kufa had done. Both these men together busied themselves with criticising the Caliph's public and private actions; and (according to Habib-al-Siyar) the opposition reached to such a pitch that Amr, who had a sister of Othmán's in his wedlock, divorced her. Every man's mouth was now full of grievous accusations against the Caliph, charging him with nepotism.

Lavish Gifts. 26 A. H.

In this year and in the year following (*i. e.*, A. H. 26-27) conquests were extended in Africa from beyond Egypt in the east to as far as Morocco in the west, comprising almost the whole territory along the sea-coast viz. Tripoli, Tunis, Algeria and Morocco. Immense spoils of war were hoarded up by the conquerors, and a fifth of the booty was sent to the Caliph for the public treasury, which was devoted to the poor. Othmán bestowed the whole of it, including the

† Abul Fida; Habib-al-Siyar.

portion which was set apart for the family of the Prophet*, upon his secretary Marwán. It amounted to five hundred thousand Dinars.¶

Marwán's father Hakam b. al As was banished from Medina for life by the Prophet and for this reason he was not recalled by either of Othmán's predecessors *i. e.* Abubekr and Omar. Hakam and Marwán were near relations of Othmán, the former being uncle and the latter a cousin to him. He recalled both of them and reinstated them †. He gave his daughter in marriage ‡ to Marwán and made him his own Secretary and beside the above mentioned gift of the war spoils he granted Marwán Fadak § (the property claimed by Fátema) as a Jaghyr, which remained in his possession and in possession of his posterity till the time when Omar b. Abd-al-Aziz in the 2nd century restored it back to its original owners, the posterity of Fátema.

Othmán bestowed lavish gifts upon his relations and parasites. For instance, once he gave one hundred thousand Dinárs to Hakam. He bestowed upon his cousin Hárith b. Hakam, who had married a daughter of Othmán's, the right of levying the tax on the sales (1/10th of the sale proceeds) conducted in the market of Medina.** This income was devoted to the poor by the Prophet. Three hundred thousand Dinárs were granted to Abdalláh b. Khálid b. Osaid, a parasite who was the son of a cousin of Othmán's father. Likewise, he gifted four hundred thousand Dinárs to his foster brother Abdalláh b. Abi Sarh, the Apostate, whom he had made governor of Egypt.

Appointment of Abdallah b. Amir as Governor of Bussorah.

In the year 28 A. H. the Caliph removed Abu Musa Ash'ari from the government of Bussorah and appointed his own cousin ††Abdalláh b. Amir, a youth of but 25 years in place of Abu Musa.

---

* W. Irving p. 161.
¶ Abul Fida.
† Ibn Abd Rabia; Abul Fida.
‡ Milal wa Nahal Shohristani.
§ Abul Fida Vol. I p. 169; Ibn. Abd Rabia; Ibn Qotaiba.
** Ibn Abd Rabia in Aqdal Farid.
†† Abul Fida.

In the same year Othmán married Náela, a Christian lady. He had built a palace for her at Medina.

In the same year Cyprus and Rhodes were captured.

During the year 29 A. H. there had been a revolt in Persia. Astakhar, Ispehan and Shiráz had to be recaptured.

Revolt in Persia.

† In the same year a woman, who gave birth to a child after only six months of her marriage, was brought before the Caliph for punishment on a presumption of fornication. Othmán ordered her to be stoned to death. They carried her for execution of the sentence, when Ali got information of it. He at once interviewed Othmán and explained to him the law of the Lord which meant that the least limit of pregnancy was six months, and therefore no woman who gave birth after this period should be suspected of adultery, unless there was evidence against her for her adultery. Othmán, ashamed of his rash and unjust decision, at once sent men forbidding her execution, but by the time the messengers reached, she had already been stoned to death.

A rash and unjust decision.

†† In the same year (29 A. H.) when Osmán made his pilgrimage to Mecca, he introduced several innovations, and amongst others he followed the practice of his heathen predecessors and erected a spacious tent on the plains of Miná under which he distributed various provisions to the pilgrims, although the Prophet had carefully abolished this custom as a relic of heathenism.

Revival of Heathenish custom.

‡ The Prophet and his two successors, Abubekr and Omar, or even Othmán himself at Miná and Arafát, used to shorten by two prostrations all the prayers which are usually read with four prostrations; but on this occasion (29 A.H. Pilgrimage) Othmán did not shorten

Action contrary to the teachings and practice of the Prophet.

† Rawdzat-al-Ahbáb.

†† Ibid; Izálatal Khifa Persian V. II. p. 248; Dr. Weil quoted by Ockley p. 280.

‡ Ibid.

the prayers. This action, being contrary to the teachings and practice of the Founder of the Faith, was resented by the Moslems in general and by the leading or prominent Companions of the Prophet in particular; and it was a cause of great indignation and prejudice against the Caliph.

Recension of the Quran 30 A. H.

"Differences arose in the recitation of the sacred text of the Qurán in the vast dominions of the Mohammedan Empire. Bussorah followed the reading of Abu Musa Ash'ari; Kufa was guided by the authority of Ibn Mas'ud, their Chancellor; and the text of Hims differed from that in use even at Damascus. Hozhaifa urged Othmán to restore the unity of the Divine Word. The Caliph called for samples of the manuscripts in use throughout the Empire and then appointed a Syndicate to collate these copies with the sacred originals still in the keeping of Hafsa. Under their supervision the variations were reconciled and an authoritative Examplar written out, of which duplicates were deposited at Mecca and Medina, Kufa and Damascus. From these Examplars, copies were multiplied and broadcasted over the Empire; all former manuscripts were called in and committed to flames; and the Standard Text was brought into exclusive use. Ibn Mas'ud at Kufa, who prided himself on his faultless recitation of the Oracle, pure as it fell from the Prophet's lips, was much displeased; and the charge of Sacrilege, in having burnt the former copies of the Sacred text, was readily circulated among the factious citizens. By and by the charge was spread abroad and was taken up with avidity by the enemies of Othmán." *Muir's Annals p. 307.*

Walid's Deposition and Sa'id's Appointment. 30 A. H.

† Walid, the Governor of Kufa, on an occasion in a state of inebriation conducted the morning Service with four prostrations, instead of the usual two as prescribed by the Prophet. The congregation which consisted of several pious persons, like Ibn Mas'ud, was much incensed and still more irritated when, finishing the four

† Mas'udi in Morawij-al-Zahb; Ibn Qutaiba; Ibn Athir.

prostrations, Walid said to the people, " What a pleasant morn! I would like to extend the Service further if ye consent." Repeated complaints were already made to the Caliph against Walid on account of his debauchery, but as often dismissed. People now reproached Othmán for not listening to their grievances, and favouring such a scoundrel. Perchance they succeeded in taking off the Signet Ring from the hand of the Governor while he lay senseless from the effects of a debauch, and carried it off to Medina. Still the Caliph was slow and hesitated to enforce punishment upon the governor, his uterine brother; giving cause to be himself reproachfully accused of ignoring the law; though at last he was persuaded to have Walid scourged with 40 stripes. He was consequently deposed from his office. Sa'id b. al As, a cousin of Othmán's was appointed to take his place.

Othman's Threats to the Public. Ammar ill-treated. 30 A. H.

It was a matter of great reproach against Othmán that he bestowed lavish gifts from the public treasury, upon his parasites and kinsmen, who were hated and abhorred by the Prophet. For instance he gave one hundred thousands Dinárs to Hakam; four hundred thousands to Abdalláh b. Abi Sarh; five † hundred thousands to Marwán. Murmurs rose against him on all sides and daily increased in virulence. His conduct, both public and private, was scrutinised. "At ‡ last in a public assembly Othmán told them, that the money which was in the treasury was sacred and belonged to God, and that he (as being the successor of the Prophet) would, in spite of them, dispose of it as he thought fit; and threatened and cursed all who should presume to censure or murmer at what he said." Upon this, Ammár b. Yásir, one of the primitive Molems of whom the Prophet himself had said that he was filled with faith from the crown of his head to the soles of his feet, boldly declared his disapprobation and began to

---

† Adul Fida. ‡ Ockley's His Sar. p. 280.

charge him with his inveterate propensity to ignore the interests of the general public; accused him with reviving the heathenish customs abolished by the Prophet in utter disregard of the sacred example set by the Founder of the Faith. Whereupon Othmán commanded him to be ¶ beaten and immediately some of the Bani Omyyads, the kindred of the Caliph fell upon the venerable Ammár, the Caliph himself kicking him down; and he was beaten till he swooned. Bani Makhzum, the descendants of Ammár's uncle, hearing all this, carried Ammár away and swore, that if Ammár died of the hurts received by him, they would avenge themselves upon Othmán.

The outrage offered to the special favourite of the Prophet was promulgated far and wide and contributed largely to raise the prevailing general discontent.

Change in the National Character of Arabs.

The conquests of Persia, Syria and Egypt produced a great effect on the national character and habits of the once simple Arabs. The everlasting luxury and soft voluptuousness of the magnificent royal cities of the conquered countries sapped the rude simplicity of the Arabian deserts. Gorgeous palaces, crowds of slaves, multitudes of horses, camels, flocks and herds, profusion of costly garments; sumptuous fare, splendid equipage, idle games and sports now became the fashion of the day throughout the Empire. For instance, Othmán had built for himself a palace, an imposing building in Medina with marble pillars, grand gates and gardens. He had built 6 other palaces, one for Náela his wife and one for each of his daughters. He had got multitudes of slaves, thousands of horses, camels and flocks. His properties at Wádi-al-Qora, Honein etc. valued at more than one hundred thousand Dinárs. He is said to have amassed vast treasures. On his death one hundred and fifty thousands of Dinárs and ten hundred thousands of Dirhams were found in cash with his treasurer. Zobeir had built palaces at Kufa, Fostat, Alexandria and most of the great cities of the

¶ Tarikh-al-Khamis; A'tham Kufi.

Empire. The one at Bussorah existed till the fourth century. His landed Estate in Iraq yielded 1,000 golden pieces a day. He had got no less than one thousand horses and as many slaves. Talha had got palaces at Kufa, Medina etc. His daily income in Iráq and Náhiya Saráh amounted to more than 2,000 Dinárs. Abd-al-Rahmán had one thousand camels, ten thousand sheep and 100 horse. He left property valued at between 3 and 4 hundred thousand Dinárs. Zaid left gold and silver in great ingots and landed property valued at 10,000 Dinárs. Mo'áwiya in Syria excelled all of them in pomp and show of wordly riches.†

Banishment of Abuzharr Ghifari, 30 A.H.

Abu Zharr Ghifári, a venerable Companion of the Prophet and an ascetic in habits, who now lived in Syria, inveighed against the riches and extravagance of the day—evils, which were altogether alien to the simplicity of the Prophet and which rushing in like a flood, were now demoralising the people. The spirit of the ascetic was stirred at the pomps and vanities so rife around him and he preached repentance to the inhabitants of Damascus. "This gold and silver of yours," he cried, "shall one day be heated red hot in the fire of hell; and therewith shall ye be seared in your forehead, sides and back, ye ungodly spendthrifts!" *Sur. IX-35*. He preached against the prevailing inroads of profligacy and the practice of forbidden pastimes, music, wine and gambling. Crowds flocked to hear him.

Uneasy at the disturbance by caused these diatribes in the public mind, ‡ Mo'áwiya, apprehensive of the spread of communistic doctrines, wrote against Abu Zharr to the Caliph, who ordered his removal to Medina at once. || Mo'áwiya, in compliance with the Caliph's order despatched Abu Zharr to Medina on a bad tempered, unsaddled camel guided by a rude and harsh driver. Abu Zharr, an old man with white hair from

† Mas'udi; Muir's Annals.

‡ Mas'udi in Morawij-al-Zahb. || Muir's Annals p. 309 & 310.

head to foot, tall, thin and lean reached Medina with his legs bruised and bleeding and his whole frame aching with pain. He was received by the Caliph with hot words, upon which Abu Zharr fearlessly declared that he had heard the Prophet say, "† When the posterity of Abul-As numbered thirty, they will count the riches of the Lord as their own and will treat His people as their own servants and slaves. They will deviate from the right path. Then they will be freed from them by their Lord." Othmán was so much displeased at this that he banished Abu Zharr subsequently to Rabazha, a wilderness in the desert of Nejd, where, two years after, he died in penury and neglect.

Abu Zharr was one of the four ¶ persons whose love was particularly enjoined by the Prophet declaring that they were loved by God. He was treated by the Prophet as a friend. When he felt his end approach, the hermit desired his daughter to slay a kid and have it ready for a party of travellers, who, he said, would shortly pass that way and bury him; then making her turn his face towards Ka'ba, he quietly breathed his last. Soon after, the expected party came up and amongst them was Málik-al-Ashtar from Kufa (according to some, Ibn Mas'ud) who, weeping over him, bewailed his fate and buried him on the spot on which he died. ††

The plaintive tale of the harsh treatment, meted to the preacher of righteousness, was fresh in every one's mouth as a serious ground of complaint against the Caliph. ||

‡ A few days after it, the death of Ibn Mas'ud who was ill-treated by Othmán forfeiting his stipend for his refusal to give up his manuscript of the Qurán for being burnt, added to the pathos of the incident.

---

† Tárikh Ibn Wádzeh; Mas'udi.

¶ Tirmizhi, Hákim, quoted by Suyuti p. 173.

†† Tárikh Ibn Wádzeh; Mas'udi.

|| Mas'udi; Rawdzat-al-Safá; A'tham Kufi.

‡ Tárikh Ibn Wádzeh; Masudi.

In the seventh year of his caliphate, an ominous incident occurred to Othmán in the loss of the Signet Ring, which was accidentally dropped and disappeared in the well Aris in the suburbs of Medina. It was a silver ring inscribed with the words 'Mohammed the Apostle of God'. It originally belonged to the Prophet, who had it made in the year 6 A. H. for sealing the letters sent by him to foreign Courts. After his death, the ring was used and worn by Abubekr and Omar as the symbol of Command. Othmán also used it as such and its loss was considered to be of sinister import. All efforts to recover the precious relic were vain. The omen weighed heavy on the mind of Othmán, though the ring was replaced by another made of the like pattern.

Loss of Othman's Signet Ring. 30. A. H.

In 31 A. H. Yezdjird the Persian Emperor, who was fleeing from fortress to fortress to save himself from the pursuing Moslems, was murdered at Merv by a mill-owner with whom he had sought shelter. Thus the Persian Government ended with its last monarch and all the territories belonging to it finally came under the sway of Islam.

End of Persian Emperor and Empire.

In 32 A. H. a riot broke out at Bussorah but was, for the moment, suppressed by Ibn Amir the Governor.

Riot at Bussorah.

About the year 33 A. H. a revolt broke out at Kufa. It was mainly due to the tyranny of the Governor, Sa'id b. al-As a consin of Othmán's. He had excited the hatred of the principal citizens, but since he particularly offended Málik b. al Ashtar, who was a leading chief and a great favourite of theirs, they assembled every day in Málik's house and criticised the Governor's public and private actions, seeking every opportunity to bring contempt not only upon the administration of Sa'id but also upon that of the Caliph. One day Sa'id sent an Officer to disperse the assemblage but they fell upon him beating him till he fainted. Sa'id appealed to the Caliph against the machinations of the ringleaders. Othmán

Revolt at Kufa.

ordered that twenty of the ringleaders might be expelled to Syria, where their conduct would be properly watched by the vigilant Mo'áwiya. Consequently Málik-al-Ashtar; Thábit b. Qais; Amir b. Qais; Komail b. Ziyád; Jondab b. Ka'b; Zaid b. Sohán; Orwa b. al-Jo'd; So'sa'a b. Sohán; Omeir b. Sábi; Amr b. al-Homaq and ten others were banished to Syria. Mo'áwiya quartered them in the Church of St. Mary; and, in regard to their being men of rank and position, endeavoured to conciliate them by mildness, but they never refrained from reviling and abusing the house of the Omyyads in general and the Caliph in particular. It happened that one day after a sharp discussion upon the subject with Mo'áwiya, they actually fell upon him aud seized his beard †. Mo'áwiya, however, only cried out, "Mind! ye are not in Kufa, if my Syrians only knew of your insults, by heavens, I shall not be able to save ye from being torn to pieces." Then Mo'áwiya, hopeless of pacifying them, wrote to Othmán all about them. The Caliph instructed him to transfer his turbulent charge to Abd-al-Rahmán son of Khálid b. Walid, who was governor at Hims, and who was expected to treat them befittingly after his own rude and rough fashion. When they reached Hims, Abd-al-Rahmán did not for a whole month grant them audience. At last he received them very rudely, reviled them whenever they happened to appear before him and made them trot by his horse talking to them while he rode out. Thus he soon reduced them to submission and at length they were permitted to return to Kufa. But Málik continued to reside at Hims till he received news that Sa'id was absent from Kufa on a visit to Medina.

Malik's return to Kufa. Abu Musa-al-Ash'ari appointed Governor. 34 A. H.

Málik-al-Ashtar repaired to Kufa in 34 A. H. in the absence of Sa'id, the Governor, and resumed his place at the head of the disaffected people of Kufa. When Sa'id returned to Kufa, he found his way barred by the inhabitants, who had

† Abul Fida.

assembled in great numbers upon the walls to intercept his entry. Alarmed at their hostile attitude, Sa'id retraced his steps to Medina. The Caliph, to make a virtue of the necessity, acceded to the wishes of the Kufa men, who desired that Abu Musa Ash'ari might be appointed in place of Sa'id.

Weakness of Othman realised by the people.

Though Othmán was already falling rapidly in popular esteem as will appear from the following illustrations, still more by yielding to the insurgents the weak Caliph committed an error fatal to his government. The people around him looked upon him with contempt, while those in distant parts of the Empire, who were suffering the hardships and tyranny of the despotic governors, realising the weakness of Othmán, were emboldened to raise their voice for redress. Seditious letters were now freely exchanged; thus even from Medina messages reached the provinces that the sword would soon be needed there at home rather than in foreign lands.†

Illustrations of Contumelious treatment of Othman.

Sa'id b. al As, the governor of Kufa being angry with Hishám b. Otba, a nephew of Sa'd b. Abi Waqqás, had the house of Hishám at Kufa burnt to ashes. Sa'd b. Abi Waqqás, a veteran Companion of the Prophet, the ex-Governor of Kufa and now a leading citizen of Medina, approached Othmán and demanded retaliatory punishment on Sa'id and amends to the injured. Waiting some time, when he saw that nothing was done by the Caliph, Sa'd, backed by Ayesha, fired the house of Sa'id in Medina and the Caliph could not take any step against him.‡

"Abdal-Rahmán b. Awf who, no doubt, felt a large measure of responsibility for the share he took in the election of Othmán, was about this time removed by death. But even he was dissatisfied, and one of the first open denunciations of Othmán's unscrupulous disregard of law—small it might be, but significant—is attributed

† Ibn Qoteiba.

‡ Zákir Hosain's History of Islam vol. iii p. 138.

to him. A fine camel, having come in with the tithes of a Bedouin tribe, was presented by the Caliph, as a rarity, to one of his kinsfolk. Abd-al-Rahmán, scandalised at the misappropriation of religious property devoted to the poor, laid hands upon the animal, slaughtered it and divided the flesh among the people. The personal reverence attaching heretofore to the successor of the Prophet of the Lord gave place to slight and disregard."

"Even in the streets, Othmán was greeted with cries demanding that he should depose Ibn Amir and the godless Abu Sarh, and put away from him Marwán, his chief adviser and confident."

"Amr (b. As), who had become a petulant mal-content ever since his deposition, is represented as speaking contumeliously of Othmán to his very face, and Othmán is represented as returning it in kind, calling him a louse in his garments." *W. Muir's Annals, p. 324.*

List of charges against Othman.

† It will not be out of place to give here, from the endless roll of charges against the caliph Othmán, a list of the most conspicuous complaints of the general public.

1. To have revived certain heathenish customs which the Prophet had carefully abolished. (See page 333.)
2. To have acted contrary to the teachings and practice of the Prophet in performing the prayers at Mina and Arafát. (See page 333).
3. To have acted against the precedents of Abubekr and Omar by his taking seat on the uppermost step of the pulpit where the Prophet used to sit.
4. To have recalled Hakam and Marwán who were banished by the Prophet. *Abul Fida.* (See page 332.)
5. To have committed to flames the sacred manuscripts of the Qurán. (See page 334.)
6. To have bestowed lavish gifts upon his relations and parasites from the religious properties devoted to the poor. (See page 331.)

---

† Imámat Wal Siyásat; Tárikh-al-Khamis.

7. To have deposed venerable Companions of the Prophet from their posts to make room for his own ungodly relations. (See pages 330, 331 and 332.)
8. To have ill-treated Ammár Yásir, a venerable Companion of the Prophet. (See page 335.)
9. To have ill-treated and banished the pious Abu Zharr, a favourite of the Prophet, to a wilderness where he died in penury, his stipened having been forfeited. (See pege 337.)
10. Te have ill-treated Abdalláh b. Mas'ud and to have forfeited his stipend. (See page 338.)
11. To have banished Málik-al-Ashtar and Ka'b from Kufa. (See page 339.)
12. To have banished Obeida b. Sámit as a punishment for his cutting open the skins-full of wine carried to Mo'áwiya. *Tarikh-al-Khamis; Imamat Wal Siyasat.*
13. To have allowed the people of his House the exclusive use of the rain water collected in cisterns for general use. *Ibid.*
14. To have reserved the pasture grounds exclusively for the use of his own animals. *Ibid.*
15. To have restricted the Seas exclusively for his own trade vessels. *Ibid.*
16. To have decried Abd-al-Rahmán b. Awf as hypocrite. The poeple said that if Abd-al-Rahmán was a hypocrite, then his choice of Othmán as Caliph was illegal; or if he was maliciously decried by Othmán then Othmán was undeserving of Caliphate. *Ibid.*

When Málik-al-Ashtar together with the other leading men of Kufa was banished, Ka'b b.

Ominous Sounds of Warnings.

Abda, a man famous for his piety, wrote to Othmán from Kufa protesting against the banishment, and warning him against the impending dangers which the tyranny of Sa'id was bringing about. On receiving the message, Othmán was very angry and desired that the messenger should be imprisoned or severely beaten, but on the interference of Ali he was allowed to go back unmolested. Othmán, however, wrote to Sa'id, who scourged Ka'b and banished him. Upon this Talha and Zobeir expostulated with Othmán and warned him that they feared lest his maladministration should result in an outburst like volcanic fires and engulf him. Othmán consequently wrote to Sa'id, who called back Ka'b from exile.†

Meanwhile, people from every province came in, asking the leading citizens of Medina their way to get rid of the oppressions and cruelties they were suffering at the hands of the despotic governors. Moved by their appeals, Ali repaired to Othmán and said: "People complaining against thy governors have come to seek redress, and they hold thee responsible for the actions of thine Governors; they blame thee for not listening to their grievances repeatedly put forward by them. Beware of treason lest it should rage like the foaming waves of the seas. Fear God and do justice to them so that they might return satisfied." Othmán replied: "I have done my best. As for the Governors, wouldst thou not concede that the governors of my appointment are not any the worse than Moghira b. Sho'ba, who was appointed by Omar to the government of Bussorah and, after he was deposed on a charge of adultery, was again appointed by Omar to the government of Kufa?" 'And Mo'áwiya too', continued the Caliph, 'was the choice of Omar. He was not appointed by me to hold the chief command in Syria.' "Yes", answered Ali, "but Omar kept strict control over his officers; they obeyed his orders, and when they did wrong he punished them; whereas thou treatest them mildly and thou dost not punish them because they are thine relations. Wouldst thou not admit that Omar's slaves stood not in so much awe of Omar as did Mo'áwiya?" Othmán had to admit. Ali continued: 'but now he doeth whatever he pleaseth and putteth thy name to the bidding, and thou, knowing it all, leaveth him unquestioned." Having thus warned the Caliph, Ali took his departure. ‡

† Tárikh-al-Khamis.
‡ Ibn Athir; Ibn Qoteiba.

In the words of Sir W. Muir "As Ali's message professed to come from the people, Othmán went straightway to the pulpit and addressed the multitudes there assembled for prayers in the Mosque. He reproached them for giving vent to their tongues and following evil leaders whose object it was to blacken his name, exaggerate his faults and hide his virtues. 'Ye blame me', he said, 'for things which ye bore cheerfully from Omar. He trampled on you, beat you with his whip and abused you. And yet ye took it all patiently from him, both in what ye liked and what ye disliked. I have been gentle with you, bended my back unto you, withheld my tongue from reviling and my hand from smiting. And now ye rise up against me.' Then after dwelling on the prosperity of his reign at home and abroad he ended thus, 'wherefore refrain, I beseech you, from your abuse of me and of my governors, lest ye kindle the flames of sedition and revolt throughout the Empire.' The appeal, we are told, was marred by his cousin Marwán who exclaimed, 'If ye will oppose the Caliph, we shall soon bring it to the issue of the sword.' 'Be silent', cried Othmán. So Marwán remained silent and Othmán descended from the pulpit. The harangue had no effect for good. The discontent spread, and the gatherings against the Caliph multiplied." *W. Muir's Annals, p. 322.*

Conference of Governors at Medina. 34 A.H. 655 A.D.

It was a custom that the governors of different provinces on their return from the annual pilgrimage at Mecca used to present themselves at the court of the Caliph in Medina. The season of the pilgrimage in the eleventh year of Othmán's caliphate having approached, Othmán issued an edict requiring the people, who had any cause of complaint against the governors, or any grievances against them, to come forward on that occasion in order that their appeals might be heard in the presence of their governors and the wrongs done to them might be redressed. After the pilgrimage the Governors attended the Caliph's court but the complainants dared not come forward to claim a redress in the presence of the governor against whom they had complaints. The Caliph, however, discussed the situation with the Governors and asked their advice to find out ways and means to check the growing discontent. One (Sa'id) suggested that the ringleaders should be put to sword; another (Abdalláh) proposed that they should be silenced by liberal gifts; a third (Ibn Amir) advised to send them out on some expeditionary force, thus to divert their energies from their present activities. The conference was, at length, broken up without any definite settlement. Nothing was done to avert the impending crisis, and the Caliph gave them leave to depart saying only that they should use every means to control the situation.

Prediction of Ka'b-al-Ahbar.

† During his sojourn at Medina, Mo'áwiya met Ka'b-al-Ahbár, the Jewish convert, who was a famous fortune teller, and asked him to foretell the issue of the prevailing discontent. He said, 'His (Othman's) end is approaching. It will be the grey mule that wins* in the long run after much bloodshed,' meaning Mo'áwiya, who from that moment resolutely kept an eye on the Caliphate. ‡

Deputations seeking redress and Othman's ficklemindedness.

On return to their seats of government the governors exhibited more high handedness and cruelty. The opressed, on the other hand, meeting in the dark, decided to send in their deputations once more to warn the Caliph, and if they still failed in their efforts to bring Othmán to reason, they were her eafter to converge upon Medina in a combined and menacing force to demand abdication of the Caliph. The deputations reached Medina in Rabi I, 35 A. H. and presenting an endless roll of their grie-

† Rawdzat-al-Safá Habib-al-Siyar.

* The Prophet had a vision relating to t family of Omyya, whom he saw mount his pulpit, and jump about in it like monkeys; upon which he said: This is their portion in this world, which they have gained by their profession of Islam. *Sale from Al-Beidzawi.*

‡ Muir's Annals, p. 327; Rawdzat-al-Safá.

vances demanded redress of their wrongs or otherwise the abdicatian of the Caliph. They were, however, by the intercession of Ali, pacified by promises of redress and with liberal donations from the Treasury. When they were gone, Marwán, the evil genius of Othmán, reproached him with what he termed as an act of weakness, and advised the Caliph to announce from the pulpit that the deputations, being led by false motives, could not achieve much and they could do no better than to return to their homes disappointed. Othmán, following blindly the advice of his Secretary, next day delivered a sermon from the pulpit repudiating the claims of the deputations. Amr. b. As, who was present in the congregation, protested against the speech, saying that the deputations had not gone back of their own accord but they were made to return with all possible care to avert the crisis. There was a murmur against this undiplomatic speech of the Caliph, and Amr b. As asked Othmán to offer contrition for his behaviour. Othmán, being displeased, insolently exchanged hot words with Amr. But instantly from every corner of the Mosque rose voices demanding Othmán to offer contrition for his sin. The Caliph was alarmed at the disrespectful attitude of the assembly, (who on this occasion, instead of adressing him as Amir-al-Mominin, as was their wont, called him by his simple name Othmán,) and offered the contrition demanded of him; and descending the pulpit, crestfallen, retired to his house. Ali, on hearing all about this sermon remonstrated with Othmán at the futility of the action and advised him to wash away the prejudices conceived by the people against him by declaring his genuine sorrow for what had passed. Othmán did as he was advised, and to prove his sincerity he invited people, who wished to come to his palace, to have a free discourse with him. When some influential men went to see Othmán at his palace, Marwán again reproached Othmán saying that the son of Abu Tálib had cleverly misled the Caliph and by making him admit his faults he had attained his object to prove that the Caliph was guilty of the various charges laid against him. The fickle-minded Caliph was easily persuaded to give him permission to turn out the visitors and Marwán addressed them in so harsh a strain that it soon roused them to tenfold fury. They all went straight-way to Ali and mentioned to him what had happened. Making sure of the facts, Ali was highly indignant and declared that he would not have anything to do with the affairs of Othmán. Náela, the wife of Othmán, who had heard the words of Marwán and beheld the keen resentment of the people, warned her husband of the storm he was bringing over his own head and prevailed upon him again to make friends with Ali, who alone, she said, could effectively mediate with his opponents.

Several minor deputations in the like manner waited upon Othmán, who promised redress but under the baneful influence of Marwán, he never kept his word. According to Major Price, "the imbecile old Caliph frequently advised with Ali, but the malignant influence of his Secretary Marwán perpetually interposed to prevent his taking advantage of the good counsel he received. Marwán, in fact, had gained an undue ascendancy over Othmán, and was the active and insinuating spirit of his government and the evil genius of Othmán. He may justly be looked upon as the principle cause of Othmán's ruin."†

Menacing deputations from Egypt, Kufa and Bussorah. 35 A. H.

The deputations referred to in the above paragraph returned to their homes, but the Egyptian deputies ‡ on reaching their destination were caught hold of by the Governor, who killed the leaders and imprisoned others. Excited at this, some six or seven hundred Egyptians including many men of note such as Abd-al-Rahmán b. Adis, Amr. b. Homaq, Kinána b. Boshar, Sodán b. Ahmar issued from Fostát headed by Gháfiqi b. Harb. Mohammed the son of Abubekr was also with them. Likewise, some two or three hundred men including many in-

† S. Ockley's His. Sar.

‡ Zákir Hosain's History of Islam vol. iii p. 149.

fluential men like Ziyád b. Sohán, Ziyád b. Nasr, Yazid b. Qais came out from Kufa headed by Málik-al-Ashtar. Bussorah also sent out a contingent headed by Harqus b. Zobeir, comprising as many men as from Kufa. Under the pretext of pilgrimage to Mecca they took their journey two months before the anuual pilgrimage and encamped within a league of Medina in separate camps like an army, in the month of Shawwál, 35 A.H. The Egyptians pitched their tents at Zi-Marwa, the men of Kufa at Al-A'was, and the Bussorah party at Zi-Khashab, all places in the close neighbourhood of the city. Hopeless of any amends or redress at the hands of Othmán, they had resolved to compel the Caliph, who was habituated to breach of promises, to abdicate and to elect another in his place. They sent a message to the Caliph, demanding the deposition of their respective governors or his own abdication from the Caliphate. Alarmed at the threatening attitude of the multitudes, Othmán sent Moghira b. Shoba and Amr b. As to persuade them to leave their complaints to be decided according to the Qurán and the Sunnat. But the mal-contents repelled both Moghira and Amr, abusing them with coarse and vulgar language. In consternation and with the advice of his wife, Náela, Othmán again applied to Ali, requesting him to go forth and pacify the rebellious mob. He consented on condition that Othmán would first make formal atonement for his errors from the pulpit. Harassed and dismayed, the Caliph mounted the pulpit and with a voice broken by sobs and tears admitted his faults and begged pardon of God, with exclamations of penitence and sorrow. The whole assemblage was moved and softened. Othmán's public repentance and the interpollation of Ali, who was reverenced on account of his personal traits and being the nearest in kin to the Prophet, produced the desired effect on the insurgents.

Appointment of Mohammed b.

The Egyptians, however, insisted that they would not be content with anything short of the deposition of Abdalláh b. Abi Sarh, the

Abubekr to replace Ibn Abi Sarh in Egypt.

Governor of Egypt, and the appoitment in his place of a man of their own choice. Othmán yielded, and they desired Ali to stand as surety for the fulfilment of Othmán's pledge. "They unanimously named Mohammed, the brother of Ayesha, who had, in fact, been used by that intriguing woman as firebrand to kindle this insurrection; her object being to get Talha appointed to the Caliphate." *W Irving's Successors of Mohammed p. 163.*

A document was drawn up, signed and sealed by the Caliph, attested by Ali, Talha, Zobeir and Abdalláh b. Omar, and handed over to the Egyptians.

†This action of the Caliph apparently satisfied the insurgents, who, now breaking their camps, retraced their steps homewards. Mohammed b. Abubekr, with the Egyptian band, took his way to Egypt to join his post. Three days had Mohammed and his train been on their journey, when they saw a black slave on a swift dromedary passing in haste at a little distance by them. They detained and brought him before Mohammed. On being questioned, he said that he was a slave of Othmán's, and was proceeding on an errand of importance to the Governor of Egypt. He was then told that he was already standing before the governor to whom he should deliver his errand. In reply he said that his mission was for Abdalláh b. Abi Sarh. He denied possession of any letter, but, on a thorough search of his person and baggage, a letter was discovered on tearing open the skin of his water-flask. It was opened on the spot before all who had assembled there and was found to contain orders from the Caliph to Abdalláh b. Abi Sarh directing him to make away with Mohammed b. Abubekr secretly along with several other leaders of the party, as soon as they should arrive in Egypt, to destroy the order of Mohammed's appointment, and to imprison, until further orders others, who had brought complaint to Medina.

The detection of the perfidious letter.

---

†Abul Fida.

It is easier to imagine than to describe what Mohammed b. Abubekr and the Egyptians with him felt. Their indignatian knew no bounds, and no ill language against the Caliph was deemed sufficient. They now resolved to avenge themselves upon the author of this perfidy. They at once turned their faces back towards Medina, and despatched swift messengers to overtake the Bussorah and Kufa delegates on their way home, to apprise them of the foul play meditated by the Caliph and to ask them to return immediately to Medina in order to help them in deposing Othmán. They themselves hastened back to Medina cursing the Caliph all the way for his dastardly attempt at their lives, and congratulating themselves on their fortunate escape from so imminent a danger.

Angry feelings against Othman.

The news of their return and of the intercepted letter excited the most angry feelings of the whole populace, who spared not to say the worst of the Caliph. With the exception of Othmán's immediate kinsmen, the whole body of the Mohájirs and the citizens of Medina were loud with reproaches with one voice and sympathised with the infuriated Egyptians. Even Ayesha, the Mother of the Faithful, was heard to say: "Slay the Na'thal, † May God kill him," and the Egyptians found a justification for their action in the fury against Othmán exhibited by the Mother of the Faithful. In short the Caliph was universally condemned and detested. Meanwhile the men of Bussorah and Kufa, having been alarmed at the evil tidings, turned back to Medina to assist the Egyptians, who were also joined by the dissatisfied faction in the city. Thus ten thousand mal-contents assembled against Othmán to force his abdication.

Denial of Othman about the perfidious letter.

Ali repaired to the Caliph and explained to him the circumstances under which the insurgents had re-appeared in Medina. Othmán denied all knowledge of the letter, and

† Na'thal was the name of a long bearded Jew in Egypt with whose resemblence Othmán was so called by his enemies, *Ibn Athir in Nihaya,*

assented to receive a deputation of the rebel leaders. The deputees produced the letter but Othmán swore solemnly that he knew nothing about it. They asked the Caliph who it was, then, that wrote it and the Caliph's answer was the same that he knew not. 'But it was carried', they pressed, 'by thy own slave, on thine own camel, at thine own order, with thine own seal, and yet thou sayest that thou wast not a privy to it.' Again Othmán affirmed that it was even so. 'It must then,' they said, 'be a forgery of Marwán's' and requested that he might be called on to explain. But Othmán would not call his Secretary, who was his cousin as well as son-in-law. Incensed at Othmán's denial and of his refusal to summon Marwán, who was at the time in the same house, they insisted that if the letter originated with Marwán, he should receive the merited punishment, and whether Othmán was speaking the truth or telling a lie, in either case he was a knave or a fool unworthy of the Sceptre he held, and therefore he should resign. In reply Othmán said that he would not put off the robes which the Lord had girded him with, and offered to make them every satisfaction that could reasonably be demanded of him, declaring his repentance for what had occurred. They answered that they could no longer put any trust in him, as he had often made promise to amend and as often broken it. The altercation became loud. Ali arose and departed to his house. Soon after, returned the men of the deputation to join their bands. Ali left Medina in disgust with the affairs of Othmán and went out.

Ayesha's part in the cold treatment of Othman.

†Ayesha zealously took her share in fomenting the discontent and instigated the insurgents to treat Othmán as an apostate. She accused him of having misappropriated the Public money to the benefit of his own relations and of having treated the Public treasury as his own. She cursed him to be deprived of Heaven's blessings

† Mir Akhond; A'tham Kufi.

for having left the people to the mercy of his ungodly relations, whom he had appointed over them as their sole masters. She said that, but for being a Mussalman, she would like to see him slain as a camel. On hearing this, Othmán (alluding to Ayesha and Hafsa's betrayal) recited, as an answer in kind, the verse 10 of *Sura LXVI*. "God gives out a similarity of the Disbelievers to the wife of Noah and to the wife of Lot, who betrayed their husbands, the two righteous devotees of the Lord, and nothing could avail them against God, who ordered them to enter the Fire (of Hell) along with other convicts". She stirred up the malcontents against Othmán, saying that the sheets wrapped over the Prophet's body had not yet changed their colour in his grave when his Doctrines of Faith have been discarded by Othmán and treated as dead letters.

As the Haj season was approaching and Ayesha intended to proceed on pilgrimage, she made up the contribution of her share towards the murder of the Caliph by stirring up the insurgents and continuously telling them "Kill this old magician, may God slay him". While she was taking her way to Mecca, Marwán told her that she was shaking herself free from the conspirators, having commanded them to do away with the Caliph. She retorted that she would like to have him suspended to her neck, inclosed in a sack, to be carried and drowned into the Red Sea. Simon Ockley in his History of the Saracens writes: "Ayesha, Mohammed's widow, was his (Othmán's) mortal enemy, certainly it would much better have become one that pretended to have been the wife of an inspired prophet, to have spent the days of her widowhood in devotion and good works, than in doing mischief and embroiling the State. But she was so prejudiced in favour of Talha and the son of Zobeir, whom she would fain have raised to the dignity of Caliph, that no consideration of virtue or decency could hinder her from doing everything in her power to compass the death of Othmán."

Violent attitude against Othman.

Othmán's palace was surrounded by the insurgents, but for several weeks he used to come out and lead the usual prayers in the Mosque. They joined the worshippers, but one day they cast dust in the face of Othmán. On a subsequent Friday when the prayers were done, † Othmán, mounting the pulpit, first appealed to the better sense of the citizens and then turning to the insurgents addressed them thus, "The Prophet cursed the people who rose up against the Caliph of the Prophet and his vicegerent, and the people of Medina condemn the lawless attitude." He advised them to repent of their evil deeds and atone for them by doing good. On hearing this sermon a tumult arose and the people threw stones at the Caliph, one of which struck Othmán and he fell from the pulpit to the ground and swooned. He was not, however, seriously hurt and for some days still presided at the daily prayers. ‡ On another occasion the Caliph was addressing the congregation in the Mosque in the same strain, leaning upon the Prophet's staff (a sacred relic which had come down from the Prophet to his successors), when an Arab seized and broke it over Othmán's head.

The blockade of Othman's palace.

The violent attitude of the mob forced Othmán to shut himself up in his palace, and a virtual blockade ensued. The entrance to the palace, however, where a guard of armed men was posted by Othmán, was still safe. As the holy month of the Haj pilgrimage was at hand, Othmán was advised by his friends to sally forth on pilgrimage to Mecca, in order that the piety of the undertaking, the sanctity of the pilgrim garb, and the sacredness of the truce months would be the sources of protection, but he rejected the advice; and coming over the roof of his palace called Abdalláh, the son of Abbás, who was one of the party guarding the gate, and bade him to lead the pilgrims' rites at Mecca. He undertook the duty and proceeded to Mecca.

† Abul Fida. ‡ Ibn Khaldun; Tárikh-al-Khamis.

As soon as Othmán was convinced that the rebels were ready to go to the extremes as they had already shown their colours, he sent urgent messages demanding succour from Mo'áwiya in Syria, Abdalláh b. Amir in Bussorah and Abdalláh b. Abi Sarh in Egypt and sent a letter to Ibn Abbás to be read out to the pilgrims at Mecca to hasten to his relief.

Talha's collusion with the insurgents.

†Talha pressed the insurgents to the strict enforcement of the blockade so that the privations of the siege might be keenly felt by the besieged. This was overheard by Othmán, who happened to listen from inside of his palace to what was going on among the besiegers outside, and the Caliph was astonished to find out that Talha had actually colluded with the insurgents, and the Caliph cursed him for his ambitious aim. The insurgents vigorously enforced the blockade and every approach to the palace was closed, allowing neither ingress nor egress. The supply of water to the palace was cut off and the privation was keenly felt by the besieged. When Othmán saw himself reduced to this strait, he sent for Ali and appealed to him for relief. According to some historians, Ali upbraided the insurgents for cutting off the supply of water and sent his sons Hasan and Hosain with some skins full of water to the palace of Othmán. The insurgents, respecting the memory of the Prophet, who had fondled the children—now grown up youths—in his lap for years, let them go unchecked and thus the water reached to the great relief of Othmán and all those shut up with him.

Apprehending from the ferocity, with which the investment was now pressed, that the end was not far, Othmán, from the flat roof of his palace offered the usual salutations preparatory to open an address to the besiegers below, but none having returned the salute, he asked if Talha was among them. Receiving a reply in the affirmative from Talha himself, the Caliph reproached him

† Ibn Qoteiba; Tabari.

for not receiving his salutation, to which Talha replied that he had answered but his voice might not have reached the Caliph's ears. Then the Caliph asked if Zobeir and Sa'd b. Abi Waqqás were also among them. Both of them shouted a reply. He then addressed them: In the words of Sir W. Muir: 'My fellow citizens. I have prayed to the Lord that when I am taken He may set the Caliphate aright.' After this he made a mention of his previous life, and how the Lord had made him successor of His prophet and Commander of the Faithful, 'And now,' said he, 'ye have risen up to slay the Lord's elect. Have a care ye men, (and here he addressed the besiegers) the taking of life is lawful but for three things, Apostasy, Murder, and Adultery. Taking my life without such cause, ye but suspend the sword over your own necks. Sedition and bloodshed shall not depart for ever from your midst.' They gave him audience thus far and then cried out that there was yet a fourth just cause for death *viz.* the quenching of truth by inequity and of right by violence, and that for his ungodliness and tyranny he must abdicate or be slain. For a moment Othmán was silent. Then calmly rising, he bade the citizens go back to their homes and himself, with but faint hopes of relief, turned to his dreary abode.

According to some traditions, we are told, that Othmán prevailed on Ali to procure for him a three days truce, under the pretence of issuing orders to the governors for reforms of the administration; and that he treacherously employed the time in strengthening the defences, and excused himself by saying that the time was too short to carry out the promised reforms. *Muir's Annals pp. 335 & 336.*

Murder of Othman.

The siege had lasted 40 days or so. After the first rising, Othmán used to preside at the daily prayers for over three weeks, after which he shut himself up in his palace on account of the violent attitude of the insurgents, and the investment became severe. The knowledge that the Caliph had summoned succour from the provinces; combined with the incident narrated below, infuriated the insurgents to precipitate matters in order to finish their operations. Major Price writes thus: "During the siege, one of the Order of the Prophet's Companions came forward and requested that Othmán would appear upon the terrace as he had some thing to his advantage to communicate. The Caliph complied and the conference was opened, when one of the besieged suddenly drew his bow from the battlements of the palace, and killed the officious adviser on the spot. The besiegers with eager vociferation demanded that the murderer should be delivered up; but Othmán firmly and magnanimously refused, declaring that those should never suffer whose only crimes were loyalty and devotion. But the issue of the contest was considerably accelerated by the useless piece of treachery. The assailants set fire to the palace gates and forcibly rushed in through the doors by the terraced roofs. On the other hand Marwán and Sa'id b. As, at the head of 500 Mamelukes, prepared to give the rebels a gallant reception. The aged and venerable Caliph now endeavoured to dissuade his adherents from a fruitless opposition. In the meantime, the insurgents had forced their way into the interior of the palace, and a short and sanguinary contest ensued in the courts. Marwán, who stood conspicuous at the head of his people, received a stroke from a scimitar, which laid him senseless, whilst Sa'id was shortly afterwards compelled by a wound to quit this scene of blood and outrage. The contest, notwithstanding, raged with unabated fury until Mohammed the son of Abubekr made his way into the apartment where Othmán sat with his eyes intently fixed on the sacred pages of the Qurán. He seized his sovereign by the beard, but Othmán appealing to the memory of his father, he retired without doing him further injury. Kinána, the son of Bashar, then entered the room and was preparing to strike when several others rushed in with naked swords and drew the first blood of the defenceless monarch. Náela, the wife of Othmán, threw herself upon her husband, and endeavoured to ward off the stroke of a scimitar, but in this effort of tenderness she lost the fingers of her hand, and the unhappy Caliph soon afterwards expired under repeated wounds. Three days elapsed before his murderers could permit his body to be buried. At length, through the intercession of Ali, permission was granted; and having placed his corpse upon one of the palace doors which they tore off as a subtitute for a bier, † they consigned his mutilated remains to a recess between the public burying place of Medina and that of the Jews, three of the Ansárs insisting that it should not be laid among true believers. At a subsequent period, however, Mo'áwaiya took the spot into the Mussalman enclosure.

Othmán was murdered at the age of eightytwo years on the 18th of Zhilhajja, 35 A. H. having reigned eleven years eleven months and fourteen days.

Salman Farsi.

At the close of Othmán's reign, during the year 35 A.H., Salmán Fársi, who was reckoned as a member of the Prophet's family, died at the age of 250 or (according to some) 350 years.

---

† Abul Fida.

CHAPTER XXI.

Ali b. Abi Talib.

Contemplations for the election of a Caliph in place of Othman.

After the murder of Othmán terror reigned in the city and the regicides had the entire mastery of it, there being no settled Government in Medina. The principal citizens, feeling the tumultuous state of the populace and apprehending civil war, clamoured for the instant election of a Caliph. The threatening attitude of those who had come from various parts of the empire *viz*. Egypt, Syria, Mesopotamia and Persia on the occasion, was a source of great alarm; because they were resolved not to disperse until they knew whom they were to look upon as their sovereign.

There were two candidates, Talha and Zobeir (both brothers-in-law of Ayesha) who aspired to claim the Caliphate with the powerful support of Ayesha, but, to their great disadvantage, she was not present in Medina at this juncture, having gone on pilgrimage to Mecca, as already observed. Talha, who had taken an active part in instigating the besiegers of Othmán's dwelling to precipitate things, and his associate Zobeir, though had their pretensions urged by some people of Bussorah and Kufa, but the majority of the general public of Medina, who enjoyed the exclusive right of electing a Caliph, looked upon a third as the man best fitted for the office. He was a man admired by his friends and foes alike for his courage, eloquence, magnanimity, piety, nobility, and his near kinship to the Prophet. This was Ali, the cousin-german of the Prophet and the father of the Prophet's posterity from his best beloved daughter Fátema. He was considered as the natural claimant to the Caliphate; and the people, now wishing to be governed by the Prophet's heir, desired to see Ali elevated to his legitimate dignity. Talha and

Zobeir, cautioned by the atmosphere, held their peace and thought it prudent to dissemble their feelings so far as to take the oath of allegiance to Ali when he was elected, with a steadfast resolve, however, of breaking it as soon as a favourable opportunity should offer.

Election of Ali.

In this dilemma several of the principal men of Medina repaired to Ali and desired him to accept the government. In reply he assured them that he had no wish for temporal power and would willingly yield obedience to any other person elected by them. They, however, insisted that there was none other so well qualified as he. But to all their remonstrances, Ali was resolute in his refusal and said that he would rather like to serve another as his adviser than take the government upon himself. The insurgents, anxious to put the city back to its nomal state, which they themselves had set to its present disturbed condition, were much annoyed at the difficulty in the choice of the Caliph, and insisted that before they quitted Medina, the citizens, in exercise of their right, must elect a Caliph within one day, as they were the proper persons to determine the controversy, or, if the choice was not made within the time allowed by them, they would put to sword the leading men of Medina. Upon this the people again came to Ali in the evening and explaining to him the situation, earnestly entreated him to reconsider their position and the menace to the religion. Overcome at length with their pathetical expostulations, Ali consented with reluctance saying: 'If you excuse me and elect another, whomsoever you may think fit to choose, I shall most submissively yield obedience to him. If not, and I must comply with your wish to accept the offer, I must say frankly at the outset that I shall conduct the administration quite independently, and I shall deal with all of you according to the Holy Book of the Lord and to the best of my knowledge and judgment.' They unhesitatingly assented and proferred to give him their hand in token of doing fealty to him; but he refused to do anything, unless it were in public, in order that no one might have cause to grumble. "Ali was apprehensive of the intrigues of Ayesha, Talha and Zobeir and the whole house of Omyya (of which Moáwiya, Othman's lieutenant in Syria, was chief), who, he knew, would avail themselves of every opportunity to oppose and disturb his government. Ockley's His. Sar. p. 289.

Inauguration of Ali as Caliph.

Next morning (on the fourth day after Othmán's murder), the people assembled in large numbers in the great Mosque, where Ali made his appearance, clad in a simple cotton gown and a coarse turban wound round his head with a bow in his right hand and his slippers in the left, which he had taken off in reverence of the place. Talha and Zobier being not present, he caused them to be sent for. When they came, they offered him their hands in approbation of his election as Caliph. But Ali paused and said to them, that if they were sincere in their hearts they might do him fealty in good earnest; assuring them at the same time, that if either of them would accept the Caliphate, he was quite willing to do him fealty with perfect sincerity and would be glad rather to serve him as his adviser than to take the government upon himself. This, however, both of them declined, and expressing their perfect satisfaction, stretched forth their hands to pay homage to Ali. Talha's right arm was maimed, having received a wound in the battle of Ohod, he could therefore stretch it forth with difficulty. As he was the first to begin with the ceremony, the audience took it as an evil omen and a by-stander remarked: 'It is likely to be a lame business that is begun with a lame hand.' The presage proved only too true by subsequent events. The audience then swore allegiance to Ali and their example was followed by the general public. None of the Omyyads and the immediate adherents of Othmán came in, nor did Ali press any one to come in and do fealty to him. There were also some prominent men in Medina, who kept themselves aloof, not liking to pay homage to Ali. These were (according to Mas'udi) Sa'd b. Abi Waqqás, Maslama b. Khálid. Moghira b. Sho'ba, Qidáma

b. Matz'un, Wahbán b. Saifi, Abdalláh, b. Salám, Hassán b. Thábit, Ka'b b. Málik, Abu Sa'id Khudri, Mohammed b. Maslama, and Abdalláh † b. Omar, Fidzála b. Abeed, Ka'b b. Ajza ; Habib-al-Siyar adds: Zaid b. Thábit, Osáma b. Zaid, Abu Musa Ash'ari, Zaid b. Ráfe,' Salma b. Saláma, Sohaib b. Sinán, No'mán b. Bashir; Tabari adds: Ráfe' b. Khadij. These people were named Mo'tazilities.

The insurgents, having themselves done homage to Ali, departed to their homes.

The cry for the revenge of Othman's murder.

After the inauguration, of Ali, Talha and Zobeir, with several others, came to Ali and asked him that the murder of Othmán ought by all means to be avenged, proferring their services to attain the end. Ali knew full well that the crime was perpetrated hardly against their own will and even before their eyes, that now their cry for vengeance was nothing but a design to foment disturbance by calling up a host of enemies. He, therefore, explained to them that the event had its foundations in old dissensions; that there were several parties different in opinion from one another; that it was not the moment to stir up a civil war; that the discontent was instigated by the devil, who, when once holds the ground, never quits it easily; and that the very measure they suggested to undertake was the devil's own proposal to foster unrest and tumult. However, he told them that he had already sent for Marwán, the Secretary of Othmán, and Náela the wife of Othmán, who were all the time in the same house with Othmán, to enquire as to the real culprits who perpetrated the murder. Marwán was not forthcoming, while Náela said that they were two persons but she could name or identify none. He added that several persons were said to be implicated in the crime but no evidence could be available against them. Under the circumstances, he swore that

† (Mas'udi stains the character of Abdalláh b. Omar by his keeping himself from paying homage to Caliph Ali and later on swearing allegiance to Yazid b. Mo'áwiya as Caliph, and again to Abd al Malik b. Marwán.

unless all parties united, if it so pleased God, it was difficult to take successful steps. He asked them what method they would propose as best suited to gain the end. They replied that they knew of none. Then he said: 'If you will point out the real assassins of Othmán, I shall not fail to vindicate the majesty of the Divine Law in putting them to their dues.' They were silent. Thus their insidious proposition being turned down they departed.

In the meantime, warned by the sudden departure of the Omyyad families, Ali began to secure the good will of the Qoreish and the Ansárs by showing his high appreciation of their worth, for he was desirous of having as many friends as possible against the apprehended trouble with the Omyyads.

Reforms contemplated by Ali.

The next matter for immediate attention of the new Caliph was the removal of the ungodly men, who governed various provinces with such tyranny that it drove the people to desperation, which cost Othmán his life. Many abuses had crept in during the reign of Othmán, which called for immediate action, and most of the governments of provinces were in the hands of persons of equivocal antecedents and suspected faith. Determined upon a thorough reform, he resolved to depose Mo'áwiya and the other governors, who had received their appointments from his predecessor. Abdalláh b. Abbás, who had returned by now from his pilgrimage at Mecca, strongly opposed this measure, especially that of Mo'áwiya's deposition, and advised him to postpone the execution of this reform for a short while, till at least, he should find himself more firmly established in authority. He argued: 'If thou deposest Mo'áwiya, the Syrians, whom he hast firmly attached to himself by his munificence, will rise up against thee in a body, will not recognise thee Caliph and worst of all, they will accuse thee of the murder of Othmán. It will be advisable, therefore, to let him continue in his place till he submits to thy authority, and when once he hast done that, it will be easy for thee to pull him out of his house by the ears whensoever thou dost desire it.' 'Besides,' he reminded Ali, 'Talha and Zobeir are not the persons to be relied upon; I have good reasons to suspect them of taking up arms against thee very soon, and perhaps they may join Mo'áwiya.' 'But the Divine Law,' said Ali, 'dost not allow of crafty deceptions. I must strictly follow the true principles of religion and therefore should not willingly allow any ungodly man to retain his office. Mo'áwiya will have nothing but the sword from me. I cannot retain him for a single day.' 'See,' continued he, 'I appoint thee, O Ibn Abbás! Thou shalt go forth thyself to Syria to turn him out.' 'That', cried Ibn Abbás, 'is quite impracticable, Mo'áwiya would not leave me alive because of my being akin to thee.'

When these arrangements were in progress, Talha and Zobeir came to Ali and applied for their appointment to the governments of Kufa and Bussorah respectively. But Ali politely refused, observing that in his present emergencies he needed such able counsellors at hand.

Having chosen his men for the government of the various provinces, Ali sent them out to their destinations in the month of Moharram 36 A.H. to replace the existing governors. Thus he sent (1) Obeidalláh b. Abbás to Yemen; (2) Qais b. Sa'd b. Obáda to Egypt; (3) Qutham b. Abbás to Mecca; (4) Samáha b. Abbás to Tiháma; (5) Awn b. Abbás to Yamáma; (6) Othmán b. Honeif to Bussorah, (7) Ammára b. Shaháb to Kufa; (8) Sa'id b. Abbás to Bahrein; and (9) Sahel b. Honeif to Syria.

Obeidalláh reached Yemen and found that Ya'la, his predecessor, had carried off to Mecca all the treasure † amounting to sixty thousand Dinárs, which he made over to Ayesha along with six hundred camels, one of which was a rarity, a big-sized, well bred animal, valued at 200 gold pieces. It was named Al-Askar and was

† Rawdzat-al-Ahbáb; Ibn Athir; Ibn Khaldun.

specially presented for the use of Ayesha. Obeidalláh, however, took possession of the govrnment of Yemen.

Qais b. Sa'd, when approaching Egypt, was opposed by a party of Othmán's in passing a frontier garrison; but by feigning attachment to the cause of Othmán, he succeeded to reach the seat of his government, which he occupied. His predecessor, Abdalláh b. Abi Sarh, being certain of his removal, had already made his way to Syria to take refuge with Mo'áwiya, as most of the Omyyads had done on the accession of Ali.

Othmán b. Honeif, who went to Bussorah, entered unopposed; but Ibn Amir, his predecessor, had also already made away with all the treasure and joined Talha and Zobeir. Othmán occupied his post but found that disaffection was rife against Ali among a considerable number of the people.

Ammára on his way to Kufa was met by Tulaiha and Qa'qá', at the stage named Zabála, and they advised him to go back to Medina as the Kufians, they said, were resolved not to part with Abu Musa Ash'ari, who was set over them by their own choice by the late Caliph. They warned him that if he attempted to enter Kufa, he would have to face strong hostilities. Ammára retraced his steps to Medina and reported the state of affairs to the Caliph.

When Sahel, the governor elect for Syria, reached Tabuk, he met a party of horsemen, who told him that the people of Syria were clamouring for the vengeance of Othmán's blood and would not receive a man of Ali's appointment whom they did not recognise as a Caliph. Being unprepared to force his advance, Sahel returned to Medina and reported the facts to Ali.

Scheme of the Omyyads to stir up the people against Ali's government.

In the meantime the Omyyads, sparing nothing which could possibly serve to disturb Ali and his government, carried, at the instance of † Omm Habiba, a widow of the Propht and the sister of Mo'áwiya, the blood-covered shirt in which Othmán was

† Mas'udi; Habib al Siyar.

murdered, together with the mangled fingers of Náela, his wife, to Mo'áwiya in Syria, where he used them as instruments to stir up the spirit of vengeance among his people. Amr b. As, the witty counsellor of Mo'áwiya, said to him: 'Show the dam her foal, it will stir her bowels'; and he accordingly suspended the shirt with the mangled fingers attached thereto on the pulpit of the Mosque at Damascus. At times these emblems were carried about in the army. These objects, daily exposed to view, exasperated the Syrians, who wept till their beards were wet with tears, and swore vengeance upon the murderers of Othmán.

Mo'awiya's defiance of Ali's authority.

When Sahel returned, Ali asked Talha and Zobier to mark the extent to which the parties were divided and which he had cautioned them against. They replied that, if they were allowed to go out of Medina, they would be answerable if the disturbance did not cease. Upon this Ali said that sedition was like fire, the more it burnt the stronger it grew and the brighter it shone; he would, however, bear it so long as it was possible, and when it became unbearable he would try to extinguish it. He resolved in the first instance, to write a letter to Mo'áwiya and also to Abu Musa demanding their allegiance. Abu Musa replied that he himself and the Kufians, with some exceptions, were entirely at his service; but from Mo'áwiya no reply was forthcoming though weeks elapsed. In fact Mo'áwiya had detained the messenger to witness the spirit of his armies clamouring impatiently to revenge the blood of Othmán, but, being faithfully submissive to him, only waited a word of command from him to march against all concerned. After several weeks Mo'áwiya permitted the messenger to go back to Medina, accompanied by a messenger of his own, who carried a despatch which was superscribed on the cover with the words 'from Mo'áwiya to Ali.' According to the instructions given him by Mo'áwiya, when his messenger reached Medina, he carried the despatch aloft upon a staff on purpose to be seen by the people in the streets. Being well aware of

Mo'áwiya's disaffection to Ali, the people thronged anxious to know what the contents of the message might be. It was just three months after the murder of Othmán that the despatch was presented to Ali, who read the address and breaking open the seal found all blank within, which he rightly took as a token of utmost defiance. Astonished at the contemptuous effrontery of Mo'áwiya, he asked the messenger to explain the enigma. † Upon this the messenger having begged and received assurance for the safety of his life answered: "Know then, I have left behind me in Syria sixty thousand warriors bewailing the murder of Othmán under his blood-stained shirt by the pulpit of the great Mosque at Damascus, all bent on revenging the death of the Caliph on thee."

"On me!" cried Ali in astonishment. "I call God to witness that I am not guilty of it. O God! I seek Thy protection against so false a charge." Ali then declared that only the sword could be the arbitrator betwixt Mo'áwiya and himself; and turning to Ziyád b. Hantala who sat by him, said that an expedition against Syria might be proclaimed, which Ziyád soon communicated to the people.

† The messenger's reply to Ali is given by Major Price thus: "Fifty thousand men are assembled about the robes of Othmán, whose cheeks and beards have never been dry from tears, and whose eyes have never ceased from weeping blood, since the hour of that prince's atrocious murder. They have drawn their swords with a solemn pledge never to return them to the scabbard, nor cease from mourning, until they have extirpated all concerned in that detested transaction. This sentiment they have left as a solemn bequest to their descendants; and the earliest principle that mothers instil into the minds of their infant offsping is, to revenge the blood of Othmán to the last extremity.' This insolent speech excited the anger of the attendants of the Caliph to such a degree, that, had not Ali interposed, serious consequences might have ensued. Strange to say, this magnanimity on the part of Ali operated like magic on the messenger of Mo'áwiya, who then declared himself convinced of his error, and solemnly swore that for the future he would never voluntarily separate from the person of Ali, or acknowledge the authority of any other sovereign to his prejudice." *S. Ockley's His. Sar. p. 295.*

Departure of Talha & Zobeir.

Talha and Zobeir, whose desire to quit Medina was twice thwarted, now, seeing how the affairs were drifting, were anxious to acquire freedom of action, which they could not effect so long as they remained in Medina. Once more, therefore, they came to Ali and asked of him leave to proceed to Mecca on pretext of performing the Lesser Pilgrimage. Ali, who understood their motive, reminded them of their declaration of free will in swearing him allegiance on the day of his inauguration and gave them leave to depart, saying that he expected strange things from them and therefore he had insisted upon them their sincerity in taking the oath.

Ali began preparations for the expedition to Syria, calling for assistance from all the provinces and endeavouring recruitment from Medina; but before clashing arms with Mo'áwiya, he had to face another serious rebellion, which is described in detail below:

Ayesha's plans for rebellion.

Ayesha, on her way back from the pilgrimage at Mecca, met Ibn Omm Kaláb at Sarif. He informed her of Othmán's murder and Ali's accession to the Caliphate. Hearing this news she cried, 'Carry me back to Mecca' and, repeating it, she said, 'By God! Othmán was innocent, I will avenge his blood.' She went instantly back to Mecca along with her confederate Hafsa † and began to propagate sedition there. Sir. W. Muir in his Annals of the early Caliphate on pages 351 and 352 gives the following account of Ayesha relating to this incident: "In the early period of Othmán's troubles, Ayesha is said to have contributed her share towards fomenting public discontent. We are told that she even abetted the conspirators, among whom her brother Mohammed son of Abubekr was a chief leader. When on receiving the tidings of the murder, on her way back from Mecca, she declared that she would avenge Othmán's death. 'What!' cried her informant, startled by her zeal, 'is this thy speech now, whilst but yesterday

† Tabari.

thou wast foremost to press the attack upon him as an apostate?' 'Yea', she replied, 'but even now he repented him of that which they laid to his charge, and yet after that they slew him.' In reply her informant recited the verses purporting to say: 'Thou wast the first to foment the discontent. Thou commendedst us to slay the prince for his apostasy, and now etc.' Anyhow it must be admitted that Ayesha was a jealous, violent, intriguing woman, a character that may well account for much that would otherwise appear strange." In fact Ayesha expected either of the two, Talha nnd Zobeir, to succeed Othmán, but now, contrary to her expectations, hearing of the election of Ali, whom she detested, she was extremely disturbed in mind and thought of adopting open hostilities. Declaring herself avenger of Othmán's blood, she induced the great and powerful clan of Omyya, to which Othmán belonged, to join her cause. Those Omyyads, who still resided at Mecca and those who had fled from Medina on the accession of Ali, readily gathered under her flag. The deposed governors of several provinces also came in, one after the other, and, persuading easily a large number of malcontents, made common cause with her. Ya'la, the ex-governor of Yemen, furnished her with ample means to carry on war by presenting her the treasure, which he had carried off from Yemen.

Talha and Zobeir join Ayesha in her rebellion.

It was nearly four months after the murder of Othmán when Talha and Zobeir reached Mecca and found things well in progress. They were near relatives of Ayesha; her youngest sister was a wife of Talha, who was also a cousin of her father Abubekr, and her eldest sister was a wife of Zobeir, whose son Abdalláh was adopted by Ayesha. Notwithstanding their oath of allegiance to Ali, which they now said they swore under compulsion and were not therefore bound to abide by it, they longed to take up her cause, which, in case of success, was sure to prove to their own benefit. Accordingly, they joined Ayesha and began to take measures against Ali, promulgating among the faction at Mecca that Ali's affairs were quite in an unsettled condition. "Ayesha, Talha and Zobeir who had always been enemies to Othmán, and were, in fact, the contrivers of his death and destruction, when they saw Ali elected, whom they hated equally, if not more, made use of Othmán's real and sincere friends as instruments of their malice against the new Caliph. So that from very different motives they all unanimously joined in demanding satisfaction for the murder of Othmán." *Simon Ockley's His. Sar. p. 294.* The standard of rebellion was raised and the tale of these distinguished persons was eagerly listened to by the factious and the revengeful Arabs at large, whose fathers and brothers were killed by Ali in defending the Prophet's cause on the occasion of various wars in his time. Many a discontented Arab flocked under the Standard. The treasure, which Ibn Amir the deposed governor of Bussorah had brought away with him, was now utilized by Talha and Zobeir in equipping the force.

War Council.

The preparations for war having been completed, the leaders of the rebellion held a council to discuss the place where the operations could be carried on with success. Ayesha proposed to march upon Medina to attack Ali in his capital and to strike at the very root; but it was protested by representations that the people of Medina were unanimously in favour of Ali, and too powerful to be assailed with success. Some suggested to proceed to Syria and to make a joint attack with the insurgents there; but Walid b. Oqba strongly opposed this suggestion, saying that Mo'áwiya would not approve of the presence of his superiors in his capital, much less the control of his armies by them in such critical times; rather he would take it ill as an interference in his designs to gain independence, which, as a matter of fact, kept him from sending succour demanded of him as a feudatory chief by Othmán, whose days of life he already expected as numbered. The objection being weighty, the suggestion was dropped. At last, Talha having assured them that he had a strong party in his favour at Bussorah and that he was confident of its surrender, it was finally resolved to march toward that city. A proclamation was accordingly made by beat of drum through the streets of Mecca that Ayesha, the Mother of the Faithful, accompanied by the distinguished chiefs, Talha and Zobeir, was going in person to Bussorah; that all those who were desirous of revenging the atrocious murder of the prince of the faithful *viz.* Othmán, and of doing service to the cause of the Faith, should join her, even if they had no equipments, which would be furnished to them as soon as they came in.

Ayesha's instigations to Omm Selma.

Ayesha desired Omm Selma, another of the Mothers of the Faithful, who had been at Mecca on pilgrimage, to accompany her in the adventure, but she indignantly refused the invitation, and reasoned with Ayesha if she was justified to venture against the dictates of the Prophet in opposing Ali, who, she pointed out, was also Caliph duly elected unanimously by the people of Medina and acknowledged by the people of several provinces. Reciting the Prophet's saying: "Ali is my vicegerent in my life as also on my death, whosoever disobeys him disobeys me," she asked Ayesha if she had heard the Prophet say so. She assented. Then Omm Selma reminded her of the Prophet's prediction, as follows, to which he had given utterance reproachfully to his wives: 'A short while after, the dogs of Hawáb shalt bark at one of my wives who wilt be amongst a rebellious mob. Oh! that I knew who she was! Beware O Homeira! lest thou shouldst be the one.' Ayesha, on these demonstrations of truth, was alarmed. Omm Selma continuing her warnings said: 'Do not let thyself be beguiled by Talha and Zobeir. They shalt entangle thee into wrong but would not be able to extricate thee from the wrath or disgrace that may befall thee.' Ayesha returned to her lodging half inclined to desist from her scheme, but the entreaties of her adopted son, Abdalláh b. Zobeir, persuaded her vindictive nature to avenge herself upon the man who had once associated himself with the Prophet in suspecting her when a false charge was laid against her. "Ayesha, spurning the restraints of her sex, prepared to join the campaign and to stir up the people of Bussorah, as she had stirred up those of Mecca. Hafsa, daughter of Omar, another of the Mothers of the Faithful, was with difficulty restrained by her brother (who had just fled from Medina and held aloof from either side) from accompaying her sister-widow." *Muir's Annals, p. 353.*

Ayesha's march on Bussorah.

At length Ayesha, mounted in a litter on the camel al-Askar, marched forth from Mecca at the head of one thousand volunteers, 600 of them being mounted on camels and 400 on horses. She was attended on her right and left by Talha and Zobeir. On her way, many a people joined her, soon swelling the number of the rebel army to three thousand.

Moghira b. Sho'ba, the ex-governor of Bussorah and of Kufa, who held these goverments in the time of Caliph Omar, and Sa'id, one of the veteran elders of Mecca and a Mohájir of the first emigration, who also accompanied the cavalcade, suspecting the motives of Talha and Zobeir, enquired of them as to who would be the Caliph in the event of victory. 'Either of us two, as chosen by the people', was the ready response. 'And why not a son of Othmán?' asked Sa'id. To this the reply was, 'Because the elders, being distinguished chiefs and Mohájirs, should not be overlooked.' 'But I think', rejoined Sa'id, 'if you are going forth to revenge the murder of Othmán, his successor should, of a right, be his own son, two of whom Abán and Walid are already in your Camp. Your succession would mean that, under the pretended cover of Othmán's blood, you sought to fight for your own good.' 'It will, however', they answered, 'depend upon the men of Medina to choose whomsoever they like.' Moghira and Sa'id, distrusting the leaders of the rebellion, resolved to retire, and accordingly they retraced their steps to Mecca along with their followers, who formed part of a body of the rebel army. Turning to the troops, as they were passing by them shouting: 'Slay the murderers of Othmán, destroy them, one and all', Moghira cried out to Marwán and others: 'whither are ye going to hunt the murderers? They are before your eyes on the humps of their camels (pointing out towards Talha, Zobeir and Ayesha), slay them and go back to your homes. They are the proper objects of your vengeance, they had as much hand in the detested affair as anybody else.' The army, however, continued their march shouting wildly as they did. It was urged that the question of succession was premature, and Ayesha declared that the choice of a successor was the exclusive right of the men of Medina and must rest with them as heretofore; and, to avoid further misgivings, she directed that Abdalláh, the son of Zobeir, should lead the daily prayers.

Ayesha at the valley of Hawab.

On their way to Bussorah, the rebel army received intelligence that Ali, the Caliph, had come out of Medina in their pursuit. In order to reach Bussorah uninterrupted and unchecked, Ayesha ordered to change the route. Leaving aside the highway, her armies took their march by an unfrequented pathway to Bussorah. The guide, to dispel the irksomeness of the long autumn nights, whiled away his time usually singing and occasionally shouting the name of each valley, desert or village they were passing by. Reaching one night a place, he cried: "The valley of Hawáb." Struck at this name, a thrill ran through Ayesha's whole frame as instantly the dogs of the village surrounding her camel began to bark at her most clamorously. 'What place is this?' she screamed aloud, and the guide repeated in his usual tone, 'The valley of Hawáb.' The Prophet's prediction recently brought to her memory by Omm Selma, as already observed, was now uppermost in her mind, and she shiveringly exclaimed, 'Inná lilláh-wa inná ilaih-i-rájiun' *i. e.* We are resigned to God and to Him we must return. Making her camel kneel, she alighted from her litter and moaned with a deep sigh: "Alas! Alas! I am indeed the wretched woman of

Hawáb. The Prophet had already warned me against this." She declared that she would not move a step farther on. that ill-omened expedition. Talha and Zobeir entreated her in vain to proceed with her journey, telling her that the guide had mistaken the name and that the place was never called Hawáb. They even suborned fifty witnesses to swear to it; but she would not believe them and refused to step further onward. This is said to be the first public false evidence produced ever since the introduction of Islam. Thus the night and the whole of the following day they halted at Hawáb. Talha and Zobeir were quite perplexed and did not know what to do. At last, hitting upon a clever stratagem, the next night they made the army raise a cry: 'Quick! Quick! Ali is fast approaching to overtake us.' So saying, they began scampering off. Ayesha, struck with terror, instantly took to her heels, found her camel and nimbly got into her litter. The march was thus resumed.

Ayesha's encampment at Khoreiba.

The army pushed forward in haste towards Bussorah and reaching near the town encamped at Khoreiba. Ayesha sent for Ahnaf b. Qais, a leading citizen of Bussorah, and asked him to join her Standard. After some discussion on the subject, he refused to take up arms against the Caliph. Resolving, however, to remain neutral, he left Bussorah with six thousand of his followers and encamped in the suburbs of Bussorah at Wádi-al-Sabá. Ayesha sent a message to Othmán b. Honeif, the Governor of Bussorah, inviting him to come to her. Immediately Ibn Honeif, putting on his armour and followed by a large number of the citizens, went forth to meet Ayesha. But to his surprise, he found the army of the insurgents arrayed on the parade-ground followed by a large number of the factious element of the citizens, who had in the meantime joined Ayesha to stand by her side. A parley ensued: "Talha and Zobeir alternately addressed the multitude, and were followed by Ayesha, who harangued them from her camel. Her voice, which she elevated that it might be heared by all; became shrill and sharp, instead of intelligible, and provoked the merriment of some of the crowd. A dispute arose as to the justice of her appeal; mutual revilings took place between the parties; they gave each other the lie, and threw dust in each other's faces. One of the men of Bussorah then turned and reproached Ayesha: "Shame on thee, O Mother of the Faithful!" said he, "murder of the Caliph was a grievous crime, but was a less abomination than thy forgetfulness of the modesty of thy sex. Wherefore dost thou abandon thy quiet home and thy protecting veil and ride forth like a man barefaced on that accursed camel, to foment quarrels and dissensions among the Faithful?" Another of the crowd scoffed at Talha and Zobeir: "You have brought your mother with you," cried he, "why did you not also bring your wives?" Insults were soon followed by blows, swords were drawn, a skirmish ensued, and they fought until the hour of prayer separated them." *W. Irving's Succ. of Mohd. p. 172.*

The gates of the city were now closely barred against the entry of the insurgents. Some days passed in skirmishes with serious loss to the Governor's party and the rebels had the advantage of gaining some footing in the town. At length a truce was agreed upon with terms that a messenger should be sent to Medina to enquire whether Talha and Zobeir paid homage to Ali on the day of his inauguration voluntarily or under compulsion. In the former case they would be treated as rebels and in the latter their partisans in Bussorah will be justified in upholding their cause. The insurgents, who were desirous to get a chance to overpower the Governor and to take possession of the city, acquiesced in this arrangement to gain time for the longed for opportunity. A messenger was sent to Medina. When he delivered his errand, the people were all silent. At last Osáma stood up and said that they were compelled. But this assertion of Osáma would have cost him his life, had not a friend of his *viz.* Sohaib, a man of influence and authority, taken him under his protection and led him home.

Seizure of Bussorah by Ayesha.

In the meantime the insurgent leaders endeavoured to draw Ibn Honeif, the Governor of Bussorah, to their Camp by friendly messages, but he suspected treachery, confined himself to his own house and substituted Ammár in office. Talha and Zobeir, taking a chosen band one stormy dark night, mixed with the congregation in the mosque in the guise of worshippers, surprised the Governor after killing forty of his guard and took him prisoner. On the following day Hakim b. Jabala tried to release the prisoner, but in his efforts lost his life together with seventy of his followers. A serious conflict raged throughout the city, resulting in the total discomfiture and heavy loss of Ali's party. Ayesha entered the city in state and the government of Bussorah, together with the Treasury, passed into the hands of the insurgents.

Soon after the capture of Othmán b. Honeif, Ayesha was asked in what way it was her pleasure to dispose of him. She passed sentence of death on him, but on the entreaties of a woman of her retinue she was moved to spare his life. He was doomed, however, to suffer still greater evils before he could escape from the hands of his captors. His beard, moustaches and eyebrows were plucked out hair by hair and he was then contemptuously turned out.

Tidings to Ali of Ayesha's revolt.

The reader might naturally be anxious to know what Ali, the Caliph, was doing so long. I will therefore leave the insurgents in possession of Bussorah and will follow Ali: Rumours of the disturbance at Mecca reached Medina, but Ali said that unless an overt action of the malcontents threatened the unity of Islam, he would not take drastic measures against them. After some time, Omm Selma, † who had spurned the proposals of Ayesha at Mecca, as already observed, repaired to Medina soon after the departure of the rebels. to Bussorah and informed Ali of the revolt of Ayesha, Talha and Zobeir. Again, an urgent

† Rawdzat-al-Ahbáb.

message was received from Omm-al-Fadzl the widow of Abbás at Mecca with news of the rebels' designs against the Caliph and of their march upon Bussorah.

On receipt of the intelligence, Ali assembled the people in the great Mosque and called them to arms and to follow him against the rebels. The Caliph's eloquent address and warm appeal was received with coldness and apathy‡ which pervaded the assembly. No one appeared ready to respond to the call; as some of them had in their consideration the fact that the person against whom they were urged to take up arms was none other than the Mother of the Faithful *i. e.* Ayesha; others dreaded a civil war; some doubted if Ali might not in some degree have been implicated in the death of Othmán, which had been so artfully charged against him. For three consecutive days Ali tried his best to move the audience to bestir themselves. At last on the third day Ziyád b. Hantzela rose and stepped up to Ali with these words: 'Let whomsoever will, hold back, I shall go forward.' Following his example two Ansárs, Abul-Hathim and Khazima b. Thábit, came forth saying: 'The Prince of the Faithful is innocent of the murder of Othmán, we must join him.' Instantly Abu Qatáda, another Ansár, a man of distinction, stood up and drawing his sword exclaimed: "*The Apostle of God, upon whom be peace, girded me with this sword. I have kept it sheathed a long while; but now it is high time to draw it against these wicked men who are always deceiving the people." Simon Ockley's His. Sar. p. 300.* Even Omm Selma ¶ in the enthusiasm of her zeal for Ali said to him: 'O Commander of the Faithful! If it were permitted by Law, I myself would have accompanied thee in thy expedition, but I know thou wouldst not allow it; so I offer the services of my son Omar b. Abi Selma who is dearer to me than my own life. Let him go with thee and partake of thy fortunes.' Ali accepted the offer and Omar b. Abi Selma accompanied him in the expedition. He was a man of valour, possessed of piety and many good qualities, and

‡ Ibn Athir. ¶ Tabari; Ibn Khaldun;

was subsequently appointed governor of Bahrein.

Ali's march against Ayesha.

In short, a levy of nine hundred men could be raised with difficulty. The cold attitude of the people of Medina at this critical juncture made Ali so dejected that he resolved not to come back among them but to change his seat of government elsewhere. However, at the head of this small force of nine †hundred men he marched out of Medina wishing to overtake the rebels on their way to Bussorah. Arriving at Rabazha (on the outskirts of Nejd), he found out that the insurgents had already passed and were beyond reach on their road. Though joined on his march by the Bani Tay and some other loyal tribes, still not being sufficiently equipped for further advance, he ordered a halt at Zhi Qár waiting for reinforcements from Kufa, where he had sent Mohammed b. Abubekr and Abdalláh b. Ja'far to Abu-Musa-al-Ash'ari, the governor, requesting him to urge the people to come over to their Caliph in order to repair with him to the rebels and to try for the re-union of a divided people.

Abu Musa-al-Ash'ari's conduct towards the Caliph.

Abu-Musa cherished no good will towards the Caliph, for his having sent Ammára b. Shaháb to supplant him, as has been noticed; and he was a man of lukewarm spirit. Ayesha had already sent him letters to dissuade his people from their allegiance to Ali and to persuade them to rise up to avenge the murder of Othmán. Apprehensive of the success of Ayesha at Bussorah, he had already begun to waver in his allegiance to Ali and to advocate her cause to the people. When the Caliph's messengers arrived at Kufa and gave out his command, there was perfect silence among the audience in the mosque. At length the people asked Abu-Musa how he advised them in the matter of going out as desired by the Caliph. He gravely replied that the going out and the sitting quietly at home were two different things. The former was the way of the world while the latter was the

† Rawdzat-al-Safá.

heavenly way. They should take their choice. Enraged at hearing him speak thus, the Caliph's envoys reproached him, to which he answered with an oath that the homage done to Othmán hung still round his neck and round the neck of his master (meaning Ali) as well as his people; so † they were resolved to see the murderers of Othmán cleared out withersoever they were; and so long as any of the murderers remained they would not go out to join an expedition. He desired Mohammed b. Abubekr and Abdalláh b. Ja'far to go back as fast as they could to Ali and tell him so.

‡ In the meantime Othmán b. Honeif, the ex-governor of Bussorah, presented himself at Zhi-Qár—his appearance was strange indeed. The Caliph recognised him and observed with a smile that he had left him an old man but he returned to him a beardless youth. In fact Othmán had a remarkably beautiful beard, the loss of which, together with the hair plucked out of his moustaches and eyebrows, gave him an uncanny appearance, which made all smile. He recounted the misfortunes he had experienced at the hands of the insurgent leaders, and the Caliph sympathised with him for his sufferings and comforted him by assuring him that his sufferings would be counted as merits. He then said that the men who were the first to accept him as a Caliph were the first to break their oath of fealty and the first to rise up in rebellion against him. He wondered at their voluntary submission to Abubekr, Omar and Othmán and their opposition to him.

As soon as Mohammed b. Abubekr and Abdalláh b. Ja'far came back and reported what Abu-Musa had said, the Caliph despatched || Ibn Abbás and Málik-al-Ashtar to Kufa to use their influence over the Kufians. Arrived at Kufa, they delivered the message and invoked the assistance of the Kufians. Abu-Musa, however, addressed them thus: "Brethren! The Companions of the Prophet know better of God and his Prophet than those who are

---

† Tabari. ‡ Abul Fida. || Ibn Athir.

not Companions. The disturbance is amongst the Companions; they know best who is to be trusted. You should not meddle with their affairs. For such an occasion the Prophet had said: 'There would be a disturbance in which he that sleepeth is better than he that is awake; and he that is awake is better than he that sitteth; and he that sitteth is better than he that standeth; and he that standeth is better than he that walketh; and he that walketh is better than he that rideth.' Wherefore sheath your swords, cut your bow strings and put off your lances. Sit quietly in your houses and receive the injured to your hospitality till the disturbance is ceased. Let the Companions of the Prophet be all agreed. You need not make war against any. Let those who have come to you from Medina return back."

Abu Musa's deposition from the government of Kufa.

Ibn Abbás and Málik-al-Ashtar went back and reported this to the Caliph, who then sent his son Hasan accompanied by Ammár Yásir, who had been for some time governor of Kufa during the reign of Caliph Omar and who for his outspoken remarks had been severely maltreated by Caliph Othmán. Málik-al-Ashtar (a man possessed of initiative and determination, exercising great influence over the Kufians), who was irritated by the prevarications of Abu-Musa in his previous mission, followed Hasan along with Qartza b. Ka'b Ansár, who was nominated by the Caliph to replace Abu-Musa in office. Abu-Musa received Al-Hasan quite respectfully, but when in the Mosque the assistance required by the Caliph was sought for, he opposed the proposal as vigorously as before, repeating the saying of the Prophet as mentioned in the foregoing paragraph *viz.* 'There should be a disturbance in which he that sleepeth is better than he that walketh etc.' Ammár Yásir, the venerable old favourite of the Prophet aged about 90, a stern soldier and veteran, now General of the Horse in Ali's forces, hearing the cunning speech of Abu-Musa, tartly replied to him that he had mis-applied the words of the Prophet which were meant to rebuke such men as Abu-Musa himself, who were far better sleeping than awake, better sitting than standing etc. Still Abu-Musa persisted in hindering the people from complying with the envoys' proposals. A tumult ensued when Zaid † b. Sohán stood up and read out a letter from Ayesha commanding him either to remain at home neutral or to join her. Having read this letter he produced another, meant for the Kufian general public to the same effect. Having read both these letters he remarked: 'She is required by the Qurán and by the Prophet to sit quietly at home in her house, and we to fight till there should be no sedition. She commands us to play her part while she has taken ours upon herself.' Some people among the audience reproached Zaid for this remark against the Mother of the Faithful. Abu-Musa again began his address in opposition to the Caliph, upon which some of the audience chided him for his unfaithfulness and disloyalty and forced him to leave the pulpit which was then occupied by Al-Hasan b. Ali.

‡ Abu-Musa had to leave not only the pulpit but also the mosque at once, as some of the men of the garrison stationed at the Governor's castle came crying to him, bearing evidence of having been severely beaten with batons or sticks. It may be explained that, while the debate was conducted in the mosque, Málik-al-Ashtar taking a party of his men seized the castle of the Governor by surprise, caused the garrison to be soundly beaten and sent them to the mosque, to cut short the debate. This prompt measure of Al-Ashtar produced the desired effect; and, moreover, it placed the cold-spirited conduct of Abu-Musa in such a ridiculous light that the feelings of the populace were instantly turned against him. He proceeded to the castle in haste only to receive orders from Málik to vacate it at once. The mob at the gate were ready to plunder his goods, but Málik interposed and granted Abu Musa twenty four hours time to take out his goods.

---

† Tabari. ‡ Ibn Athir ; Ibn Khaldun

Hasan b. Ali raising a levy of 9000 Kufians.

From the pulpit Al-Hasan very fluently addressed the congregation. "He maintained the innocence of his father in regard to the assassination of Othmán. His father, he said, had either done wrong, or had suffered wrong. If he had done wrong, God would punish him. If he had suffered wrong, God would help him. The case was in the hands of the Most High. Talha and Zobeir who were the first to inaugurate him, were the first to turn against him. What had he done, as Caliph, to merit such opposition ? What injustice had he committed ? What covetous or selfish propensity had he manifested ?" ***W. Irwing's Succ. of Mohd. p. 177.*** Wherefore come on and command that which is good and forbid that which is evil. The eloquence of Al-Hasan was powerfully effective ; the heads of the tribes were telling each other that they had given their hands in allegiance to Ali. He had done them the honour by wishing to make them arbitrators in such an important affair. They were sorry for not giving heed to the messengers which necessitated the Caliph to depute his own son to come to them asking their assistance. They finally concluded that they ought to obey their Caliph and must comply with such a reasonable demand. Hasan told them that he was going back to his father and that those who thought fit to accompany him might do so, while others may follow by land or by water. Accordingly †nine thousand Kufians came over to Ali, some by land and some by water. Welcoming them, Ali said to them : "I have called you hither to be witnesses between us and our brethren of Bussorah. If they submit peaceably, it is what we desire ; if they persist we will heal them with gentle usage, unless they fall upon us injuriously. We, on our part, will omit nothing that may, by any means, contribute to an accomodation, which we must prefer to the desolation of war." *S. Ockley's His. Sar. p. 306.*

The army of the Caliph, having been reinforced from other quarters as well, now numbered twenty thousand

† Tabari.

strong, and with this army he advanced towards Bussorah. ‡While staying at Zhi-Qár, Ali wrote letters to Ayesha, Talha and Zobeir warning them against the unwise steps they had taken and telling them that none of them could stand as legitimate avengers of the blood of Othmán, who was an Omyyad while none of them belonged to Bani Omyya. Ayesha sent a reply that affairs had already reached a stage at which warnings were useless; while Talha and Zobeir gave no written answer but sent word to inform him that they were not prepared to obey his dictates and that he was at liberty to do whatever he wished.

Ali's arrival at Bussorah.

Ayesha's army numbered thirty thousand, but it consisted mostly of raw recruits, while that of Ali's was composed principally of veterans and men who had seen service and the Companions of the Prophet. When Ali appeared with his forces marshalled in an imposing battle array before Bussorah, Ayesha and her confederates were struck with terror. ¶ Approaching Bussorah, Ali sent Qa'qá b. Amr, a Companion of the Prophet, to the rebel leaders to negotiate peace if possible. Ayesha replied that Ali should personally negotiate with them. †When Ali arrived, messages passed between the hostile forces with a view to compromising the matter. Ali, Talha and Zobeir were seen holding long conversations, walking about together backward and forward in the sight of both the armies, and the negotiations went so far that every one expected that a peace would be effected; for Ali, with his impressive eloquence, touched the hearts of Talha and Zobeir warning them against the judgement of Heaven and challenging them to the Ordeal of invoking heavenly wrath on those who promoted and prompted the murder of Othmán instigating the malefactors. In one of their conferences Ali asked Zobeir: "Hast thou forgotten how the Apostle of God once asked

‡ Rawdzat-al-Ahbáb. ¶ Al-Murtudza; Abbási.

†Tabari; Rawdzat-al-Ahbáb; Imámat-wal-Siyásat.

thee if thou did not love his dear son Ali, and when thou answered 'Yes', dost thou not remember the Prophet's prophecy: that 'nevertheless, there will come a day when thou wilt rise up against him and bring many miseries upon him and upon all the Mussalmans.' Zobeir answered that he remembered it perfectly well and he felt sorry, that had he remembered it before, he would never have taken up arms against him. Zobeir appeared determined not to fight against Ali. He returned to his Camp and acquainted Ayesha with what had passed between himself and Ali. "It is said that upon this hint he declined fighting with Ali, but that having acquainted Ayesha with the circumstances, that woman was so envenomed against him (Ali), that she would not listen to an accomodation on any terms. Others say, that his son Abdalláh (adopted by Ayesha) turned him again by asking him whether or no he was afraid of Ali's colours. Upon Zobeir answering 'No, but that he was sworn to Ali', Abdalláh bade him expiate his oath, which he did by giving a slave his liberty, and forthwith prepared without further hesitation, to fight against Ali." *S. Ockley's His. Sar. p. 307.*

The two armies were lying opposite to one another on the same field. During the night one party fell upon the other, each blaming the other for occasioning the necessity of a drawn battle. The reader may find out which of the two parties was to blame for this night attack. Which party attempted at pacification to avoid bloodshed, and which thwarted the attempts. The circumstances related above are only too clear to indicate the truth.

The battle of the camel; 'Jamal.'

Early next morning, Friday the 16th of Jamádi II, 36 A.H. (November 656 A.D.) Ayeshá took the field, mounted in a litter on her great camel Al-Askar and riding up and down among her troops, animating them by her presence and by her voice. In history the battle is named 'the battle of the camel' after the strange animal on which Ayesha was mounted, though it was fought on the field of Khoreiba close to Bussorah. Ali's army faced the enemy in battle array, but the Caliph ordered them not to take the offensive unless the enemy began the onset. He further gave stringent orders that no wounded should be slain, no fugitive pursued, no plunder seized nor the privacy of any house violated. In the meantime, showers of arrows were pouring in from the enemy; still Ali forbade his soldiers to return the shot and bade them wait. "To the very last moment Ali evinced a decided repugnance to shed the blood of a Mussalman; and just before the battle, he endeavoured to turn the adverse party to their allegiance by a solemn appeal to the Qurán. A person named Muslim immediately offered himself for the service; and uplifting a copy of the sacred volume with his right hand, this individual proceeded to admonish the enemy to recede from their unwarranted designs. But the hand which bore the holy Manuscript was severed from his arms by one* of the infuriated multitude. Seizing the charge with his left, that limb was also divided by another scimitar. Still, however, pressing it to his bosom with his mutilated remnants, he continued his exhortations until finally despatched by the swords of the enemy. His body was subsequently recovered by his friends and prayers pronounced over it by Ali in person; after which, taking up a handful of dust, and scattering it towards the insurgents, that prince imprecated upon them the retribution of an avenging Deity. In the meantime, the impetuosity of Ali's followers could no longer be restrained. Drawing their swords and pointing their spears, they rushed impetuously to the combat, which was supported on all sides with extraordinary fierceness and animosity " *Price's Mohd. His. quoted by S. Ockley p. 308.*

Talha's fate.

†During the heat of the battle when the victory began to incline towards Ali, Marwán b. al-Hakam (Secy. of the late Caliph Othmán) one of the Officers in Ayesha's army, noticed Talha urging his troops to fight valiently. 'Behold the traitor,' said he to

*According to Tabari (Persian) by Talha.

†Rawdzat-al-Ahbáb.

his slave attendant, 'but recently he was one of the murderers of the aged Caliph, now he stands the pretended avenger of his blood. What a mockery! All to gain worldly grandeur.' So saying he, in a fit of hatred and fury, shot Talha with an arrow which pierced his leg right through and struck his horse, who reared and threw the rider to the ground. In the anguish of the moment, Talha cried: "O God, take vengeance upon me for Othmán according to Thy will!" and then called for help. Seeing his footwear full of blood, he asked one of his men to pick him up behind him on his horse and convey him to Bussorah. Finding his death approaching, he called one of Ali's men, who happened to be present, 'Give me thine hand,' said the dying penitent, 'that I may put mine in it and by this act renew my oath of fealty to Ali.' With these words Talha breathed his last. It touched the generous heart of Ali when he heard it, and he said, 'Alláh would not call him to heaven until He had blotted out his first breach of his word by this last vow of fidelity.' Talha's son Mohammed was also killed in this battle.

Zobeir's fate.

Remorse and compunction had been aroused in the heart of Zobeir at Ali's reminding him of the Prophet's prophecy. He had entered, no doubt, into the battle at the instance of Ayesha and his own son, but his heart was heavy. Now he saw that †Ammár Yásir, the venerable old Companion of the Prophet, noted for his probity and uprightness, was a General in the Caliph's army; he recollected having heard from the Prophet's lips that Ammár was a person that would always be found on the side of justice and right and that he would fall under the sword of rebels. It all looked ominous to Zobeir and with a boding spirit he withdrew from the field of battle and all alone took the road to Mecca. When he came to the valley crossed by the brook Sabá where Ahnaf b. Qais was encamped with a horde of Arabs (as already observed), awaiting the issue of the battle, he was identified by

†Ibn Athir.

Ahnaf at a distance. 'Can not any one bring me tidings of Zobeir,' said he to his men. One of his men, Amr b. Jarmuz, understood the hint and immediately set off. Zobeir, seeing him approach, suspected some evil intent and bade him keep his distance. But after some discourse they made friends and both dismounted to offer prayers as it was the time for prayers. When Zobeir prostrated himself in the prayers, Amr took his opportunity and struck off Zobeir's head with one stroke of his scimitar. He carrid the head to Ali, who shed tears at the sight of it. It was the head of one who was once his friend. Turning to the man he said, 'Go, villain! Carry thy news to Ibn Safiah in hell.' This unexpected malediction so enraged the wretch, who expected a reward, that he uttered a rhapsody of abuse upon Ali; and in a fit of desperation he drew his sword and plunged it through his own heart.

Defeat of Ayesha.

Such was the end of the two great leaders of the rebels. As to Ayesha, the implacable soul of the revolt, the brave lady was still screaming unceasingly with her shrill voice, 'slay the murderers of Othmán, urging her men to fight. But the troops, bereft of their leaders, had already lost heart and were falling back upon the city. Seeing, however, that she was in peril, they stayed their flight and turned to her rescue. Rallying round her camel, one after another rushed to seize the bridle and the Standard, and one after another they were cut down. Thus seventy men perished by the bridle of the ill fated animal. Her litter, steel-plated and constructed like a cage, bristled all over with darts and arrows, and over the hump of the huge beast looked like a startled and angry hedgehog. "Convinced that the battle must remain in suspense as long as the camel continued to exhibit a rallying point to the defenders of Ayesha, Ali signified his desire to those around him that their efforts should be directed to bring down the animal. After repeated and desperate assaults, Málik-al-Ashtar succeeded at length in forcing a passage and immediately struck off one of the camel's legs. The animal preserved its posture, notwithstanding, erect and unmoved. Another leg was struck off equally without effect, and Málik-al-Ashtar, under an impression of astonishment and awe, was hesitating whether he should proceed, when Ali drew near and called out to him to strike boldly, though the animal might appear to be under the care of a supernatural agency. Thus stimulated, Málik smote the third leg, and the camel immediately sank to the earth. The litter of Ayesha being thus brought to the ground, Mohammed, the son of Abubekr, was directed by Ali to take charge of his sister and protect her from being injured by the missiles which still flew from all quarters. He drew near accordingly, but introducing his hand into the litter and happening to touch that of Ayesha, she loaded him with abuse and execration, demanding what reprobate had presumed to stretch his hand where none but the Prophet's had been permitted to intrude. Mohammed replied, that though it was the hand of her nearest in blood, it was also that of her bitterest enemy. Recognizing, however, the well known accents of her brother, the apprehensions of Ayesha were speedily dispelled." *Price's Mohd. His. as quoted by S. Ockley p. 310.*

Ali's magnanimity towards the enemy.

"Ayesha might have looked for cruel treatment at the hands of Ali, having been his vindictive and persevering enemy, but he was too magnanimous to triumph over a fallen foe." *W. Irving's Succ. of Mohd. p. 179.* When all the confusion of the battle was over, Ali came to her and asked her how she fared. Finding that she was all right and had escaped without injury, he reproachfully said to her, 'Had the Prophet directed thee to behave in this way?' She replied, 'You are victorious, be good to your fallen foe.' Ali reproached her no more and directed her brother Mohammed, who took her to the house of Abdalláh b. Khalaf a Khozáite, who was a leading citizen of Bussorah and was killed fighting for Ayesha. She asked her brother to trace out Abdalláh, the son of Zobeir, who was subsequently found lying wounded on the battlefield among the dead and wounded. As desired by Ayesha, he was brought before Ali for pardon and forgiveness. The generous-hearted conqueror magnanimously announced general amnesty to all the rebels and their confederates along with Abdalláh b. Zobeir. In spite of all this, Marwán and the Omyyads fled to Mo'áwiya in Syria or to Mecca.

Carnage in the battle.

The losses in the battle were very great. Some † historians say that 16,796 men of Ayesha's forces and 1,070 of Ali's army were killed in the battle. Others ‡ say that 10,000 of Ayesha's followers and 5,000 of Ali's men were slain. The field was, however, covered all over with the dead bodies of the slain. A trench was dug and the dead bodies of the friends and foes together were buried by order of the Caliph.

Retirement of Ayesha.

When all was quiet, Ali sent ¶ Abdalláh b. Abbás to ask Ayesha to go to Medina, but she declined, saying that she would not go to a place where the Bani Háshim were to be found. Some reproachful discourse passed between the two, after which Ibn Abbás came back to Ali and reported her refusal. Málik-al-Ashtar was then sent to her, but he also failed in his attempts to persuade her. Then Ali himself went to her and told her that she was required to sit quietly at her home where she should now go to take her abode in the place where the Prophet left her, forgetting the past. 'The Lord pardon thee,' he said, 'for what hath passed and have mercy upon thee.' But she paid no heed to his words. At || last, he sent his son Hasan with the message that if she persisted in her refusal to go to her house in Medina, she would be treated in the way of

† Habib-al-Siyar; Kashf-al-Ghamma.

‡ Tabari.

¶ Mas'udi ; Rawdzat-al-Ahbáb.

|| Rawdzat-al-Ahbáb ; Manáqib Murtadzavi ; Habib-al-Siyar ; A'tham Kufi.

which she was well acquainted. When Hasan visited her, she was dressing her hair, but hearing the message she was so perplexed that leaving her head half dressed she got up and ordered preparations for the journey. Hasan retired, but the ladies of the house enquired of her what it was in the boy that made her so uneasy after her rejecting Ibn Abbás, Málik-al-Ashtar and even Ali's suggestion. Then she narrated the incident which showed that the Prophet had authorized Ali to divorce any of the Prophet's wives during his life or after. Hasan, said she, was the bearer of a warning from Ali to enforce that authority, which made her so uneasy. Ali made proper arrangements for Ayesha's journey and directed his two sons, Hasan and Hosain, to escort her to a day's march, himself accompanying her for some distance, "By the direction of Ali, Ayesha was escorted by a retinue of women (40 or 70), apparelled as men, and their familiar approach afforded a constant subject of complaint. On her arrival at Medina, however, she discovered the delicacy of the imposture, and became as liberal in her acknowledgments as she had before been in her reproaches." *Price's Mohd. His. as quoted by S. Ockley p. 310.*

The Spoils of war.

It has been noticed that Ali had forbidden his armies to seize any plunder. "So carefully were Ali's orders against plundering observed, that whatever was found on the field, or in the insurgent Camp, was gathered together in the great mosque, and every man was allowed to claim his own. To the malcontents, who complained that they were not allowed to take booty, Ali replied that the rights of war, in this case, lasted only so long as the ranks were arrayed against each other, and that immediately on submission, the insurgents resumed their rights and privileges as brother Moslems. Having entered the city, he divided the contents of the Treasury amongst the troops which had fought on his side, promising them a still larger reward when the Lord should have delivered Syria into his hands." *Muir's Annals, p. 366.*

Ali's stay in Bussorah was not long. Having appointed Abdalláh b. Abbás as Governor, the Caliph repaired to Kufa in the month of Rajab, 36 A. H. Apprehensive of Mo'áwiya's designs against him, Ali considered Kufa suitably situated to check any encroachment in Iráq or Mesopotamia; or, in recognition of the assistance he had received from the Kufians, he transferred the seat of his government to Kufa from Medina and made it the centre of Islam and the capital of the Empire, as topographically it was in the centre of his dominions.

Transfer of the seat of government.

The conspiracy of Ayesha, Talha and Zobeir having been crushed at the Khoreiba battlefield, this victory had given Ali quiet and complete sway over the territories from Khorásán in the east to Egypt in the west with the exception of the provinces in the north-west of Arabia, which were under the Governor of Syria *viz.* Mo'áwiya.

Ali's dominion.

It has already been observed that during his sojourn at Medina on the occasion of his visit to Caliph Othmán, Mo'áwiya one day happened to ask Ka'b-al-Ahbár how the prevailing disturbances against Othmán would end. Ka'b predicted that Othmán would be murdered and that in the long run the Grey Mule (meaning Mo'áwiya) would succeed in rising to power. Relying on this prophecy, Mo'áwiya looked forward to chances of his rise to the sovereign authority and lost no opportunity of taking measures to promote the object in view. Thus was it:—that, he was slack in sending succour † demanded by Othmán when he was besieged; that, when Othmán was murdered, he was busy in stirring up the Syrians to avenge his blood by exhibiting from the pulpit the gory shirt of the murdered Caliph; that, to let the spirit of revolt ripen among the Syrians, he long detained the envoy from Ali and evaded a definite answer to the invitation of the Caliph demanding homage from him; that, he gathered around him

Mo'awiya's preliminary activities.

† Rawdzat-al-Safá.

several discontented men of note, such as † Obeidalláh (the son of Caliph Omar, the murderer who had escaped for fear of being summoned to the tribunal before Ali), Abdalláh b. Abi Sarh (the ex-governor of Egypt who was displaced when Ali came to power), Marwán (the secretary and the evil genius of Caliph Othmán) and almost all the immediate adherents of that Caliph, and the Omyyads who had fled to him when Ayesha was defeated at Bussorah; that, he secured the alliance of Amr b. As, the conqueror of Egypt and the ex-governor of that country, now residing in Palestine as a landlord but as a discontented man; (With the ‡ stipulation of his restoration to the same government as the reward for his successful co-operation in deposing Ali, he took the oath of allegiance to Mo'áwiya acknowledging him the lawful Caliph, in the presence of all the army, who also took the oath of fealty. They were followed by the Syrian public who joined in the acclamations at this grand ceremony); that, he sought allegiance ¶ of several distinguished Companions of the Prophet, such as Sa'd b. Abi Waqqás, Abdalláh b. Omar, Osáma b Zaid, Mohammed b. Maslama, who were noted for not having done fealty to Ali on his inauguration as Caliph, but they chose to remain aloof from either party and wrote reproachful answers to Mo'áwiya. At this period Abu Horeira, Abu-al-Darda, Abu Osáma Báhili and No'mán b. Bashir Ansári were the only Companions in attendance at the court of Mo'áwiya; that, being for over twenty years governor of the rich province of Syria and pursuing a far-sighted policy from the very beginning as noticed on page 313, he had amassed an immense treasure and had a powerful army at his command. Now he had in his favour the prejudices of the Syrians in general and of his armies in particular, who had been artfully taught to implicate Ali in the murder of Caliph Othmán. The blood-stained shirt of Othmán was still hung over the pulpit in the great mosque of Damascus, and the people, inflamed by its sight, sobbed

† Rawdzat-al-Safá. ‡ Mas'udi. ¶ Habib-al-Siyar.

aloud and cried for vengeance on the murderers and those who sheltered them. Such was the formidable adversary with whom Ali had to deal after he had done with Ayesha, Talha and Zobeir.

Ali's march to Syrian frontier.

Apprised of these commotions in Syria, Ali once more tried (Sha'bán 36 A. H. or Jany. 657 A. D.) to use conciliatory means by deputing a Chief of the Bani Bajila named Jarir, the Governor of Hamdán, who happened to be at Kufa, having been summoned to pay homage to the Caliph, and who was known to entertain friendly relations with Mo'áwiya. His return was anxiously awaited. At length, † he came back after three months with an oral message from Mo'áwiya that the allegiance sought for could only be tendered if punishment were meted out to the murderers of Othmán. Málik-al-Ashtar accused him for having wasted time in effeminate pleasures with Mo'áwiya, who purposely kept him so long to mature his plans of hostilities. Pretending to be offended with this imputation, Jarir left Kufa and joined Mo'áwiya.

Finding Mo'áwiya hopelessly alienated, Ali resolved to march upon Syria without any further delay. In the month of Zi-Qa'da, 36 A. H. or April 657 A. D. sending out a detachment as an advance guard to meet him at Riqqa, he himself with his army proceeded to Medáen. He despatched a contingent from Madáen and marched crossing the Mesopotamian desert.

The Miraculous fountain in the Mesopotamian desert.

On his way he had to halt at a place where no water was avilable and the want was keenly felt by the army. A Christian hermit, who lived in a cave near the camping grounds, was sent for and asked to point out some well. He assured Ali that there was no well in the vicinity all around but there was a cistern near by, which contained not more than three buckets of rain water. Ali then said, 'I know, however, that some of the Bani Israel prophets of ancient times had fixed their abode in this

† Ibn Khaldun.

place and had dug a pit for their stock of water.' The hermit replied that he also had heard of it, but it had been shut up for ages and all traces of it were lost; and that there was an old tradition that none but a prophet or one sent by a prophet would discover and re-open it. "He then, says the Arabian tradition, † produced a parchment scroll written by Simeon bin Safá (Simon Cephos), one of the greatest apostles of Jesus Christ, predicting the coming of Mohammed, the last of the Prophets, and that this well would be discovered and re-opened by his lawful heir and successor. Ali listened with becoming reverence to this prediction; then turning to his attendants and pointing to a spot, 'dig there,' said he. They digged, and after a time came to an immense stone, which having been removed with difficulty, the miraculous well stood revealed, affording a seasonable supply to the army, and an unquestionable proof of the legitimate claim of Ali to the Caliphate. The venerable hermit was struck with conviction; he fell at the feet of Ali, embraced his knees, and never afterwards would leave him." *W. Irving's Succ. of Mohd. p. 180.*

Having offered thanks to God, and taking water sufficient for the army, Ali resumed his march. Crossing the Mesopotamian desert, he reached Riqqa on the banks of the Euphrates. A bridge of boats was constructed and the army crossing the river advanced westward, where they met the Syrian outposts at Sur-al-Rum. After some skirmishes between the vanguards of the two armies, the enemy gave way and Ali's army advancing forward came in sight of the main body of Mo'áwiya's forces, already stationed at Siffien, (Zhilhajja 36 A. H. or May 657 A. D.)

Ali's Camp at Siffien.

The following interesting circumstance is related by Major Price as having taken place at the commencement of the war:—"As Siffien commanded, to a considerable distance, the only access to the waters of the Euphrates, Mo'áwiya had stationed Abul Awr, one of his Generals, with ten thousand

† Rawdzat-al-Safá vol. ii, p. 292; Jame'-al-Tawárikh, p. 183 etc.

men, to guard the communication from the troops of Ali. He had not long placed his army in this advantageous position, when Ali approached and pitched his Camp in the same neighbourhood, and his followers soon found that their expected supply of water was intercepted. Under these circumstances, Ali sent a deputation to Mo'áwiya to request he would relinquish an advantage which appeared so inconsistent between kindred, though at present hostile tribes, assuring him that had he been possessed of it, the passage should have been equally free to both armies. Mo'áwiya immediately made known the message to his courtiers, most of whom contended that as the murderers of Othmán had cut off all supplies of water when they besieged his palace, so on the present occasion it would only be just to retaliate. Amr. b. As, however, dissented from this opinion, declaring that Ali would not suffer his army to perish of thirst with the warlike legions of Iráq at his heels and the Euphrates before his eyes, and added that they were contending for the Caliphate not for a skin of water. But the first counsel prevailed, and the messenger was dismissed with the reply that Mo'áwiya was resolved not to forego what he considered to be the earnest of future victory. The result of this application occasioned Ali considerable vexation and perplexity, till at length the privations became unbearable, and Málik-al-Ashtar and Ash'as the son of Qais begged to be allowed to open the communication with their swords. Permission being granted, and proclamation being made throughout the Camp, in less than an hour, ten thousand men had flocked to the Standard of Málik-al-Ashtar, and an equal number to the tent of Ash'as. Disposing these troops in convenient order, the two chieftains conducted each their army towards the channel of the Euphrates, and after vainly warning Abul Awr to quit the banks of the river, Málik at the head of the Cavalry and Ash'as at the head of the Foot, immediately closed upon the enemy. During the action that succeeded, Málik was nearly exhausted with thirst and exertion, when a soldier by his side begged him to accept a draught of water, but the generous warrior refused to accept the indulgence till the sufferings of his followers had been allayed, and at the same time being assailed by the enemy, he laid seven of their bravest soldiers in the dust. But the raging thirst of Málik and his troops became at length intolerable, and he directed all that were furnished with water bags to follow him through the ranks of their opponents without quitting his person until they should have filled all their vessels. Piercing the line of the adverse party, Málik made good his way to the river whilst his followers supplied themselves with water. The conflict raged with unabated fury in the bed of the Euphrates, till Abul Awr, finding his troops give way before the resistless attack of their assailants, and being already beaten from his post, despatched a messenger to Mo'áwiya who immediately sent Amr b. As with three thousand horse to his relief. The arrival of that General, however, seems to have rendered the victory of Málik more signal and decisive. No sooner did the latter descry the approach of Amr than, covering himself with his shield, he urged his courser towards him with irresistible impetuosity, and Amr only eluded the fury of his adversary by retiring within the ranks of the Syrians. The latter, however, were put to the sword in great numbers, many were drowned in the Euphrates, whilst the remainder fled for refuge to the camp of Mo'áwiya; and the troops of Ali having thus successfully dislodged the enemy, established themselves in quiet possession of the watering place and its approaches. Smarting under the reproaches of Amr, Mo'áwiya now found himself reduced to the necessity of applying to his adversary for the indulgence which he had so recently withheld; but Ali, with the liberality and magnanimity so congenial to his general character, readily granted to his troops a free communication to the Euphrates, and from this time the followers of either army passed and re-passed to the river with equal confidence and freedom of intercourse." *S. Ockley's History Sar. p. 312.*

Ali divided his forces, which numbered 90,000, into seven columns each commanded by a Companion of the Prophet or a Chieftain of renown. The Commanders were; Ammár Yasir, Abdalláh b. Abbás, Qais b. Sa'd b. Obáda, Abdalláh b. Ja'far, Málik-al-Ashtar, Ash'as b. Qais Kindi and Sa'id b. Qais Hamdáni.

Desultory fighting for one month.

Mo'áwiya had similarly divided his men, 1,20,000 which greatly outnumbered the army of Ali, into seven or eight columns under the following commanders: Amr b. As, Abdalláh b. Amr b. As, Obeidalláh b. Omar, Abul Awr, Zhul Kalá' Homeiri, Abd-al-Rahmán b. Khálid b. Walid, and Habib b. Maslama. Every day one of these columns from each army took the field by turn and engaged in skirmishing or single combat, in which case only one champion from each side fought till the heat of the sun became intolerable. In this way the contest was kept up for the whole month of Zhilhajja, as Ali was desirous to avoid serious loss of the Moslems in a decisive battle.

The next year (37 A. H.) having set in with Moharram, in which fighting was forbidden, both the armies lay encamped in sight of one another without practical activities. During this month of truce Ali earnestly wished to conciliate Mo'áwiya in order to avert the impending crisis and re-opened negotiations. The whole month passed in sending or receiving deputations but all to no purpose. Ali clearly pointed out that, as Caliph, he was ready to vindicate the majesty of the Divine Law on the murderers of Othmán, if they were only named by Mo'áwiya. But Mo'áwiya, entertaining ambitious designs upon the Caliphate under cover of the pretended revenge of the blood of Othmán, which had so far been his strength and had secured him so big an army, would not accede to any terms before the murderers of Othmán were exterminated.

The hostilities were resumed with the beginning of the next month (Safar, 37 A. H.). For a week the battles raged with unceasing fury till sunset separated the contesting parties. Every

Furious battles at Siffien.

day the conflict became severer and more embittered. In the second week Ali made up his mind to bring on a decisive engagement. The authorities quoted by Price, enter very minutely into various individual contests which took place during this protracted campaign. †"In several of these Ali was personally engaged; but his extraordinary strength and skill was so well known to the opposite party, that he was obliged to disguise himself before an assailant would attack him. On one occasion, being mounted on the horse and arrayed in the armour of one of his Chiefs, he was attacked by a warrior from Mo'áwiya's army; and we are told that with a single sweep of his scimitar, the Caliph severed the upper from the lower half of his body. It is said that such was the keenness and temper of the steel, and the rapidity and precision of the stroke, that the man thus severed in twain continued fixed in the saddle; the spectators concluding that Ali had missed his blow, until the horse chanced to move, when the two halves of the body fell to the ground."

Ammar's fall in the battle.

"The carnage, chiefly in the ranks of Mo'áwiya, was very great in these battles. Among the ranks of Ali the loss of certain distinguished Companions was regretted by friends and foes alike. Ammár Yasir was deeply grieved when Háshim b. Otba, the hero of Qádisia fell fighting by his side. As he saw Háshim fall, he exclaimed to his fellows: 'O Paradise! how close thou couchest beneath the arrow's point and the falchion's flash! O Háshim even now I see heaven opened, and black-eyed maidens, all bridally attired, clasping thee in their fond embrace.' So singing, and refreshing himself with his favourite draught of milk and water, the aged warrior, fired again with the ardour of youth, rushed into the enemy's ranks and met the envied fate. It had long been in every one's mouth both in town and Camp, that Mohammed had once said to him: 'By a godless and rebellious race, O Ammár, thou shalt one day be slain;' in other words (so the saying was interpreted), Ammár would

† S. Ockley's His. Sar. p. 314.

be killed fighting on the side of right. Thus his death, as it were, condemned the cause of the ranks against whom he fought; and so it spread dismay in Mo'áwiya's host. When Amr b. As heard of it, he answered readily: 'And who is it that hath killed Ammár, but Ali the Rebellious, that brought him hither?' The clever repartee ran through the Syrian host, and did much at once to efface the evil omen." *Muir's Annals p. 382*. Other versions of Ammár's last words run as follows: 'The thirsty man longeth for water; and here, close by, it welleth up. Descend to the spring (death) and drink. This is the joyful day of meeting with friends, with Mohammed and his Companions.' *Wackidi quoted in Muir's Annals p. 382*. "By Alláh! I do not know a deed more pleasing to God than to war against these lawless vagabonds. I would fight them even if I was assured of being run through with a lance; for the death of a martyr, and the paradise beyond, are only to be acquired in the ranks of Ali. However courageously our enemies may fight, still justice is on our side; they desire not to revenge Othmán's death, but ambition drives them to revolt. Follow me, Companions of the Prophet! the gates of Heaven are opened, and houris are waiting to receive us. Let us triumph here, or meet Mohammed and his friends in Paradise!" With these words he gave his charger the lash, and plunged with desperate violence into the hottest of the fight, till, at length, he was surrounded by the Syrians, and fell a sacrifice to his own courage. His death stirred up Ali's troops to revenge, whilst even the Syrians regretted his loss, from the high esteem in which Ammár had been held by the Prophet." *Weil, Geschicte der Chalifen quoted in Ockley's His. Sar. p. 314*. Beholding Ammár fall, Mo'áwiya cried to Amr b. As, who was sitting by him, 'Do you see, what precious lives are lost in our dissensions?' 'See'! exclaimed Amr, 'would to God I had not lived to see such a catastrophe.' Ammár Yasir, the patriarch of Moslem chivalry was ninety three years of age; he had served the Prophet in Bedr and several other engagements. He was now Ali's

General of the Horse. He lived reverenced and died lamented by all. Having fallen wounded by a lance of Joweir Oskoni, he was brought to his tent where Ali, taking his head into his lap, shed tears of sorrow and offered prayers for the dead friend.

Ali's furious charge on the enemy.

Ali was as much annoyed as grieved at the loss of his brave General and friend. Putting himself at the head of twelve thousand of his Cavalry, he made a furious charge on the enemy, trying to reach Mo'áwiya, whose pavilion was surrounded by five compact rows of his own body-guard behind the lines of the fighting ranks. Breaking the ranks, Ali confronted the body guard. They also could not withstand the fierce shock of the charge. All the rows were broken and coming within earshot of Mo'áwiya, Ali called him saying: 'Come forth O Mo'áwiya! How long shalt the blood of the Moslems flow over the battle-field in the strife between we two? Let us have a duel and let God decide our fate, whoever kills his adversary shalt be the master.' 'Fairly spoken,' said Amr b. As to Mo'áwiya and he urged him to accept the challenge, telling him that his refusal would discredit him for ever. But sneering at Amr, Mo'áwiya replied that the provocation was prudently made to secure for him the Government of Syria, because he knew full well that Ali's antagonist in fight never escaped death.

Scandalous plight of Amr b. As.

†"Amr b. As, however, does not seem to have possessed a much larger share of personal valour than Mo'áwiya on this occasion. Price tells us that a short time afterwards, Ali, having changed his armour and disguised himself, again appeared in the lists. Unconscious of his identity, Amr b. As advanced a few steps, and Ali, pretending a degree of apprehension, still further encouraged him to proceed. They were both on horse back, and as Amr neared his foe, he repeated certain bragging lines, importing discomfiture and havoc he intended to carry into the

†S. Ockley's His. Sar. P. 315.

enemy's army, even though a thousand such as Ali were numbered in their ranks. Ali replied in a strain which rather unexpectedly announced his identity. Away went Amr b. As, without a moment's delay, whipping and spurring as fast as possible, whilst Ali pursued with the utmost eagerness, and making a well directed plunge, the point of his lance passed through the skirts of Amr's coat of mail, and brought him, head foremost, to the earth. Unfortunately (rather fortunately) as Amr wore no drawers, and his heels were in the air, that part of his person became exposed which we shall forbear to particularize. In this situation Ali scorned to do him any further injury, and suffered him to escape with the contemptuous remark, that he was never to forget the circumstance to which he was indebted for life and safety. A very humorous account has been preserved of the conversation that ensued between Amr and Mo'áwiya at their next interview which we here insert:—

Mo'áwiya.—I give thee credit, Amr, for thy ingenuity, and believe thou art the first warrior that ever escaped the sword by so scandalous an exposure. You ought to be grateful to those organs to the day of thy death.

Amr b. As.—Cease thy railing, Moáwiya! hadst thou been in my place, thy pride had been completely humbled, and thy wives and children widowed and fatherless. These sarcasms come not well from you who turned pale and trembling at Ali's challenge.

Mo'áwiya.—Pray, Amr, how didst thou breathe with thy legs swinging in the air? If thou hadst known how thou were to be disgraced thou surely wouldst have worn a pair of drawers.

Amr b. As.—I only retreated from the superior strength of my enemy.

Mo'áwiya.—Oh, I do not consider it disgraceful to yield to Ali, but I maintain it was scandalous to make flag-staffs of thy legs, and expose thyself so shamefully to him and all the world.

Amr b. As.—It cannot be surprising that Ali should have spared me when he recollected me to be his uncle's son.

Mo'áwiya.—Nay Amr, ‡ this is too arrogant. The Prophet declared that Ali was of the same descent as himself, and we all know that his father was a Chief of the illustrious race of Háshim, whereas thine was a common butcher, of the tribe of Qoreish.

Amr b. As.—Great God! Your remarks are worse than the swords and arrows of the enemy. Had I never involved myself in thy quarrel, nor bartered my enternal welfare for worldly profit, I should never have been forced to bear with such speeches, or endure such a burden of labour and anxiety."

Hotly contested battle.

† "One day, towards the close of the campaign, Ali prepared for battle with unusual solemnity. Clad in the Prophet's mail and turban, and mounted on the Prophet's horse, Riyáh, he brought out the old and venerated Standard of Mohammed. The appearance of the sacred relic, now worn to shreds, brought sobs and tears from the illustrious Companions who had so often fought and conquered under its shadow, and the enthusiastic troops drew out in formidable strength beneath the holy banner. Mo'áwiya had assembled twelve thousand of the best warriors of Syria, when Ali, sword in hand, rushed upon them at the

‡ " He (Amr) was the son of a courtezan of Mecca, who seems to have rivalled in fascination the Phrynes and Aspasias of Greece, and to have numbered some of the noblest of the land among her lovers. When she gave birth to this child, she mentioned several of the tribe of Qoreish who had equal claims to the paternity. The infant was declared to have most resemblance to As, the oldest of her admirers, whence, in addition to his name of Amr he received the designation of Ibn-al-As, the son of As." *W. Irving's Life of Mohammed p. 48.*

† S. Ockley's His. Sar. p. 315.

head of his impetuous veterans to the cry of Alláh o Akbar, and threw the enemy into immediate confusion. The Syrians at length recovered from the disorder. The tribe of Awk on the side of Mo'áwiya and that of Hamdánites on the part of Ali, each made a solemn vow never to quit the field whilst one of their opponents remained to dispute it. A dismal slaughter among the bravest of both armies was the result. Heads rolled about like tennis balls, and streams of blood polluted the field in all directions; but in the issue, the Syrians suffered a total defeat, and retired in the utmost confusion." *Price's Mohammedan History.*

Decisive battles at Siffien. Valiant fight of Malik-al-Ashtar.

The battles of Siffien at last were fought desperately on the 11th, 12th and 13th of Safar, 37 A.H. War continued raging in the moon-lit night of 13th rather more furiously than in the day. Like the night of Qádisia field, this night was called a second Lailat-al-Harir or 'Night of Clangour.' Málik-al-Ashtar mounted on a piebald horse, wielding a two-edged broad sword repeatedly shouted Alláh o Akbar. At every stroke of his terrible scimitar fell a warrior cleft down. History has it that he was heard to utter this awful exclamation no less than four hundred times during the night. The hero of the battle, resolved on victory, was pushing his attacks with sustained vigour and persistence. The morning dawned more disadvantageous to the Syrians, who were pressed hard to their encampment by the brave assailants. Mo'áwiya, who was eyeing the field with great anxiety grew more and more nervous when the ranks of his body-guard were cut to pieces. He despairingly bethought himself of flight and even called for his horse, when Amr b. As, who stood by, said to him: 'Courage, Mo'áwiya, be not disheartened! I have devised means to avert the crisis. Call the enemy to the Word of God by raising aloft the Holy Book. If they accept, it will lead to thy victory; if any refuse to abide thereby, it will sow discord amongst them.'

Trick to avert the crisis.

Mo'áwiya eagerly caught at the words, and in a moment † five hundred copies of the Qurán were raised aloft at the point of the lance. 'Behold', cried they, 'the Book of God, let it decide our differences.' This stratagem produced a magical effect on Ash'ath ‡ b. Qais and his followers and some Kufians, as if the artifice was anxiously awaited by them. They at once leaped forward and with one voice re-echoed the cry, 'The Book of God, let it decide our differences,' and they dropped their weapons. Hearing the tumult, Ali stepped forth and remonstrated with them: 'It is a trick.' he said, 'afraid of defeat the evil men have sought their safety by guile.' 'What!' they cried, 'Do you refuse to submit to the decision of the Qurán to which they call you?' 'That it is,' said Ali, 'which I have been fighting so long to bring them to, but they rebelled. Go on and fight your enemy. I know Mo'áwiya, Amr b. As, Ibn Abi Sarh, Habib and Dzohák better than you do. They ¶ have no regard for the religion or the Qurán.' 'Whatever that might be,' they persisted, 'but we are now called to Qurán and we must not decline it.' Thus they would not listen to any argument. At last in a revolting attitude, they threatened the Caliph, that unless he agreed, they would all desert him, or deliver him into the hands of his enemies, or serve him as Othmán was served. Further protest with such determined soldiery being of no avail, Ali said: 'Hold your wild and treasonable language, obey me and fight, but if you are intent upon disobedience, do as you like.' They refused obedience and pressed Ali to call back Málik-al-Ashtar from the field. (These men turned Sectaries and are known in the history as Khárijities). Málik-al-Ashtar, being summoned, at first refused, saying, 'I cannot leave the field. The victory is at hand.' On this answer of Málik the tumult of the Khárijites increased, insisting Ali to call him back at once. He then again sent for Al-Ashtar, saying: 'Of what avail is

† Mas'udi. ‡ Rawdzat-al-Safá. ¶ Ibn Khaldun.

victory when treason is rife in my own camp. Come back at once before I am murdered or delivered over to the enemy.' Málik-al-Ashtar reluctantly gave in and hurried to the Caliph. "A fierce altercation ensued between him and the angry soldiery. 'Ye were fighting', he said, 'but yesterday for the Lord, and the choicest among you lost their lives. What is it but that ye now acknowledge yourselves in the wrong, and the martyrs gone to hell?' 'Nay,' they answered; 'it is not so. Yesterday we fought for the Lord; and today, also for the Lord, we stay the fight.' On this Ashtar upbraided them as, traitors, cowards, hypocrites, and villains. In return they reviled him, and struck his charger with their whips. Ali interposed. The tumult was stayed." *Muir's Annals p. 384.*

Proposals for arbitration.

*Ash'ath b. QaisKindi, stepping forth from amongst the Khárijites, asked permission of Ali to visit Mo'áwiya to enquire of him what his precise meaning was in raising the Qurán aloft. He went to Mo'áwiya and on his return said that Mo'áwiya and his party wished that the differences should be left to the arbitration of two Umpires, who might decide it according to the true sense of the Qurán, each party to nominate an Umpire and their verdict to be final. "Ash'ath the son Qais, one of those who had the greatest credit and influence among the soldiers of Iráq, and whose fidelity it was suspected † had been tampered with by Mo'áwiya, asked Ali, how he approved of this expedient. Ali answered him coldly, saying, 'He that is not at liberty cannot give his advice. It belongs to you to manage this affair according as you shall think fit among yourselves." *S. Ockley's His. Sar. p. 317.* The army, however, determined to follow it, shouted assent; and they named Abu Musa-al-Ash'ari, the late governor of Kufa who was deposed by Ali for his

* Ash'ath is the same man who in 17 A. H. had travelled all the way from Iráq to Kinnisrin in Syria in expectation of bounty from Khálid b. Walid, who gave him 1000 pieces of gold.

† According to Rawdzat-al-Safá a gift of one hundred thousand dirhams was promised by Mo'áwiya fo Ash'ath.

disloyalty as already noticed. 'This man,' said Ali, surprised at the designation, 'has already forsaken us; neither he hath now been fighting with us. The son of the Prophet's uncle *viz*. Abdalláh b. Abbás can preferably be chosen instead.' 'More preferably,' they ironically answered, 'name thy own self, why namest thou thy cousin?' They said they would have none but one who should deal impartially between him and Mo'áwiya. Ali then proposed Málik Al-Ashtar, but they obstinately forced him to accept none other than Abu-Musa as his representative. "It was a bitter choice for Ali, but he had no alternative. Abu-Musa had kept aloof from the battle, but must have been in the neighbourhood. When told of the arbitration, he exclaimed, 'The Lord be praised, who hath stayed the fighting'! 'But thou art appointed Arbiter on our side.' 'Alas! Alas!' he cried; and so in much trepidation, he repaired to Ali's camp. Ahnaf Ibn Qais asked to be appointed joint Umpire with Abu Musa, who, he said, was not the man to stand alone, nor had he tact and wit enough for the task:—'There is not a knot which Abu-Musa can tie, but I will unloose the same; nor a knot he can unloose, but I will find another still harder to unravel.' This was too true; but the army was in an insolent and perverse mood, and would have none but Abu-Musa. The Syrian arbiter was Amr b. As for whose deep and crafty ways Abu-Musa was no match." *Muir's Annals. p. 385*.

The Deed of Arbitration.

†The two referees (Abu-Musa and Amr b. As), having presented themselves in Ali's camp, a truce was put in writing. Dictated by Ali, it was begun thus: 'In the name of God, the most Gracious and Merciful. This is what had been agreed upon between the Commander of the Faithful Ali and......' Amr b. As objected to this and said, 'Ali is your commander but not ours; write down simple names Ali and Mo'áwiya.' Upon this Ali, remembering the prophecy uttered by the Prophet at Hodaibiya, told the people around him that a similar objection was raised by the Qoreish to delete

†Rawdzat-al-Safá; Habib-al-Siyar.

the words 'Apostle of God' appended to the name of the Prophet in the Treaty; that the Prophet yielded and erased out the words with his own hands when he saw me hesitating; that he then predicted that 'the day will come when I shall also have to yield to make a similar concession.' Hearing this, Amr b. As cried out, 'Dost thou represent our similarity to the Pagan Arabs in spite of our being good believers.' 'And when,'said Ali, 'an evil-born son had not been a friend of the wicked and a foe of the righteous?' Upon this Amr swore that he would never again seek the company of Ali, and Ali expressed his wish that God may keep him free of such a Companion. However, Ali yielded and the truce was written with simple names of Ali and Mo'áwiya, and signed, by which the contracting parties bound themselves to ratify and confirm the decision of the referees, which was to be determined some six or eight months later at some place midway between Kufa and Damascus. The Umpires swore that they would judge righteously in accordance with the Holy Book and without regard to partiality. This deed of Arbitration was executed on Wednesday, the 13th of Safar, 37 A. H. or 31st July, 657 A. D.

The Carnage at Siffien.

†Ninety battles were fought at Siffien. The carnage had been very great. Most of the historians give the number of the slain on both sides, from first to the last, as seventy thousand. Of these forty five thousand were Syrians and twenty five thousand Iráqians. Ammár Yasir, Háshim b. Otba, Khazima b. Thábit, Abdalláh b. Bodail and Abul Hathim b. Teihán were the leading chiefs killed on Ali's side; while the men of distinction killed on Mo'áwiya's side were Zhul-Kalá' Homeiri, Obeidalláh b. Omar, Hoshab b. Zhi-Tzalim and Hábis b. Sa'd-al-Tai.

Return of the armies.

The truce having been arranged, Mo'áwiya escaped a defeat and gained his point for the present with bright hopes for the future The armies having buried their dead, left the ill-starred battlefield.

† Abul Fida.

Mo'áwiya retired to Damascus and Ali repaired to Kufa.

Decision of the Umpires.

The time for arbitration having come, the Umpires proceeded to Dumat-al-jondel or Azroh, each with a retinue of four hundred horsemen according to the agreement. Many a leading Chief from Mecca, Medina, Iráq and Syria went there to watch the proceedings, which were to decide the future of Islam. Abdalláh b. Abbás, who accompanied Abu-Musa to preside at the daily prayers, while having a discourse with Abu-Musa upon the topic of arbitration, urged him to beware of the crafty ways of his astute colleague and to keep particularly in his mind the fact that Ali had no blemish to render him incapable of government, nor Mo'áwiya any virtue to qualify him for it. When Abu-Musa reached Duma, Amr b. As received him with great deference. A private conference was held between the two alone in a pavilion erected for the purpose. Amr was already well aware of the weaknesses in Abu-Musa's character. He treated Abu-Musa with utmost respect and civility till he brought him completely under his influence. Having won his confidence, he made him admit that Othmán was foully murdered. Then he asked him why the avenger of his blood, a near relation of his and an able administrater *viz.* Mo'áwiya should not be taken as his successor. To this Abu-Musa replied that the succession should not be determined on such a basis which would give preference to Othmán's sons as legitimate claimants; but that they must above all things take care lest a mutiny should be kindled or civil wars break again. Upon this Amr b. As asked Abu-Musa how he would then propose to decide. 'Set aside,' said Abu-Musa, 'both Ali and Mo'áwiya, and let the Faithful elect a third. This is the simplest and safest solution of the problem.' 'I agree,' said Amr, 'let us go forth to pronounce.' A tribunal was erected from which each of the Umpires was to declare publicly his decision. Abu-Musa wished Amr to go up first, but Amr, alleging reasons to give preference to Ali's man, overcame all his scruples and insisted upon Abu Musa going up first. Abu-Musa ascended and addressed the people thus: 'Brethren! I and Amr b. As, both of us, have given full consideration to the matter and have come to the conclusion that no other course to restore peace and to remove discord from the people can possibly be better than to depose both Ali and Mo'áwiya in order that people may have their choice of a better man in their stead. I therefore depose both Ali and Mo'áwiya from the Calihate to which they pretend, in the manner as I draw this ring from my finger.' Having made this declaration Abu-Musa came down. Amr b. As now took his turn and went up to announce what he had to declare. 'You have heard,' he said, 'how Abu-Musa on his part has deposed his chief Ali; I, on my part, do depose him too and I invest my chief Mo'áwiya with the Caliphate and I confirm him to it, as I put this ring upon my finger. I do this with justice because Mo'áwiya is the avenger of Othmán and his rightful successor.' So saying, he came down. This arbitration took place in the month of Ramazán, 37 A. H. or February 658 A. D.

Amazement at the decision.

The audience were quite amazed at the unexpected issue of the arbitration. Neither the Kufians dreamt of Amr b. As so shamefully over-reaching Abu-Musa, nor the Syrians ever thought of Mo'áwiya achieving such a triumph. Abu-Musa, confounded and bewildered, assailed from every side, said, 'what can I do, I have been duped by Amr, who first agreed with me then swerved aside.' As much as the Syrians applauded the decision, so much so the Kufians were enraged. In the heat of his indignation, Shureih, the commander of the Kufa escort, rushed upon Amr b. As and was roughly handling him when the people interposed and set them apart to have recourse only to mutual revilings. Laughed at by the Syrians and reproached by the Kufians, Abu-Musa felt deeply ashamed of having been outwitted by his colleague. Apprehending mischief, he made good his escape and fled to Mecca, where he thenceforth lived in obscurity and was not heard of any more, though he died in 42 A. H. or according to others in 52 A. H.

"Many of the angry speeches at Duma by the chief men, who were bewildered at the strange denouement, have been preserved. These are some of them; The son of Omar: 'See what a pass Islam hath come to. Its great concern committed to two men: one who knoweth not right from wrong, the other a nincompoop.' Abubekr's son: 'Would that Abu-Musa had died before this affair; it had been better for him.' Abu-Musa himself is represented as abusing Amr in the language of the Qurán: 'His likeness is as the likeness of a dog, if thou drive him away, he putteth forth his tongue, and if thou leave him alone, still he putteth forth his tongue.' (*Sur. VII-77*). 'And thou,' retorted Amr, 'art like the donkey laden with books, and none the wiser for it.' (*Sur. VI-25*). Shureih, Commander of the Kufa escort, flew at Amr, and they belaboured each other with their whips till they were separated by the people. Shureih exclaimed that he only wished he had used his sword instead." ***Muir's Annals p. 394.***

Amr b. As returned to Damascus, where Mo'áwiya, amidst the acclamations of joy, was salutad Caliph by the Syrians. Henceforward Mo'áwiya's interests began to prosper, and the prediction of Ka'b-al-Ahbár appeared to accomplish in the near future; while Ali's power began to wane.

The Kharijites.

The truce having been concluded on 13th Safar, 37 A. H. at Siffien, when Ali was returning homeward with his army, a body of 12,000 men had separated themselves from the ranks and marched at some little distance in the same direction as the main body towards Kufa. They murmured at the compromise agreed upon, and were even loud in their reproaches to one another for having abandoned the cause of the Faith to the ungodly compromise. These were the Khárijites (Khárijite means one who turns out rebelling against the established tenets of a religion,—a Sectary or Schismatic or Seceder), who had refused fighting at the battlefield after the trick played by the enemy, and had pressed the Caliph to accept the arbitration and the particular arbitrator. Approaching Kufa, these seceders encamped at a village named Harora in the vicinity of Kufa. Their religious notions were developed into fanatic zeal that the Believers were all of equal standard and nobody should exercise authority over another. They formulated their creed with the phrase 'La hukm illálilláh,' *i. e.* no judgement but Lord's alone; consequently there should be no Caliph nor oath of allegiance sworn to any human being. They blamed Ali as having sinned in consenting to refer to human judgment that which belonged to God alone, and demanded of him repentance for his apostasy. They said that Ali ought not to have given quarter to the enemy, who could be pursued and put to sword. Proceeding to their camp, the Caliph firmly remonstrated with them, that they had given wrong interpretation to the phrase La hukm illá lilláh; and that in accepting the arbitration he had followed the provisions contained in the Qurán; and that he had committed no sin to repent of. He pointed out that the sin lay at their own door, because with their persistent obstinancy they refused to continue fighting with the enemy; and that with their revolting attitude they forced him to call back Málik-al-Ashtar, who was beating the enemy back to their camp and was at the point of gaining a complete victory; and that they pressed him to accept the arbitration and the particular arbitrator. He added that he entertained, however, that the arbitrators were as well bound by the terms of the truce to deliver their judgment righteously in accordance with the Qurán; and that if the judgment turned out to be in disregard of righteousness, he would at once reject it and would again set out against the enemy. Concluding, he said that it was wrong of them if they desired him to break the truce, which they themselves had driven him to arrange. To all this reasoning they simply answered, 'we do admit of our sin, but we have repented of our apostasy; and thou must repent of it likewise.' To this Ali replied that he being a true believer he would not belie himself by admitting his apostasy.

Revolt of the Kharijites. 37 A. H.

The Sectaries were not satisfied and they resolved on rebellion; but awaiting the issue of the Umpire's decision, they for the present postponed any overt action. Soon after the judgment of the arbitrators, they determined to raise the standard of revolt and prevailed on Abdalláh b. Wahab, one of their chiefs, to accept (contrary to the principles of their creed) the command, as a temporary expedient, to meet the emergency. Fixing their headquarters at Nehrwán, a few miles from Bagdad, in the month following the arbitration, they began to take their way, to meet at the rendezvous, either singly or in small batches for fear of raising an alarm. Some five hundred malcontents from Bussorah also joined the insurgents at Nehrwán. In the meantime, Ali, having received intelligence of the deceitful arbitration at Duma, took little notice of these fanatic zealots, his thoughts being more occupied with the affairs of Mo'áwiya and raising levies for Syria for the renewal of hostilities. Hearing about the Khárijite insurgents, Ali wrote to them that as he was preparing to march against Mo'áwiya, it was high time for them to join his Standard. To this they sent an insulting reply that they had cast him off as an ungodly heretic unless he acknowledged his apostasy and repented thereof, in which case they would see whether anything could be arranged between them.

The battle of Nehrwan.

Ali had commenced his march on Syria when he received tidings that the Khárijites had attempted a raid on Madáen but were beaten back to their camp; that they were committing horrible outrages in the country all around their camp, condemning as impious all those who did not fall in with their sentiments; that they had put to death a traveller who refused to accept their creed, and ripped up his wife who was great with child. The followers of the Caliph, whose families were left behind unprotected at Kufa, apprehending danger from these barbarous fanatics desired that before proceeding on to Syria these outlaws should be dealt with first. A messenger was sent to make enquiries but he too was put to death by them. Seeing the attitude of the insurgents, Ali thought that immediate measures to check them were necessary; he therefore changed his course eastward, crossed the Tigris and approaching Nehrwán sent a messenger to demand of them the surrender of the murderers. They replied that no particular person was responsible; they all deserved equal merits for the blood of the apostates slain by them. Still Ali, avoiding bloodshed, tried to win over these misguided fanatics by gentle means. He had, therefore, a Standard planted outside of his camp and a proclamation made that the malcontents rallying round it or those who retired to their homes would be safe. The proclamation produced the desired effect. The rebels began to disperse, deserting their camp, till Abdalláh b. Wahab was left with only 1800 adherents, who resolved to fight against the Caliph at any cost. Ali said that those men were the true Khárijites, who would go forth against Islam as quick as an arrow from the bow. At last, headed by their leader, Abdalláh b. Wahab, they desperately rushed upon Ali's army and met their fate. All of them were slain except only nine, who escaped to serve as firebrands to rekindle the future fire. On Ali's side only seven men were killed. The zealots, who had escaped, promulgated their creed and cause in secret at Bussorah and Kufa and appeared in the following year in bands of insurgent fanatics, but were easily put to flight or cut to pieces.

Syrian expedition frustrated.

The Khárijites having been disposed of at Nehrwán, Ali retraced his steps towards the Tigris which he re-crossed with his army to march upon Syria, but the Chiefs of his followers urged him to give the army some rest preparatory to the long journey and to enable them to refit their armour for war with the well equipped enemy. Ali consented to the proposal. They marched back towards Kufa and encamped at Nokheila in the vicinity of the town. A proclamation was made that any one who had any business in the town may leave the Camp for one day returning on the next. In a short time the Camp was almost empty of its soldiers, who all went one after the other to the town. None returning after one day, Ali became impatient and at length himself entering the town harangued the people to go forth with him to the Syrian expedition, but no response was forthcoming and nobody came forward. The Caliph was disappointed and at last the project for the expedition had to be abandoned, never to be resumed.

Affairs in Egypt 38 A. H.

Mohammed † the son of Abu Hozhaifa, a distinguished Companion of the Prophet, was an orphan, his father having been killed at Yamáma. He was adopted by Othmán and was brought up under his care. When he grew up, he asked Othmán, the then Caliph, to give him some Command, but the Caliph would not accede to his demand unless he proved himself on the field capable of undertaking the responsibilities of so important a charge. Dissatisfied with this reply, Mohammed fled to Egypt and took shelter with Abi Sarh the governor. Being a man noted for his piety, Mohammed soon gained great influence over the people at large and in the court. Abi Sarh on the occasion of his proceeding to Medina to the relief of Caliph Othmán, who had demanded succour of him when besieged by the insurgents, entrusted the charge of his office to Mohammed. On his way to Medina, Abi Sarh received intelligence of Othmán's murder and of the accession of Ali to the Caliphate. Being a tyrant and an unprincipled man, his guilty conscience urged him to escape the tribunal of Ali. Abi Sarh, therefore, hurried to Syria to seek refuge with Mo'áwiya and did not go back to Egypt. Thus Mohammed b. Hozhaifa held the government of Egypt till the approach of Qais b. Sa'd the governor elect of Ali. So long as Mohammed held the office, he reproachfully

† Rawdzat-al-Safá.

counted the faults of Othman's character. Before the arrival of Qais to the seat of government, Mohammed, while visiting Amr b. As at Arish, a bordering town, in a friendly invitation, was captured by him and taken as a prisoner to Mo'áwiya, who had deputed Amr for the purpose. Qais assumed the command of Egypt as Ali's viceroy during the absence of Momommed. He was a man of distinction, the son of Sa'd, the son of Obáda the rival of Abubekr at the Saqifa election. He was an able adminis- of trator and acquitted himself of his charge with great prudence. He sagaciously secured the oath of fealty from the Egyptians in behalf of Ali and managed to hold the reins of government firmly. A strong † faction of Othmán's partisans at Kharamba, however, stood aloof demanding loudly the satisfaction for Othmán's blood. He wisely let them alone for the present, waiving even the demand for the tithes. Mo'áwiya, afraid of so wise and firm a ruler commanding on the borders of his frontier, apprehended disadvantages to his designs on Egypt and he made every effort to detach him from his allegiance to Ali, by promises to confirm him in the government of Egypt and to provide good offices to his relatives in the Hejáz. Being a loyal follower of Ali, Qais spurned all his tempting offers. Mo'áwiya, having failed in his attempts to win him over to his side, had recourse to foul play to dislodge him from his position. He gave out that Qais was a friend of his and acted in concert with him. He had the report assiduously reach the ears of Ali, on purpose to have the fidelity of Qais doubted by him. To promote the design, he forged a letter meant to have been sent by Qais addressed to Mo'áwiya, wherein Qais agreed not to take measures against the Othmánly party at Kharamba. This letter, as it was intended for Mo'áwiya managed to let fall into the hands of Ali, and it produced the desired effect. The fidelity of Qais was doubted and he was put to the test by being ordered to take severe steps against the malcontents of Kharamba imme-

† Tabari.

diately. Qais, unaware of the underhand fiction of Mo'áwiya, with his usual sincerity remonstrated against the order. His protest was taken as a proof of his complicity. He was deposed and Mohammed the son of Abubekr was sent to replace him.

Mo'awiya's encroachment upon Egypt. 38 A. H.

As soon as Mohammed b. Abubekr was established in authority (38 A.H.), he began to chase out Othmán's party. These steps caused immediate strifes and dissensions, which led to disorder throughout the country. Desirous of restoring pe.ce, the Caliph wished to change the governor, and, summoning Málik-al-Ashtar from his command at Nisibin, sent him in haste to take over the government of Egypt. Mo'áwiya, who was at the bottom of all the troubles in Egypt, kept himself well informed of even the minutest incidents there. Receiving intelligence of Málik's appointment, Mo'áwiya apprehended frustration of his designs at the hands of this strong and able man, who was already a terror to the Syrians in general and to him in particular. It was a matter of vital importance to Mo'áwiya to get rid of Málik. He therefore instigated a Chief, who lived on the confines of Arabia and Egypt and with whom Málik was to lodge on his way to his seat of government, to poison him, on the promise of immunity, for ever afterwards, from the payment of tithes and revenues which he collected in that quarter. This man, tempted by the vile promises, actually poisoned his unsuspecting guest with so deadly a poison in a cup of honey that Málik died before he could stir out of the house. As soon as Mo'áwiya heard it, he said: 'Verily † God hath armies of honey;' and he immediately sent Amr b. As with six thousand horse to seize upon Egypt in its present disturbed state. Amr gladly hastened to the country of his own conquest and which he had peacefully ruled for years. Reaching Alexandria, he was joined by Ibn Sharigh, the leader of the Othmánly party, and with this combined force he proceeded to engage Moham-

† Abul Fida.

med b. Abubekr, who still retained the name and authority of Governor for Ali. Having been routed by Amr, Mohammed b. Abubekr fell into the hands of his enemies, who inclosed him alive in the skin of an ass and the bundle was thrown into flames to be burnt to ashes. Thus the government of Egypt was lost to Ali and passed into the hands of Amr b. As as viceroy of Mo'áwiya. Ayesha was extremely grieved to hear the cruel fate of her brother at the hands of Amr b. As and Mo'áwiya, and in the agony of her heart she invoked † curses upon them at each and every prayer thereafter. It is said that the roasted head of Ayesha's brother was severed from the body and sent to Ayesha as a present. At the sight of it, she was inconsolable at her brother's fate and thence forward she ate no roasted meat until her death.

Mo'awiya's encroachment upon Bussorah 38 A. H.

Ali was as deeply afflicted at the tragic murder of his faithful General, Málik-al-Ashtar, and the cruel death of Mohammed b. Abubekr, as excited at the treacherous conduct of Mo'áwiya, in encroaching upon Egypt. He felt his helplessness to avenge the wrongs, as he could raise no armies against Mo'áwiya, in spite of all his eloquent speeches, which he vainly made continually for fifty days to move the people to take up arms. His cousin Abdalláh b. Abbás, the governor of Bussorah, leaving the Chancellor in charge of his office, came to Kufa to comfort Ali. Taking advantage of Abdalláh's absence from Bussorah, Mo'áwiya, who was watchful of every opportunity to give trouble to Ali, sent one of his Captains, named Abdalláh Hadzrami, with two thousand horse to seize upon Bussorah. The Charge d'Affaires, not having forces sufficient to stand against the invader, left the city to him and demanded urgent succour from the Caliph. Prompt assistance was sent by Ali under the command of Járiya b. Qidáma. After a hard and bloody contest, Hadzrami was defeated and driven for refuge to a neighbouring castle, which was surrounded

†Abul Fida.

and set on fire. The rebel, along with seventy of his followers, perished in the flames. The city was re-taken by the Caliph's forces and Abdalláh b. Abbás, having in the meantime come back from Kufa, resumed his Office. This was in the 38th year of Hegira.

Other revolts of the Kharijites.

During the same year, the Khárijites in considerable bands, revolted against Ali on five or six occasions, but on each occasion they met the common fate of slaughter and dispersion. The most remarkable of those risings was that of Khirrit, who instigated the Persians, Kurds and Christians of Ahwáz and Ram Hurmuz and raised the standard of rebellion. An army to suppress the revolt was sent from Bussorah. Khirrit was killed in the battle and the Caliph's authority was re-established.

Mo'awiya's aggressive policy. 39 A. H.

In the year 39 A. H. several raids on Ali's territory were made by Mo'áwiya without any result of importance. Sometime the raid was made to ravage the country; sometime to exact the tithes from the people; sometime to show his power in superiority to Ali's. The main object of these inroads was to give annoyance to Ali and, at the same time, to create a sense of insecurity under Ali's rule among his subjects. Some eight or ten raids of the kind were made in different parts of Ali's dominion during the year. For instance: Sofyán b. Awf was sent with a large force to ravage the country round Hit, Anbár and Ain Tamr. Abdalláh b. Mas'ud Fizári was sent to exact tithes from the Bedouines of Taima. Dzohák b. Qais was sent to surprise the citadels of Sa'labiya and Qatqatána. During the pilgrimage season, an officer was deputed to lead the pilgrims in their pilgrimage rites at Mecca. Qotham b. Abbás, Ali's governor, was forced to hold back from performing his duties, while Mo'áwiya's man Othmán b. Sheiba Abdari led the rites. The force, sent by Ali to check this, reached Mecca when the Syrians had retraced their steps homeward. They were, however, pursued and overtaken at Wádi-al-Qora where, after some skirmishing, they took to flight. Some of them were captured and brought as prisoners to the Caliph, who had them exchanged with his men who were prisoners with Mo'áwiya. Though these raids were not always successful yet the aim with which they were made was gained to a considerable extent, as the people betrayed, now more clearly than ever, their lukewarmness in the cause of Ali, as they would not stir to repel the invaders who forced upon them their allegiance to Mo'áwiya. Once to repel the raiders, Ali's captain had pursued them as far as Ba'lbak, in the heart of the Syrian territory and thence returned unchecked to Iráq via Riqqa. In return for this, Mo'áwiya made an incursion as far as Mossul in Ali's territory and encamped there for several days to show his contempt for the power of Ali. He went back to Damascus without being questioned for his intrusion.

Mo'awiya's raids in Hejaz 40 A. H.

In the beginning of the 40th year of Hegira, Mo'áwiya sent Bosar b. Artáh, a cruel captain of his host, with three thousand horse to seize upon Medina and Mecca, the sacred cities of the Hejáz and to secure for him the allegiance of the inhabitants. When Bosar approached Medina, the governor Abu Ayyub fled to Kufa, and Bosar entered Medina unopposed. Putting some inhabitants to a cruel death, he threatened the leading men to a general massacre if they refused to acknowledge Mo'áwiya as their Caliph. They were thus forced to swear allegiance to Mo'áwiya. Having done this, he passed on to Mecca and enacted the same scene there. Taking the oath of fealty to Mo'áwiya from the citizens of Mecca, the tyrant proceeded to Yemen, where he put to sword some thousands of Ali's adherents. Obeidalláh b. Abbás, Ali's viceroy in Yemen, managed to escape to Kufa but his two little sons were left behind, who fell into the hands of the tyrant, and they were barbarously put to death along with their Bedouin attendant, who ventured to protest against the cold-blooded murder of the boys. Ali, having received intelligence of the incursion, immediately sent an army of four thousand horse in command of Járiya b. Qidáma but he was too late to stop the outrages. Bosar was already on his way back to Syria, when Ali's army reachad Yemen. Járiya pursued the Syrians to Najrán where they were being hailed with welcome. On his approach, they took to flight, but Járiya put to sword the inhabitants whose complicity in inviting Mo'áwiya's horde was now no secret and who had already risen up against the local governor. Then Járiya proceeded to Mecca in pursuit of the fugitives but they were gone. He forced the Meccans to recall the oath they had recently taken in allegiance to Mo'á-wiya, and again do homage to Ali. After this he went to Medina, where Abu-Horeira, of the opposite faction, who led the daily prayers on behalf of Mo'awiya, hid himself somewhere. Járiya made the citizens of Medina swear homage to Hasan the son of Ali, and staying only for a day at Medina he took his way to Kufa. Abu-Horeira reappeared after Járiya's departure and led the prayers as before.

The cruel fate of the two infant sons of Obeidalláh (Ali's cousin) occasioned great grief to their father and mother and it preyed on Ali more, perhaps, than all his other troubles. He invoked the wrath of Heaven on Bosar, praying that he might lose his intellect, and in answer to the prayer he became a hopeless, drivelling lunatic. During his insanity he was always calling for his sword. His friends provided him with one made of wood and another hollow one full of air. The wretch struck his wooden sword against the other and imagined that he killed an enemy at each stroke.

Still there were some more griefs in store for Ali.

Misbehaviour of Abdallah b. Abbas.

Complaints having reached the Caliph of frauds and misappropriation of public money of the Bussorah treasury, the Caliph called upon the Governor to submit the accounts of the Treasury. Abdallàh b. Abbás received the order with scorn, and, without complying with the demand, threw up his office and made good his way to Mecca, carrying great riches with him. He was pursued by the citizens of

Bussorah, but after some fighting he managed to get off to Mecca without further molestation. Ali was greatly mortified at this behaviour of his cousin Abdalláh b. Abbás. Obeidalláh b. Abbás, the late governor of Yemen, who was still staying with Ali, his cousin, was sent to replace Abdalláh.

The defection of Aqil.

About the same time another great calamity befell Ali. "His brother Aqil went over to Mo'áwiya, who received him with open arms, and assigned to him large revenues. Aqil alleged no other excuse for his defection, but that his brother Ali had not entertained him according to his quality." *Simon Ockley's His. Sar. p. 326.*

† "Aqil had complained to Ali of the slenderness of his means, and requested that an addition to his salary might be made him from the public treasury. This Ali refused to do, but upon being repeatedly urged by his brother, he at length desired Aqil to meet him at night, when they would break into the house of a wealthy neighbour, and find ample means for his wants. 'Are you serious?' demanded Aqil, with a mixture of surprise and indignation. 'On the great day of account,' replied Ali, 'how much easier shall I acquit myself against the accusation of a solitary individual, than against the united cry of the whole community of Islam, individually possessed of that property which you wish me to give to thee?' Other writers, however, say, that when Aqil applied to his brother for an augmentation of his pension, the latter desired him to wait for a moment, and withdrawing into his own house, he presently returned with a piece of red-hot iron, which he requested Aqil to hold in his hand. The latter of course declined. 'Nay, then,' said Ali, 'if you cannot sustain the heat which has been produced by man, how can you expect me to expose myself to the fire which God will kindle.' Aqil thus seeing that his application would not be attended to, left Kufa, and joined Mo'áwiya." *Price's Mohammedan History.*

† S. Ockley's His. Sar. p. 326.

Designs of the Kharijites to get rid of the rulers.

The period of Ali's Caliphate was one of continued struggles. He was never left to live in peace. The revolt of Ayesha, Talha and Zobair; the rebellion and treacherous outrages of Mo'awiya and Amr b. As; the risings of the Khárijite fanatics; the lukewarmness and apathy of his own people; the unfaithfulness of his cousin Abdalláh b. Abbás and, last of all, the defection of his own brother Aqil affected his spirits a great deal. These troubles crowding rapidly one upon another entirely disturbed his mind.

Still the Khárijites were impatient for the destruction of Ali in particular and the despotic rulers in general as they recognized no power and authority but the Lord's—their creed being formulated by the phrase 'La hukm illa lillah' *i.e.* no command but the Lord's alone. They expected that the ungodly (as they said) rulers *i. e.* Ali and Mo'áwiya would perish of themselves in their strife, and the reign of the Lord would prevail at last. Tired of their long drawn stay, three fanatics, happening to meet at the holy precincts of the Ka'ba, brooded over the blood that had been shed in vain at Nehrwán and other fields of battle and groaned over the ruthless tyranny and apostasy (as they said) pervading throughout the Islamic world. Suddenly an idea brightened the face of one of them with gleaming hopes, and he spoke thus: 'It is useless to bemoan the losses we have sustained, we must act to mend matters. Let not our blood be shed in vain. Let each of us kill one of the three oppressors of the Faithful. Islam may yet be free and the reign of righteousness may yet be established.' The other two warmly approved of the suggestion. The three zealots swore to a compact for the sacrifice of their lives in the cause, and they said that no other plan would work better to restore unity and peace in Islam than the destruction of the three ambitious apostates *viz.* Mo'áwiya, Amr b. As, and Ali. Each of them undertook to dispatch his allotted victim on a certain fixed day at an appointed hour with a poisoned weapon to ensure a mortal blow.

The three conspirators *viz.* Borak b. Abdalláh Tymi, Amr b. Bekr Tymi, and Abd-al-Rahmán b. Muljim undertook to kill Mo'áwiya, Amr b. As and Ali respectively. The third Friday in the month of next Ramadzán was fixed as the date for the preparation of the heinous deed at the morning Service in the Mosques at Damascus, Fostát and Kufa. Having poisoned their swords each man took his way, Borak to Damascus, Amr to Fostát and Abd-al-Rahmán to Kufa.

Attempt on the life of Mo'awiya.

Having reached Damascus, Borak mingled with the worshippers in the mosque on the appointed day at the morning Service and stabbed Mo'áwiya in the groin. He considered that the blow was fatal, but it was not so. Mo'áwiya's surgeon examining the wound, declared that his life could be saved either by cautery or by drinking a potion that would render him impotent for life. Mo'áwiya was given his choice either to be cauterized or to drink the draught. He chose the latter and was impotent for the rest of his life. The culprit was instantly seized, mutilated of his hands and feet and suffered to live. He was sent to his home in Bussorah, where some years later he got a son born to him. Then Ziyád, the then governor of Bussorah, put him to death saying, 'Villain! Thou hast begotten a son thyself and hast made the Caliph impotent. Thou shouldst die.'

Attempt on the life of Amr b. As.

Amr b. Bekr, the second of the conspirators, was in the mosque at Fostát on the fixed Friday of the month of Ramadzán. He dealt a blow at the Imám, who was leading the Service. The victim fell dead, but he was not Amr b. As, who could not attend on this occasion to lead the prayers on account of colic pain, which proved so fortunate for him that day. It was Khárija, who officiated for Amr b. As. The assassin was caught and taken before Amr to his court, where he discovered his mistake. 'I intended thee, O tyrant!' cried the prisoner to Amr b. As, who calmly retorted, 'Thou intended me, but the Lord intended thee,' and ordered his immediate execution.

Attempt on the life of Ali.

The third of these conspirators, Abd-al-Rahmán b. Muljim, having reached Kufa, put up with a woman, a beautiful maid of the Khárijite sect, whose father, brother and other near relations were all killed at Nehrwán. Abd-al-Rahmán became violently enamoured of this damsel and made proposals of marriage to her. Qettámah, as she was named, answered that her spouse could only be a man who would bring her a dowry consisting of Ali's head, 3000 dirhams of silver, a slave and a maid. He instantly accepted the conditions. Qettámah then introduced him to two other miscreants named Werdan, a Khárijite bent upon avenging himself on Ali and to another named Shuheib, both of whom gladly undertook to assist Abd-al-Rahmán in his nefarious design. Proceeding to the mosque on the appointed Friday early in the morning when Ali appeared to lead the Service, Werdan and Ibn Muljim managed to take their stand just behind him. As soon as the Service was begun, Werdan aimed a blow at Ali but missed him. Next the blow from Abd-al-Rahmán was instantly struck with fatal precision.

It struck Ali upon his head just in the same place where he had received a wound in a battle in the life-time of the Prophet. In the confusion which ensued, the three assassins managed to escape. Werdan ran to his house, followed by a pursuer who overtook and killed him. Shuheib made good his escape and was never heard of again. Abd-al-Rahmán concealed himself for some time. When Ali was asked as to who was his assassin, he answered, 'You shall soon see him.' Abd-al-Rahmán, having been discovered hidden in a corner of the Mosque with his blood-stained sword, was asked if he was the culprit. He faltered for a moment but was constrained by his own conscience to confess the guilt. He was dragged forth and brought before Ali, who consigned him to the custody of his son Hasan, directing with his accustomed clemency: 'Let him not want for anything, and if I die of my wound, let his death be by a single blow.' The wouud was pronounced to be fatal, as it proved. Ali felt thirsty and a cup full of syrup was brought to him. At the same time the prisoner asked for some water to drink. With a generosity, which is past understanding and which was a characteristic trait of Ali throughout his life, Ali had his own cup of syrup made over to him to drink.

Ali's presages about his death.

During all the month of Ramadzán, in which he was killed, Ali had several presages of his death, and in private, among his friends, used occasionally to let drop some words to that purpose. Once, after he had undergone a great deal of uneasiness, he was heard to say, 'Alas! my heart, there is need of patience, for there is no remedy against death.' In short, Friday, the 19th of this month being come, he went out of his house early in the morning to go to the mosque, and it was observed that the house-hold birds made a great noise as he passed through his yard; and that one of his slaves having thrown a cudgel at them to make them quiet, he said to him, 'Let them alone, for their cries are only lamentations foreboding my death.' *S. Ockley's His. Sar. p. 328.*

The death of Ali. 40 A. H.

Ali was wounded on Friday, the 19th of Ramadzán in 40 A.H. in the Mosque at Kufa, where he had been to conduct the usual morning Service. He was immediately brought to his house. He survived three days. "He called his sons Hasan and Hosain to his bedside and counselled them to be steadfast in piety and resignation to the will of God, and to be kind to their younger brother (Abbás) the son of his Hanifite wife. After that he wrote his testament, and continuing to repeat the name of the Lord to the end so breathed his last." *W. Muir's Annals p. 414.* He died of his wound on Monday, the 21st of Ramadzán 40 A. H. at the age of sixtythree. "His remains were interred about five miles from Kufa; and in after times a magnificent tomb, covered by a Mosque, with a splendid dome, rose over his grave, and it became the site of a city, called Mashed Ali, or the Sepulchre of Ali, and was enriched and beautified by many Persian monarchs." *W. Irving's Succ. of Mohd. p. 187.* It is said that the Sepulchre of Ali was kept hid during the reign of the Omyyads.

Ali's literary works.

"Among all the Mohammedans alike, Ali has a great reputation for wisdom. There is extant of his a 'Centiloquium,' or a hundred sentences which have been translated out of Arabic into Turkish and Persian. There is likewise a collection of verses by him under the title of 'Anwar-al-Aqil.' And in the Bodleian library there is a large book of his sentences. But his most celebrated piece is that entitled 'Jafr wa Jáme'. It is written on parchment in a mystic character intermixed with figures, which narrate or typify all the grand events that are to happen from the foundation of Mohammedanism to the end of the world. This parchment, which is deposited in the hands of his family, has not up to this time been deciphered. Ja'far Sádiq has indeed succeeded in partially interpreting it; but the entire explication of it is reserved for the twelfth Imám, who is surnamed by way of excellence, the Mahdi, or 'Grand Director.' *S. Ockley's His. Sar. p. 332.*

The scholar of the Arabic language owes great gratitude to Ali, who regulated the correct composition of the language by introducing † its Grammar, the absence of which was a great defect to the literature, and its want was keenly felt by the literary man.

Anecdotes of Ali.

‡ The following anecdotes of Ali are chiefly extracted from 'Oriental Table Talk,' translated by Jonathan Scott Esqr. See Ouseley's 'Oriental Collections':—

Once when Mohammed and Ali were eating dates together, the former placed all the shells on the plate of the latter unperceived, and on finishing their repast, he said, 'He who has most shells must have eaten most.' 'No,' says Ali, 'he surely must have eaten most who has

† Major Jarret's trans. of Suyuti, p. 184. ‡ Ibid.

swallowed the shells also.'

A Jew said to the venerable Ali, in argument on the truth of their respective religions, 'You had not even deposited your prophet's body in the earth when you quarrelled among yourselves.' Ali replied, 'Our divisions proceeded from the loss of him, not concerning our faith; but your feet were not yet dry from the mud of the Red Sea when you cried unto Moses, saying, make us Gods like those of the idolaters, that we may worship them.' The Jew was confounded.

A person complained to Ali, saying, 'A man has declared, he dreamed that he slept with my mother, may I not inflict upon him the punishment of the law?' 'What is it?' Ali replied, 'Place him in the sun, and beat his shadow; for what can be inflicted on an imaginary crime but imaginary correction?'

Ingenious decision of Ali.

† The following decision is creditable to the ingenuity of Ali:—Two travellers sat down to dine; the one had five loaves, the other three. A stranger passing by, asked leave to eat with them, and they hospitably agreed thereto. After dinner, the stranger laid down eight pieces of money for his fare, and departed. The owner of the five loaves took up five pieces and left three for the other, who insisted upon getting half. The case was brought before Ali for his decision, and he gave the following judgment: 'Let the owner of the five loaves take seven pieces of money and the other but one.' And this was the exact proportion of what each furnished for the stranger's entertainment; for, dividing each loaf into three shares, the eight loaves gave twentyfour shares, and as they all fared alike, each person's proportion was a third of the whole or eight shares. The stranger therefore ate seven shares of the five loaves and only one of the three loaves; and in this manner the Caliph divided the money between the owners. *S. Ockley's His. Sar. p. 336.*

‡ The signet ring of Ali bore this inscription, 'Ex-

---

† Major Jarret's trans. of Suyuti's Tárikh-al-Kholafa p. 183.
‡ Ibid.

cellent is the Omnipotent God,' or according to another tradition. 'The Kingdom belongs to the only Mighty Lord.' † Ali used to sweep the Public Treasury and then pray within it, in the hope that it would be testified in his favour that he did not keep the State property within it withheld from the Moslems.

‡ Five hundred and eighty six traditions are ascribed to Ali, on the direct authority of the Apostle of God.

Some Traditions from Tárikh-al-Kholafá of Jaláluddin-as-Suyuti as translated from the original Arabic
by
MAJOR H. S. JARRET,
Calcutta Edition,
1881.

Regarding the Merits of Ali.

1. The Imam Ahmad b. Hanbal says: There hath not come down to us regarding the merits of any one of the Companions of the Apostle of God, what hath been transmitted concerning Ali. (Al Hákim.)
2. Ibn Asákir from Ibn Abbás says: There hath not been revealed in the Book of God regarding any one what hath been revealed concerning Ali, and that 300 (three hundred) verses have been revealed concerning Ali.
3. At-Tabráni and Ibn Abi Hátim record from Ibn Abbás that he said: The Lord never revealed the words 'O True Believers' but that Ali was understood to be the lord and chief of them; and verily the Lord hath reproved the Companions of the Prophet in various places, but hath never mentioned Ali save with approval.
4. At-Tirmizhi, An-Nasái and Ibn Mája from Habshi b. Jonáda say that the Apostle of God said: Ali is a part of me and I of Ali.

---

† Major Jarret's trans. of Suyuti, p. 183.
‡ Ibid p. 172.

5. At Tabráni records in the Awsat from Jábir b. Abdalláh that the Apostle of God said: The people are of various stocks but I and Ali are of one stock.
6. At-Tabráni records in the Awsat and Saghir from Omm-Selma that she narrates, 'I heard the Apostle of God say: Ali is with the Qurán and the Qurán with Ali, they shall not be divided until they arrive at the fountain of Kauthar in Paradise'.
7. Ibn Sa'd records on the authority of Ali that he said: By Alláh a verse of the Qurán was never revealed but I know regarding what it was revealed and where it was revealed and concerning whom it was revealed, for my Lord hath given unto me a wise heart and an eloquent tongue.
8. Ibn Sa'd and others on the authority of Abu Tofail record that Ali said: Ask ye me regarding the Book of God, for verily there is not a verse but I know whether it was revealed by night or by day, in the plains or on the mountains.
9. At Tirmizhi and Al-Hákim record from Ali that the Apostle of God said: I am the city of Knowledge and Ali is its gate.
10. Ibn Mas'ud says that the Prophet said: To look upon Ali is Devotion.
11. Ibn Asákir on the authority of Caliph Abubekr records that the Prophet said: Looking upon Ali is worship.
12. Muslim records on the authority of Ali that he said: By Him who hath cleft the seed and created the soul, verily the Prophet promised me that none but a true believer should love me, and none but a hypocrite hate me.
13. At-Tirmizhi from Abu Sa'id al Khudri says that he said: We used to distinguish the hypocrites by their hatred of Ali.
14. At-Tabráni from Omm Selma says that the Apostle of God said: He who hath loved Ali, verily he hath loved me, and he who hath hated Ali, verily he hath

hated me, and who hath hated me, verily he hath hated the Lord.

15. Abu Ya'la and Al-Bazzár from Sa'd b. Abi Waqqás say that the Apostle of God said: Who grieveth Ali, grieveth me.

16. Ahmad records and Al Hákim verifying it on the authority of Omm Selma that she narrates, 'I heard the Apostle of God say: He who hath reviled Ali, verily he hath reviled me.'

17. Sai'd b. Al-Mosyyeb says that Omar b. Al-Khattáb used to beg God to preserve him from a perplexing case which the father of Al-Hasan was not present to decide; and that Omar said: None of the Companions used to say 'ask ye of me', except Ali.

18. At-Tabráni says in the Awsat from Ibn Abbás that he said: Ali possessed 18 eminent qualities which belonged to no other of this people.

19. Al-Bazzár records on the authority of Sa'd, that the Apostle of God said to Ali: It is not lawful for anyone to be in the Mosque, while under the obligation of performing a total ablution, except for me and for thee.

20. Abu Ya'la from Abu-Horeira says that Omar b. al-Khattáb said: Verily Ali hath been endowed with three qualities, of which had I but one, it would be more precious to me than were I given high bred camels. It was asked of him what they were; he replied: His marriage with Fátema, the daughter of the Prophet: His remaining in the Mosque while that is permitted to him, which is not lawful for me; and his carrying the Standard on the day of Khaibar.

21. The two Sheikhs (Bokhári and Muslim) record on the authority of Sa'd b. Abi Waqqás, that the Apostle of God left Ali b. Abi Talib behind, as his Vicegerent during the expedition of Tabuk, and Ali said, O Apostle of God, dost thou leave me behind among the women and children? He repied: Art thou not content to be to me in the relation of Aaron tc Moses, save that there shalt be no prophet after me?

22. And from Sahl b. Sa'd that the Apostle of God said on the day of Khaibar: I will surely give the Standard tomorrow to a man, at whose hands the Lord will give victory, one who loveth God and His prophet and whom God and his prophet love; and the people passed the night in perplexity as to the one among them to whom it would be given. And when they entered upon the dawn, they went early to the Apostle of God, each of all of them hoping that it would be given to him, but he said: Where is Ali the son of Abu Talib? They said to him, 'he complaineth of pain in his eyes.' He replied, 'then send for him;' and they brought him and the Apostle of God spat upon his eyes and prayed for him, and he was healed so that it was as if he had no pain, and he gave him the Standard.

23. Muslim records on the authority of Sa'd b. Abi Waqqás, that when this verse 'Let us call together, our sons and your sons etc. *Sur. iii-54* was revealed, the Apostle of God summoned Ali, Fátema, al-Hasan and Hosain, and said, O God! these are my family.

24. At-Tirmizhi and al-Hákim verified on the authority of Boreida that the Apostle of God said: Verily the Lord enjoined upon me the love of four men, and declared unto me that He loved them. They said to him, 'O Apostle of God, name them to us.' He replied: Ali is among them, this he said three times, and Abu Zharr and Miqdád and Salmán.

25. Abu No'aim records in the Daláel, on the authority of the father of Ja'far b. Mohammed that two men having an altercation, were brought before Ali who sat himself at the foot of a wall, and a man said to him 'the wall will fall down,' and Ali said, 'Go to......God is a sufficient protector' and he decided between them, and arose, and then the wall fell.

26. At-Tabráni records in the Awsat and Abu No'aim in the Daláel on the authority of Zádán, that Ali was relating a tradition when a man accused him of speaking falsely, and Ali said to him, 'shall I curse thee if I

have lied' and he said 'curse,' and Ali cursed him. and he did not quit the place till his sight left him.

27. Abul Qásim-al-Zajjáji narrates in his Dictations that Ali composed a work on the principles of the Arabic language, the Grammar of the Arabic language.

INDEX.

INDEX TO VOL. II.